The Tyndale New Testament Commentaries

General Editor: PROFESSOR R. V. G. TASKER, M.A., B.D.

THE ACTS OF THE APOSTLES

To
FREDERICK FYVIE BRUCE
on his seventieth birthday

THE ACTS OF THE APOSTLES

AN INTRODUCTION AND COMMENTARY

by

I. HOWARD MARSHALL M.A., B.D., Ph.D.

Professor of New Testament Exegesis, University of Aberdeen

Wm. B. Eerdmans Publishing Company
Grand Rapids, Michigan

© I. Howard Marshall 1980
First edition published 1980
by Inter-Varsity Press, England
First American edition published 1980
through special arrangement
with Inter-Varsity by Wm. B. Eerdmans Publishing Co.,
255 Jefferson Ave. S.E., Grand Rapids, MI 49503

Reprinted April, 1981

ISBN 0-8028-1423-9

WILLIAM B. EERDMANS PUBLISHING COMPANY
GRAND RAPIDS, MICHIGAN

GENERAL PREFACE

THE original *Tyndale Commentaries* aimed to provide help for the general reader in his study of the Bible. They concentrated on the meaning of the text without going into scholarly technicalities. They aimed at a mean between being too short to be useful and being too extensive for the present reader. Most who have used the books agree that there has been a fair measure of success in reaching that aim.

Times, however, change. The first *Tyndale Commentaries* appeared over twenty years ago and it is felt that some volumes do not meet the changed needs. New knowledge has come to light in some areas. The discussion of critical questions has moved on. Bible-reading habits have changed. In an earlier day most people read the Authorized Version and comments could be based on that. This situation no longer obtains and indeed the last commentary in the original series was based on the Revised Standard Version. In all the circumstances it is felt that the needs of students will best be served by replacing some of the original volumes. This is not meant as an expression of dissatisfaction with them. They served the needs well, but in these days some new needs will be better served by new books.

The original aims remain. The new commentaries are neither minuscule nor unduly long. They are exegetical rather than homiletic. They do not aim to solve all the critical questions, but none is written without an awareness of the critical questions that engage the attention of New Testament scholars. Serious consideration is normally given to such questions in the Introduction and sometimes in Additional Notes. But the main thrust of these commentaries is not critical. These books are written to help the non-technical reader to understand his Bible better. They do not presuppose a knowledge of Greek, and all Greek terms discussed are transliterated; but the authors have the Greek text before them and the commentaries are written in the light of the originals. The English text used is normally the Revised Standard Version, though

5

it is borne in mind that these days readers use a variety of translations.

The original series owed an immense debt to Professor Tasker. He edited the whole, and wrote four of the commentaries himself. It is fitting to place on record this acknowledgment of our debt. I can therefore conclude in no better way than by echoing what Professor Tasker said of the original series. It is the hope of all concerned with these replacement volumes that God will graciously use them to help readers understand as fully and clearly as possible the meaning of the New Testament.

LEON MORRIS

CONTENTS

AUTHOR'S PREFACE

A T a time when there are almost innumerable commentaries on the books of the New Testament anybody who dares to add to their number is under some obligation to justify producing yet another. In the present case it is not enough to claim that the demands of a series had to be fulfilled, since the *Tyndale New Testament Commentaries* already contained a volume on Acts by the distinguished Classical scholar, Professor E. M. Blaiklock. A number of factors, however, made a replacement of this work desirable.

In the first place, Professor Blaiklock deliberately set himself the limited task of writing 'an historical commentary', in the sense that he concentrated on illustrating and expounding the book of Acts against its historical background in the Graeco-Roman period. The course of study since his commentary was published has emphasized the *theological* importance of Acts, and it has become desirable that some account should be taken of this interest. It is significant that F. Bovon's excellent survey of recent scholarship on the works of Luke is entitled *Luc le théologien*.

The historical problems cannot be set aside in favour of a purely theological approach, however, and this leads to a second reason for attempting a fresh study. Shortly before the appearance of Professor Blaiklock's work there appeared another commentary in German from the pen of Professor E. Haenchen; with much learning and great attention to detail the author made Luke out to be something more like a writer of historical fiction than a serious historian. Haenchen's case needs to be taken seriously and evaluated. If, therefore, the present work appears at times to be over-polemical and one-sided in its concentration on historical questions, this may be explained by the fact that so far commentators (with the notable exception of R. P. C. Hanson) have made little attempt to come to terms with Haenchen's approach. It should perhaps be emphasized that although this commentary is frequently critical of what I consider to be Haenchen's unjustified

9

scepticism regarding the historicity of Acts, his work is an outstanding piece of scholarship which has done much to rekindle interest in the study of Acts.

In keeping with the expressed aim of the series, the commentary is primarily exegetical, although it is hoped that sufficient pointers have been given to the expository value of the text. While the commentary is intended to serve a wide range of readers, I have also tried to make it useful for the theological student, and to this end I have attempted to give some reference to the literature on Acts which has appeared subsequently to the publication of Haenchen's commentary and is not listed in his bibliographies.

I should like to express my warm thanks to Dr Leon Morris, the general editor of the series, and to Dr Colin J. Hemer for their helpful comments on the manuscript, and also to Miss T. Clark and Mrs P. Henderson for help with the typing.

The commentary has been written in the University of Aberdeen where Sir William Ramsay was a professor and Professor F. F. Bruce a student. It will be obvious how much I have been influenced by these distinguished writers on the book of Acts, and it gives me the greatest of pleasure to express something of my gratitude to the latter for his friendship and encouragement in many ways by dedicating this book to him.

I. HOWARD MARSHALL

CHIEF ABBREVIATIONS

AG — *A Greek-English Lexicon of the New Testament and Other Early Christian Literature* edited by W. F. Arndt and F. W. Gingrich (Cambridge, 1957).

AHG — *Apostolic History and the Gospel* edited by W. W. Gasque and R. P. Martin (Exeter, 1970).

BC — *The Beginnings of Christianity* edited by F. J. Foakes-Jackson and K. Lake (London, 1920–33).

Bib. — *Biblica.*

BJRL — *Bulletin of the John Rylands University Library of Manchester.*

CBQ — *The Catholic Biblical Quarterly.*

EQ — *The Evangelical Quarterly.*

ET — *The Expository Times.*

GNB — The Good News Bible (Today's English Version), Old Testament, 1976; New Testament, Fourth Edition, 1976.

HTR — *The Harvard Theological Review.*

JB — The Jerusalem Bible, 1966.

JBL — *The Journal of Biblical Literature.*

Jos. — Josephus (*Ant.: Antiquities; Ap.: Against Apion; Bel.: War*).

JSNT — *The Journal for the Study of the New Testament.*

JTS — *The Journal of Theological Studies.*

LS — *A Greek-English Lexicon* compiled by H. G. Liddell and R. Scott, new edition revised by H. S. Jones and R. Mackenzie, 2 vols. (Oxford, 1940).

LXX — The Septuagint (pre-Christian Greek version of the Old Testament).

MT — Masoretic Text.

NBD — *The New Bible Dictionary* edited by J. D. Douglas *et al.* (London, 1962).

NEB — The New English Bible, Old Testament, 1970; New Testament, Second Edition, 1970.

NIDNTT — *The New International Dictionary of New Testament Theology* edited by Colin Brown (Exeter, 1975–78).

11

CHIEF ABBREVIATIONS

NIV	The New International Version, Old Testament, 1979; New Testament, 1973.
Nov.T	*Novum Testamentum.*
NTA	*New Testament Abstracts.*
NTS	*New Testament Studies.*
PLA	*Perspectives on Luke-Acts* edited by C. H. Talbert (Danville and Edinburgh, 1978).
RSV	American Revised Standard Version, Old Testament, 1952; New Testament, Second Edition, 1971.
SB	*Kommentar zum neuen Testament aus Talmud und Midrasch* by Herman L. Strack and Paul Billerbeck, 1956.
SJT	*The Scottish Journal of Theology.*
SLA	*Studies in Luke-Acts* edited by L. E. Keck and J. L. Martyn (Nashville, 1966).
TDNT	*Theological Dictionary of the New Testament*, a translation by Geoffrey W. Bromiley of *Theologisches Wörterbuch zum neuen Testament*, vols. 1–4 edited by G. Kittel, 5–10 edited by G. Friedrich (Grand Rapids, 1964–76).
TNT	The Translator's New Testament, 1973.
Tyn. B.	*Tyndale Bulletin.*
TZ	*Theologische Zeitschrift.*
ZNW	*Zeitschrift für die Neutestamentliche Wissenschaft.*
ZTK	*Zeitschrift für Theologie und Kirche.*

BIBLIOGRAPHY

Books listed here are referred to in the commentary simply by the author's surname, unless there are two or more books by the same author, in which case the shortened titles given here are used.

Barrett, C. K., *The New Testament Background: Selected Documents* (London, 1956). (Barrett, *Background*).
Luke the Historian in Recent Study (London, 1961). (Barrett, *Luke*).
Blaiklock, E. M., *The Acts of the Apostles* (*Tyndale New Testament Commentaries*, London, 1959).
Bovon, F., *Luc le théologien: Vingt-cinq ans de recherches (1950–1975)* (Neuchâtel and Paris, 1978).
Bruce, F. F., *The Book of the Acts* (*New International Commentary*, Grand Rapids: *New London Commentary*, London, 1954). (Bruce, *Book*).
The Acts of the Apostles: The Greek Text with Introduction and Commentary (London, 1951). (Bruce, *Acts*).
Burchard, C., *Der dreizehnte Zeuge* (Göttingen, 1970).
Conzelmann, H., *Die Apostelgeschichte* (*Handbuch zum neuen Testament*, Tübingen, 1963). (Conzelmann, *Apostelgeschichte*).
The Theology of St Luke (London, 1960). (Conzelmann, *Theology*).
Dibelius, M., *Studies in the Acts of the Apostles* (London, 1956).
Dunn, J. D. G., *Jesus and the Spirit* (London, 1975). (Dunn, *Jesus*).
Baptism in the Holy Spirit (London, 1970). (Dunn, *Baptism*).
Dupont, J., *Études sur les Actes des Apôtres* (Paris, 1967). (Dupont, *Études*).
The Sources of the Acts: The Present Position (London, 1964). (Dupont, *Sources*).
Edwards, D. M., *Good News in Acts* (London, 1974).
Ellis, E. E., *Prophecy and Hermeneutic in Early Christianity* (Tübingen and Grand Rapids, 1978).
Franklin, E., *Christ the Lord* (London, 1975).

13

BIBLIOGRAPHY

Gasque, W. W., *A History of the Criticism of the Acts of the Apostles* (Tübingen and Grand Rapids, 1975).

Haenchen, E., *The Acts of the Apostles* (Oxford, 1971).

Hanson, R. P. C., *The Acts* (*New Clarendon Bible*, Oxford, 1967).

Harvey, A. E., *The New English Bible: Companion to the New Testament* (Oxford and Cambridge, 1970).

Hengel, M., *Acts and the History of Earliest Christianity* (London, 1979).

Jervell, J., *Luke and the People of God* (Minneapolis, 1972).

Knowling, R. J., *The Acts of the Apostles*, in W. R. Nicoll, *The Expositor's Greek Testament* (London, 1912), Vol. II.

Knox, W. L., *The Acts of the Apostles* (Cambridge, 1948).

Kremer, J., *Les Actes des Apôtres: Tradition, rédaction, théologie* (Gembloux and Leuven, 1979).

Lindars, B., *New Testament Apologetic* (London, 1961).

Löning, K., *Die Saulustradition in der Apostelgeschichte* (Münster, 1973).

Marshall, I. H., *Luke: Historian and Theologian* (Exeter, 1970, 1979²). (Marshall, *Luke*).

  The Gospel of Luke (*New International Greek Testament Commentary*, Exeter, 1978). (Marshall, *Commentary*).

Metzger, B. M., *A Textual Commentary on the Greek New Testament* (London, 1971).

Neil, W., *The Acts of the Apostles* (*New Century Bible*, London, 1973).

O'Neill, J. C., *The Theology of Acts in its Historical Setting* (London, 1970²).

Ramsay, W. M., *St Paul the Traveller and the Roman Citizen* (London, 1895).

Scharlemann, M. H., *Stephen: A Singular Saint* (Rome, 1968).

Schmithals, W., *Paul and James* (London, 1965).

Schürer, E., *The History of the Jewish People in the Age of Jesus Christ* (revised and edited by G. Vermes, F. Millar and M. Black, Edinburgh, I, 1973; II, 1979).

Sherwin-White, A. N., *Roman Society and Roman Law in the New Testament* (Oxford, 1963).

Stählin, G., *Die Apostelgeschichte* (*Das Neue Testament Deutsch*, Göttingen, 1970).

Stanton, G. N., *Jesus of Nazareth in New Testament Preaching* (Cambridge, 1974).

Stolle, V., *Der Zeuge als Angeklagter* (Stuttgart, 1973).

van Unnik, W. C., *Sparsa Collecta*, I (Leiden, 1973).

Wilckens, U., *Die Missionsreden der Apostelgeschichte* (Neukirch-en-Vluyn, 1974³).

Wilcox, M., *The Semitisms of Acts* (Oxford, 1965).

Williams, C. S. C., *A Commentary on the Acts of the Apostles* (*Black's New Testament Commentaries*, London, 1957).

Wilson, S. G., *The Gentiles and the Gentile Mission in Luke-Acts* (Cambridge, 1973).

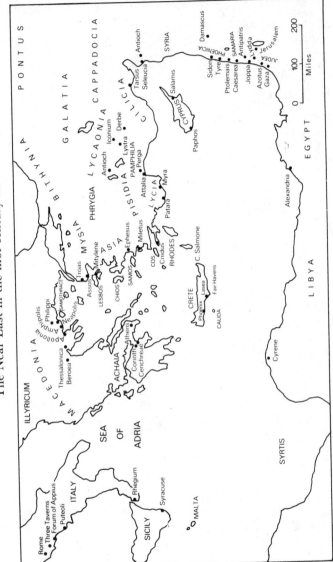

The Near East in the first century AD

INTRODUCTION

I. THE PURPOSE OF ACTS

WHAT a reader gets out of a book and how he assesses its quality are determined to a considerable extent by the expectations with which he approaches it. These expectations may be based partly on the expressed purpose of the author and partly on the presuppositions with which the reader approaches it.

It is probable that the average reader approaches the Acts of the Apostles as *the history book of the early church*. He reads it in order to discover what happened in the first years of the church's existence. He will certainly find a story that answers such expectations. It begins with the ascension of Jesus, the event which marked the end of the earthly ministry of Jesus (Lk. 24:50–53) and which also pointed forward to the ongoing work of Jesus through the church. After describing the equipping of Jesus' disciples for their work with the gift of the Spirit, the book goes on to tell the exciting story of the beginnings of the church in Jerusalem, its spread throughout the wider areas of Judea and Samaria, and then its rapid movement from Antioch in Syria through Asia Minor and Macedonia and Greece, until eventually the arrival of Paul in Rome symbolizes the presence of the gospel in the central city of the ancient world. There is a wealth of detail in the telling of the story. Colourful, dramatic scenes alternate with straightforward reporting. Vigorous personalities stand at the centre of the action. The author has a talent for portraying the variety of life in the ancient world, as he takes us from backwater country towns like Lystra to the intellectual centre of Athens and brings us into touch with unforgettable characters, Jewish and Greek, nobles and slaves. His book is 'a story full of interest, told by a master story-teller'.[1]

Almost without realizing it, we have found ourselves moving

---

[1] Edwards, p. 9. Edwards' book is a most lively introduction to Acts.

17

from what Luke tells us to how he tells it, and have realized that this piece of history is told with conscious artistry. It is *a work of literature*, something that would have been very evident to the ancient reader from the moment he picked up the book with its introductory dedication to 'Theophilus' in the typical manner of an ancient work of letters. The language and style of Luke stand out in the New Testament and show that he was perhaps the most conscious of all its writers that he was writing literature for an educated audience and not merely pamphlets for use within a church that had no literary aspirations or interests.

But if Luke was writing what looks like history, and he was doing so with deliberate literary skill, the question inevitably arises as to what was his purpose in doing so. Why did he write the story of the early church? It was not, after all, the most obvious of things for a Christian writer to do, a fact demonstrated by the recollection that Acts is the only first-century example that we have of this particular kind of literature. Other Christians wrote Letters and Gospels, but only Luke wrote a history of the early church: what led him to do so? A whole variety of reasons have been suggested, and it is probable that we should seek for a compound rather than a simple answer to the question.

Two important preliminary points must be made. The first is that one of the most striking literary features of the writings of Luke is that they are *written in the style of the Greek Old Testament*, the Septuagint (LXX). Since Luke can write in a different style (Lk. 1:1–4), this is something deliberate. Probably he regarded himself as recording *sacred history*. He believed that the events which he was recording were the fulfilment of the prophecies contained in the Scriptures and that consequently they were the same kind of divinely wrought events as were already recorded in the Scriptures. Luke may not have claimed the description of 'Scripture' for what he himself was writing, but implicitly he was claiming that the story of the early church was part of the ongoing story of the work of God, and that the story itself was of similar character to the Old Testament Scriptures.

The second point is that the book of Acts is *the second part of a two-volume work* whose first part is the Gospel of Luke.[1] It is one of the unfortunate effects of the present ordering of the books in the New Testament that it leads us to think of Acts as a separate work on its own. But it was common in the ancient world for a writer to organize a work into several shorter sections (known as 'books') and to furnish each with its own brief introduction. Luke's contemporary Josephus wrote an apology for the Jews divided into two books, the second of which begins thus: 'In the first volume of this work, my most esteemed Epaphroditus, I demonstrated the antiquity of our race... I also challenged the statements of Manetho, Chaeremon, and some others. I shall now proceed to refute the rest of the authors who have attacked us' (Jos., *Ap.* 2:1). This extract is interesting for the way in which it parallels the details of Luke's own introduction to his work (Acts 1:1f.), but our present point is that it underlines the fact that Acts and the Gospel form the two parts of one single work. It follows that to ask questions about the purpose of Acts in isolation from the broader question of the purpose of Luke-Acts is to set off from the wrong starting-point, a practice which generally leads to arrival at the wrong destination.

It emerges that we must ask about the purpose of Luke-Acts as a whole. If we nevertheless concentrate our attention here on Acts, the right way of posing the question will be to ask why Luke, in contradistinction to the other evangelists, chose to add a second volume to the Gospel instead of being content merely to write a Gospel.

One possible answer to this question is that Luke was attempting to write *the story of 'Christian beginnings'* in a broad sense. When Mark headed his Gospel 'The beginning of the gospel of Jesus Christ, the Son of God', he indicated that the ministry of Jesus, from his baptism to his resurrection, was the beginning and basis of the gospel. Luke, however, gathers together the story of Jesus *and* the story of the early church, and sees these as forming together the foundational narrative of the church. He was explaining how the good news had started, and how it had spread to cover the Mediterranean world from Jerusalem to Rome. He does in fact state at the beginning of Acts that his first volume dealt with 'all that

---

[1] With the vast majority of scholars I am assuming the common authorship of the Gospel and Acts.

Jesus began to do and teach', and it seems very probable that by implication the second volume deals with 'all that Jesus continued to do and teach'.[1] In this way the two volumes cover the beginning of the gospel, the establishment of salvation in the ministry of Jesus and the proclamation of salvation by the early church. This basic insight can be developed in various ways.

First, in an important article W. C. van Unnik argued that the book of Acts is the confirmation of the Gospel.[2] He suggested that in the Gospel Luke was presenting the saving activity of Jesus and showing its reality. Then in Acts Luke shows how the church proclaimed and confirmed this salvation. What Acts does in effect is to show how the salvation which was manifested by Jesus during his earthly life in a limited area of country and for a brief period became a reality for increasing numbers of people over a wide geographical area and during an extended period of time. As a result of this, Luke-Acts could be regarded as *an evangelistic work* which proclaims salvation to its readers. Similarly, J. C. O'Neill has insisted that the main purpose of Acts is evangelistic, and makes the specific suggestion that the intended audience consisted of educated Romans.[3] This is an interesting possibility, but it does not seem to do justice to the considerable amount of material in Luke-Acts which appears to be directed to a wider audience.

Secondly, a key point in Acts is that it shows how the gospel was meant *for the Gentiles as well as for the Jews*. Part of the demonstration lies in Luke's claim that what took place in the early church was in accordance with prophecy. Luke's purpose was to show not only that the coming of Jesus fulfilled prophecy, but also that the rise of the church and the spread of salvation to the Gentiles fulfilled the prophecies in the Old Testament and the promises of Jesus (see Lk. 24:47; Acts 1:4f.; 20; 2:16–21; 3:24; 10:43; 13:40f., 47; 15:15–18; 28:25–28).[4]

Thirdly, while Luke's central concern is no doubt with salvation,[5] it is questionable whether we should regard his *main*

---

[1] Marshall, *Luke*, p. 87 n. 2.
[2] Van Unnik, pp. 340–373; originally as 'The "Book of Acts" the Confirmation of the Gospel', *Nov.T* 4, 1960, pp. 26–59.
[3] O'Neill, p. 176.
[4] Dupont, pp. 393–419; Bovon, *Études*, pp. 343–345.
[5] Marshall, *Luke*, pp. 88–94; Bovon, pp. 255–284.

audience as non-Christians. At this point we must take seriously what Luke himself tells us about his purpose in the prologue to his work.[1] He specifically addresses himself to 'Theophilus', who, according to the most plausible understanding of Luke 1:1–4, was already a Christian, and who can be regarded as typical of Luke's readers. Luke's explicit purpose was to confirm his faith by providing him with an orderly account of the things which he had learned in the course of his Christian instruction. A sceptic might have tried to persuade Theophilus that his faith was based on nothing more than 'cunningly devised myths'; Luke's reply was to present him with an account of the beginnings of Christianity based on what had been handed down 'by those who from the beginning were eyewitnesses and ministers of the word' (Lk. 1:2). If the Gospel gave the facts about the ministry of Jesus, Acts demonstrated how the preaching of Jesus as the Christ corroborated and confirmed the facts recorded in the Gospel; when the good news was preached, the Spirit made the word effective and brought the hearers into the experience of salvation. On this view of things, the book of Acts was intended as an account of Christian beginnings in order to strengthen faith and give assurance that its foundation is firm. Obviously, a book written with this aim has an evangelistic purpose, but the scope of Luke-Acts stretches beyond material that is purely evangelistic.

If we adopt this view of Luke-Acts, it becomes highly unlikely that the *primary* purpose of Acts was to provide some kind of *political apologetic* for Christianity. It has sometimes been argued that the aim of Acts was to show that Christians were innocent of the political charges that were brought against them, and that in fact the Roman officials who examined such cases were agreed that the Christians had not in any way offended against the laws of the Roman Empire. It has even been suggested that Acts was written to supply the evidence needed for Paul's defence when he appeared before the Emperor Nero. This suggestion clearly goes too far. We are not denying that Luke had an apologetic motive in the composition of Luke-Acts, especially in the case of Acts. But

[1] The prologue to the Gospel is probably meant to cover the entire work; Marshall, *Commentary*, p. 39.

it is a subordinate aim as compared with the main theme of the presentation of the historical basis for Christian faith.

It also becomes unlikely that the main purpose of Luke-Acts was *to refute Christian heresies* or *to promote some particular theological emphasis* of the author. It has been argued, for example, that Luke's aim was *to refute a Gnostic type of heresy*,[1] but it has been convincingly shown that Luke does not refer explicitly to any specific heresies of a Gnostic character and that there is no indication of any conscious polemic.[2] Another suggested aim is *the rehabilitation of Paul* over against his detractors in the church,[3] but this cannot be more than a subordinate purpose. A much more important aim of Luke is to show *how the church, composed of Jews and Gentiles, stands in continuity with Judaism*, and this can be regarded as a vital aspect of Luke's main theme. A further, extremely important view is that Luke was attempting to come to terms with the problem caused for the church by the fact that the second coming or parousia of Jesus had not yet happened despite the church's expectation of it in the very near future; Luke, it is claimed, wrote *to produce a new theological outlook, in which the coming of the Spirit and the mission of the church filled the gap caused by the delay of the parousia*.[4] It is not clear whether the proponents of this view regard it as providing the conscious and deliberate motive of Luke for composing his work, or as the underlying and unconscious motivation which led him to frame his work in the way he did. In any case, it seems most unlikely that the delay of the parousia constituted a major conscious motive for Luke's work, and it is also unlikely that it was a decisive unconscious factor in the structuring of his work.[5] The view that Luke's theological outlook was determined largely by the delay of the parousia leads to a distorted understanding of Acts.

---

[1] C. H. Talbert, *Luke and the Gnostics* (Nashville, 1966).
[2] Van Unnik, pp. 402–409; originally as 'Die Apostelgeschichte und die Häresien', *ZNW* 58, 1967, pp. 240–246.
[3] E. Trocmé, *Le 'Livre des Actes' et l'histoire*, (Paris, 1957); A. J. Mattill, Jr, 'The Purpose of Acts: Schneckenburger Reconsidered', *AHG*, pp. 108–122.
[4] Conzelmann, *Theology*.
[5] Marshall, *Luke*, pp. 77–79, 84–88.

II. THE THEOLOGY OF ACTS

Although we have emphasized that Luke was writing a historical narrative about the beginnings of Christianity, and although we have rejected the view that he wrote to put over a particular theological point of view, we must nevertheless ask about the nature of the theological outlook which comes to expression in Acts. There is no doubt that Luke does see the story as having theological significance and that he has brought out its significance in the way in which he tells it. This is of course something different from saying that he has reinterpreted the history by presenting it in an alien theological framework.

1. The continuation of God's purpose in history

The story recorded in Acts is seen as *standing in continuity with the mighty acts of God recorded in the Old Testament and with the ministry of Jesus.* The phrase which has become current in theological jargon to express this characteristic is 'salvation history'. In this context the phrase refers to an understanding of the various events in the life of Jesus and the early church as historical actions in which the activity of God himself is revealed. Christian faith is directed towards the God who has revealed himself as Saviour on the stage of history. This understanding of faith is sometimes compared with an 'existentialist' view, according to which faith is essentially independent of historical facts.[1] Indeed, it has been claimed that originally the Christian message had a basically 'existential' character; it was a proclamation of God's salvation with little or no backing from history and demanding faith and obedience from the hearers. Luke, it is claimed, transformed this 'message' into a historical report about Jesus, and thus made the story of Jesus into part of an ongoing set of acts of God in history; what had originally been 'the end of history' now became 'the middle of history'.[2] This is a misinterpretation of the evidence. There never was an 'existential' message independent of history, but rather the kind of presentation of

[1] See O. Cullmann, *Salvation in History* (London, 1967), for a comparison of the two approaches and a defence of a salvation-historical understanding of the New Testament as a whole.
[2] Conzelmann, *Theology*, pp. 9–17. The thought is already present in R. Bultmann, *Theology of the New Testament*, II, (London, 1955), pp. 116–118.

salvation history offered by Luke was the original understanding of Christianity. To contrast the 'salvation-historical' and 'existentialist' approaches is to produce a false antithesis. The truth is rather that the historical facts, in which God was seen to be active, demand an existential response of commitment and obedience to this God. Apart from those historical facts there can be no basis for faith. This does not mean that Christian faith is faith *in* certain events, or that faith is possible only if certain events can be *proved* to have taken place and to have been acts of God. It does mean that if the reality of the events is denied, then there is no basis for faith: 'If Christ has not been raised, your faith is futile and you are still in your sins' (1 Cor. 15:17).

A number of important facets of this basic point must be noted. First, the events recorded in Acts are seen as being brought about *by the will and purpose of God*. The story of the death and resurrection of Jesus is the most obvious example of an event which is traced to 'the definite plan and foreknowledge of God' (2:23), but the same is true of the events in the life of the church; thus it is implied, for example, that the opposition which the church experienced was of the same character as the divinely foretold opposition to Jesus (4:27–29).

It follows, secondly, that the life of the church was regarded as taking place *in fulfilment of Scripture*. The prophecies made in the Old Testament governed the course of church history – the outpouring of the Spirit and the proclamation of salvation (2:17–21), the mission to the Gentiles (13:47) and their incorporation in the church (15:16–18), and the refusal of the Jews as a whole to respond to the gospel (28:25–27).

Thirdly, the life of the church was *directed by God* at crucial stages. Sometimes the Spirit directed the church what to do (*e.g.* 13:2; 15:28; 16:6). At other times angels spoke to Christian missionaries (5:19f.; 8:26; 27:23), or messages were mediated by prophets (11:28; 20:11f.). On occasion the Lord himself appeared to his servants (18:9; 23:11).

Fourthly, the power of God was seen in *signs and wonders* which were performed by the name of Jesus (3:16; 14:3). As a result the work of the Christian mission can be said to be carried out by God (15:4).

2. *The mission and the message*

Acts is a book about mission. It is not unfair to take 1:8 as a summary of its contents: 'You shall be my witnesses in Jerusalem and in all Judea and Samaria and to the end of the earth.' The purpose of the Christian church was to bear witness to Jesus. This was in a special sense the task of the Twelve, who had been with Jesus during his earthly ministry and had seen him risen from the dead (1:21f.), and were therefore especially equipped to bear witness to Israel. But the task was by no means confined to the Twelve, and many other Christians took their share in evangelism.

The *message* which was proclaimed is expounded in a series of public addresses scattered throughout the book. Broadly speaking, it was concerned with the fact that Jesus, who had been raised from the dead by God after being put to death by the Jews, had been declared to be the Jewish Messiah and the Lord, and hence the source of salvation. It was through him that forgiveness of sins was offered to men, and it was from him that the gift of the Spirit had come down to the church. The way in which Jesus functions as a Saviour is not made clear in Acts; there is no very close link made between his death and the possibility of salvation (except in 20:28), and the impression gained is rather that it was by virtue of being raised from the dead and exalted by the Father that Jesus received the authority to bestow salvation and to carry out his mighty acts in the church. It is thus the resurrection and exaltation of Jesus which stands at the centre of the preaching in Acts.[1]

The blessings associated with salvation are summed up as the forgiveness of sins and the gift of the Spirit. The latter was manifested in experiences of joy and spiritual power. Acts has little to say about the Pauline experience of union with Jesus, and one might be tempted to assume that Luke's religion is less mystical. It would be more correct to say that Luke describes the same basic Christian experience as Paul in different terminology. The place given to prayer and to visions in Acts, as well as to such charismatic experiences as speaking in tongues and prophesying, indicates that there is a real and profound element of communion with God in this book.

---

[1] Luke does not ignore the atoning significance of the death of Jesus, but he does not go out of his way to stress it; Marshall, *Luke*, pp. 169–175.

INTRODUCTION

The main story-line in Acts is concerned with *the spread of this message*. It begins with the existence of a small group of followers of the earthly Jesus gathered in Jerusalem, and describes how under the impact of the gift of the Spirit they became witnesses to Jesus and gathered an increasing number of converts. The early chapters portray the growth and consolidation of the group in Jerusalem. From chapter 6 onwards we are conscious of widening horizons. Many priests are converted, and at the same time the Christian witness reaches various synagogues associated with the Jewish Dispersion in Jerusalem. As persecution led to the flight of many Christians from Jerusalem, so the message began to spread in the broader area of Judea, and then took a decisive step forward with the conversion of some Samaritans and even a traveller from Ethiopia. By the middle of chapter 9 the author can speak of 'the church throughout all Judea and Galilee and Samaria'. But with the inclusion of Samaria the first important move had been made towards people who were not fully Jews, and soon afterwards various events convinced the church that it was called to take the good news to non-Jews. At first, the contacts were with Gentiles who already worshipped God in the synagogues, but it could not be long before other Gentiles too were attracted by the message. Once the church had become firmly established in Antioch, the Gentile mission became established policy, and from Antioch deliberate, organized mission took place. If Peter had been the leading figure in the early days of the church in Jerusalem, guiding it from its infancy to the point where it recognized that the gospel was for the Gentiles, so Paul plays the leading part in the development of the mission from Antioch; the second part of Acts is essentially the story of how Paul, in co-operation with other evangelists, proceeded to establish churches in Asia Minor and Greece, so that by chapter 20 the gospel has been effectively proclaimed throughout the Eastern Mediterranean world, and Paul can speak as though his work there is complete. But we are in fact only at chapter 20, and there is still something like a quarter of the book to come. What we have is an account of how Paul returned from his travels to Jerusalem and was arrested on a trumped-up charge; the story describes his various appearances before courts and governors in the course of which he defends himself over against both the Jews and the Romans, protesting his innocence and in effect having it confirmed by the Roman authorities. Finally, at considerable length we have the account of his journey to Rome. In the broad sense it can be said that the purpose of the account is to show how the gospel, in the person of Paul, came to Rome, but it is clear that the story in Acts, which starts off as a story of missionary expansion, has other aims also. We must ask whether other theological elements have a place in Acts.

3. Progress despite opposition

Acts is much concerned with *the opposition which surrounds the spread of the gospel*. 'Through many tribulations we must enter the kingdom of God' (14:22). Luke recognizes that, just as the way of Jesus took him through opposition culminating in judicial murder, so too the path of the Word of God is beset by opposition. It begins with the mockery of the apostles on the day of Pentecost and continues with the attempts of the Sanhedrin to force them to remain silent about Jesus. It comes to a swift climax in the death of the first martyr, Stephen, and the wave of persecution that followed his death. A Jewish king attempted to curry favour with the people by putting James to death, and only a miracle saved Peter from the same fate. When the missionaries moved out into the Roman world, they were dogged by opposition. Usually it began with the Jews who viewed the evangelism of the Gentiles with disfavour; but in many cases the Jews were able to gain support from pagan sympathizers in acts of violence against the missionaries. This led on occasion to the missionaries being brought before the magistrates. The attitude of the latter was ambivalent. On occasion they were quite prepared to administer summary justice against people who appeared to be responsible for breaches of the peace. At other times, however, they appear not so much as defenders of the missionaries but rather as unbiased and disinterested upholders of the law who recognize that the activities of the missionaries are in no way contrary to Roman law and custom.

The paradigm case is that of Paul, and it is Luke's interest in this theme which has led to the remarkable amount of space devoted to his period of captivity. Here Luke makes it quite plain that Paul had not offended against the laws of Rome and that, in a sense, only a legal technicality prevented his being set free by the Roman governor. At the same time, however, the story suggests that Roman governors were not free from blame in their handling of the affair. So long as governors were prepared to buy favour from the Jews and to seek bribes from defendants, Christians must expect to receive less than justice. Luke thus shows an awareness of the hard realities of life; no matter how innocent Christians might be, they could still expect to be victims of injustice.

So far as the Jews were concerned, the charges against Paul were that he tried to profane the temple, and more generally that he was promoting a Jewish heresy wherever he went. The first of these charges (which was little more than a pretext for his arrest) is simply denied; on the contrary, Paul is presented as a law-abiding Jewish worshipper. The second charge is refuted by the argument that Paul was simply worshipping and serving God in the way that had been laid down in the Old Testament, and that he was and remained a Pharisee in his convictions. In other words, *Christianity is true Judaism.* This basic point is made at length, but it is clear that it cut no ice with the Jews, although some of the Pharisees were sympathetic to it. Here again Luke can only present the hard reality that many Jews refused to accept the Christian claim that Christianity is the fulfilment of Judaism. At the same time, Luke is using the motif to indicate that from a Roman point of view Christianity should be regarded as a legitimate development of Judaism, and should therefore receive the same privileged position as a tolerated religion within the Empire; the quarrels between Jews and Christians are theological in nature, and do not come within the cognizance of Roman law.

In face of this opposition two important facts emerge. The first is that Christians are called *to stand firm and to be faithful* despite the tribulations which they must endure. When they are commanded to stop preaching, their answer is a defiant refusal to do so. True, they find it necessary to retreat from towns where they are forbidden to continue preaching, but they simply carry on evangelism wherever they find opportunity to do so; the gospel command did not require them to continue to battle on in situations where they were unwelcome, but having faithfully borne their witness they were required to move on elsewhere (Lk. 9:5). In the trial of Paul a different feature emerges. Paul uses the courtroom as a place to bear witness; his concern is not so much to defend himself as to proclaim the gospel (Lk. 21:12–15). Opposition becomes an occasion for evangelism. This, of course, was also true of Peter and Stephen when they appeared in court scenes.

The other fact is that despite the opposition *the Word of God continues its triumphal progress*. The hand of God is upon the missionaries even in the midst of persecution. It does not remove them from danger and suffering, but on occasion they find divine protection from their enemies. Here again Luke's realism comes out; James dies, but Peter survives to fight another day. Paul is brought safely from Jerusalem to Rome despite every kind of obstacle and danger. God's declared purpose will be fulfilled, no matter what the opposition. Acts is the story of the triumphant progress of the Word of God.

4. The inclusion of the Gentiles in the people of God

Acts reflects the tremendous tensions which existed in the early church over *the basis of the Gentile mission*. Although the Gospels record the commission given by Jesus that his disciples should take the gospel to all nations, at first the church was composed of Jews and carried out its evangelism among Jews. Contrary to a widespread popular belief, Luke makes no mention of Gentiles being present on the day of Pentecost other than Jewish proselytes (2:10). But within a few years the church found itself preaching the gospel to Samaritans, uncircumcised God-fearers and finally to pagan Gentiles. This progression is seen by Luke as divinely willed and prophesied; it was a turn of events that came about apart from any conscious planning by the church. The church had to come to terms with this fact.

The essence of the problem was whether the rise of the church had produced a new society that was different from Judaism. Since the first Christians were Jews, it was natural for them to live as Jews – to circumcise their children and to live according to the law of Moses, although admittedly there could be variations in the interpretation of the law, and Jesus himself had displayed considerable freedom with regard to certain aspects of it. The same way of life could be expected of Jewish proselytes who were converted to Christianity. Christianity could then be seen as the true and proper fulfilment of Judaism; the promised Messiah had come and brought renewal to his people.

Two factors disturbed this easy assumption. On the one hand, it became increasingly obvious that the Jewish leaders and many of the people were not prepared to accept Jesus as the Messiah, and an easy evolution from first-century Judaism to Christianity simply by incorporating the Christian message of Jesus as the Messiah was ruled out. In fact the Judaism of the early church's contemporaries had turned aside from the truth. It was Stephen who voiced criticism of the Jews of his time, alleging that they had failed to follow truly the law of Moses and that their worship of God in the temple was displeasing to him. Not surprisingly this attack provoked strong opposition from the Jewish leaders, and we may suspect that Stephen's outlook was not immediately shared by all members of the church. Nevertheless, it was bound to become increasingly obvious that official Judaism was opposed to the church and regarded its views as heretical.

On the other hand, there was the problem of the entry of the Gentiles into the church. This not only intensified the opposition against the church from Judaism. It also raised acute questions within the church regarding its character and its way of life. There has been much discussion regarding the way in which Luke envisaged the nature of the church. One view is that he saw it as essentially a Jewish institution, the people of God, consisting of Jews, and from which Jews who refused to repent cut themselves off, and to which believing Gentiles can be joined.[1] The other view is that Luke saw God's purpose as the gathering of a new Israel, composed of both Jews and Gentiles, and that he describes the progressive separation of the church from Judaism.[2] The truth probably lies somewhere between these extremes; in our view Luke stresses the Jewish origins of the church and its roots in Old Testament prophecy, but shows that it is a people of God, composed of believing Jews and Gentiles, in which Jews may find the fulfilment of Judaism and Gentiles are not required to become Jews.

But how was this possible on a practical level? The problem was twofold. First, could Jewish Christians have fellowship with Gentiles without becoming 'unclean' through contact with people who did not observe the law of Moses? Secondly, could Gentiles come into a true relationship with God and his people merely by accepting Jesus as the Messiah? Were they not required to accept the Jewish law, including circumcision?

[1] Jervell, pp. 41–74.
[2] O'Neill. See the discussion in Wilson; also Bovon, pp. 342–361.

Luke was quite certain that Gentiles did not need to be circumcised. But this solution led to searching struggles of conscience for Jewish Christians, and for many years a group of strictly law-abiding Jewish Christians continued to exist in Palestine in isolation from the rest of the church.

Luke depicts how the problem was solved in the early days. When God poured out the Spirit on the Gentiles, Peter was prepared to accept them as members of God's people, and to eat with them. The vision which he received from God showed him that there was no longer to be a distinction between clean and unclean foods. But it is doubtful how quickly other Jewish Christians came to share Peter's viewpoint (and even he found it difficult to maintain it consistently). When the Jerusalem church met with representatives from Antioch to consider the matter, the fundamental point that was accepted was that the Gentiles did not need to be circumcised. At the same time, however, they were asked to avoid alienating their Jewish colleagues by abstaining from food sacrificed to idols and from meat not slaughtered in the Jewish manner, and by observing Jewish standards of sexual behaviour. These requirements bear some relationship to the rules already accepted by God-fearers who worshipped in the synagogues. The only really difficult point was the rule about meat, and this may have applied only to common meals with Jews. In this way it was possible for strictly law-abiding Jews to recognize the validity of the Gentile mission. How long the regulations continued in force is not known. They were probably taken seriously in Jerusalem, especially under mounting Zealot pressure in favour of the preservation of Jewish national and cultural identity. Paul himself lived as a law-abiding Jew among Jews, although he strongly protested his freedom of conscience. It is unlikely that the Jerusalem regulations had a long or wide currency, however, and they probably fell into disuse. When they are echoed in Revelation 2:14, 20, the ruling about meat appears to have been quietly dropped.

Alongside the acceptance of the Gentiles Luke chronicles the increasing refusal of the Jews to accept the gospel. Paul's regular practice was to begin his mission in the local synagogue, and we almost gain the impression that only when the Jews refused the gospel did he turn to the Gentiles (Acts 13:46). It may be better to say that the Gentile mission took place once the Jews had had an opportunity to hear the gospel

first.[1] Paul recognized that the gospel was for 'the Jew first
. . . and also the Greek' (Rom. 1:16). When the Jews rejected
the gospel, they were rejected by God from his people, a fact
symbolized when the missionaries shook off the dust from
their feet against them and turned to the Gentiles.[2] The point
which is made in Acts 13:46 is repeated with tremendous
emphasis at the climax of the book in 28:25–28. Yet one factor
strangely absent from Acts is any reference to the divine judgment upon Jerusalem which figures so prominently in the
Gospel (Lk. 13:34f.; 19:41–44; 21:20–24; 23:28–31). Jerusalem,
which figures in the Gospel as the place of the Lord's rejection,
becomes the place where he rises from the dead, where the
Spirit is poured out, and where the church begins its work. In
Acts it is official Judaism rather than Jerusalem which stands
under condemnation for refusing the gospel.

5. The life and organization of the church

Luke is concerned to offer a picture of *the life and worship of the
church* no doubt as a pattern to provide guidance for the church
in his own time. From the brief summaries in the early chapters
of Acts (2:42–47; 4:32–37) we gain a picture of small groups
meeting together for teaching, fellowship, prayer and the breaking of bread. Entrance to the church is by baptism with water.

Luke particularly stresses the importance of the Spirit in
the life of the church. The Spirit is the common possession of
every Christian, the source of joy and power, and Christian
leaders are people who are especially filled with the Spirit to
perform their various functions. The Spirit guides the church
in its choice of leaders and in its evangelistic activity to such
an extent that Acts has sometimes been described as the book
of 'The Acts of the Holy Spirit'.[3]

Initially the leadership of the church was in the hands of
the apostles in Jerusalem together with the elders, and the
church in Jerusalem occupied an important place in relation
to the other churches which grew up subsequently. There

---

[1] Jervell, pp. 60f., does his best to play down the force of 13:46. He is at
least correct, however, in insisting that the Gentile mission is not motivated
solely by the refusal of the Jews to accept the gospel.
[2] Perhaps the motive indicated in Rom. 11:13f. is implied.
[3] J. H. E. Hull, *The Holy Spirit in the Acts of the Apostles* (London, 1968); F.
F. Bruce, 'The Holy Spirit in the Acts of the Apostles', *Interpretation* 27, 1973,
pp. 166–183.

were elders in the local churches, and special significance is attached to prophets and teachers, some of whom appear to have been resident while others were more itinerant. Luke says so little about how such people were appointed and what they did that we can only conclude that he did not regard this as important. Yet we are told how an apostle was appointed to replace Judas, and how seven men to assist the apostles were chosen. We hear briefly how missionaries were sent out by the church at Antioch and how Paul appointed elders in the churches which he founded. This is sufficient evidence to show that for Luke the significant factors were the spiritual qualities of the persons chosen and the guidance of the Spirit in the meetings that appointed them.

We also learn something about the work of missionaries. The principle of team work was established from the start, and for the most part the missionaries travelled in groups of two or more; Peter and Philip (chapters 8–10) were exceptions to the rule. Luke's manner of presentation has suggested to many readers that we should think of Paul and his colleagues as carrying on 'missionary journeys', but a closer study of the narrative shows that in fact Paul stayed in important centres of population for considerable periods of time. Whether Luke fully recognized Paul's principles of working is not clear, but he certainly gives us the evidence that Paul's journeys were far from being whistle-stop tours.

Luke records several sermons as examples of the way in which the gospel was preached, and one example of Paul speaking to Christian leaders about their responsibilities (20:17–35). The variety in these missionary sermons and the speeches of Christians on trial before Jewish and Roman bodies is no doubt meant to illustrate the different ways in which the gospel was presented to different groups of people, Jews and Greeks, cultured and uncultured, and it is hard to resist the impression that the sermons are presented as models for Luke's readers to use in their own evangelism. It is material of this kind which has led to the characterization of Acts as 'edifying'. Although the term, as used by Haenchen (pp. 103–110), seems at least mildly derogatory, it is a proper and respectable word to describe this book, intended as it is to show the Christians of Luke's day what it means to be the church and how they should continue to live according to the pattern established in the early days.

INTRODUCTION

Luke's story is very much structured on the careers of the two Christian leaders, Peter and Paul. There are interesting parallels between the two men, and one can also trace some parallelism between the careers of Jesus and Paul. Some scholars have shown great ingenuity in discerning this parallelism in detail and have probably exaggerated its presence.[1] In broad terms, however, the claim is persuasive, and shows that Luke saw a pattern for the life of the church and its missionaries in the life of its earthly Master.

III. THE HISTORICITY OF ACTS

In the preceding section we have seen some of the theological interests which are apparent in the composition of Acts. Their presence has led an increasing number of scholars to question the historical value of Acts.[2] In the nineteenth century the so-called Tübingen school of criticism regarded Acts as a late attempt to varnish over the conflict between Peter and Paul which (it was alleged) had dominated the early years of the church; Acts presented a picture of smooth compromise and glossed over the harsh realities of the conflict.[3] Towards the end of the century the researches of Sir William Ramsay in particular did much to discredit this interpretation of Acts and to reaffirm the high historical quality of Luke's work.[4] Ramsay no doubt put the point much more strongly than many of his contemporaries would have been prepared to accept, and he was capable of making assertions about Luke's historical accuracy which went beyond what could be shown by the available evidence. Essentially the same point of view was presented more moderately in the major work of Anglo-American scholarship on Acts in the early twentieth century, *The Beginnings of Christianity*. The contributors to this work came from various schools of thought and most certainly displayed no blind adulation towards Luke; on the contrary, they estimated his work by the standards of liberal scholarship and

[1] M. D. Goulder, *Type and History in Acts* (London, 1964); W. Radl, *Paulus und Jesus im lukanischen Doppelwerk* (Bern and Frankfurt, 1975).

[2] For a history of criticism with special reference to this question see Gasque.

[3] H. Harris, *The Tübingen School* (Oxford, 1975).

[4] W. M. Ramsay, *St Paul the Traveller and the Roman Citizen* (London, 1895, 1920[56]); *The Bearing of Recent Discovery on the Trustworthiness of the New Testament* (London, 1914).

in general recognized Acts as a historical work of considerable value. This verdict was endorsed in the post-war commentaries by F. F. Bruce and C. S. C. Williams.

Meanwhile a powerful reaction was developing. In Germany a much more sceptical attitude to the historical value of Acts was expressed in a series of essays by M. Dibelius, who applied the methods of form-criticism to the book. Then came the development of redaction-criticism, in which the function of the New Testament writers as creative theologians, working freely on the traditions available to them, was emphasized. Although H. Conzelmann's major study of Luke's theology, published in 1954, concentrated attention on the Gospel, it established for many readers that Luke was primarily a theologian and cut a poor figure as a historian. Two years later there followed the first edition of a mammoth commentary on Acts by E. Haenchen. Anyone who may have thought that R. Bultmann represented the ultimate in historical scepticism as regards the New Testament was in for a rude shock. Haenchen's method was to ask at every point in Acts 'What was Luke trying to do?' and he found that he could explain most of Acts in terms of Luke producing an edifying account of the early church that owed nothing to written sources and was based on the scantiest of oral traditions. The result was that Luke's historical accuracy was apparently torn in shreds; the narrative was claimed to have little basis in tradition, to be full of historical inconsistencies and improbabilities, and to be basically the product of the fertile mind of a historical novelist with little or no concern for such tiresome things as facts. Essentially the same line was taken in a somewhat later commentary by H. Conzelmann, although the brevity of his treatment means that his historical scepticism appears much more arbitrary and ill-founded than that of Haenchen. For the moment the Haenchen-Conzelmann approach appears to be dominant and largely uncontested on the Continent.[1]

[1] For a recent summary of this approach see E. Plümacher, 'Apostelgeschichte', in *Theologische Realenzyklopädie* III (Berlin, 1978), pp. 483–528. A much less sceptical approach is adopted by G. Stählin in his commentary which stands in the scholarly Pietist tradition.

Most recently M. Hengel, *Acts and the History of Earliest Christianity* (London, 1979), has strongly defended Luke and affirmed that he 'is no less trustworthy than other historians of antiquity' (p. 60).

INTRODUCTION

1. Historical scepticism

What factors have led to this estimate of Acts? First, there is the general background of *historical scepticism* associated with form-criticism and redaction-criticism. It is commonly assumed that the circles in the church which preserved and handed on traditions and then incorporated them in writing were theologically motivated and *therefore* uninterested in what actually happened and/or incapable of checking up to see what the historical facts were. The early church, we are told, was not interested in history. But this general conclusion is logically unjustified – the *therefore* italicized above has no probative value – and is in any case inherently unlikely. It has been shown time and again that theological motivation does not exclude historical interest, particularly when a writer like Luke deliberately states that his theological purpose led him to produce a historical account of the beginnings of Christianity.[1] It should perhaps be added that form-criticism and redaction-criticism are perfectly legitimate approaches, and that there is no need for them to be characterized by historical scepticism.[2]

2. Historical background in Acts

One of the major contributions of Ramsay to Lucan study was his demonstration that on matters of detailed historical background *Luke shows remarkable accuracy*. Indeed, it was precisely this observation which led Ramsay to abandon his earlier acceptance of the Tübingen view of Acts as a second-century romance. But the evidence needed to be reconsidered, and today we are in a better position to affirm the essential reliability of Acts in this area. The major work here is that of A. N. Sherwin-White, and his approach is currently being carried further by C. J. Hemer.[3] Sherwin-White writes cautiously and does not claim more than is justified from the evidence. He is quite prepared to admit that Luke makes

[1] See Marshall, *Luke*, pp. 13–76; *idem, I believe in the historical Jesus* (London, 1977), for fuller discussion of this point.
[2] See the treatment of these disciplines by S. H. Travis and S. S. Smalley in I. H. Marshall (ed.), *New Testament Interpretation* (Exeter, 1977), pp. 153–164 and 181–195 respectively.
[3] C. J. Hemer, 'Luke the Historian', *BJRL* 60, 1977–78, pp. 28–51. Hemer is the co-author with W. W. Gasque of a forthcoming major critical commentary on Acts.

mistakes, but the main thrust of his book is to demonstrate that for the most part Luke portrays the first-century Roman scene accurately. The conclusion to be drawn is that if Luke is right about the details of the story he is likely also to be right about the main episodes. The fruits of this approach can be seen in the brief, but helpful, commentary by R. P. C. Hanson, who attributes to Luke a far higher level of historical accuracy than is customary in German-speaking scholarship.

German-speaking scholars seem in general either to ignore Sherwin-White or to argue that, even if a writer is accurate on background, it does not necessarily follow that he is accurate on the main plot: a historical novelist, it is argued, can go to great pains to get his background authentic. This suggestion is totally unconvincing. It assumes that Luke wrote like a modern novelist, striving for verisimilitude; this is sheer anachronism. It also ignores the fact that Luke's accuracy extends to trivial details of the sort that a writer would be hardly likely to research specially. The very casualness of the accuracy suggests that it is not artificial. Further, we should need some good evidence to show that Luke was writing a historical novel before we put on one side his own claim to be writing reliable history and the evidences of his accuracy.[1]

3. The problem of sources

One big problem with Acts is *the difficulty of discovering any sources* used by the author. Even if we assume that the book was written by a companion of Paul, he himself does not appear on stage until chapter 16, and he must, therefore, have been dependent on information from other people for what happened in the earlier sections. Writing in 1964 J. Dupont commented: 'It has not been possible to define any of the sources used by the author of Acts in a way which will meet with widespread agreement among the critics.'[2] Nothing has happened subsequently to alter this estimate in any significant way. The general view is that Luke has successfully managed to conceal whatever sources he used beneath a uniform editorial style. Moreover, the fact that some stories can be ana-

---

[1] W. W. Gasque, 'The Book of Acts and History', in R. A. Guelich (ed.), *Unity and Diversity in New Testament Theology* (Grand Rapids, 1978), pp. 54–72; *cf.* Hanson, pp. 2–21.
[2] Dupont, *Sources*, p. 166.

lysed form-critically may imply that the author was not dependent on direct eyewitness accounts of what happened, and redaction-critical analysis of others indicates that they can be explained at least partly in terms of his own composition. If we cannot trace the sources of an allegedly historical work, we can have little grounds for confidence in the reliability of the information which it contains, even if the author was well-intentioned and careful.

The difficulty of the problem must be admitted, but it is not insuperable. First, in an important essay on 'The Problem of Traditions in Acts' Jervell (pp. 19–39) has argued that there is independent evidence that the activities of the apostles and the establishment of congregations were events that formed part of the missionary proclamation of the church, and thus conditions were favourable to the preservation of traditions about the history of the church. Secondly, it so happens that in the Gospel we can to a considerable extent check Luke's use of his sources. If we grant that he made use of Mark and also of a lost source which he shared with Matthew,[1] we can see how he used these sources. It emerges that although he employed a certain measure of editorial freedom and did not simply retail his sources verbatim, he was remarkably faithful to them: 'What concerns us here,' said F. C. Burkitt, 'is not that Luke has changed so much, but that he has invented so little.'[2] It is reasonable to assume, until the contrary has been proved, that he acted similarly in Acts.

Thirdly, Dupont's somewhat pessimistic conclusion does not mean that some theories regarding the sources of Acts may not be more plausible than others. In the second part of Acts certain sections have been written in the first person plural form (16:10–17; 20:5 – 21:18; 27:1 – 28:16). The most natural explanation of this phenomenon is that these sections are based on material composed by a participant in the events described, and that the author of Acts has not changed the style to the usual third-person narrative. Many efforts have been made to explain these passages otherwise. It has been suggested that the use of 'we' is a literary device used in the context of sea voyages or with a view to claiming that the

---

[1] For a cautious defence of both these points see L. Morris, *Luke (Tyndale New Testament Commentaries*, London, 1974), pp. 47–59.

[2] *BC*, II, p. 115.

author is a far-travelled and hence competent writer.[1] Such an explanation says little for the writer's honesty, but in any case the parallels which have been adduced do not prove the point. It is more convincing that the first-person style points to the use of eyewitness material, and that this is how Luke's readers would have evaluated it.[2]

As for the earlier chapters of Acts, the most likely hypothesis is still that Luke obtained information from the various churches and possibly from some of the chief actors in the story. The possibility that he obtained information from such places as Jerusalem, Caesarea and Antioch is strong. Indeed, it is almost inconceivable that a writer on the early church would not have done so. But it must be admitted that Luke has so thoroughly worked over his sources that it is impossible to distinguish them stylistically. The verdict of F. J. Foakes-Jackson (cited by Bruce, *Acts*, p. 21) is especially true of Acts: 'We should constantly remember that source-criticism in the New Testament is largely guess-work.' In individual passages the critic may be able to detect places where the author is using tradition, but it must be remembered that an author can rewrite a source so completely in his own words that it is almost impossible to recover its original form. In Acts there is constant danger that the all-pervading presence of the author's own style may tempt scholars to conclude that he was not dependent on sources; this temptation must be resisted.

Within the scope of this commentary source-analysis is not practicable, and it must be left to larger works to undertake this task.

4. Luke's theological motivation: the speeches in Acts

We have already mentioned the question of *the presence of Lucan theology* in Acts. The chief medium through which this is believed to have happened is the spoken matter. British scholarship has in general defended the view that the various

[1] V. K. Robbins, 'By Land and by Sea: The We-Passages and Ancient Sea Voyages', in *PLA*, pp. 215–242; E. Plümacher, 'Wirklichkeitserfahrung und Geschichtsschreibung bei Lukas', *ZNW* 68, 1977, pp. 2–22.

[2] Barrett, *Luke*, p. 22; R. Jewett, *Dating Paul's Life* (London, 1979), pp. 12–17. Barrett does not think that the author of the we-sections was Luke, and Jewett emphasizes that, even if they are from Luke, this does not necessarily guarantee the factuality of every detail in the account. Hengel, pp. 66f., states that Luke is probably the author of the we-passages and of Acts.

speeches placed in the mouths of Peter, Paul and others were, if not verbatim accounts of what was actually said, at least compositions based on tradition and expressing the structure and the details of the earliest Christian preaching.[1] Another trend in scholarship, represented especially by M. Dibelius and U. Wilckens,[2] claims that the speeches had little, if any, basis in tradition and were almost entirely the composition of Luke himself, reflecting his own late theological outlook. The basis for this sceptical verdict lies in an analysis of the speeches themselves. It is argued that their contents do not correspond with the fragments of early preaching which can be detected elsewhere in the New Testament, that the speeches follow a common structure (with individual variations to suit the occasion), that their language and style is Lucan, and that together they offer a compendium of Lucan theology, each speech making its own contribution to the total effect.

These arguments are less forceful than they may appear.[3] First, it is noteworthy that in the most recent edition of his book Wilckens had to make some important qualifications of his earlier statements, and admit that there was more of a traditional basis to some of the speeches than he had previously allowed. The extent of his change of mind must not be over-estimated, but it is of some significance.

Secondly, a number of scholars have drawn attention to the presence of primitive elements in the speeches, especially Jewish patterns of use of the Old Testament.[4] The style of the speeches is not as polished as one would expect if these were careful literary productions; there are in fact the kind of redundancies and minor incoherences which mark the incorporation of traditions into a redactional framework.

Thirdly, while a common structure can be traced in the

[1] C. H. Dodd, *The Apostolic Preaching and its Developments* (London, 1936); F. F. Bruce, *The Speeches in the Acts of the Apostles* (London, 1943).

[2] Dibelius, pp. 138–191, *et passim*; Wilckens; E. Schweizer, 'Concerning the Speeches in Acts', *SLA*, pp. 208–216. The major English-speaking work representing this approach is H. J. Cadbury, 'The Speeches in Acts', *BC*, V, pp. 402–427.

[3] F. F. Bruce, 'The Speeches in Acts – Thirty Years After', in R. Banks (ed.), *Reconciliation and Hope* (Exeter, 1974), pp. 53–68; W. W. Gasque, 'The Speeches of Acts: Dibelius Reconsidered', in R. N. Longenecker and M. C. Tenney (eds.), *New Directions in New Testament Study* (Grand Rapids, 1974), pp. 232–250.

[4] Wilcox, *passim*; Ellis, pp. 198–208.

speeches, it shows considerable variety in individual application, and there is some agreement between the speeches and the admittedly meagre evidence of early preaching that can be gleaned from elsewhere in the New Testament. One may justifiably ask: What sort of things would Peter have said to the Jews, if he did not say the things that Luke ascribes to him? It is very difficult to imagine him taking a line very different from that which he is alleged to have taken.

These points indicate that the speeches in Acts are based on traditional material, although they are insufficient to demonstrate that all the speeches were actually delivered on the occasions specified – a point which probably lies beyond historical proof in any case.[1] In fact, there are a number of points which indicate that the speeches were never meant to be verbatim reports.

First, it would take only a few minutes to read out loud any of the speeches. It is wholly improbable that in reality the speakers were so brief, as 20:7 clearly demonstrates. At best, then, we cannot have any more than summaries of the kind of things that were said.

Secondly, while it is very probable that the teaching of Jesus was especially remembered by his disciples, and indeed that they specifically learned some of what he taught them, it is much less likely that audiences remembered what early Christian preachers said, or that the speakers themselves kept full accounts of what they said. Paul did not speak from a prepared manuscript at Lystra (14:15–17), or write up his sermon afterwards. At most a general account of what he said will have been passed on to Luke.

Thirdly, in some places it can be demonstrated that Luke was not concerned to give a word-for-word account of what was said. The brief message of the angel to Cornelius appears in slightly different forms in 10:4–6 and 31f. But from 10:22, 33 it is plain that the angel said more to Peter than is contained in the two reports just listed. It follows that Luke was not attempting to give more than the general sense of the message. The same is true of the various versions of what was said to Paul at his conversion by the heavenly voice and by Ananias.

Fourthly, there are occasions where it is inherently imposs-

---

[1] Paul's speech in Athens, however, is closely integrated with its specific occasion.

41

ible that Luke can have known what was said. Luke could hardly know what Festus and Agrippa said to each other in their private apartments (25:13–22; 26:30–32), nor could the Christians learn exactly what the members of the Sanhedrin said in closed session (4:15–17; 5:34–40). In the former case, Luke could express the kind of thing that the public behaviour of the rulers indicated that they had probably said in private, and in the latter case some sympathizer from the Sanhedrin may have given the Christians the gist of what had been said about them, but in neither case is a word-for-word reproduction of the conversations at all likely.

The effect of these comments is to show that Luke could and did compose appropriate remarks for his speakers, and that we do him an injustice if we expect from him verbatim accounts of each and every speech. This does not mean that the speeches are his own undisciplined inventions; we have already seen that they are based on source-material of various kinds. In the speeches Luke has done his best to report what was said by preachers in the early church. It is still most reasonable to believe that his practice was similar to that of Thucydides: 'It was in all cases difficult to carry the speeches word-for-word in one's memory, so my habit has been to make the speakers say what was in my opinion demanded of them by the various occasions, of course adhering as closely as possible to the general sense of what they really said' (*History*, 1.22.1).

5. Luke's portrait of Paul

Finally, some mention must be made of *Luke's portrait of Paul, his activities and his theology*. It is this point, perhaps more than any other, which has led to sceptical estimates of the historical value of Acts. The case against Luke is summarized in an essay by P. Vielhauer which argued that Luke's presentation of Paul's attitude to natural theology, to the Jewish law, to christology and to eschatology was quite inconsistent with the picture that we get from Paul's own letters.[1] This article has had an extraordinary influence in persuading scholars of the unhistorical character of Acts. In fact, however, the case has been strongly criticized, and in our opinion convincingly de-

---

[1] P. Vielhauer, 'On the "Paulinism" of Acts', in *SLA*, pp. 33–50. *Cf.* Haenchen, pp. 112–116.

stroyed, in a brief discussion by E. E. Ellis.[1] Some general observations by F. F. Bruce confirm the point.[2] This is not to say that there are no points of tension between Luke's portrait of Paul and his own writings; it is to affirm that in our opinion they are not so substantial as to make us dismiss Acts as unhistorical.[3]

Other points might be brought into the discussion of the historical value of Acts, but these are probably the most important. The effect of our admittedly brief comments is to show that there is a strong case for regarding Acts as an essentially reliable account of what it reports. But it must be observed that arguments of the kind that we have been using cannot *prove* its historicity in detail. Nor should we expect more from Luke than what he claimed to offer. He could not be expected to give the kind of report that might be obtained by a newsman present at every incident with a tape recorder – and even such a report could be one-sided and misleading. He has given us an account of the history of the early church, which deals only with certain aspects of its development and ignores others,[4] and which is based on the sources available to him and written up in a sympathetic manner. If we approach

---

[1] E. E. Ellis, *The Gospel of Luke* (London, 1974²), pp. 45–47.

[2] F. F. Bruce, 'Is the Paul of Acts the Real Paul?', *BJRL* 58, 1976, pp. 282–305. *Cf.* Hanson, pp. 24–27.

[3] E. Plümacher (see p. 35 n. 1), p. 519, lists the following points: (1) Luke's Paul is proud of his Pharisaic piety and ties himself to the law (16:3; 21:18–26; 26:5), while the real Paul sees this as only one possibility which must not be allowed to limit his freedom in Christ (1 Cor. 9:19–23; Gal. 2:5, 11). (2). Above all, Luke's Paul is brought directly into the church and into the closest union with the Jerusalem apostles (9:10–19, 23–30), while the real Paul lays the highest worth on his distance from the apostles and his independence of them. (3). While the historical Paul passionately claims the title of apostle (Gal. 1:1), Acts refuses it to him (with the strange exception of 14:4, 14). None of them is really expressive of a contradiction. Luke stresses the willingness of Paul to live as a Jew among Jews, but says nothing to suggest that he compromised his own freedom or that of his Gentile converts. There is nothing in Acts 9 to suggest that Paul was in any way subordinate to the apostles or dependent upon them. And Acts 14:4, 14, shows that Luke knew that Paul was an apostle, even though he is more interested in the place of the Twelve.

[4] The differences between Luke's portrait of Paul and the picture we get from Paul's own writings are basically due to the different interests of the two writers. Luke is principally concerned with the evangelistic mission of Paul and with his relations to the Jewish Christians, while Paul's letters reflect his concern for problems within the new churches and for the freedom of the Gentiles from Judaistic and syncretistic perversions of the gospel.

it for what it is, we shall appreciate it better than if we demand from its author what he did not try to provide.

IV. THE ORIGINS OF ACTS

1. Authorship

Throughout the preceding discussion we have been content to refer to the author of Acts by his traditional name of 'Luke'. But was the author in fact the person known in the New Testament by this name, the physician, friend and colleague of Paul (Col. 4:14; Phm. 24; 2 Tim. 4:11)?[1] Two lines of argument favour this identification.

First, there is the internal evidence of Acts. Certain passages are written in the first person plural, and the most plausible interpretation of them is that they come from the pen of a companion of Paul, and that they were incorporated in Acts without change of style because the author of this source was himself the author of the book.[2] When we ask who this companion of Paul was, we can eliminate various persons who are mentioned by name in Acts, such as Timothy and Aristarchus; among the various persons whom Paul mentions as his companions in Rome (or in Caesarea, if that be the place of origin of the prison letters), Luke stands out as an obvious name.[3]

Secondly, there is the external evidence from early church writers. The clearest evidence is that of Irenaeus (*c.* AD 180) who names Luke as the author of the third Gospel and Acts. From this point onwards the tradition is firmly attested. It is to be found in the Muratorian Canon[4] and in the so-called Anti-Marcionite Prologue to the Gospel of Luke.[5] The evidence of other writers shows that from the beginning of the third

---

[1] See L. Morris, *Luke*, pp. 14–22; Bruce, *Acts*, pp. 1–8.

[2] See above, p. 38.

[3] The old argument that this identification is proved by the use of medical phraseology at certain points in Luke–Acts has been seriously weakened. The presence of a few medical terms cannot do more than provide some corroboration of a view already held on other grounds.

[4] This is commonly dated at the end of the second century. A. C. Sundberg Jr, 'Canon Muratori: A Fourth-Century List', *HTR* 66, 1973, pp. 1–41, has argued for a later date, but his views do not seem to have gained scholarly assent.

[5] The dating of this document is much disputed. See Haenchen, p. 10 n. 1, and E. E. Ellis, *The Gospel of Luke*, pp. 40f., who date it in the time of Irenaeus or later.

century the tradition is undisputed. It can probably be traced back earlier in the second century. Marcion, who was a fanatical follower of Paul, and whose New Testament consisted only of the Pauline Letters and one Gospel, chose the Gospel of Luke as his Gospel; this very probably implies that he regarded it as being written by a colleague of Paul and expressing a Pauline outlook. Marcion did not include Acts in his 'canon', but his probable recognition of the Lucan authorship of the Gospel can be used to strengthen the case for the Lucan authorship of Acts.[1] There is also a variant text of Acts 20:13 in an Armenian source, which in turn rests upon the Old Syriac version of Acts. It reads: 'But I, Luke, and those who were with me went on board.' This has no claim to be the original text of Acts, but it does indicate how an early scribe interpreted the we-passages. There is some reason to believe that this interpretation may go back to the time of the compilation of the so-called Western text of Acts 11:28, which can be dated early in the second century[2]. The Western text of Acts 11:28 also introduces a 'we' into the text; since tradition held that Luke was a native of Antioch, this variant reading could reflect a belief that Luke was the author of Acts.

It would not be wise to place too much weight on this evidence from the Western text. The important question is whether the verdict of Irenaeus and of others who shared his outlook is merely an intelligent deduction from the we-passages in Acts or rests, at least in part, on some independent tradition regarding the authorship of Acts. Here two points are valid. The first is that the tradition which we have outlined is uncontested. There is no evidence for any other identification of the author of Acts. The second is that, if the tradition were merely a deduction from the New Testament evidence, it is possible that some other companion of Paul might have been named. In fact the tradition in favour of Luke's authorship of the Gospel and Acts is as good as that for any other of the Gospel writers. The argument against it essentially rests on the alleged incompatibility of Luke's portrait of Paul with

---

[1] Marcion could well have rejected Acts, just as he excised certain passages from Paul's Letters, because he did not like the Jewish Christianity which he found expressed in it.

[2] Bruce, *Acts*, 5.

the historical Paul; we have already seen that this argument is lacking in force.[1]

Note on the Western text. Modern Greek texts of Acts are essentially based on the Egyptian manuscripts, Codices, Vaticanus and Sinaiticus. There are many differences (additions and omissions of words, changes of words, and so on) in the version of the text found in Codex Bezae and other manuscripts which mainly come from the western area of early Christendom; this form of text can be traced back to the second century. Arguments that it represents the original text of Acts, or a second edition of the text by the original author, have failed to produce conviction. It is generally thought that it represents an early scribal revision of Acts, although on occasion it may preserve the original wording of Acts when the Egyptian text goes astray. But the whole matter is far more complicated than the present brief summary indicates. Metzger (pp. 259–272) gives a good introduction to the problem, and the major differences between the two textual traditions are discussed *ibid.*, pp. 272–503.

2. *Date of composition*

A decision regarding the date of composition of Acts rests on three factors.

First, there is *the relationship of Luke's writings to other documents.* If we assume that the Gospel of Luke shows literary dependence on Mark, it follows that the date of Luke-Acts will be after that of Mark. Probably the majority of modern scholars would date Mark after AD 70, the year when Jerusalem fell to the Romans after a lengthy siege, on the grounds that Mark appears to recognize in this event the fulfilment of the prophecy made in Mark 13. Luke, it is often argued, has made the allusion to the events of AD 70 all the clearer in Luke 21:20–24 (*cf.* 19:41–44; 23:28–31). Adoption of this view, it should be emphasized, does not necessarily mean that the predictions ascribed to Jesus are to be regarded as fictitious 'prophecies after the event'; it is equally possible that genuine prophecies were remembered, cited, and perhaps edited simply because of the author's desire to show that what Jesus prophesied had in fact come true.

Nevertheless, it has been argued with good reason that the prophecies show no sign of having been written or edited after the event, and that the early church's interest in preserving them may be sufficiently explained by the fact that anybody with any political sense could see in what direction events

[1] The case against Lucan authorship is strongly presented by W. G. Kümmel, *Introduction to the New Testament* (London, 1966), pp. 102–105, 123–132.

were moving in Palestine in the sixties of the first century.[1] The case for dating any of the Synoptic Gospels after AD 70 is thus not a conclusive one, and there is not the slightest reference in Acts to the fall of Jerusalem.[2]

Secondly, there is the question of *the relationship between the writing of Acts and the death of Paul*. Acts does not record the death of Paul which was a judicial execution by the Romans during the reign of Nero (AD 54–68). It ends the story with Paul still active in Rome for two years after his arrival there. Luke gives us prophecies of Paul's appearance before Caesar and his death as a martyr, and yet there is nothing to suggest that the proceedings against him in Rome were likely to lead to his condemnation. It is thus uncertain whether Luke broke his story off because he had brought it up to the time of writing or because for some reason he felt that he had taken it as far as he wished. The latter possibility is the more likely, since Luke's purpose was to show how the gospel reached Rome rather than to write the life story of Paul, and it leaves open the question whether Paul was martyred at the end of the two-year period in Acts 28:30 or at a later point.

Thirdly, there is the question of *the outlook of Acts*. We have seen that its author does not present a mere chronicle of events but has thought carefully about the significance of the story which he records. He presents an interpretation of the history of the early church. It is arguable that a writer cannot do this successfully unless he stands at some distance from the events so that he can see them in perspective. Luke, it can then be claimed, wrote at a point when he could look back at the period which he describes.

But how late is this point? Those who hold that Luke gives us an erroneous picture of Paul will naturally suggest a late date for the book. We have already argued against the basis of this dating. The objection can be strengthened by the observation that Acts does not manifest the interests and outlook typical of the early catholicism which developed late in the first century. There is little interest in the crystallization of

---

[1] B. Reicke, 'Synoptic Prophecies on the Destruction of Jerusalem', in D. E. Aune (ed.), *Studies in New Testament and Early Christian Literature* (Leiden, 1972), pp. 121–134; J. A. T. Robinson, *Redating the New Testament* (London, 1976), chs. 2 and 4.

[2] It has been suggested (Williams, pp. 14f.) that Luke wrote Acts before the Gospel.

sound doctrine, in the doctrine of the church, in the sacraments, and in the development of a hierarchical ministry standing in a line of succession from the apostles. Nor are there any clear references in Acts to the deaths of James (AD 62) and Peter (a victim of Nero). Nor, again, does Luke appear to have read the Letters of Paul, a fact which becomes odder the later we date Acts.[1] To date Acts in the second century becomes manifestly impossible,[2] and a date in the eighties or nineties of the first century is also improbable.

If, however, it is reasonable to hold that Luke could attain to a nuanced picture of the early church comparatively soon after the events which he records, then a somewhat earlier date becomes possible. We have seen that the evidence is ambiguous. On the one hand, Acts betrays no knowledge of any events after Paul's two years in Rome, except perhaps his death. On the other hand, it looks back on his career with a certain sense of perspective. There is therefore much to be said for the view of F. F. Bruce[3] that the composition of Luke-Acts may have taken place over an extended period of time and the completed work may have been issued 'towards AD 70'. On this view, Luke brought his story up to a significant point, the completion of the process of bringing the gospel to Rome, as symbolized by Paul's unhindered preaching there for two years. This was a fitting climax to the story, and here Luke was happy to terminate his account.

3. Place of composition

If the date of Acts is uncertain, the place of its composition and the location of its intended readership are even more uncertain. We have seen that tradition connects Luke with Antioch, and there is some slight evidence for connecting the Gospel with that church. Another suggestion is Rome, since

---

[1] Luke's ignorance of the Letters is odd whatever the dating of Acts. C. K. Barrett, 'Acts and the Pauline Corpus', *Exp. T* 88, 1976–77, pp. 2–5, thinks that the author of Acts belonged to a non-Pauline group and did not know them; in any case their thought would not have fitted into his picture of Pauline theology. If Luke was a companion of Paul, however, his disuse of the Letters may be connected with his lack of interest in the internal problems of Paul's churches.

[2] This view, advanced by O'Neill, pp. 1–58, has not found any significant scholarly support.

[3] F. F. Bruce, 'The Acts of the Apostles', in D. Guthrie *et al.*, *The New Bible Commentary Revised* (London, 1970), pp. 968f.

this is where the story in Acts concludes. Yet another possibility is Ephesus, a city in which Acts shows considerable interest; it is to the leaders of the church there that Paul directs his pastoral 'farewell'.[1] It must be confessed, however, that we simply do not know the answer to this question.

4. Conclusion

Identification of the author, date, and place of composition of Acts does not offer us much help in understanding the book unless we know something independently about each of these factors which can then be used to shed light on the book. Certainly, if Acts was written at an early date by Luke, the companion of Paul, it is likely to have a better basis in history than if it were composed by an unknown author in the early second century. Again, it would be helpful to know if there was some specific historical situation in the church which led to the composition of the book. There is, however, no evidence that Luke was attempting to cope with some specific crisis in the life of the church. His motives were less sharply defined.

Fortunately the intelligibility and value of the book are largely independent of a knowledge of the precise situation in which it was written. While the finer points of the interpretation of Acts can still cause intense discussion among scholars, the essential themes of the book are basically clear and simple.

V. THE PERMANENT VALUE OF ACTS

The particular problems in the church which concerned Luke have in some cases disappeared. No longer is the church concerned with the problem of Jews and Gentiles and all the subsidiary questions that arose out of this basic one. Yet the book retains its value for the church of today in many ways. One or two examples may suffice.

First, Luke himself is seen to be a writer with *a pastoral concern*. He writes in order to help and succour the church. He demonstrates once and for all that church history is not a cold academic discipline but can be the means of encouraging the people of God.

Secondly, Luke makes it clear that in his view *the essential task of the church is mission*. He says remarkably little about the

---

[1] I owe this suggestion to the Rev. D. G. Deeks.

inner life of the church and concentrates most of his attention on this aspect of the church's task. Moreover, for Luke mission means evangelism, the proclamation of the good news of Jesus and the challenge to repentance and faith.

Thirdly, Luke demonstrates that in the purpose of God there can be *no racial discrimination* within the church. The church is called to witness to all people, and salvation is offered to all on the same terms.

Fourthly, Luke stresses *the place of the Spirit* in guiding and empowering the church for its mission. Mission is no mere human achievement. The gifts of the Spirit are given for the purpose of mission and not for the private edification of the church or its individual members.

Fifthly, all this is summed up in the fact that Luke sees *the church as raised up and directed by God* so that it will achieve his intended purpose. In this sense Luke can be said to believe in a *theologia gloriae*. He believes in the ultimate triumph of the gospel. At the same time, however, he is well aware that the triumph of the gospel is achieved only through suffering and martyrdom; in this sense he most emphatically believes in a *theologia crucis*.

Twenty years ago I visited the town of Kassel in Germany. Much of it was still a devastated ruin after the battering it had received during the Second World War. But amid the wrecks of old buildings there still stood the broken-down shell of a church. Only fragments of the building had survived, but at one end a spire still pointed to the sky, and an inscription remained carved in stone over a doorway: 'But the Word of God abides for ever.' Luke would have appreciated the symbolism; this is what he has to say to us.

ANALYSIS

I. THE BEGINNING OF THE CHURCH (1:1 – 2:47)

    a. Prologue (1:1–5)

    b. The ascension of Jesus (1:6–11)

    c. The return of the disciples to Jerusalem (1:12–14)

    d. The twelfth apostle (1:15–26)

    e. The pouring out of the Spirit (2:1–13)

    f. Peter preaches the gospel (2:14–42)

    g. A summary of the life of the early church (2:43–47)

II. THE CHURCH AND THE JEWISH AUTHORITIES (3:1 – 5:42)

    a. The healing of a lame man (3:1–10)

    b. Peter explains the incident (3:11–26)

    c. The arrest of Peter and John (4:1–22)

    d. The disciples pray for further boldness (4:23–31)

    e. A further summary of the life of the early church (4:32–37)

    f. The sin of Ananias and Sapphira (5:1–11)

    g. The continuing growth of the church (5:12–16)

    h. The second arrest of the apostles (5:17–42)

III. THE CHURCH BEGINS TO EXPAND (6:1 – 9:31)

    a. The appointment of the Seven (6:1–7)

ANALYSIS

COMMENTARY

I. THE BEGINNING OF THE CHURCH (1:1 – 2:47)

a. Prologue (1:1–5)

The Gospel of Luke and the Acts of the Apostles were intended by their author to be regarded as Part 1 and Part 2 of one single work. It was common in the ancient world for a single work to consist of several parts or 'books' in this way, and for the author to provide a brief introduction to each part. In the Gospel Luke has provided a carefully phrased introduction at the beginning (Lk. 1:1–4); its language, style and content clearly distinguish it from the main body of the story which begins in Luke 1:5. In Acts Luke follows traditional practice in reflecting the wording of the preface to the Gospel, but in this case the introduction is not sharply distinguished from the following narrative, and the latter flows out of the former. Moreover, while Luke tells us what he had done in the Gospel, he does not state explicitly what is the purpose of the Acts. The effect of the introduction, therefore, is to give the reader a brief summary of the Gospel before he goes on to the next stage of the story. By writing in this way Luke has emphasized the unity between the story of the ministry of Jesus and the story of the beginning of the church. The Gospel tells what Jesus began to do and teach; Acts relates what he continued to do and teach through the agency of his witnesses. Since verses 1–5 are largely a recapitulation of the last chapter of the Gospel, we may regard the introduction as comprising this section before fresh material is added in verses 6ff. Luke sets the scene for what follows by emphasizing the commandments which Jesus gave to the disciples, the reality of his resurrection appearances, and the promise of the coming of the Spirit. These points form the foundation for the continuing work of the followers of Jesus.

1. Luke dedicates his book to *Theophilus*. The name means 'dear to God', but it is doubtless the real name of a real person and not just a symbolical name. The omission of the courteous 'most excellent' used in Luke 1:3 is quite natural at the second occurrence of the name. Theophilus was probably already a Christian, and Luke wrote his book to help him and others like him to have a reliable account of the beginnings of Christianity. The *first book* is of course the Gospel, which is summed up as an account of *all that Jesus began to do and teach*. The phrasing has two slight peculiarities. First, Luke has included a Greek particle (not translated in RSV) equivalent to our 'on the one hand' in describing his composition of the Gospel; this leads us to expect a further statement outlining 'on the other hand' what is going to be related in Acts, but no such statement follows. Luke makes the same omission elsewhere, and we should probably supply the contrast from the context. This leads us to the second peculiarity, the use of the word *began* in relation to the earthly ministry of Jesus. Although some scholars think that the word is redundant (as it often can be in ancient writing), it seems more probable that it is deliberately used here, so that Luke is associating what Jesus began to do during his ministry with (implicitly) what he continued to do after his ascension; the ministry of Jesus was the beginning of Christianity.

2. The story of the 'beginning' covered the time until Jesus *was taken up* by God to heaven. The Gospel ends with a brief reference to this incident (Lk. 24:51), which was preceded by important teaching given by Jesus to his disciples. So important was this teaching that we have three accounts of it. Luke records it in the Gospel (Lk. 24, especially verses 44–49); he then summarizes it briefly in this introductory part of Acts, and then he covers certain aspects of it once again in the story of the ascension which is the first incident in the main narrative in Acts (1:6–11). The repetition is partly for emphasis, and at the same time it indicates that the period from Easter Sunday to the ascension is both the conclusion of the earthly ministry of Jesus and the beginning of the work of the church. This period had two important characteristics. It provided evidence that Jesus was alive (1:3) and it was the time when Jesus gave his marching orders to the apostles (1:4f.; *cf.* 1:7f.).

Two significant points come out incidentally before Luke develops these characteristics. The first is that the followers of Jesus are designated as *apostles*. To understand this word we have to look at its earlier use in the Gospel where it refers to the twelve disciples whom Jesus chose and sent out to act

56

as missionaries and witnesses (Lk. 6:13; 9:10; 11:49; *cf.* 17:5; 22:14; 24:10). Later it will become clear that it refers to people who were with Jesus during his ministry and were specifically chosen to be witnesses to his resurrection (1:21f.). The thought is of the twelve disciples (with Judas replaced by Matthias, 1:15–26), but the word can also be used of Paul and Barnabas (14:4, 14; see note there). The other point is the reference to the *Holy Spirit* as the source of guidance for Jesus in choosing the apostles.[1] One of the concerns of Luke is to demonstrate how both Jesus and the church were directed by the Spirit to fulfil the purpose of God for them.

3. Luke explains that the instructions given by Jesus were delivered during the period between his death and ascension. His death is described as his *passion*, literally 'suffering', a word that is not infrequent in the New Testament and brings out the element of torture inflicted on the innocent Jesus at his death (17:3; 26:23). After it Jesus showed that he was *alive* by *appearing* to his disciples on several occasions. The stress lies on the factuality of the evidence, as we have it in the stories in Luke 24 where the initial unwillingness of the disciples to believe that Jesus was risen was overcome by the clear evidence presented to them. Nor did their conviction rest on one single experience, but rather on repeated pieces of proof. Although in Luke 24 the resurrection appearances of Jesus are presented as if they all took place on Easter Sunday, here Luke relates that they happened over an extended period of *forty days*. This may be simply a round number, but it fits in with the fact that there were fifty days between Easter and Pentecost. During this period the theme of Jesus' teaching is said to have been the *kingdom of God*, a phrase which elsewhere sums up the theme of his earthly ministry (Lk. 4:43), and signifies the saving, sovereign action of God through him. The point is that this is to continue to be the theme of the witness of the church, which will thus follow on from the preaching of Jesus (8:12; 19:8; 20:25; 28:23, 31), although there will inevitably be new elements and a new emphasis as Jesus himself becomes part of the message (28:31). It follows that

[1] The RSV links *through the Holy Spirit* with *after he had given commandment*, but it probably should go with *whom he had chosen*; the unusual word-order in the Greek is probably for emphasis.

the church can take up the message of Jesus, as recorded in the Gospels, and make it part of its own.

4. One particular instruction of Jesus is recorded from the time while he was *staying* with them. The word used here (Gk. *synalizomai*) is unusual and appears to refer to some special kind of fellowship (Wilcox, pp. 106–109); NIV 'while he was eating with them' (*cf.* RSV mg.) brings out the probable meaning and shows that the instruction probably took place during the meals held by Jesus with the disciples after the resurrection (*cf.* Jn. 21:9–14). Jesus instructed the apostles to stay in Jerusalem until they received *the promise of the Father*. Here *promise* means concretely 'the thing promised by the Father' and must refer to the Holy Spirit (2:33, 38f.; Gal. 3:14; Eph. 1:13); the Father's promise is contained in the Scriptures, Isaiah 32:15 (*cf.* Lk. 24:49) and Joel 2:28–32. But when did the disciples hear this promise from Jesus himself? One possibility is that Luke 24:49 is in mind, but it is more likely that the present verse is a recapitulation of the saying in the Gospel, expressed in slightly different wording. We should, therefore, think perhaps of such teaching about the coming of the Spirit as we find in Matthew 10:20 (*cf.* Lk. 12:12) and John 14 – 16. The disciples might have been tempted to return to Galilee (Jn. 21 indicates that this did in fact happen), but Jerusalem was the divinely intended scene for the giving of the Spirit; the place where Jesus was rejected was to be the place where fresh witness to him would begin.

5. Jesus' promise is strengthened by a reminder of the testimony of John the Baptist; he had claimed to baptize merely *with water*, but prophesied the coming of One who would baptize *with the Spirit* (Lk. 3:16), and Jesus now alludes to this statement (*cf.* Peter's citation of these words of Jesus in 11:16). To baptize literally means to immerse a person in water or to deluge him with it, usually as a means of cleansing. When the term is applied to the Spirit, it appears to refer to the pouring out of the Spirit from on high by God and is associated with the forgiveness of sins (2:38). But the metaphor of pouring out a liquid is ultimately inadequate to do justice to the gift of the Spirit who comes to God's people, bringing power, wisdom and joy; as a result the term 'baptism' is considerably widened in its metaphorical use, and no one synonym can do justice to its range of meaning as a Christian technical term for the reception of the Spirit.

b. The ascension of Jesus (1:6–11)

Although we have entitled this section 'The ascension', it is doubtful whether the actual act of ascension is the central feature in the story. Luke is more concerned with what was said than with what happened. The vital question was the one posed by the disciples: now that Jesus had been raised from the dead, was God going to complete his purpose by finally establishing his rule? The answer given was twofold. First, the time of this event remained God's secret; what was more important was the immediate task of the disciples which was to act as witnesses to Jesus from Jerusalem to the end of the earth. The spread of God's rule was to take place by means of the disciples, empowered by the Spirit. This was the final command of Jesus before he left the disciples. Secondly, the departure of Jesus was interpreted as a pattern for his ultimate return to the earth to inaugurate the final establishment of the rule of God. These verses thus spell out God's purpose and the place of the church in it. They postulate that the period of witness and mission must precede the return of Jesus. They were thus in effect a warning to the disciples not to expect a speedy winding up of history. For Luke's readers some forty or more years later they were a reminder of an ongoing task: the gospel must still be taken to the end of the earth. At the same time the words contain a note of promise in that the departure of Jesus is compensated for by the coming of the Spirit, given by Jesus himself (2:33).

Luke alone describes the ascension of Jesus as a visible event, although the fact of the ascension is firmly attested elsewhere (1 Tim. 3:16; 1 Pet. 3:21f.), especially in the many passages where the resurrection of Jesus is understood to be not simply his raising from death but also his exaltation to the right hand of God (2:33–35). The historicity of the scene has been strongly questioned by scholars who hold that Luke has created a dramatic representation of the theological truth of the exaltation of Jesus.[1] There are of course difficulties if we interpret the story over-literally and draw from it the concept of a heaven 'up there' somewhere in space. The story is rather like those of the creation of the world or of the incarnation of Jesus or of his resurrection, in which events that bring together the transcendent reality of God and the physical world – and

[1] G. Lohfink, *Die Himmelfahrt Jesu* (München, 1971).

which therefore cannot be described fully in terms and categories that belong to the latter – are expressed in a symbolical, pictorial manner. The symbolism of 'ascension' expresses the way in which the physical presence of Jesus departed from this world, to be replaced by his spiritual presence. To say this is obviously not to deny the factuality or historicity of what happened, but to admit that what happened lies beyond simple, literal description. It is in this kind of way that the story of the ascension of Jesus is best understood.

6. Luke portrays a fresh scene in which the disciples take up the reference to the kingdom of God in verse 3. Their question is whether Jesus intends to *restore the kingdom to* (or 'for') *Israel.* This may reflect the Jewish hope that God would establish his rule in such a way that the people of Israel would be freed from their enemies (especially the Romans) and established as a nation to which other peoples would be subservient. If so, the disciples would appear here as representatives of those of Luke's readers who had not yet realized that Jesus had transformed the Jewish hope of the kingdom of God by purging it of its nationalistic political elements. Another possibility is that Luke's readers might think that the 'times of the Gentiles', during which Jerusalem was to be desolate, ought now to be coming to an end and giving place to the coming of the kingdom (Lk. 21:24, 31); in this case there would be a secondary interpretation of the disciples' question in terms of the expectations of Luke's readers. It is less likely that the question is in effect whether the coming of the Spirit is to be interpreted as the restoration of the kingdom. Rather, we have a question about how soon the end is to come, which was natural enough in the context of the resurrection appearances of Jesus: it would be very natural to wonder whether these marked the beginning of the last stage in God's plan.

7–8. But no direct answer is given – at least in terms of time. In language reminiscent of Mark 13:32 Jesus roundly states that the matter of the time of God's action is his own affair, and it is not open to men to share his knowledge. Since this is God's secret, there is no place for human speculation – a point that might well be borne in mind by those who still anxiously try to calculate the probable course of events in the last days. Instead of indulging in wishful thinking or apocalyptic speculation, the disciples must accomplish their task of being *witnesses* to Jesus. The scope of their task is worldwide.

It begins with *Jerusalem, Judea and Samaria,* and it stretches *to the end of the earth.* While some have thought that this expression designates Rome, it is much more probable that it has a wider sense;[1] the end of Acts does not mark the completion of the task proposed here, but simply the completion of the first phase. Nevertheless, in a broad sense the programme outlined here corresponds to the structure of Acts as a whole. For this task the disciples are promised the power of the Spirit (Lk. 24:49), a promise primarily fulfilled at Pentecost and secondarily fulfilled on many other occasions. These words have special emphasis as the last words of Jesus before his departure; they are closely parallel to his last recorded words in the Gospel (Lk. 24:46–49), given just before he left the disciples, and are perhaps to be understood as an alternative version of them (we may compare the way in which Luke gives us slightly different versions of the conversation associated with Paul's conversion in the three accounts of it).

9. Immediately afterwards Jesus was *lifted up* and *a cloud took him* away before the eyes of the disciples. The function of the disciples as eyewitnesses to the ascension is underlined by the threefold repetition of the thought in this verse and the next. The cloud is at one and the same time the vehicle which envelops Jesus and transports him away, and the sign of the heavenly glory of God (*cf.* Lk. 9:34f.; Rev. 11:12). It is thus a supernatural and symbolical cloud.

10–11. The disciples are portrayed as looking intently into the sky as Jesus disappears, a detail which suggests that they are longing for the reappearance of Jesus or some other happening which will indicate that what they have seen is not the final act in the drama. Their unspoken prayer is answered by the appearance of two figures dressed in white. The description is that of angels (Lk. 24:4; Acts 10:30) who wear bright, shining clothes. Their function is to give a commentary on what has happened. They ask the disciples why they are gazing into heaven; the question is an implicit reproach of them for dawdling there and longing for Jesus to remain with them. Already the disciples have had a command as to what they are to do. Now they are given an assurance that the ascension of Jesus is a guarantee that, as it was possible for Jesus to ascend into heaven, so it will be possible for him to

---

[1] van Unnik, pp. 386–401.

return in the same way, *i.e.* on a cloud at the parousia (Lk. 21:27; Mk. 14:62; *cf.* Dn. 7:13). Thus the promise of the parousia forms the background of hope against which the disciples are to act as the witnesses to Jesus. In effect the present passage corresponds to Jesus' statement in Mark 13:10 that the gospel must first be preached to all nations before the end can come.

c. The return of the disciples to Jerusalem (1:12–14)

The story of the ascension is completed with the account of how the disciples obeyed Jesus and returned to Jerusalem to await the promised Spirit in an attitude of prayer.

12. Only at the end of the story of the ascension do we learn that it happened at 'the Mount of Olives'. In the parallel account in Luke 24:50 Jesus is said to lead the disciples to Bethany, which was a village lying on the east slope of the hill (*cf.* Lk. 19:29). *A sabbath day's journey* was about 1.2 km (¾ mile); the expression is a Jewish one, and is not meant to imply that the event took place on a sabbath. The point is rather that the ascension (like the resurrection appearances of Jesus in Lk. 24) took place in the near vicinity of Jerusalem.

13. The disciples had established themselves in an upstairs room in a house in Jerusalem; this would give them privacy (*cf.* 9:37) and would be suitable for prayer (Dn. 6:10). Whether this particular room should be identified with that where the Last Supper was held (Lk. 22:12 – a different Greek word for 'room' is used) and located in the house of Mary, the mother of John Mark (12:12), cannot be stated with any certainty. Luke gives a list of the eleven apostles at this point, which corresponds with his earlier list in Luke 6:14–16 and demonstrates that the intimate disciples of the earthly Jesus formed the core of the church.

14. If the Holy Spirit is the divine gift which empowers and guides the church, the corresponding human attitude towards God is *prayer*. It is as the church prays that it receives the Spirit. So at the outset Luke emphasizes that the disciples spent the time of waiting for the Spirit in an attitude of continuous and united prayer (*cf.* 2:46f; 4:24ff.). They included among their number *the women* who were disciples of Jesus (Lk. 8:2f.; 23:49; 24:10), at least some of whom had seen the empty tomb, and in particular *Mary*, the mother of Jesus, together with his *brothers* (Mk. 6:3; Jn. 7:3–5). The family of

Jesus were thus among those who became part of the church, and one of them, James, was to assume a leading position in it.[1]

d. The twelfth apostle (1:15–26)

Luke relates one incident which in effect fills up the time gap between the ascension and Pentecost. It may, therefore, be regarded as of particular importance in his eyes. The story is concerned with the choice of a successor to Judas to become a witness to the resurrection and take his place among the twelve apostles; woven in with this is an account of how Judas died and lost his place. There can be no doubt that the choice of Matthias instead of the alternative candidate is historical. Problems are raised, however, by the account of Judas's death (which differs in some particulars from the record in Mt. 27:3–10) and also by the speech of Peter.[2] According to Haenchen, (pp. 163f.), Luke's purpose was to show that in the apostles the church possessed reliable guarantors of the truth of its message. But there is probably more to it than this.[3] In the Gospel the Twelve had a special function as apostles to the Jews and could look forward to sitting on thrones to judge the twelve tribes of Israel (Lk. 9:1–6; 22:28–30); the filling up of the number was probably meant to indicate that the task of witness to Jesus as the Messiah for the Jews was to be continued after the resurrection. It is not so likely that we are to see here information about how the leadership of the church ought to be organized.

15. The initiative in the story is assigned to Peter, who had been the most forceful personality among the disciples in the Gospels and now naturally took the lead with his proposal. The story is interrupted by an awkwardly placed parenthesis which indicates that the number of 'brothers' present was about 120. Here we have the first use of 'brothers' to designate

[1] For the relation of the brothers of Jesus to Mary see R. V. G. Tasker, *James* (*Tyndale New Testament Commentaries*, London, 1957), pp. 22–24.

[2] For the death of Judas see especially A. Gordon, 'The Fate of Judas according to Acts 1:18', *EQ* 44, 1971, pp. 97–100; J. A. Motyer, in *NIDNTT*, I, pp. 93f. For the latter see M. Wilcox, 'The Judas-Tradition in Acts i. 15–26', *NTS* 19, 1972–73, pp. 438–452, who argues that Luke has used a tradition as the basis of the speech (found in verses 17, 18, 19b).

[3] K. H. Rengstorf, 'The Election of Matthias, Acts 1, 15ff.', in W. Klassen and G. F. Snyder (eds.), *Current Issues in New Testament Interpretation* (New York, 1962), pp. 178–192.

Christians; Hanson (p. 46) thinks that this was the earliest Christian designation for members of the church. The reason for the parenthesis about the number of disciples is that in Jewish law a minimum of 120 Jewish men was required to establish a community with its own council; in Jewish terms the disciples were a body of sufficient size to form a new community.

16–17. Peter's speech begins by claiming that it was necessary for the Scripture to be fulfilled in the case of Judas, the betrayer of Jesus. The reference to *David* as the writer through whom the Holy Spirit made his prophecy directs our attention to the two quotations in verse 20 which come from the Psalms, and in particular to the former one which deals with Judas's fate. The long gap before the actual quotation is due to the way in which verses 18–19 have been inserted as a parenthesis which does not form part of Peter's speech (*cf.* NEB and NIV punctuation). The reason why the Scripture had to be fulfilled was that Judas belonged to the number of the Twelve and had his appointed share in the task of ministry or service instituted by Jesus. This share would need to be taken over by somebody else. Behind the wording may lie the wording of the Palestinian Targum to Genesis 44:18 which refers to 'Benjamin who was numbered with us among the tribes and will receive a portion and share with us in the division of the land'; if this is a correct identification, it confirms that Luke is here dependent on Palestinian traditions. The wording underlines the enormity of Judas's sin as a betrayer of Jesus.

18–19. The next two verses form a digression, describing for the reader how Judas died. The wording in verse 19, with its reference in the third person to the inhabitants of Jerusalem and their language, indicates that this is not part of Peter's address. The story is that Judas *bought a field* or property with the money he obtained for betraying Jesus. He fell down prone and ruptured himself with the result that his entrails poured out (like Amasa, 2 Sa. 20:10). The result was that the people of Jerusalem nicknamed the place *Akeldama* (Aramic *hᵃqēl dᵉmā*) which means *Field of Blood, i.e.* 'the bloody field'. This story raises problems: *a*. It leaves the manner of Judas's death very unclear; *b*. It differs in important respects from Matthew's story. Matthew tells us that Judas committed suicide by hanging, and that, when Judas returned the blood-money to the temple, the priests bought the 'potter's field' to serve as a graveyard and it became known as 'field of blood'. It is quite possible that Matthew or Luke is simply reporting what was commonly said in Jerusalem, and that we are not meant to harmonize the two accounts. If we do try to harmonzie them, the following possibilities arise: (1). Judas hanged himself (Mt.), but the rope broke and his body was ruptured by the fall (possibly after he was already dead and beginning to decompose); (2). What the priests bought with Judas's money (Mt.) could be regarded as his purchase by their agency (Acts); (3). The field bought by the priests (Mt.) was the one where Judas died (Acts).

20. Two scriptural quotations follow. The first is from Psalm 69:25, and represents a threat against the enemies of a godly person who was seen by Jesus and the early church as typifying the Messiah; hence it would be natural to find in this Psalm a prophecy or type of the betrayer of Jesus. The application is made by altering the original 'their habitation' of the Psalm to *his habitation*. The *habitation* is the field which Judas bought and over which a curse will rest: nobody will live in it (as Matthew indicates by saying that it became a cemetery). C. H. Dodd[1] suggests that the effect of the citation was to show that Scripture allowed for the creation of a vacancy in the apostolate, caused by apostasy and not by death (hence there was no need to elect a successor to James, Acts 12:2); moreover, a further scripture gave warrant for the filling of the vacancy. The second text is Psalm 109:8[2] where the Psalmist utters a string of curses against his enemy and wishes that somebody else may take over his occupation. This is used as justification for handing over the office of Judas to somebody else.[3]

21–22. The real reason, however, for seeking a successor to Judas, lay not in Old Testament prophecy, which provided confirmation for the action rather than its original inspiration; rather it arose from the character of the task which required

[1] C. H. Dodd, *According to the Scriptures* (London, 1965), p. 58n.

[2] 'Let someone else take over his office', JB; the RSV rendering 'may another seize his goods' is possible, but less likely.

[3] We may note in passing that in both cases the interpretation could be made on the basis of the Hebrew text, and that it is false to claim that the quotations could have been used only on the basis of the Greek text; the Greek text, however, does use the word *episkopē* 'oversight' which is related to *episkopos*, used as a later term for Christian leaders.

that the full number of witnesses be made up. According to Paul the qualifications of an apostle, such as himself, were that he should have seen (the resurrected) Jesus and have received a commission to be his witness (1 Cor. 9:1f.; 15:8–10; Gal. 1:16f.). Here too the need is for a *witness to his resurrection*, but the choice is to be made from the group of people who had been associated with the other apostles throughout the ministry of Jesus, from its beginning at *the baptism of John* right through to the ascension of Jesus. This 'extra' qualification has seemed strange to many readers, but it is entirely natural in seeking a successor for one of the Twelve who had been disciples of Jesus and whose task (we may reasonably suggest) was linked with witness to the Jews. It is a different question whether in Acts apostleship is thought to be limited to the Twelve (see 14:4, 14 and notes).

23–25. The audience put forward two possible candidates for the post. *Joseph Barsabbas* is distinguished from other persons called Joseph by his patronymic, 'Son of the Sabbath' (*cf.* 15:22); he also had a Latin name, *Justus* (*cf.* Col. 4:11), following a practice adopted by many Jews. Nothing further is known about him, although a legend sprang up that he drank poison and suffered no harm. *Matthias* is an abbreviated form of Mattithiah, another common name. The real choice, however, was left to the *Lord*, since apostleship is not a humanly ordained office. The assembly, therefore, prayed that he would exercise his choice in virtue of his knowledge of men's hearts (*cf.* 15:8 and especially 1 Sa. 16:7). It is not clear whether God the Father or Jesus is addressed in the prayer, but in view of the fact that in 1:2 the same verb is used of Jesus choosing the apostles, it is more probable that he is addressed here. The task of apostleship is described as a *ministry*; the Greek word *diakonia* means 'service' (originally service at a meal table), and it is used of Christian work of all kinds, which takes its pattern from the One who came not to be served but to serve (Mk. 10:45). The *place* to which Judas went represents a current euphemism for one's ultimate destination, whether heaven or hell.

26. The casting of *lots* was the device employed to allow the Lord to make his choice (Pr. 16:33). It was a practice also followed by the Qumran sect (1QS 5:3), but it seems doubtful whether it was copied by the church from Qumran. Likewise, it is unnecessary to regard the number of twelve apostles as

66

patterned on the twelve lay persons who (together with three priests) made up the council of the Qumran sect (1QS 8:1; it is not clear whether there were fifteen or twelve members in all). Some commentators have argued that the recourse to the lot typifies the situation of the church before Pentecost when it did not have the guidance of the Spirit, and others have gone further and claimed that the church acted wrongly in choosing Matthias: it should have waited for the 'twelfth man' of God's own choice, Paul, instead of giving God his choice between two others who are never heard of again. But we never hear any more of the other members of the Twelve (apart from Peter, James and John) in Acts, and Paul did not possess the essential qualifications to be one of the Twelve. The most that might be said is that in the period before Pentecost the church had to seek other means of divine guidance than the aid of the Spirit, but the method which it adopted (prayer and the casting of lots) was entirely proper. In fact the church was asking the Lord to make *his* choice of the right man, who was then *enrolled* as an apostle; the church cannot be said to have 'elected' him.

e. The pouring out of the Spirit (2:1–13)

When the days of waiting were over, the Holy Spirit came upon the assembled group of disciples in a new way, accompanied by supernatural signs and causing them to burst out into the praise of God in languages other than their own. As the disciples moved out into the streets, their strange activity attracted the attention of the people who were nonplussed by what they heard. Many were amazed, but some were ready to seek a rationalist and somewhat discreditable explanation of what was happening.

Luke alone refers to the story of how the Spirit came upon the church for the first time, but the essential historicity of the incident is firmly assured.[1] Its placing in Acts corresponds to the position of the birth of Jesus in the Gospel, and its significance is that the church is now equipped for the task of witness and mission, and proceeds straightaway to undertake it. The story contains the fulfilment of the prophecy in 1:4f.,

---

[1] See J. Kremer, *Pfingstbericht und Pfingstgeschehen* (Stuttgart, 1973); Dunn, *Jesus*, pp. 135–156; I. H. Marshall, 'The Significance of Pentecost', *SJT* 30, 1977, pp. 347–369.

and thus describes how the disciples were baptized with the Holy Spirit; more correctly, it is the first occurrence of this experience. At the same time, the event fulfils the prophecies of Isaiah 32:15 and Joel 2:28–32, and thus indicates that the last days have arrived. Some scholars have detected in the story a deliberate contrast to the story of Babel (Gn. 11) and a Christian counterpart to the giving of the law at Sinai. The former of these possibilities has no basis in the text, while the evidence for the latter is stronger but not altogether convincing.

1. *Pentecost* is the New Testament name for the Feast of Weeks, when the wheat harvest was celebrated by a one-day festival during which special sacrifices were offered (Ex. 23:16; Lv. 23:15–21; Dt. 16:9–12). Just as other festivals were associated with important events in Israel's history (*e.g.* Passover with the exodus from Egypt), so in Judaism the festival was associated with the renewal of the covenant made with Noah and then with Moses (*Jubilees* 6); in second-century Judaism Pentecost was regarded as the day when the law was given at Sinai. It is interesting that there was a rabbinic tradition that the law was promulgated by God in the languages of the seventy nations of the world, but we cannot be certain that this tradition was current in the first century. The disciples were still in Jerusalem; some scholars think that they were in the temple, in view of the word 'house' in verse 2, but 'house', used on its own like this, cannot mean the temple. The whole company of 120 people is doubtless meant, and not just the reconstituted twelve apostles.

2–3. Since elsewhere the Spirit is likened to *wind*, and the word used (Greek *pneuma*) can have either meaning, it is not surprising that the first of two symbols which accompanied his arrival was a noise like that of wind; Luke describes it as almost palpable when he says that *it filled all the house*. The language, it should be noted, is that of analogy – a sound *like* that of wind – and indicates that we have to do with a supernatural occurrence. The symbolism is reminiscent of Old Testament theophanies (2 Sa. 22:16; Job 37:10; Ezk. 13:13): the wind is a sign of God's presence as Spirit. A second symbol was *fire*. A flame divided itself into several *tongues*, so that each rested upon one of the persons present. Again the description is analogical – *as* of fire. And again we are reminded of Old Testament theophanies, especially of that at Sinai (Ex. 19:18), but the primary background is probably John the Baptist's association of the Spirit with fire as a means of cleansing and judgment (Lk. 3:16).

4. With these outward signs came *the Holy Spirit* as an inward, invisible reality that demonstrated his presence by the effects wrought upon the disciples. Luke uses the word *fill* to describe the experience. This word is used when people are given an initial endowment of the Spirit to fit them for God's service (9:17; Lk. 1:15) and also when they are inspired to make important utterances (4:8, 31; 13:9); related words are used to describe the continuous process of being filled with the Spirit (13:52; Eph. 5:18) or the corresponding state of being full (6:3, 5; 7:55; 11:24; Lk. 4:1). These references indicate that a person already filled with the Spirit can receive a fresh filling for a specific task, or a continuous filling. It is also important to observe that what is here called a 'filling' is called a 'baptizing' (1:5 and 11:16), a 'pouring out' (2:17f; 10:45), and a 'receiving' (10:47). The basic act of receiving the Spirit can be described as being baptized or filled, but the verb 'baptize' is not used for subsequent experiences.[1] A good deal of theological confusion would be avoided if we were careful to use these terms in the biblical manner. We should also note that what happened later to Cornelius and his family was the same as what happened at Pentecost (11:15); at conversion the believer experiences his own 'Pentecost'. It is probable that Luke has used the term 'filled' in the present context because the Spirit inspired the recipients *to speak in other tongues.* Verses 6, 8 and 11 show that human languages are meant. This raises two difficulties. First, most commentators think that the gift of tongues described in 1 Corinthians 12, 14 was the ability to speak in non-human languages (the tongues 'of angels', 1 Cor. 13:1). On the assumption that it is unlikely that there were two different types of phenomenon, it is then often claimed that Luke has either misunderstood or deliberately reinterpreted an earlier tradition which described the Pauline kind of tongues. Secondly, this conclusion is held to be confirmed by modern linguistic analyses of the tongues spoken in modern Pentecostalist movements as non-human languages. It is difficult, however, to set aside the evidence of

[1] The noun-phrase *'baptism* with the Spirit' does not occur in the New Testament.

modern people who have claimed to hear their own languages being spoken by persons with the gift of tongues. Nor is it altogether impossible that Paul was referring to human languages,[1] or that both human and heavenly tongues were used (1 Cor. 13:1 – 'the tongues of men *and* angels'). Dunn (*Jesus*, pp. 151f.) suggests that what happened was that the hearers thought that they heard and recognized words and phrases of praise to God in their own languages.

5. We must assume that at some point the disciples moved outside from the upper room and came in contact with the crowds assembled in Jerusalem for the feast; *dwelling* need not necessarily imply permanent residence, although many Jews did return to Jerusalem from the Dispersion to end their days there. Their presence and participation in what happened constituted an indication of the worldwide significance of the event. True, they were all Jews or proselytes and not pagans, but they acted as a symbol of the universal need of mankind for the gospel and of the church's consequent responsibility for mission.

6–8. The *sound* of the disciples calling out loud *bewildered* the crowd since they could not understand how *Galileans* could speak in their own languages. It has been objected that probably most of the crowd would speak Aramaic or Greek, the two languages which the disciples also would speak, and that therefore the miracle of tongues was unnecessary. But this difficulty must surely have been obvious to Luke also. What was significant was that the various *vernacular* languages of these peoples were being spoken. We may wonder how the crowds knew that the disciples were Galileans. But a glance at the saying attributed to the crowds in verses 7–11 will indicate that this is no more than a summary of the different things that were being said, combined for literary reasons into one choral statement, and therefore we need not suppose that more than a few of the crowd were able to recognize the disciples as Galileans.

9–11. Still continuing his omnibus version of what the various members of the crowd are likely to have said, Luke now gives us a list of the nationalities represented. It begins with three countries to the east of the Roman Empire in the area known as Persia or Iran, and then (with a change of construc-

---

[1] R. H. Gundry, '"Ecstatic Utterance" (NEB)?', *JTS* 17, 1966, pp. 299–307.

tion) moves westward to Mesopotamia, modern Iraq, and Judea. Next come various provinces and areas in Asia Minor, (modern Turkey), and then Egypt and the area immediately westwards, followed by Rome. Then we have a general statement applicable to all the peoples in mind: there was a considerable Jewish population in each of these areas, and the presence of Jews often led to the conversion of Gentiles to become proselytes. Finally, and somewhat surprisingly, the list includes people from Crete and Arabia. It is an odd list, and nobody has been able to explain satisfactorily why it includes the particular selection of countries that it does, and why they come in this strange order.[1] It certainly was not invented by Luke himself. It must suffice to observe that the list is clearly meant to be an indication that people from all over the known world were present, and perhaps that they would return to their own countries as witnesses to what was happening. All of them as worshippers of Yahweh could tell that the Christians were celebrating the mighty works of God.

12–13. The primary reaction was one of incomprehension. The crowds were very naturally at a loss to know what was happening, and this situation created the opportunity for Peter to address them and explain what it was all about. More particularly, he was given a 'lead-in' to his speech by the fact that some people were ready to explain the speaking in tongues as the result of drunkenness; this would be a very natural explanation to offer if one heard people making unintelligible noises, as some of the sounds must have seemed to those of the hearers who did not recognize the particular language being used.

f. Peter preaches the gospel (2:14–42)

The assembled crowd provided Peter with his opportunity to explain the significance of what was happening. His speech or sermon begins with an allusion to the pouring out of the Spirit as the fulfilment of prophecy and concludes with a further reference to the same event (2:33). But in between these references Peter explores more deeply the significance of the event. He traces the gift of the Spirit back to Jesus. This man

---

[1] See B. M. Metzger, 'Ancient Astrological Geography and Acts 2:9–11', in *AHG*, pp. 123–133; E. Güting, 'Der geographische Horizont der sogennanten Völkerliste des Lukas (Acta 2:9–11)', *ZNW* 66, 1975, pp. 149–169.

of God had been rejected by the Jews, but raised from the dead by God, as the apostles could testify. But his resurrection had to be seen also in the light of prophecy. A Psalm of David which spoke of deliverance from death must, said Peter, be understood as applying to the Messiah, since clearly it could not apply to David himself. Since God had raised Jesus from death, it followed that he was the Messiah, and it was in consequence of this that he had poured out the Spirit (Lk. 24:49; Jn. 20:22). Thus the resurrection of Jesus and the pouring out of the Spirit both testified that Jesus was the Lord and Messiah. When the audience demanded to know what this implied, Peter urged them to be baptized in the name of Jesus so that their sins might be forgiven and they might share in the gift of the Spirit which was freely promised to them. Many responded to his appeal and began to share in a new way of life.

We cannot prove that Luke has recorded verbatim what Peter said on this occasion, and in any case the speech recorded here is too brief to be a full account of what was said. Nevertheless, we have a good example of the kind of thing that was probably said on this occasion, and there can be no doubt that the speech fits admirably into the situation of the day of Pentecost. It has been argued that it fits into the pattern of other speeches in Acts and that this pattern and the way in which it is filled out reflect Luke's own theology; but, although the wording is largely that of Luke himself, and although the pattern is a common one in Acts, both the pattern and the basic theology are older than Luke and probably reach back into the early days of the church. One might well ask: what else would Peter have said on this occasion? It is interesting that the heart of the speech is built around the exposition of Old Testament prophecy and that there is some reason to believe that this exposition shows primitive features.[1]

14. Peter is represented as *standing* up to speak in the open air, backed up by the other apostles; he acts as their spokesman. The verb *addressed* can be used of inspired utterance: Peter's sermon is regarded as being the work of a man filled

---

[1] I. H. Marshall, 'The Resurrection in the Acts of the Apostles', in *AHG*, pp. 99–101. For the case against the authenticity of the speech see R. F. Zehnle, *Peter's Pentecost Discourse* (Nashville, 1971).

with the Spirit. He begins by summoning the attention of his hearers, both resident Jews and visitors to Jerusalem.

15. As on other occasions (3:12; 14:15) the preacher's first task is to correct a misapprehension by his audience, in this case to point out the absurdity of suggesting that men were likely to be drunk before nine o'clock in the morning. The point is that Jews did not ordinarily eat so early in the day, still less drink wine.

16–21. The correct explanation lay on a different level of understanding. What was happening was to be seen as the fulfilment of a prophecy by *Joel*, and here Peter proceeded to cite the relevant passage, Joel 2:28–32. A further phrase from the same passage is to be found in verse 39, and the same passage is also cited in Rom 10:13 and Rev. 6:12.[1] The quotation follows the LXX, but with a number of small alterations to adapt the prophecy to its context.[2] One of the more important of these changes is the way in which Joel's 'And it shall come to pass *afterward*' has been altered to 'And *in the last days* it shall be'. Peter regards Joel's prophecy as applying to the last days, and claims that his hearers are now living in the last days. God's final act of salvation has begun to take place.

The first and main theme of the prophecy is that God is going to pour out his Spirit upon all people, *i.e.* upon all kinds of people[3] and not just upon the prophets, kings and priests, as had been the case in Old Testament times. The evidence will be seen in prophecy and visions. Since tongues could be broadly described as a kind of prophecy, this passage provided the nearest equivalent to tongues in Old Testament phraseology: it is true that Paul distinguishes tongues from prophecy (1 Cor. 12:10), but he was not limited by having to find an Old Testament phrase with which to express himself. A second element in the prophecy is the occurrence of cosmic *signs* of the type associated with apocalyptic pictures of the end of the world; the same language is in fact used in Revelation 6:12. Here it may be noted that Peter has altered Joel's 'wonders

---

[1] These citations show that the prophecy was one that was used in the early church, and not one first introduced into the speech by Luke himself.

[2] It was natural for New Testament writers to adopt the form of Old Testament text which best suited their purpose or to adapt the wording as necessary. The meaning was more important than reproduction of the exact wording; see E. E. Ellis, 'Quotations (in the New Testament)', *NBD*, p. 1071.

[3] Luke may have seen a reference to Gentiles as well as Jews.

in the heavens and on the earth' to *wonders in the heaven above and signs on the earth beneath*. The signs are probably the gift of tongues and the various healing miracles which are shortly to be recorded. But what about the wonders? If we do not accept that the reference is to the cosmic signs which accompanied the crucifixion (Lk. 23:44f.), then Peter is looking forward to the signs which will herald the end of the world; these are still future, and they belong to the 'end' of the last days, rather than to their 'beginning' which is just taking place. The third element in Joel's prophecy is the event which these signs portend: *the day of the Lord*, *i.e.* the day of judgment. For Joel of course the *Lord* was Yahweh himself. For Peter and Luke the question arises whether *Lord* here does not implicitly mean 'Jesus', since in verse 36 Jesus will be declared to be Lord. In any case, the prophecy concludes, fourthly, with a promise that *whoever calls on the name* of this *Lord*, *i.e.* appeals to him for help, will *be saved*; for Christians this certainly meant seeking salvation from Jesus (Rom. 10:13f.; 1 Cor. 1:2). Admittedly, if Peter were citing the text in Hebrew, the reference would be clearly to Yahweh, and therefore an application to Jesus would be clear only to readers or hearers of the text in Greek.

It is hard to know in what way Joel envisaged the fulfilment of his oracle. It comes in the context of a plague of locusts upon Israel, which the prophet saw as a warning judgment. When the people responded with repentance, the Lord heard them and reversed their fortunes, promising them plenteous harvests. Then comes this prophecy of what will happen 'afterward', as the prophet looks forward to yet future events and envisages the final vindication of Israel and the defeat of her enemies. Thus the prospect appears to be a distant one, associated with the day of the Lord, and therefore no injustice is done to the passage when Peter sees that it is beginning to be fulfilled in the events of Pentecost.

22. Once again Peter calls for his hearers' attention; what he has to say is addressed to the people of *Israel*, who claimed to be God's people. Somewhat abruptly he directs their attention back to *Jesus*, the man of *Nazareth*, who had been marked out by God to them through the various miracles and signs which God had performed publicly through him. Peter assumes the reality of these signs, claims that his audience are well aware of them, and states that they were worked by God. He is prepared to argue from the miracles to the hand of God.

Already in his lifetime, therefore, Jesus was singled out as an unusual person, although Peter does not yet say what his particular role or status may have been. In a world which accepted the possibility and reality of the miraculous Peter's claim would have considerable weight. Later Jewish polemic against Jesus did not deny that he had wrought miracles, but rather claimed that he was a sorcerer, and already in his own lifetime his opponents attributed to Beelzebul the exorcisms which he performed (Lk. 11:15). Something more was needed to convince the Jews that God was at work in the life of Jesus.

23. For instead of recognizing Jesus as a man of God the Jews had taken steps to crucify him and so kill him. The *lawless men* are usually taken to be the Romans who actually executed Jesus. Nothing is said to minimize the fact of Jewish guilt in crucifying Jesus (*cf.* verse 36). Nevertheless, at the same time the crucifixion took place according to the *plan* and purpose of God (*cf.* 4:28). Here we have the paradox of divine predestination and human freewill in its strongest form. Even in putting Jesus to death, the Jews were simply fulfilling what God had already determined must take place and indeed had foretold in the prophetic writings.

24. Now comes the decisive contrast. *God raised* this Jesus *up* from the dead. Here is the key fact, stressed time and again by the first preachers; they did not need to prove that it had happened, they simply proclaimed it and bore witness to it. The divine plan took Jesus through suffering to exaltation as Saviour and Lord. Peter goes on to argue that it could not be otherwise. God raised up Jesus *because it was not possible for him to be held by* death. The Greek expression here is slightly odd. The word *pangs* refers to the pains of childbirth. The verb *loosed* goes oddly with this object. It has been suggested that the difficulty is due to the adoption of a phrase from the LXX (*cf.* Job 39:2) in which the unvocalized Hebrew word *ḥbl* has been understood as *ḥēbel*, 'pangs', instead of (correctly) as *ḥebel*, 'cord, bond'. Lindars (pp. 39f.) has suggested that Psalm 18:4 has been understood in terms of Psalm 16:6, so that Peter could speak of the cords of death being loosed; this phrase was then misunderstood by Luke. However, this interpretation does not explain how Luke used the wrong object with the verb. It is preferable to adopt the older view of F. Field, that the verb used can mean 'to bring to an end'. Then we have 'a remarkable mixed metaphor, in which death is regarded as being in labour and unable to hold back its child, the Messiah'.[1] If we ask why death could not hold back Jesus, Peter's reply would be that Jesus was the Messiah (see the evidence in verse 22), and that the Messiah could not be held by death.

25–28. This last point is defended by a quotation from Psalm 16:8–11, which is regarded as a statement by David about the Messiah. The Psalm is a prayer by a godly man, in which he professes his faith in God and declares his confidence that because the Lord is, as it were, his right-hand man, he can be joyful and sure that he will not be abandoned to Sheol or *corruption* but will rejoice in the *presence* of God. Commentators differ whether (on the one hand) the Psalmist is declaring his confidence that he will be rescued from disaster or premature death and continue to enjoy a ripe old age under the blessing of God, or (on the other) is affirming his belief that after death he will not descend to Sheol but be taken into the presence of God. It is undoubtedly the latter interpretation which is adopted here, and it seems likely that *thy Holy One* was understood as a reference to the Messiah (*cf.* 13:35 where the same Psalm is quoted).

29. The Davidic authorship of the Psalm was common ground between Peter and his Jewish listeners. Peter argues, however, that the Psalm cannot be taken as referring to *David* himself. Since he died and was buried, and since for the Jews to be buried was the same thing as to suffer corruption and descend to Sheol, it followed that he himself was abandoned to Hades (the Greek word for Hebrew Sheol) and suffered physical corruption. Peter was entitled to make his point with confidence; after all, the proof of David's burial was visible for all to see.[2]

30. If David was not speaking about himself, it followed that he must have been speaking prophetically. Two factors suggested this. First, David himself was gifted with prophetic powers.[3] The same assumption is made in 1:16 and Mark

[1] AG, *s.v. lyō*.

[2] A monument known as the tomb of David is also attested by Josephus. Unfortunately we cannot be sure whether the mediaeval building now known by this name near Siloam to the south of the city is on the ancient site. See J. Wilkinson, *Jerusalem as Jesus Knew It* (London, 1978), pp. 166–170.

[3] J. A. Fitzmyer, 'David, "Being therefore a prophet . . ." ', *CBQ* 34, 1972, pp. 332–339, notes that the activity of David is described as prophetic in 11 QPsª 27:11.

12:36, and is implicit in Jewish understanding of some of the Psalms as having a future reference. Second, David knew that God had promised faithfully that *one of his descendants* would sit on *his throne*. Here Peter has in mind Psalm 132:11f. with its divine oath, 'One of the sons of your body I will set on your throne' (*cf.* 2 Sa. 7:12–16; Ps. 89:3f., 35–37). To be sure, these references indicate that David would be the father of a line of kings; the throne would remain in his family and not be taken over by usurpers from some other family. Nevertheless, Peter takes it that one descendant in particular is in mind.

31. He therefore claims that what David was doing in Psalm 16 was to utter a prophecy regarding the Messiah, who would be his descendant. Instead of being abandoned to Hades, the Messiah would be raised from the dead. The wording of Psalm 16:10 is slightly altered to fit its new context; the word *flesh*, which has been taken over from Psalm 16:9, refers to the person of Jesus as a whole, and does not suggest that a flesh/soul dualism is in mind.

32. The conclusion of the immediate argument is now drawn. What was prophesied has been fulfilled in *this Jesus*. The Old Testament prophesied that the Messiah would rise from the dead. Jesus has risen from the dead (verse 24), and therefore it followed that he must be the prophesied Messiah; for it can be assumed that nobody else was expected to rise from the dead in advance of the general resurrection. Peter's argument obviously does not mean that Jesus *became* Messiah by being raised from the dead, but rather that since the Messiah must rise from the dead, and since Jesus rose from the dead, it follows that Jesus was already the Messiah during his earthly life.

There are two difficulties in the argument. First, the *prima facie* interpretation of Psalm 16 is that David was expressing his own hope of being saved from Sheol to enjoy communion with God, especially since the same hope is expressed elsewhere in the Psalms (Ps. 73). Secondly, it is not obvious that Ps. 132 refers to one specific descendant of David as being the Messiah. It is probable, however, that Peter's hearers shared a belief that the passages about David's descendants included a reference to the Messiah in particular; a Qumran text (4Q Florilegium) clearly interprets 2 Samuel 7:10–16 as a reference to the Messiah, and Psalm 132 would no doubt be understood in the same way. As for the use of Psalm 16, here it looks as though Peter was giving a fresh interpretation to the Psalm by claiming that it could not be true in the fullest sense for David, and that therefore he must be regarded as foreseeing the resurrection of the Messiah and speaking in his name. Peter's point is thus that David was consciously prophesying the resurrection of the Messiah, and not that there was a deeper sense in David's words than he himself was conscious of. We may compare how Abraham and Isaiah are credited with similar insight (Jn. 8:56; 12:41; *cf.* also perhaps Moses, Heb. 11:26). To Christians it seemed obvious that the great saints of past ages must have had prophetic knowledge of the Messiah. It must be remembered, however, that Peter himself reminds us of the limited nature of this prophetic knowledge (1 Pet. 1:10–12): 'it did not involve a distinct knowledge of the events foretold . . . ; that which the Holy Ghost presignified was only in part clear to the prophets, both as to the date of fulfilment and also as to historical shaping' (Knowling, pp. 87f.).

33. Having established that Jesus as the Messiah must rise from the dead, Peter can now go on to give the explanation of the pouring out of the Spirit. The resurrection is to be understood as the exaltation of Jesus. It was not simply a revivification but an ascension to be with God. Peter regards this as self-evident, but probably one factor in the early church's understanding was the use of Psalm 110:1 (see on verse 34 below) which is echoed here. Jesus has now become God's right-hand man (contrast verse 25). It may be that, as Lindars suggests, there is a hidden allusion to the same phrase in Psalm 16:11 which refers to the pleasures in store at God's right hand. This position is one of authority, and so Peter claims that it is in virtue of his exaltation that Jesus has received from the Father the promised gift of the Spirit and that he has poured it out upon his people. Here again there may be an Old Testament allusion, this time to Psalm 68:18.[1] In the MT this reads, 'Thou didst ascend the high mount, leading captives in thy train, and receiving gifts among men', but another version, cited in Ephesians 4:8, reads, 'When he ascended on high, he led a host of captives, and he gave gifts to men.' Peter's rendering and Paul's quotation indicate the

[1] J. Dupont, 'Ascension du Christ et don de l'Esprit d'après Actes 2:35', in B. Lindars and S. S. Smalley (eds.), *Christ and Spirit* (Cambridge, 1973), pp. 219–228. See, however, Wilckens, p. 233.

existence of an early Christian interpretation of the Psalm whose wording could easily be taken to mean 'thou hast received gifts for men'. The same understanding is reflected in the Targum, only here it is the words of the law which are the gift to men. If this interpretation of the words of the Psalm goes back to the first century, it is possible that the present verse contains an implicit contrast between the gift of the law to men (which, as we noted above, was associated with Pentecost in second-century Judaism) and the gift of the Spirit, but it must be emphasized that this view is somewhat speculative, and it is doubtful whether Luke himself had detected the allusion. But, however Peter came to his deduction that the Spirit was the gift of the exalted Jesus, the important fact is that the bestowal of the Spirit offers further testimony that Jesus is the Messiah. Whereas the resurrection could only be a matter of testimony by the disciples, acting as witnesses (verse 32), the effects of the pouring out of the Spirit were manifest to all Peter's hearers.

34–35. The argument is not quite complete. In verse 33 Peter argued from the exaltation of Jesus to the fact that he was the giver of the Spirit, but his ultimate aim was to claim that Jesus was not only Messiah but also Lord – with all that this implied for his hearers. So he now introduces the key Old Testament quotation which expresses the lordship of Jesus. He does so by pointing to a verse which might conceivably be taken as applying to an ascent of David into heaven, Psalm 110:1. It is not clear whether anybody actually believed that David had done so, although the Psalm might have been understood in this sense if it was regarded as addressed to David. Most modern scholars would in fact regard the Psalm as the words of a prophet to an Israelite king, expressing metaphorically the honour and authority given to him by God. But for the Jews and for Jesus and the early church David himself was understood as the speaker, and, in the same way as in verses 29–31, he was regarded as speaking of the Messiah. It is the Messiah, then, who is addressed by God as David's Lord and invited to sit at his right hand. We may note that there is an ambiguity in the English use of the word 'Lord' which is not present in the Hebrew Psalm where the first word translated 'Lord' is YHWH, the name of God, and the second word is *'ādôn* which can be used of human lords and masters. In both cases the Greek text has *kyrios*, and this

79

facilitated the transfer to Jesus of other Old Testament texts which referred to Yahweh. Here, however, it is simply the attribute of lordship which is given to Jesus; he is not equated with Yahweh.

36. From all this evidence it follows that *God has made* Jesus *both Lord* (verses 34f.) *and Christ* or Messiah (verses 25–32). Nothing suggests that this act of installation took place at or after the resurrection. We have seen that it was because he was the Messiah (*cf.* 2:22; 10:38ff.) that Jesus was raised from the dead, and it was one who was already called Lord who was summoned to sit at God's right hand. How terrible, then, was the act of the Jews in crucifying Jesus! Well might they tremble at the thought that by this act they had numbered themselves among the 'enemies' who would be overcome and defeated by the Messiah (verse 35).

37. Peter's hearers took his words as applying to them personally. Many of them had perhaps tacitly agreed with the action of their leaders in putting Jesus to death. Peter's revelation of the status and dignity of Jesus came as a drastic shock to them, and they were pierced *to the heart* by what he said. The phrase used is thought to be drawn from Psalm 109:16, the Psalm already quoted in 1:20b, but if so it is nothing more than a use of Old Testament language with no deeper significance. The thought is of being brokenhearted and standing under conviction of sin. It was natural to ask what response should be made by those thus convicted (although the question may represent Luke's dramatization of the situation).

38. Peter's reply sums up what was to be the standard call by Christian preachers to their audiences. It contained two requirements, which are in effect one. The first was a call to *repent* (*cf.* 3:19; 8:22; 17:30; 20:21; 26:20). This echoed the preaching of John the Baptist with his baptism of repentance for the forgiveness of sins (Lk. 3:3) and of Jesus himself (Mk. 1:15; Lk. 13:3, 5; 24:47). The word indicates a change of direction in a person's life rather than simply a mental change of attitude or a feeling of remorse; it signifies a turning away from a sinful and godless way of life. In one sense this is something of which man is incapable by himself, and therefore, although men can be commanded to repent, it can also be said that repentance is a gift of God (5:31; 11:18; 2 Tim. 2:25). It should also be noted that it is an essential part of conversion and response to the gospel; Calvin insisted that 'repentance not only always follows faith, but is produced by it' (*Institutes* III.iii.1), but it would be truer to say that repentance and faith are the two sides of the same coin. So it is that here repentance is linked with being baptized. Since elsewhere repentance and faith are closely linked (20:21; Mk. 1:15), it is certain that, whatever else it may be, baptism is an expression of faith. For John the Baptist, baptism was an expression of repentance. The early Christians took over the same rite, but its meaning was enlarged.

Baptism was performed *in the name of Jesus*, a phrase which may represent a commercial usage, 'to the account of Jesus', or a Jewish idiom, 'with reference to Jesus'. However precisely the phrase be understood,[1] it conveys the thought that the person being baptized enters into allegiance to Jesus, and this would tie in with the evidence that at baptism it was customary to make a confession of Jesus as Lord (Rom 10:9; 1 Cor. 12:3). Thus Christian baptism was an expression of faith and commitment to Jesus as Lord. Just as John's baptism had mediated the divine gift of forgiveness, symbolized in the act of washing, so too Christian baptism was regarded as a sign of forgiveness (5:31; 10:43; 13:38; 26:18; *cf.* 3:19). But Christian baptism conveyed an additional blessing. John had said that he baptized (only) with water but the Messiah would baptize with the Holy Spirit, and this gift accompanied water-baptism performed by the church in the name of Jesus. The two gifts are closely linked, since it is the Spirit who accomplishes the inner cleansing of which baptism is the outward symbol.

39. Peter urged that his hearers would find that this promise of forgiveness and the gift of the Spirit was true, because God had made it to them and their descendants (*cf.* 13:33). This phrase has sometimes been taken as a justification for infant baptism, but this is to press it unduly. If we are to link it with the context, we note that the prophecy in verse 17 thinks of children who are old enough to prophesy, and that verse 38 speaks of receiving forgiveness and the Spirit; in neither case are infants obviously involved. The point of the phrase is rather to express the unlimited mercy of God which embraces

[1] For details see H. Bietenhard, *TDNT*, V, pp. 274–276; L. Hartman, ' "Into the Name of Jesus" ', *NTS* 20, 1973–74, pp. 432–440; J. A. Ziesler, 'The Name of Jesus in the Acts of the Apostles'. *JSNT* 4, 1979, pp. 28–41.

the hearers and subsequent generations of their descendants and in addition *all that are far off* (Is. 57:19; Eph. 2:13, 17), a phrase which certainly includes Jews scattered throughout the world and (in Luke's eyes, whether or not Peter had yet reached this insight) the Gentiles also; a reference to the Gentiles is highly probable in view of the rabbinic understanding of the phrase in Isaiah 57:19, which is shared by Paul (Eph. 2:13, 17). In all cases, however, the promise is mediated by the call of God – and with these words Peter rounds off the quotation from Joel 2:32 with which his discourse had begun. The stress is on the primacy of God's call and the graciousness of his invitation to all mankind.

40. Luke indicates that he has given only a summary of Peter's remarks by this comment. He said more by way of argument than is recorded here, and he added a sense of urgency to his words by appealing to his hearers to escape from the fate which would otherwise befall the *crooked generation* to which they belonged. 'Perverse generation' is an Old Testament phrase for the people of Israel who rebelled against God in the wilderness (Dt. 32:5) and is applied in the New Testament to those who reject Jesus (Phil. 2:15; *cf.* Lk. 9:41; 11:29; Heb. 3:10).

41. The result of the church's first evangelistic message was impressive. Many of Peter's hearers accepted what he said and indicated their acceptance by being baptized, with the result that 3,000 are said to have been added (*sc.* to the church). Although the number may seem large and is often regarded as a figment of Luke's imagination, there is in fact nothing incredible about it. It would have been perfectly possible for a crowd of that size and greater to hear Peter in the open air (if John Wesley and George Whitefield could be heard, so could Peter), and if the other disciples shared in the actual baptizing, there would have been plenty of time to accomplish the task. It has been objected that the Romans would not have tolerated the assembly of so large a crowd, but there is no reason to suppose that they would have suppressed a peaceable assembly. And although the population of Jerusalem was small,[1] it was immensely swollen at the time of the pilgrim festivals.

[1] J. Jeremias, *Jerusalem in the Time of Jesus* (London, 1969), p. 83 n. 24, estimates the population at 55,000 – 95,000.

42. Finally, Luke records what happened to the new converts. Four activities are listed in which they took part. These are generally regarded as four separate things, but a case can be made out that they are in fact the four elements which characterized a Christian gathering in the early church, and on the whole this is the preferable view.[1] First, there was the *teaching* given by the *apostles*, who were qualified for this task by their companionship with Jesus. They may have been regarded as in a special sense the guardians of the traditions about Jesus as the church grew and developed.[2] Secondly, there was *fellowship*; the word means 'sharing', and, while it could refer to the sharing of goods described in verses 44f., it is more likely that here it refers to the holding of a common meal or to a common religious experience. Thirdly, there was *the breaking of bread*. This is Luke's term for what Paul calls the Lord's Supper. It refers to the act with which a Jewish meal opened, and which had gained peculiar significance for Christians in view of Jesus' action at the Last Supper and also when he fed the multitudes (Lk. 9:16; 22:19; 24:30; Acts 20:7, 11). It has been claimed that the thought is simply of a fellowship meal, perhaps a continuation of the meals held with the risen Lord, without any specific relation to the Last Supper or the Pauline form of the Lord's Supper which celebrated his death, but it is much more likely that Luke is simply using an early Palestinian name for the Lord's Supper in the proper sense. Finally, there is mention of *prayers*. If the reference is not to part of a Christian meeting, it will be to the way the Christians observed the set Jewish hours of prayer (3:1). Here are the four essential elements in the religious practice of the Christian church.

g. A summary of the life of the early church (2:43–47)

One of Luke's characteristics is to separate off the various incidents in the first part of Acts by means of short summary paragraphs or verses which indicate the situation of the church at the several stages of its progress. This is the first such section, and it bridges the gap between the story of Pentecost and the next set of incidents in which the relation of the church to the Jewish authorities is depicted. Others follow in

---

[1] Marshall, *Luke*, pp. 204–206.
[2] H. Riesenfeld, *The Gospel Tradition and its Beginnings* (London, 1957).

4:32-37 and 5:12-16, and have much the same general content as the present passage. Some scholars have found a parallelism between the four items in verse 42 and the contents of the present summary (apostles; all things in common; breaking of bread; praising God), but the parallelism is not especially exact.

43. One effect of the growth of the infant church was a sense of fear or awe on the part of the people. Luke means that the non-Christian population felt a certain apprehension over against a group in whose midst supernatural events were taking place (*cf.* 5:5, 11; 19:17). *Wonders and signs* – the words used are those which were also used to describe the mighty works of Jesus (2:22) – were being wrought by the apostles, and Luke will shortly relate specific examples.

44–45. A distinctive feature was the way in which the believers lived *together* and practised some kind of joint ownership of possessions.[1] What this means is made clearer in verse 45 where it appears that people sold their possessions so that the proceeds might be used to help the needy. The first impression we get, then, is that of a society whose members lived together and had everything *in common* (4:33). This would not be surprising, since we know that at least one other contemporary Jewish group, the Qumran sect, adopted this way of life (1QS 6); in their descriptions of the Essenes (with whom the Qumranites are usually identified) Philo and Josephus say the same thing. It may well be that in the first flush of religious enthusiasm the early church lived in this kind of way; the sayings of Jesus about self-renunciation could have suggested this way of life. It appears from the account in 4:32 – 5:11, however, that the selling of one's goods was a voluntary matter, and the way in which special attention is given to Barnabas for selling a field may suggest that there was something unusual about his act. We should not, therefore, conclude that becoming a believer necessarily entailed living in a tight-knit Christian community. What actually happened may have been that each person held his goods at the disposal of the others whenever the need arose. We have avoided the use of the term 'communism' in describing this practice, since modern communism is a description of a political and economic

[1] D. L. Mealand, 'Community of Goods and Utopian Allusions in Acts II–IV', *JTS* 28, 1977, pp. 96–99.

system of such a different character that it is anachronistic and misleading to use the term in the present context.[1]

46. The religious devotion of the early Christians was a daily affair. They met together in a spirit of unanimity in *the temple*. This could simply mean that they used the courtyard of the temple as a meeting place (*cf.* 5:12), but it is also implied that they took part in the daily worship of the temple (3:1). The daily worship consisted of the offering of a burnt offering and incense in the morning and the afternoon; it was carried on by the priests, but there was always a congregation of people who stood where they could see the priests going about their duties and entering the sanctuary; they took part in prayer, and they received a blessing from the priest. Since the early Christians believed that they had a true relationship with God through the Messiah, it was natural for them to take part in the worship of God in the accepted manner. Theological questions about the replacement of the temple sacrifices by the spiritual sacrifice by Jesus had probably not yet occurred to them. Nor were the Christians excluded from the temple by the religious authorities. At the same time, however, the Christians met together for their own religious gatherings. They met in one another's *homes* and broke bread together in a spirit of intense and sincere joy.[2] The idea is that they held common meals which included the breaking of bread; we may compare Paul's description of the common church meal at Corinth, which included the celebration of the Lord's Supper (1 Cor. 11:17–34). The joy that characterizes these gatherings was no doubt inspired by the Spirit (13:52) and may have been associated with the conviction that the Lord Jesus was present with them (*cf.* 24:35).

47. The sentence structure may indicate that the disciples ate together both in the temple and in their homes. As they did so, they praised God; this is one of the few references in Acts to the Christians worshipping God in the sense of rendering thanks to him. The fewness of such phrases reminds us that according to the New Testament witness Christian gatherings were for instruction, fellowship and prayer; in other

---

[1] See Marshall, *Luke*, pp. 206–209.
[2] The word translated *generous* suggests the frankness and openness of spirit that characterized the early Christian fellowship; AG translate as 'simplicity', NIV has 'sincere'.

words for the benefit of the people taking part; there is less mention of the worship of God, although of course this element was not absent. A final comment notes that the evangelistic activity of the church continued daily. As the Christians were seen and heard by the other people in Jerusalem, their activities formed an opportunity for witness. Once again Luke refers to the process of becoming a Christian as *being saved, i.e.* from belonging to the sinful people around who were under God's judgment for their rejection of the Messiah (2:40, *cf.* 2:21).

II. THE CHURCH AND THE JEWISH AUTHORITIES (3:1 – 5:42)

a. The healing of a lame man (3:1–10)

The main theme of Acts 3–5 is the way in which the witness of the first Christians brought them into conflict with the Jewish leaders, who fruitlessly attempted to put a stop to their preaching. Two such incidents are recorded (3:1 – 4:31; 5:12–42) which are separated by an account of one of the internal problems of the Christian community (4:32 – 5:11). On each occasion the power of the apostles to perform miracles led to an attempt by the Jews to stop them. There is sufficient similarity between the two stories (along with other material in chapters 1–2) to make some scholars suspect that we have two separate but parallel accounts of the same basic events, but the differences are sufficient to outweigh the similarities. The first incident falls into three parts. The story of a miracle is followed by an explanatory discourse by Peter (compare the similar pattern found several times in the Gospel of John, *e.g.* Jn. 6:1–24/25–59), and then by the story of the arrest of the apostles.

The healing story itself is similar to those related in the Gospels, but is related with a fair amount of detail. Peter is able to do the kind of thing that Jesus did by acting in the name of Jesus: thus the continuity between the ministry of Jesus and the witness of the church is expressed. One may also note how this incident and others in the career of Peter have counterparts in the career of Paul (14:8–10). But the main point in the story is the continuing power of the name of Jesus to perform the same gracious and healing acts which were signs in the Gospels of the coming of the kingdom or rule of God.

1. The story provides an example of the wonders and signs mentioned in 2:43 and takes place in the context of the visits to the temple mentioned in 2:46. The *ninth hour*, 3.00pm, was the time of the afternoon sacrifice which was accompanied by prayer by the congregation (2:46 note). The mention of *John* alongside *Peter* has puzzled some commentators, since he plays no significant part in the story, and it has been suspected that his name is an addition to the story (*cf.* verse 4, where it is almost an afterthought), perhaps to provide two witnesses to defend the Christian cause before the Sanhedrin later in the story. But the presence of John can equally well be historical in view of the early Christian habit of working in pairs and of the association of John (the son of Zebedee, Lk. 5:10) with Peter (1:13); since no convincing reason for the addition of the name has been given, it probably rests on tradition.

2. The occasion for the healing miracle arose from the presence of a man who was being carried at the same time by his friends in order that he might be laid down to beg at the entrance to the temple. Since the giving of *alms* was a particularly meritorious act in Jewish religion, it would be appropriate for a beggar to place himself where pious people might be expected to pass on their way to worship. The fact that the man had been *lame from birth* underlines the wonder of the miracle which was about to be performed. Some uncertainty surrounds the identity of the *Beautiful* Gate of the temple. There are three possibilities: (1) The 'Shushan' Gate which was on the east side of the wall enclosing the whole of the temple; it gave access from outside the temple to the Court of the Gentiles. (2) Within the Court of the Gentiles was the Court of the Women, to which there was an access on the east side; only Israelite men and women were allowed within this court. Josephus tells us that the 'Nicanor' Gate (otherwise known as the Corinthian Gate, and made of bronze) was situated here, and most scholars regard this as the Beautiful Gate. (3) From the Court of the Women a further gate led to the Court of Israel, into which only Jewish men were admitted. The rabbinic sources call this the Nicanor Gate, but there is some evidence that their picture of the temple is a confused one. Most scholars adopt view (2).[1] Christian tradition from the fifth century favours view (1), but it has been pointed out

[1] J. Jeremias, *TDNT*, III, p. 173 n. 5; G. Schrenk, *TDNT*, III, p. 236.

that the east gate of the temple complex would have been a poor place for collecting alms; far more people would enter the temple from the west side, direct from the city.

3–5. The beggar began to call out for alms from the people entering the temple, and these included *Peter and John*. They replied by suggesting that they would have something to offer him, and the man then directed his attention to them. The description is perhaps a little pedantic at first sight, but Stählin, p. 59, rightly comments that the narrative shows how the beggar's usual feelings of uncertainty, expressed in a combination of pressing entreaty and of indifference resulting from frequent disappointment, are replaced by a genuine expectation of receiving something. What could have been simply the occasion of mechanical charity is turned into a personal encounter as the lame man and the apostles look intently at one another.

6. Peter's reply, with its deliberate word-order 'Silver and gold I do not have' (NIV), would initially disappoint the hopes that had been raised, but it was swiftly followed by an offer of something better. What Peter could offer was healing, and this he gave by commanding the man to walk. '*In the name of Jesus*' (2:38 note) here means 'by the authority of Jesus'. Similar formulae were used in ancient magic, but that does not make Peter's phrase into a magic formula. Here the thought is of the continuing power of Jesus which has been bestowed upon the apostles; Jesus himself had no need to appeal to a higher authority such as the name of God (see further 3:16; 4:10). It is to be noted that Peter did have access to *silver and gold* (2:45); the point was that in this case he could offer something better that went to the root of the man's problem. The story is in no sense a prohibition of giving material help to the poor and needy, nor should it be used to suggest that the church should offer spiritual salvation rather than physical or material help – it is after all physical healing rather than spiritual salvation which is given here! There is, however, a lesson about the church's priorities.

7–8. Peter's invitation was accompanied by a hand outstretched to raise the beggar to his feet, and the miracle took place as the man's joints were cured and became active. He was able not merely to stand, but to walk and leap for joy, and his first action, when healed, was to accompany the apostles into the temple and praise God in thankfulness for what had happened to him. As in the lifetime of Jesus, so now the scripture was being fulfilled: 'then shall the lame man leap like a hart' (Is. 35:6).

9–10. The sight of the once-lame man *walking and praising God* was proof to the crowds that he had been truly cured. He was such a well-known figure after his years of begging that there could be no doubt about his identity and therefore about the reality of the cure. Although a description of *wonder and amazement* is a stereotyped feature at the end of the story of a miracle (*e.g.* Lk. 4:36; 5:9, 26; 7:16), this is precisely the reaction that would be expected. Such a reaction, however, is not necessarily the same thing as faith in the One who performed the miracle; one can be impressed by the spectacular without responding to what it signifies, the power and the grace of God.

b. Peter explains the incident (3:11–26)

The pattern of incidents on the day of Pentecost repeats itself as the unusual event is followed by a speech of Peter to the astonished people, which begins by explaining what has just happened. In this case Peter again begins by dealing with a possible misunderstanding of the situation and then proceeds to explain how the power of Jesus, raised from the dead, has healed the man. He seizes the opportunity to press home the point that it was the Jesus whom the Jews had killed who had been glorified by God and was now still active. There the speech might have stopped, having accomplished its immediate purpose, but Peter was too keen an evangelist to let a valuable opportunity slip. Having already begun to convict his hearers of their share in putting Jesus to death, he went on to argue that they had acted ignorantly. In reality God was accomplishing his plan for the Messiah, and so it was now possible for the Jews to repent and look forward to the blessings associated with the return of Jesus. This appeal was reinforced by an appeal to prophecy: Jesus was the prophet whose coming was foretold by Moses. Disobedience to him would lead to judgment. At the same time, however, those who were listening to Peter were the inheritors of God's covenant and had, as it were, first claim on the blessings brought by Jesus. Let them, then, turn away from their wickedness and accept Jesus as the Messiah. Although nothing is said explicitly, there is probably the implication that if the Jews will not listen, the blessings of the gospel will be offered elsewhere.

The particular interest of this sermon lies in the way in which it gives further teaching about the person of Jesus, describing him as God's servant, the Holy and Righteous One, the Author of life and the prophet like Moses. This indicates that a considerable amount of thinking about Jesus, based on study of the Old Testament, was taking place. While some scholars would attribute this maturity of thinking to Luke himself, there is good reason to believe that it belongs to the primitive church, in the first years of whose existence there took place an unparalleled development in theological thinking. The other main theological element in the speech, the association of blessings with the parousia, is unparalleled, and this is a further sign that here we have primitive tradition.

11. The healed man kept close to his benefactors, and the people came towards them in crowds when they reached the colonnade of Solomon which ran along the east side of the Court of the Gentiles. If the man had been healed at the Shushan Gate, this would be immediately adjacent. If the healing took place on the way into the Court of the Women, then we must presume that by this time Peter and his companions were on their way out again. This would be natural enough, since the Court of the Women would be a less suitable place for a public meeting, and Luke saw no need to fill in every detail of the actors' movements.

12. Peter grasped the opportunity to explain the significance of what had happened. If what follows represents what Luke thought that he probably would say, rather than being a summary of his remarks, it certainly catches the spirit of the occasion. Peter seizes on the way in which the crowds were quite naturally gazing at John and himself as the possessors of the remarkable power which had healed the man. They would have regarded them either as being possessed of remarkable powers of their own or as being so devout that God would respond to their prayers with miraculous signs. But, whatever they thought, Peter wanted to direct their attention away from the apostles to the source of the miracle.

13. The immediate explanation does not come until verse 16; first of all, Peter had to set the scene. Ultimately what had happened was due to the action of *God*, the very same God who had revealed himself to the patriarchs and constituted himself the God of the people of Israel; the reason for stressing this will become apparent in verses 25f. This God had *glorified his servant*, a phrase drawn from Isaiah 52:13, the first verse of the last and most important of the passages dealing with the Servant of Yahweh. In other words, prophecy was now being fulfilled, for Peter was claiming that what had happened to Jesus was the divine glorification of God's Servant. The identification of Jesus as the Servant is found in 3:26; 4:27, 30. These are the only places in the New Testament where the name is applied to him, but the prophecies about the suffering of the Servant are cited or alluded to in Mark 10:45; 14:24; Luke 22:37; John 12:38; Acts 8:32f.; 1 Peter 2:22–24; and elsewhere. This combination of references suggests a primitive understanding of Jesus which is remarkably absent from the Letters and later writings.

It might seem odd to declare that Jesus had been glorified as God's Servant. After all, he had died on a gallows. But Peter insisted that this had taken place because of the action of the Jews themselves in denying him when he was on trial before Pilate, even though Pilate regarded him as innocent of any capital crime and wanted to release him (*cf.* 13:28).

14–15. Peter presses home his point against the Jews. He has already dwelt on the enormity of the Jews' action in condemning an innocent man to death. Now he emphasizes that the One who was thus *denied* by the Jews was *Holy and Righteous*. It is not clear whether these would have been regarded by the Jews as attributes of some particular person or functionary. The full phrase 'the holy one of God' is used of Elisha (2 Ki. 4:9) and Aaron (Ps. 106:16), and is used in a unique way of Jesus as a confession by demons (Mk. 1:24) and men (Jn. 6:69); it recurs as a designation of Jesus in 1 John 2:20 and Revelation 3:7, and this suggests that Christians regarded it as a title for the Messiah. Here, however, the point may be simply to underline the fact that Jesus belonged in a special way to God (*cf.* Lk. 1:35; Acts 4:25, 27). Similarly, the use of *righteous* stresses the moral uprightness of Jesus (7:52; 22:14; 1 Jn. 2:1); there may well be a link with the description of God's Servant in Isaiah 53:11. By contrast, it was a *murderer*, Barabbas, whom the Jews wished to have released by Pilate (Lk. 23:25). Then once again the contrast is made with Jesus who is called *the Author of life*. The word *archēgos* recurs in 5:31 (*cf.* Heb. 12:2) where it has more the sense of a leader, but

91

here (*cf.* Heb. 2:10) it seems to mean 'source' or 'originator'. The thought of salvation as life (both words represent the same Aramaic word) is found here and in 5:20; 11:18; 13:46, 48; here there is probably a deliberate antithesis with *you killed*. But God raised him from the dead – this was his 'glorification' (verse 13) – as the apostles could testify.

16. Against this background the healing of the lame man could now be understood. The Greek construction is obscure and the sentence is repetitious. Two basic points are clearly made, however. First, the miracle which resulted in a well-known man being made perfectly sound in body before the very eyes of the crowd depended on the power associated with the *name* of this Jesus. Second, this power became effective through *faith* in the name of Jesus. Such faith was possible *through Jesus*: the proclamation of his power made it possible for people to believe. True, we are not told in the story that the man displayed faith, but the way in which he praised God after his cure could well imply this; alternatively, the faith might be that of Peter. In any case, any suggestion that there was something magical about the miracle is deliberately ruled out.[1]

17. The immediate occasion of the speech has now been dealt with. But, having already spoken of the guilt of the Jews in this section, Peter could not leave the matter there, and he now moves over into the specifically evangelistic and hortatory part of the speech. He begins by conceding that what the Jews and their leaders had done to Jesus sprang from *ignorance* (13:27; *cf.* 1 Cor. 2:8) and, therefore (it is implied), it could be forgiven (Lk. 23:34; 1 Tim. 1:13). The unspoken thought is that, if the Jews now fail to admit their sin committed in ignorance and repent of it, it will become a witting sin which is much more culpable (the Mosaic law made no explicit provision for atoning for such sins).

18. Yet what the Jews did in ignorance had in reality furthered the plan of God, *foretold by the prophets*, that the Messiah *should suffer* (2:23; 17:3; 26:22f.). Luke is fond of the phrase *all the prophets* (3:24; 10:43; Lk. 24:27), but we may well ask how

---

[1] This needs to be stressed against the view of J. M. Hull, *Hellenistic Magic and the Synoptic Tradition* (London, 1974), who claims that for Luke the church has a magical power distinguished from that of pagan wonder-workers only by being stronger.

references to the suffering of the Messiah can be found in literally *all* the prophets. The phrase is doubtless to be taken hyperbolically. Since the Old Testament nowhere speaks of a *suffering* Messiah (even the term 'Messiah' does not occur as a title in the Old Testament) we should probably think primarily of the teaching about the suffering of God's Servant (Is. 53), and also of other passages in the prophets and the Psalms which may have been taken as typological or prophetical of the sufferings of the Messiah (Je. 11:19; Dn. 9:26; Zc. 13:7; Pss. 22, 69); this would give us material from three of the four books of the 'latter prophets' (Isaiah, Jeremiah, and the Book of the Twelve; omitting Ezekiel) and also from the Psalms.

19. God's action has now created the conditions in which the Jews may repent and be forgiven for their sins. The meaning of *repent* (2:38) is clarified by the addition of *turn again* (RSV) or rather 'turn to (*sc.* God)' (so other modern versions). This verb signifies the act of turning away from one's former way of life, especially from the worship of idols, to a new way of life, based on faith and obedience to God (9:35; 11:21; 14:15; 15:19; 26:18, 20; 28:27; *cf.* Is. 6:10; Joel 2:12–14). The immediate result will be the 'blotting out of their sins'; the list of accusations against them will be obliterated (*cf.* Col. 2:14), which is another way of saying that their sins are forgiven (2:38).

Two further results will follow. The first (verse 19b in RSV, NEB; verse 20a in GNB, NIV) is that *times of refreshing* will come from the Lord. This is a unique phrase which commentators generally take to refer to the final era of salvation. If so, the plural *times* may perhaps indicate the length of the period in question (*cf.* perhaps the 'times of the Gentiles', Lk. 21:24). There may be a link with the 'times' in 1:7 associated with the restoration of the rule of God for Israel.

20–21. The second result will be the coming of Jesus from heaven. He is described as 'the Messiah foreordained for you', *i.e.* for the Jews; some scholars have taken this to mean that Jesus has been foreordained to *become* the Messiah at the parousia, the implication being that this is a piece of primitive christology which envisaged Jesus as becoming Messiah only in the future at the parousia. But this is a faulty understanding of the text. It states rather that the Jesus who will return at the parousia is the one who had already been ordained as the

93

Messiah for the Jews. That is to say, the coming of the 'messianic age' or the future kingdom of God, for which the Jews longed, was dependent upon their acceptance of Jesus as the Messiah. Yet the parousia would not happen immediately. It could not in any case take place until the times of the fulfilment of all that God had spoken by the prophets right back from the beginning. The word 'fulfilment' (RSV *establishment*) is from the same root as the word translated 'restore' in 1:6; hence we should take the phrase to signify God's perfect realization of the things that he had promised through the prophets, the chief of which was the setting up of his rule or kingdom. The 'times', therefore, refer not to the period before the parousia during which the various prophetically foretold events which must precede it must take place, but rather to the period of fulfilment of the prophecies concerned with the parousia itself. All this indicates that a certain time must elapse before the parousia. Whether this should be called a 'delay' is problematic; that would imply that the early church originally expected the parousia immediately, and that only when nothing happened over a period of some years did it begin to refashion its hopes (and the texts which expressed them) to take account of a much longer period of waiting than it originally envisaged. It is quite probable, however, that there were some people who expected the parousia to happen speedily, and the church had to remind them that, as Jesus had taught, the parousia would not take place immediately. It has been suggested that the present passage also suggests that Jesus was thought of as being inactive in heaven between the ascension and his return. This is most improbable in view of the other evidence in Acts which shows that Jesus was in fact very active by pouring out the Spirit and by working signs and wonders through the apostles.

22–23. The speech now takes a fresh tack as Peter makes a new point. He uses a quotation based on material from Deuteronomy 18:15–19 and Leviticus 23:29. In this passage Moses was warning the people of Israel against using magical practices to find out the Lord's will. God would raise up *a prophet* for them with the same ability as *Moses* to know and declare God's will, and the people should obey what the prophet said; if anybody refused to obey, God would hold him responsible and cut him off from the people. The original sense of the passage may have been that God would raise up prophets on different occasions as required. The formulation of the passage in the singular seems to have led the Jews to expect *one* prophet, although the evidence is scanty (*cf.* Jn. 1:21, 25; 7:40); at the same time, there was an expectation that the Messiah would be a second Moses.[1] In particular, the Qumran sect looked forward to the coming of a prophet in the end-time (1QS 9:10f.), and one of their documents cites this text (4QTest 5–7). Certainly in Samaritan and Christian circles the passage was interpreted as referring to one successor of Moses.[2] In the present passage Peter implicitly assumes that Jesus is the prophet in question (*cf.* 7:37). Moses, therefore, is a prophet of the coming of Jesus, and gives his backing to the warning against disobeying Jesus.

24. But the same thing is also true of *all the* (other) *prophets*. They too looked forward to the days which had now proved to be the days of fulfilment. The whole of the Old Testament could thus be seen to bear witness to Jesus and the setting up of the church. For all the prophets were concerned with eschatological events and not simply with what was to happen in their own time. This was the accepted understanding of the prophets in New Testament times; we may compare how the Qumran sect saw the details of their own experiences foretold in the Scriptures, admittedly at the cost of some unconvincing exegesis. But was the Christian exegesis any better based? Modern scholarship has emphasized that the prophets were primarily concerned with events in their own time and the imminent future. In what sense could *Samuel*, in particular, few of whose utterances are in any case recorded (1 Sa. 3:19 – 4:1), be regarded as a prophet of Jesus? In general, it must be replied that in many prophecies there is an element of future hope which was unfulfilled at the time or only imperfectly fulfilled, and that the prophetic hope of God's final intervention and establishment of his perfect rule was certainly not fulfilled in Old Testament times; it awaited a still-future realization. The reference to Samuel is admittedly difficult; the most that can be said is that Christians may have regarded his prophecies of David's kingdom as finding ultimate fulfilment in the rule of the Son of David (Bruce, *Book*, p. 93).

25. These prophetic promises were made for the Jewish

[1] J. Jeremias, *TDNT*, IV, pp. 848–873.
[2] *BC*, I, pp. 404–408.

people. They were the 'descendants of the prophets', and therefore they could expect to see the fulfilment of the promises made to the people of Israel and to benefit from them. The point could be reinforced by the reminder that the Jews were also the heirs of the still earlier *covenant* which God had made with Abraham. In this covenant God had promised blessings to his descendants, but had also affirmed that through his *posterity* all the families of the earth would be blessed (Gn. 12:3; 18:18; 22:18; 26:4; Gal. 3:8). This is an interesting quotation. The original version (the LXX) has 'nations', a word that might be interpreted to mean the Gentiles; Peter's citation uses a word of similar meaning, but one that leaves it open whether the Gentiles are in view (Hanson, p. 76). However, in view of the next verse ('to you first'), it is likely that the word 'families' is meant to refer to both Jews and Gentiles, although the reference to the Gentiles is at this stage a quiet hint (contrast 13:46). Again, the original saying refers to Abraham's 'seed'. The ambiguous RSV rendering *posterity* leaves it uncertain whether the reference is collective to Abraham's descendants or singular. In Galatians 3:16 Paul makes it clear that the 'seed' is to be interpreted as a singular noun, referring to Jesus: he is the descendant of Abraham through whom blessings will come to all nations. Peter had exactly the same thought in mind here.

26. This is brought out clearly by the way in which Peter goes on to state how God has raised up his servant to *bless* the audience by *turning* them away from their sin. The blessing bestowed in the covenant with Abraham by means of Jesus thus consists in enabling men to depart from the way of sin and thus to be fit to receive the other spiritual gifts associated with the Messiah. *Raise up* is probably used in the same way as in verse 22 of bringing somebody on to the stage of history; it is just possible that it means to raise from the dead (*cf.* 13:33f.). The little word *first* should not be overlooked. Here is the first explicit statement in Acts that historically the gospel came first to the Jews. But the promise in the previous verse suggests that the thought 'and also for the Gentiles' is implicit, and there may well be the warning that if the Jews fail to respond the Christian mission will turn to the Gentiles.

c. The arrest of Peter and John (4:1–22)

The healing of the lame man and Peter's sermon made a great impression on the ordinary people, but it aroused the opposition of the Jewish leaders who arrested the two apostles and then brought them before a meeting of the Sanhedrin in order to make enquiries as to what they were doing. This was the first time that official cognizance had been taken of the church. Peter's brief speech repeated the essential facts concerning the resurrection of Jesus, with the added emphasis that he alone could save people. The authorities realized that the apostles were acting in the same way as Jesus had done, but because of the popular support for them were unable to take stern measures. They contented themselves, therefore, with issuing a warning to the apostles to stop their teaching, an action which led to a bold denial of their competence to issue such a command by Peter. The church cannot obey orders to give up its most characteristic activity, witness to the risen Lord, although it must be prepared to pay the price of its refusal to keep quiet.

There is a not dissimilar story in 5:17ff., and it has sometimes been suggested that it and the present narrative are variant traditions of the same event. Another suggestion is that the relationship between the two incidents is to be explained in terms of the Jewish law which laid down that in certain cases a person could not be punished on a first offence; rather he had to be warned that what he was doing was culpable (since he might have been acting in ignorance of the law), and then, if he knowingly committed the same fault again, he could be punished on the second occasion. On this view the present story contains the warning, while the second story deals with the possibility of punishment for a witting offence. Although there are some difficulties about establishing the legal details, this suggestion may provide the key to the situation.

1. The preaching came to an end with the arrival of the Jewish authorities to arrest the apostles. It is not clear whether we are to regard the sermon as being interrupted before its intended conclusion; in any case Luke, as a skilful writer, has included all that he wished to convey to his readers, and the appeal, which we might have expected at the end of the sermon, in fact comes in verse 19. Although John is Peter's silent partner, he is reckoned along with him as speaking to the people. The police action is taken by a group of people responsible for public order within the temple area. It includes some of the *priests* who were on duty at the time. They were led by the *captain of the temple*, the official in charge of the temple police, and usually identified as the *s^egān*, the priest who ranked next to the high priest. The *Sadducees* were not a legal body. The name was applied to a political grouping which drew most of its support from the priesthood and the lay readers of the community (the 'elders'). We are probably, therefore, to think here of lay people who sided with the priests in their opposition to the church. Luke has used the term 'Sadducees' to indicate their religious and political outlook. It is interesting that, although the Pharisees were the group most opposed to Jesus during his ministry, in Acts they are almost friendly to the church, while the Sadducees (who do not figure in the Gospels until the last days of Jesus) have become the leaders of the opposition.

2–4. Their hostility is ascribed to their dislike of the message of the *resurrection*. The Sadducees objected to the idea of resurrection (Lk. 20:27–40), as Jewish sources confirm. They were particularly opposed to the Christians because they claimed to have concrete evidence of the resurrection in the case of Jesus. That this teaching should be going on in the temple made the crime all the worse in their eyes. So they had the apostles arrested, as they had the legal right to do in the case of what might be regarded as a breach of the peace in the temple precincts. Since it was too late in the day to do anything more, the apostles were given a night in prison, no doubt with the hope that it might sober them up and give them a warning. Nevertheless, Luke emphasizes, the attack on the apostles in no way hindered the effectiveness of the evangelism. Many who had listened to Peter responded to the message, so that the total of Christians now reached about 5,000. Critics have protested that this presupposes an audience of thousands for Peter's speech, and also that the total is disproportionate with the total population of Jerusalem. But the church was growing daily (2:47), and it is not necessary to ascribe the increase since 2:41 simply to this one public meeting. Estimates of the total population of Jerusalem range from 25,000 to about ten times that figure, and Hanson (pp. 76f,), opting for the larger figure, claims that Luke's estimate of the size of the church could well be fairly accurate;

but a lower figure for the population of Jerusalem seems more likely (2:41 note). Luke's figure for the size of the church may include Christians from the country districts as well as the city.

5. On the next day there was a meeting of the authorities. The three groups mentioned are probably the three components of the Sanhedrin. The *elders* were the lay leaders of the community, no doubt the heads of the principal aristocratic families, mostly of Sadducean outlook. The *scribes* were drawn from the class of lawyers, and mostly belonged to the Pharisaic party. The other group mentioned, the *rulers*, must be identified with the priestly element in the Sanhedrin; sometimes called the chief priests, these were the holders of various official positions in the administration of the temple.[1]

6. Luke mentions certain important priests who were present. *Annas* had been high priest in AD 6–14, but had been deposed by the Romans and succeeded by various members of his family, including his son-in-law *Caiaphas* (AD 18–36). Despite his deposition Annas was doubtless still possessed of great influence and he retained his title (Lk. 3:2). *John* is otherwise unknown, unless this name is a variant for Jonathan (the reading of D), another son of Annas, who was high priest in AD 37. *Alexander* is unknown. The other members *of the high-priestly family* will be those who held the various official positions in the temple administration. Verse 6 thus details more precisely the members of the first group mentioned in verse 5. We may note in passing how the temple affairs were very much in the hands of a few powerful families.

7. When the apostles were brought before the meeting they were asked *by what power* or *by* the authority of *what name* they had been acting. The question presumably related primarily to the healing miracle, as Peter assumed (verse 9), and was in effect an invitation to the apostles to explain the authority which enabled them to perform such a miracle. The use of the term *name* could be Christian language, rather than Jewish, and may be Luke's paraphrase of *by what power*, in the light of Peter's use of the term name. It has been objected that the theme of the inquiry (the miracle) has shifted from the reason for the arrest (the preaching of the resurrection); but the two themes hang together, and the court begins at the beginning.

[1] *TDNT*, III, pp. 270f.

8–10. The promise of Jesus in Luke 12:11f.; 21:14f. is fulfilled as Peter receives a special inspiration from the Spirit to enable him to reply effectively in the court.[1] Peter's address, *rulers of the people and elders*, covers the two main groups in the court. He begins his brief remarks skilfully by drawing attention to the fact that the subject of the enquiry is a good deed done to a needy person who has been healed. *Healed* reflects the same Greek word as is used in verse 12 with the wider meaning of 'save'; the speech takes advantage of the word's range of meaning. Appearing before the supreme court, Peter states solemnly to those present, as representatives of all Israel, that the healing is to be ascribed to the power of *the name of Jesus Christ of Nazareth* (note the solemn use of the full name; *cf.* 3:6), and reiterates that this person whom they had put to death was the One whom God had raised from the dead.

11. This last point is now reinforced by being expressed metaphorically in the language of Psalm 118:22, with a pointed application: the *builders* in the Psalm are identified with Peter's audience. The text used figured in the teaching of Jesus (Lk. 20:17) and also in apostolic teaching (1 Pet. 2:7), where it was linked with other 'stone' sayings. The saying has a proverbial ring, so that it could simply mean: 'The old proverb about the stone which the builders thought was useless, but which proved to be the right one to use as a cornerstone, can be applied to this situation.' But in its original context the verse in the Psalm may have referred to the position of Israel in the eyes of the nations or of the king as the leader of the nation. Jesus and the early church applied it to God's raising of the Messiah from death.

12. It was Jesus, then, who *saved* the lame man. Peter claims that only Jesus can offer salvation in the fullest sense; his is the only name which has received power from God to give salvation to men. Hence there is an implicit appeal to the audience to cease their rejection of Jesus. The thought is not uncommon in the New Testament (Jn. 14:6; Heb. 2:3; *cf.* 1 Tim. 2:5). It arose from the conviction that God had exalted Jesus to his right hand, a position that obviously could not be

[1] The objection that this fresh filling represents a different theological outlook from that which ascribes the continual presence of the Spirit to Christians (Haenchen, pp. 187, 216) misunderstands the theology of the Spirit; see 2:4 note.

shared with anybody else; it followed that if God had declared Jesus to be a Saviour, there could be nobody else alongside him.

13–14. The thing that struck the court about Peter's remarks was the *boldness* with which they were uttered. The whole demeanour of Peter and John was one of confidence and unashamedness which enabled them to speak freely in the face of what must have been a daunting audience. It was the quality for which the disciples were later to pray (4:29, 31) and which characterized their public speaking (9:27f.; 13:46; 14:3; 18:26; 19:8; 26:26; *cf.* Eph. 6:20; 1 Thes. 2:2). It was all the more surprising to the court because the apostles had had no particular training in theology or rhetoric. *Uneducated* could mean illiterate, and the word translated *common* (Gk. *idiōtēs*) refers to lay persons who had no interest in public affairs. C. H. Dodd, however, has claimed that the two Greek words translate a Hebrew phrase which refers to people ignorant of the Torah or Jewish law,[1] and this is no doubt the sense here. The implication is that the apostles' eloquence was inspired by the Spirit. Since the apostles had been with Jesus and now spoke about him, the court seized on this fact (this is the force of *recognized*, according to Bruce, *Book*, p. 102) and presumably recollected that he had behaved in the same fashion (*cf.* Jn. 7:15). The verse does not mean that the apostles' eloquence led the court (for the first time) to realize that they were connected with Jesus. Perhaps the Jewish leaders remembered how difficult it had been to win an argument with Jesus. They were having the same difficulty now, and it was compounded by the fact that the healed man was there for all to see. It is not clear why he was present. Had he been arrested as well? Or was the court meeting held in public? Luke has not bothered to tell us. What mattered was that the court was left bereft of an answer to the situation; Luke's readers might have remembered the promise in Luke 21:15 and seen it now being fulfilled.

15–17. The court was therefore cleared while the authorities decided what to do. The *council* here means in effect the 'council chamber'. Whether Luke had information about what went on behind the closed doors, or deduced what happened in the light of the later open proceedings, cannot now be

---

[1] *The Interpretation of the Fourth Gospel* (Cambridge, 1954), p. 82n.

known. The perplexity of the members of the council in face of an undeniable miracle of healing has already been described, and the remarks ascribed to the council members simply reflect their obvious feelings. In the same way, the decision of the council reflects what they said when they recalled the apostles to appear before them. Their fear was the spread of Christianity, which might have serious repercussions for the life of the community (*cf.* the attitude expressed in Jn. 11:47–53), quite apart from the fact that the rehabilitation of Jesus among the people at large would cast the strongest aspersions on their own earlier action against him which had culminated in his execution.

18. For the moment they contented themselves with issuing a stern warning to the apostles to cease their preaching. There was probably in fact little more that they could do. While one could make a show of legality in condemning Jesus as a messianic pretender, it is difficult to see what law the apostles could be regarded as having broken, and the extent of popular support for them probably prevented the authorities from getting away with applying more drastic sanctions at this stage. The best they could do was to forbid the preaching of the gospel on their own authority; at a later stage the apostles could in effect be indicted for contempt of court.

19–20. The apostles knew that they could not obey such a command, and told the court so. It was a clear act of defiance. It had an illustrious precedent in the story of the Greek philosopher Socrates who told the court which condemned him to death for his teachings, 'I shall obey God rather than you.' The statement can be seen as an affirmation of the freedom of the individual's conscience over against the state, and so in a sense it is: the individual claims the freedom to obey what he believes to be the command of God. But the important point is that it is the higher obedience due to God which is at issue, and this obedience stands above the commands of any religious or political system (for the Jews these were one and the same system). Here is the limit which is implicit in Romans 13:1–7. The problem was of course that the Jewish court would have liked to think that it was speaking with the voice of God, but Peter reminded it that it was a human institution, and that there could be no doubt that God must be obeyed rather than men, whenever it came to a clash between the two. The apostles had been called to be witnesses to Jesus Christ; they were duty-bound to continue their witness.

21–22. Faced by this defiance of their command, the authorities could do no more than repeat their threats of what would happen if the apostles landed in court again. Then they released them. Luke explains their action as being due to fear of the people, who for the moment at any rate were under the impact of a miracle wrought on a man who had been lame for over forty years and whose cure was thus all the more remarkable.

d. The disciples pray for further boldness (4:23–31)

The released apostles went, naturally enough, back to their friends, and their first action was to pray to God. Their prayer recognized him as the sovereign God; it was therefore in accordance with his foreknowledge and by his permission that the Jewish leaders had attacked them. But instead of regarding the attacks as directed against them personally, they looked to a passage of Scripture which spoke of the attacks made by earthly rulers on the Lord (Yahweh) and the Messiah, and saw them fulfilled in the unholy conspiracy of Herod and Pilate, of Jews and Romans, against Jesus. They thus regarded what was happening now as simply a continuation of this attack, and their prayer was that, despite it, they might carry on witnessing boldly with the backing provided by the miracles which testified that Jesus was still alive and active. Their prayer was heard and answered in an impressive manner, and they were enabled to do precisely what they had asked God to enable them to do, to carry on speaking boldly.

Although the prayer is ascribed to the church as a whole, it is hard to believe that a whole group could speak together in this way without some form of written prayer available for them all to read simultaneously or without a common form of words being learned off by heart previously; the view that the Spirit inspired each member to say exactly the same words reflects an impossibly mechanical view of the Spirit's working. It is, therefore, more likely that one person spoke in the name of the whole company.[1]

The prayer itself reflects the use of the Old Testament, not

[1] Possibly early Christian congregations repeated prayers a phrase at a time after a 'precentor'.

merely Psalm 2, which is explicitly quoted, but also the prayer of Hezekiah in Isaiah 37: 16–20 which has supplied the general pattern and suggested some of the phraseology. Haenchen (pp. 228f.) argues that the prayer must have been composed by Luke himself; he has to claim this since the prayer reflects the situation described earlier in the chapter, which he regards as largely a Lucan creation. We have found no reason to follow this view of the earlier part of the story, since the difficilties which Haenchen finds in it are largely of his own creation. So far as the present prayer is concerned, Haenchen has to admit that the picture of Herod and Pilate does not quite correspond to the Lucan picture, according to which the two rulers were not exactly enthusiastic to put Jesus to death; he also has to admit that the link between the attacks on Jesus and those on the apostles is a rather loose one (we might have expected Luke, as a competent writer of historical fiction, to have made a better job of it!). We might also observe that the Greek style of verse 25 is pretty atrocious, and (if the text is reliable) we might have expected Luke to make a better job of it if he was freely composing. In short, the theory of free composition has to face some obstacles, and it is wiser to admit that Luke was making use of an existing prayer.

As it stands, the prayer indicates that the early church turned to God in time of persecution, found comfort in the fact that he knew beforehand what would happen, and claimed strength to carry on its witness. This may be Luke's idea of how the church ought to have behaved – and an object lesson for the church of his own day when it faced persecution – but how does any critic know that this was not how the early church actually did behave, and hence dare to suggest that this is an example of 'the author's freedom as a writer'?

23. The apostles went back after their release to their close circle of *friends* and supporters – obviously a smaller group than the whole Christian community of 4:4. The reference to *the chief priests and the elders* suggests that in Luke's view the scribes, who represented the Pharisaic outlook, were less closely involved in the matter.

24. The immediate reaction of the group was to join together in prayer. Luke stresses the oneness of spirit which was evident (1:14; 2:46; 5:12; 15:25; Rom. 15:6); the effect of persecution was to bind the members of the church together so that there was a common desire to pray. Whatever may have been the manner in which the prayer was conducted (see introduction to section), the wording that follows expresses the common sentiments of those assembled. The prayer began with an address to God that reflected his sovereign control over all that was happening. The title *Sovereign Lord* (Gk. *despotēs*) is comparatively infrequent in the New Testament (and also in the LXX), perhaps because the word suggested a despotic, arbitrary kind of lordship. Here, however, it is appropriately used to stress the powerful control exerted by God (*cf.* Lk. 2:29; 2 Pet. 2:1; Jude 4; Rev. 6:10). This control is seen in his creation of the universe, here described in typical Old Testament language (Ps. 146:6; Is. 37:16).

25–26. It was this sovereign Lord who had prophesied in the Psalms the fruitless efforts of the rulers of the world to rebel against him and the Messiah. The unspoken thought is quite clearly that it is futile for men to scheme against a God who not only created the whole universe but also foresaw their scheming. The citation is prefaced by an introductory formula which is expressed in a rather confused Greek phrase, whose difficulty is reflected in the variety of readings in the manuscripts. The sense is plain enough: the text says that God spoke by means of the *Holy Spirit* (the inspirer of prophets) and by means of *the mouth of* his servant *David* (as the human instrument). This is what is said more simply in 1:16. It is, however, not clear how the corrupt Greek of the sentence arose; if the text in the earliest manuscripts is reliable, it would seem that Luke had not fully revised his work or that the text suffered corruption at an early stage. David is interestingly described as God's *servant* (*cf.* Jesus, verse 27), following Old Testament usage (2 Sa. 3:18; 1 Ki. 11:34; Ps. 89:3, 20).[1] The actual quotation is from Psalm 2:1f.; verse 7 of the same Psalm is cited elsewhere in the New Testament (13:33; Heb. 1:5; 5:5; *cf.* the echoes of verse 9 in Rev. 2:27; 12:5; 19:15). The use of the term *Anointed* (*i.e.* Messiah) made the application to Jesus inescapable. In its original context the Psalm is generally regarded as an address to the king, either at his coronation or at some subsequent period of crisis when it was helpful to recall the coronation, in which the promises of God to him

---

[1] The use of *pais* here rather than the Septuagintal *doulos* may be by parallelism with verse 27, but may also represent an independent Jewish usage; *cf.* Lk. 1:69; Didache 9:2.

are rehearsed as encouragement in the face of foreign enemies who threaten to overthrow him; the God who addresses the ruler as 'my son' will certainly overthrow these boastful princelings. The reapplication of the words to the Messiah was natural, and they are reflected in the heavenly address to Jesus at his baptism (Lk. 3:22). In the present context it is the opening words of the Psalm which speak of the fruitless plotting of the peoples and their rulers against the Messiah which were relevant to the immediate situation.

27-28. The quotation is broken off,[1] and the prayer proceeds to comment on it. The Psalm truly expresses what had happened in that here in Jerusalem there had been an alliance against God's anointed One (10:36-38 note), his *holy servant*, Jesus. The description emphasizes how Jesus belonged to God (*holy*, 3:14), and was appointed by him to be Messiah. The term *pais*, 'servant', could here have its alternative meaning of 'child, son', in view of the way in which the use of the Psalm evokes the thought of divine sonship, but the usual rendering should be retained (as in 3:13; 4:25). The 'kings . . . and the rulers' in the Psalm are equated with *Herod* and *Pilate*; the fact that only one example of each can be produced is unimportant. As for 'the Gentiles . . . and the peoples' (two terms used in synonymous parallelism in the Psalm), these are equated with *the Gentiles* (*i.e.* the Romans) *and the peoples of Israel*.[2] The inclusion of Israel among the foes of the Messiah marks the beginning of the Christian understanding that insofar as the people of Israel reject the Messiah they cease to be the Lord's people and can be ranked with unbelieving Gentiles. Yet all that was plotted and done against Jesus was no more than God had foreordained to happen (2:23; 3:18). The reference to God's *hand* predestining what happened is a stretching of language; the thought is of God's mighty hand which carried out what his will ordained, and this will include not only the plotting of his enemies, which he allowed, but also their frustration and defeat.

29-30. In view of all this, the church could now bring its own situation before the Lord, confident that this too was

[1] Grammatically it is still part of the address to God with which the prayer begins.
[2] The unusual use of the plural *peoples*, as against the normal 'people', for Israel is due to assimilation to the wording of the Psalm.

under his control. It prayed to him to *look upon* the *threats* (verses 17, 21) of their opponents, *i.e.* to take note of them and act accordingly (*cf.* Is. 37:17). '*Their* threats' refers back loosely to the opponents of Jesus in verse 27 who are thought of as still active against the church; it is a natural looseness of speech. The prayer, however, is not primarily that the opponents will be brought to naught. Rather, on the assumption that this will inevitably happen, the church asks for strength to carry on witnessing during the time while they still continue to be able to exercise their opposition. The Lord's servants need courage (verse 13) to stand up to the threats against them and continue to proclaim the Word. At the same time, they are conscious how much the effectiveness of their preaching was aided by the healings and other miraculous signs worked by the Lord through the name of Jesus, and they prayed for the continuation of these.

31. The effect of the prayer was remarkable. The room in which the disciples were gathered shook as if an earthquake was taking place. This was one of the signs which indicated a theophany in the Old Testament (Ex. 19:18; Is. 6:4), and it would have been regarded as indicating a divine response to prayer.[1] The point is, then, that God signified that he was present and would answer the prayer. Again the *Holy Spirit* came upon the disciples and they were given the confidence they desired to speak the Word of God. Some commentators have suggested that behind this brief description there lies a variant tradition of the supernatural phenomena at Pentecost; it has even been suggested that originally the tradition described an outbreak of speaking in tongues. Both suggestions are unlikely. The story undoubtedly means that the disciples received a fresh filling with the Spirit to enable them to bear witness to Jesus on subsequent occasions (2:4 note).

e. A further summary of the life of the early church (4:32–37)

The sequel to the previous story begins at 5:12. The temporal gap between the two incidents involving the arrest of the apostles for preaching is neatly filled by the account of another event from these early days of the church. We are given a further summary of the inner life of the church and a contrast

---

[1] For the motif in pagan thought see Virgil, *Aeneid* 3: 88–91.

is drawn between the attitudes of Joseph Barnabas and Ananias and his wife to the practice of sharing property for the sake of the poor. The greater length of the story of Ananias and Sapphira should not lead to the conclusion that it is the important incident, the preceding section being merely an introduction to give it a setting; on the contrary, it is more likely that 4:32–35 describes the pattern of life, and is then followed by two illustrations, positive and negative, of what happened in practice.

The passage shows considerable parallelism with the earlier summary in 2:43–47. It stresses the common mind and the generosity of the disciples in their life together. This close fellowship accompanied the preaching of the apostles. Haenchen (p. 232) suggests that Luke was trying to emphasize that the gift of the Spirit (verse 31) led not only to inspired preaching but also to Christian fellowship and generosity.

32. Two facts characterized the life of Christian community. The choice of word (*company*) reflects the growth in size of the Christian group. Despite its size it had a common mind and purpose; in other words, it was united in its devotion to the Lord (for the expression used see 1 Ch. 12:38). The other thing was the fact that nobody regarded his property as being under his own control but was prepared to regard it as for the use of the community as a whole. This way of putting the matter brings out the fact that the things which each person *possessed* evidently continued to be his own property until it was found necessary to sell them for the common good. The two characteristics thus described correspond broadly to the two great commandments of love (or devotion) to God and love to one's neighbour. It has also been noted that the phraseology used to describe them is reminiscent of that used by the Greek philosopher Aristotle in expressing ideals for human life in community. Christian ideals are none the less Christian for being also recognized by secular moralists.

33. Meanwhile, the apostles, as those especially called to be witnesses of the resurrection of Jesus, continued their witness *with great power* despite the Jewish prohibition of their preaching. The point is that they spoke in such a way under the guidance of the Spirit that their words were effective in leading other people to belief in Jesus. (Spirit-filled preaching can also lead to the hardening of opposition against the speaker, as in 6:10f.; 7:55–58. The point is that such utterances cannot be ignored by the hearers but force them to decision, for or against the gospel.) *Great grace was upon them all* may mean that the grace of God worked powerfully through them (6:8; Lk. 2:40); alternatively the Greek word *charis* may have its other meaning of 'favour', and the point will be that the preaching was well received by the people (2:47; Lk. 2:52). The former view is preferable in view of the parallelism of construction with Luke 2:40. If *them all* refers only to the apostles, the case for this verse being out of place and having originally followed verse 31 gains some support. If, however, it refers to the whole church, then we get a link with verse 34. The activity of God's grace was seen not merely in the preaching, but also in the way in which the members of the church were freed from material need.

34–35. The Old Testament promise to God's people that there would not be any poor among them (Dt. 15:4) was brought to fulfilment in the church by the generosity of the better-off members. Those who had estates or houses sold them and brought the proceeds to the apostles who then distributed them to the needy.[1] The reference to the *feet* of the apostles (4:37; 5:2) suggests some kind of legal transfer expressed in formal language; it is unnecessary to go along with Stählin's suggestion (p. 79) that the apostles sat on high chairs, the prototypes of later ecclesiastical thrones! We now see incidentally why the preaching of the apostles was mentioned in verse 33. They also had the additional burden of dealing with the common fund of the church; and, while at first this may not have been too heavy a task, it was not long before new arrangements were needed (6:1–6).

36. The example of generosity shown by *Barnabas* is singled out for special mention, possibly because it was an outstanding one, and certainly because Barnabas will appear later in the story as a Christian leader conspicuous for his sheer goodness (11:24). His original name was Joseph but he had been given a by-name by the apostles which presumably reflected his character. The path from 'Barnabas' to 'son of consolation' is not absolutely clear, and there are various explanations of the name.[2] A *Son of encouragement* is a person who gives encourage-

---

[1] Luke knows that not all the members of the church sold their property (12:12).

[2] See S. Brock, 'Barnabas: *huios paraklēseōs*', *JTS* 25, 1974, pp. 93–98.

ment, and Barnabas was certainly that (9:27; 11:23; 15:37). He was a Levite by birth, a member of the Jewish tribe from which some of the minor temple staff were drawn (Lk. 10:32; Jn. 1:19), but his family must have emigrated to Cyprus where there was a sizeable Jewish population (*cf.* 11:19; 13:4f.).

37. The ancient law forbidding Levites to own land (Nu. 18:20; Dt. 10:9) seems to have been a dead letter (Je. 32:7ff.). Whether the land owned by Barnabas was in Cyprus or Palestine is not clear; presumably the latter is meant, since verse 35 need not imply anything more than that Barnabas had been born in Cyprus.

f. The sin of Ananias and Sapphira (5:1–11)

The second example drawn from the area of the church's communal life is negative in character. It is the story of how two members of the community attempted to gain credit for a greater personal sacrifice than they had actually made by offering only part of the proceeds of a sale to the apostles and passing it off as if it were the whole amount. When Ananias found that his deception was discovered and was accused of lying to the Spirit, he fell down dead; and when his wife showed the same intent to deceive, she heard what was in effect a sentence of death passed upon her and also died.

The story must be ranked among the most difficult for modern readers of Acts. It portrays Peter as a man of supernatural insight who is able to pronounce effective curses upon sinners, just like Paul in 13:8–11. The story appears to present the working of the Spirit in almost magical fashion. Neither Ananias nor Sapphira is apparently offered any chance of repentance, and the way in which the former was buried without his wife's knowledge sounds heartless, to say nothing of being improbable. For such reasons the story is often regarded as legendary: its historical kernel may be an attempt to account for the sudden death of Ananias, the story of his wife's death being a legendary heightening of the grim warning thus offered to sinners.

It is certainly true that the story introduces us to a different world of thought from that of today.[1] It is a world in which sin

[1] See J. D. M. Derrett, 'Ananias, Sapphira, and the Right of Property', *Downside Review* 89, 1971, pp. 225–232, for several important insights incorporated in what follows.

is taken seriously, and in which a person convicted of sin against the Spirit might well suffer a fatal shock at the thought of having broken a taboo. This will at least account for Ananias's death; it remains the case that Peter pronounces a curse on Sapphira, the shock of which may have had the same effect on her. The lack of opportunity for repentance solves itself in the case of Ananias if we are right in thinking that he died of shock; as for his wife, Peter did give her the opportunity to alter her former attitude (verse 8). As for the difficulty that she was not informed of her husband's death and burial, it may be helpful to remember that 'it is always risky methodologically to assume that a writer does not see the contradictions in his own narrative'.[1] The difficulty, if there is one, must surely have been known to Luke. One possibility is that hot eastern conditions demanded immediate burial (though admittedly 9:37 gives a different picture), and for reasons unknown to us it may have been impossible to contact Sapphira at the time. More plausible is Derrett's view that a sinner such as Ananias was shown to be by his divinely inflicted death would have been buried forthwith without ceremony or mourning. The early church accepted the possibility of serious judgments following upon acts of sin (1 Cor. 5:1–11; 11:27–32; Jas. 5:14–16), and this is the background to the story.

1–2. The opening *But* contrasts *Ananias* and *Sapphira* with Barnabas. They sold a piece of land, but kept back part of the price which they had received for it[2] before bringing the proceeds to the apostles for the common-good fund of the church; placing the money *at the apostles' feet* means that it was given as a trust, not as a personal gift. The verb *kept back* is identical with that used to describe the action of Achan in holding on to some of the spoil from Jericho which was meant to be handed over to the house of the Lord or to be destroyed (Jos. 7:1). There are further similarities between the stories of the two men's sins and their consequent punishments, but these are insufficient to show that one story was created on the pattern of the other; at most they show that Luke was conscious of a typological resemblance between them.

3–4. Peter is assumed to have the power of spiritual in-

---

[1] R. E. Brown, *The Birth of the Messiah* (London, 1978), p. 307.
[2] It was possibly regarded as the wife's *ketubah* or share of her husband's estate (Derrett).

sight and to be able to recognize when he is being told lies;
God's power to see into men's hearts (Heb. 4:13) is given to
the apostle. Ananias's action is attributed to the inspiration
of *Satan* who is the evil counterpart to the Spirit. The expression *filled your heart* may represent a Semitic idiom which means
'has made you dare' (Est. 7:5; Ec. 8:11; Metzger, pp. 327f.).
Peter's words make it clear that Ananias was entirely at liberty
to keep or sell his property as he thought fit. His sin lay in his
lie to the Holy Spirit, and thus consisted not in giving merely
part of the proceeds to the common fund but in alleging that
the money represented the whole and not just part of the price
of the property. Nor was it simply an attempt to deceive the
human leaders of the church. The leaders were men inspired
by the Spirit, and so they were God's representatives.

5. The immediate aftermath to Peter's declaration was
that Ananias fell down dead. The death is no doubt to be
regarded as a divine judgment upon his sin, although there is
no sentence of death contained in Peter's words. From a medical point of view it was probably a case of heart-failure due
to shock; 'To offend against the Spirit of this community was
for the superstitious a fearful and terrifying thing' (Dunn,
p. 166). The effect upon the observers must have been quite
devastating; the RSV's *great fear* has become too conventional
in our ears to convey the sense of dread that there must have
been. Harvey (p. 417) notes that other communities punished
similar faults equally drastically. The Qumran community
dismissed such culprits from its midst, and, if they took
seriously the rules about eating only the community's food,
they were in danger of death by starvation. Another group in
Spain punished those who secretly kept back any of their
private property with death. Derrett argues that the death of
the sinner would have been regarded as an atonement for his
sin in line with Jewish thinking on the matter, but this is
dubious.

6. The death was followed by summary burial. The body
was *wrapped up* in a cloth and carried out to a grave, possibly
outside the city. There is no need to suppose that the *young
men* constituted a particular group of church officials, entrusted
with the more mundane duties, still less a group of 'novices'
on the analogy of the set-up at Qumran.

7. The *interval of about three hours* can be reckoned from the
death or the burial. *Sapphira* is portrayed as not knowing what

had happened. Critics have insisted that this is quite impossible, and that the detail has been thoughtlessly invented to
create the right situation for the ensuing conversation. The
normal customs with regard to burial and mourning may not
have applied, however, in the case of a sinner struck down by
what must have seemed to be the hand of God.

8. The seriousness of the situation is underlined by Peter's
words. Instead of informing the widow of her loss, he goes
straight to the matter of her sin. In view of the horror with
which an ancient community would regard such a sin, we
need not find this surprising, even if we would adopt a different
attitude in our different cultural setting. Sapphira is given the
opportunity to tell the truth and thus to show some sign of
repentance from her former attitude. When asked whether the
sum given to the church represented the actual price obtained
for the property, she persisted in claiming that it was. Haench-
en's claim (pp. 238f.) that the verse is not intended to indicate
an opportunity for repentance but merely to allow her to
implicate herself fully in her husband's guilt has no stronger
basis than his desire always to credit Luke with the worst
motives.[1] In fact the figure named by Peter in verse 8 might be
the actual amount of the sale, in which case Sapphira's reply
would be a confession.

9–11. The action of the guilty couple is represented as an
agreement *to tempt the Spirit, i.e.* to test God (as the Israelites
did in the wilderness, Ex. 17:2; Dt. 6:16) to see how much
they can get away with. Peter asks rhetorically what led them
to do it. Then comes the devastating announcement that the
people who buried her husband are ready to bury her. This
is nothing less than a sentence of death, and it is followed
immediately by the collapse of Sapphira on the spot. Again
we must remember that similar occurrences can be attested
from primitive societies where a curse of this kind can have a
cataclysmic effect in causing death by shock. The double punishment deeply affected both the Christians and everybody
else who heard of it.

It is in this inauspicious context that Luke uses the word
church (Gk. *ekklēsia*) for the first time to designate the Christian

---

[1] Haenchen's picture of the apostle still sitting on his chair without inter-
mission three hours after Ananias's death with the money lying at his feet is
pure fantasy.

community. The word means an assembly, and hence the people who compose it. The old view that it means the 'called out' people should be abandoned once for all, resting as it does on a false derivation of meaning from etymology. Rather behind the term lies the Jewish use of *ekklēsia* and *synagōgē* to translate Old Testament words referring to the assembly or congregation of God's people. The term *synagōgē* had come to be used especially of Jewish places of worship, and its associations with the Jewish law made it an unsuitable term for Christians to use. They took over the other word and used it to describe themselves as the people of God or of Christ. Luke's usage here is of course editorial and does not imply that this was the historical occasion when the term came into use; but he judged that by this time the disciples did have a corporate identity and were claiming to be the true people of God.[1]

g. The continuing growth of the church (5:12–16)

Before coming to the account of the second attack on the church by the Jewish authorities Luke recounts in general terms how the church's activities were increasing to such an extent that the authorities felt that they must again take action against it. The general picture is of a powerful healing ministry that made a deep impression on the people and helped to spread the gospel outside Jerusalem. At the same time there was a paradoxical combination of fear on the part of the populace as the story of Ananias and Sapphira's deaths got around, coupled with a desire to join the church. The combination of these two attitudes is not improbable – superstitious people would feel that the gospel was confirmed by the miraculous powers of the apostles, even when these powers were seen in punitive actions. But the way in which the statements are joined together (verses 13a and 14 fit together rather harshly, and verse 15 is added very loosely) suggests that Luke has utilized a number of separate traditions in writing this general statement.

12. The section links up directly with the prayer in 4:30 that God would help the church's witness by performing *signs and wonders*. The deaths of Ananias and Sapphira could be

[1] See further I. H. Marshall, 'New Wine in Old Wineskins: V. *Ekklēsia*', *ET* 84, 1972–73, pp. 359–364; L. Coenen, *NIDNTT*, I, pp. 291–307.

regarded as examples of these, but Luke is now thinking of the healing ministry exercised not only by Peter (3:1–10) but also by the other apostles; unfortunately we have no details of the activities of the latter. The account of the healings is continued in verses 15–16, and this has raised the suggestion that the order of the verses was altered at an early date (Stählin, p. 186). Verse 12b thus proceeds to a new theme. It describes how *they* – presumably the Christians in general, and not just the apostles – gathered together in *Solomon's Portico* (3:11).

13. *The rest* is a puzzling expression, and it has been suggested that the text originally referred to the Jewish rulers, in contrast with the people mentioned in the second part of the verse. In Luke 8:10, however, the word is used of non-disciples, and it seems that it became almost a technical term for non-believers (1 Thes. 4:13; 5:6); this will be the sense here. A further problem is caused by the word translated *join* (*kollaomai*), especially in view of the statement in verse 14. C. Burchard has shown that it means 'to come near',[1] and hence the clause simply means that the unbelieving Jews kept away from the Christians and left them alone. They may have been frightened lest half-hearted allegiance would lead to judgment. But if fear kept them away, they nevertheless could not help praising them as they were impressed by what they did.

14–15. Despite the awe which kept the people from meddling with the Christian group as they met together, there were nevertheless increasing numbers of converts who believed and were added to the Lord (11:24). As a result of the reputation of the Christians more and more people sought physical healing from the apostles, and especially from Peter. Sick people were carried out *into the streets* where Peter might pass by (*cf.* the similar description in Mk. 6:56). People hoped that even if only *his shadow* fell across them they would be healed. The idea that shadows had magical powers, both beneficent and malevolent, was current in the ancient world and explains the motivation of the people.[2] Similar beliefs about Paul's powers are attested in 19:12. Luke relates this detail as a special

[1] C. Burchard, 'Fussnoten zum neutestamentlichen Griechisch I', *ZNW* 61, 1970, pp. 159f.
[2] P. W. van der Horst, 'Peter's Shadow: the Religio-Historical Background of Acts 5:15', *NTS* 23, 1976–77, pp. 204–212.

proof of Peter's reputation among the people; he was regarded as having exceptional healing powers. Whether, however, Peter or Luke would have shared the superstitions which the people undoubtedly showed is another matter; see 19:12 note.

16. A new feature is the spread of the reputation of the church to *the towns around Jerusalem*. The implication is that at this stage Peter and the other apostles confined themselves to Jerusalem, so that the sick had to be brought to them. Later they would begin to itinerate as missionaries.

h. The second arrest of the apostles (5:17–42)

The climax of the present section of the story is the arrest and trial of the apostles for (in the case of Peter and John) a second time. The present incident is distinguished from the previous one by the way in which the apostles were set free from their prison at night and went and resumed their preaching in the temple. Luke obviously enjoyed the humour of the situation as the council sat waiting for the prisoners to be brought, quite unaware that they were back in the temple. The apostles were reminded of the previous prohibition of their preaching, and responded with a plain refusal to obey. The court could have proceeded to punish them – whether it could legally have had them executed is doubtful – but it was restrained by the intervention of Gamaliel who counselled a moderate approach, pointing out that it was folly to attack a movement that could conceivably have divine backing (his pupil Saul evidently did not share his point of view, 8:1–3; 9:1): did Gamaliel think there might be something in the story of the resurrection of Jesus as God's vindication of his servant? His counsel prevailed, but the court was not minded to ignore the way in which its authority had been flouted, and ordered a beating for the apostles. They for their part were quite prepared to continue their witness despite the risk of punishment. Indeed, for the moment they were safe, since there was nothing more that the court could do, so long as it followed Gamaliel's policy.

The historical problems of this story in relation to that of the earlier trial scene have already been discussed briefly (4:1–22 note). Apart from the problem of parallelism with the earlier story, criticism has taken up three features of the present narrative. First, the apostles' midnight departure from prison: 'an extremely vague and casual angelic deliverance, which we can hardly take as serious history' (Hanson, p. 85). The story is similar to that in 12:1–11, but much less detailed. The lack of detail may well be because Luke wants to avoid anticipating the later story and spoiling its effect. Luke plainly intends to report a supernatural occurrence (whose effect was not lost on Gamaliel), whether or not it is suspected that one of the Lord's earthly messengers may actually have opened the prison doors. A second problem area surrounds the role of Gamaliel and the historical value of his speech. Haenchen (pp. 257f.) regards it as a faulty Lucan composition, and then claims that there is no historical reason to suppose that Gamaliel did take the apostles' side, especially since the court did in fact proceed to punish them. Haenchen, however, fails to realize that the fact that Luke reports something is historical evidence for its having happened, even if confirmatory evidence is, in the nature of things, lacking. What is lacking is any evidence that Gamaliel did not act in the way described. The information that we have about Gamaliel indicates that he was a respected teacher and a firm upholder of the law, and this is certainly not inconsistent with what is said about him here. The third problem area is that of the expansion of the church. Following Dibelius (p. 124), Haenchen (p. 258) claims that in reality the earliest church was a small group, living a quiet existence, and not likely to come into sharp conflict with the authorities. Even, however, if the few colourful episodes presented by Luke may tend to make us think of the church as exercising a public influence greater than was in fact the case, there still remains not the slightest reason to dispute that the church expanded at a very fast rate and that it came into collision with the Sadducees in the early days of its existence; Haenchen's assertions to the contrary cannot take the place of solid evidence.

17–18. The initiative against the apostles was again taken by the *high priest* and the Sadducean group in the Sanhedrin (4:1); the Pharisaic group, represented by Gamaliel, does not appear until later in the narrative. The motive of the *Sadducees* is said to be *jealousy*, *i.e.* irritation at the success of the church (13:45; it is just possible, however, that here the word *zēlos* means 'religious zeal' directed against opponents of the Jewish traditional religion; *cf*. Phil. 3:6). They seized the apostles and put them in prison.

19. During the night the apostles escaped from the prison.

Their release is ascribed to *an angel of the Lord*. This is an Old Testament figure (7:30, 38) who also appears in the New Testament to bring important messages (Lk. 1:11; 2:9) or to perform miraculous acts (8:26; 12:7, 23). Luke certainly regards the incident as miraculous, or at least he presents it in this manner. Stories of doors opening miraculously and prisoners' fetters being loosed are common enough in the ancient world,[1] but this proves nothing regarding the historicity of this particular incident.

20. The angel acts as the spokesman of God in commanding the apostles to go and speak in the temple *all the words of this Life*. The *temple* was the appropriate place for such proclamation, not only because it was a well-frequented place but above all because it was the place where God had chosen to make himself known to the people of Israel. The phrase *all the words of this Life* is similar to 'the message of this salvation' (13:26; in Syriac 'life' and 'salvation' are rendered by the same word). The use of *this* is odd (*cf.* 22:4), but is perhaps simply a Lucan trick of style.

21. Although it was still early, the apostles found an audience in the temple; this is by no means surprising, since daily activity began quite early. It was, however, too soon for news to reach the members of the Sanhedrin. *The council and all the senate of Israel* is a hendiadys, only one body being meant. It is not certainly known where the council chamber was situated, but it was probably not within the temple precincts.

22–23. The council's officers were sent on a fruitless errand to the prison, where they found everything secure, but no prisoners inside. It must be concluded that, as is implied in the story in 12:18f., the guards had been unconscious during the escape of the prisoners and that the doors had been re-locked after their departure; consequently there was no cause for suspicion that the prisoners had vanished until this point.

24–26. The effect of the news was to make the members of the council perplexed about what was going on. Some of them, such as Gamaliel, must have reckoned with supernatural influences at work. Only at this point did news come from the temple that the apostles were at liberty and carrying on their preaching. A second attempt to apprehend the apostles was made, and this time it was successful. Luke notes that the

[1] J. Jeremias, *TDNT*, III, pp. 175f.

arrest was made peaceably, an indication of how the authorities realized that the apostles had the people on their side
and that the latter might react violently to the use of force. It
may be observed that neither here, nor anywhere else, do the
Christians respond with violence to being arrested; the lesson
of Luke 22:50f. had been learned.

27–28. The high priest opened the proceedings by reminding the apostles of the prohibition of their preaching which
had been made earlier (4:18); although the warning had been
addressed to Peter and John, it obviously was directed against
the church as a whole. So far from being obedient, the apostles
had filled Jerusalem with their teaching. Further, they were
accused of wanting to lay the guilt for the death of *this man* –
the high priest avoids mentioning the name of Jesus – on the
Jewish authorities. By accusing the Jewish leaders of murder-
ing the Messiah, whom God had then raised from the dead,
the Christians were in effect publicly calling for divine retribution upon them. The Jewish leaders regarded the death of
Jesus as the result of the legal trial of a malefactor; the Christians were making it out to be an act of murder, and thus
claiming that the Jewish leaders were guilty men.

29. Peter's reply to the accusation is a plainer and more
direct reaffirmation of what he said in 4:19. A command of
God, such as that given in 5:20, takes precedence over human
commands. It is the price of being a Christian that one must
be prepared to *obey God rather than men* – and bear the cost of
doing so.

30. Having answered the first part of the charge in verse
28, Peter proceeded to reaffirm the statement attributed to the
apostles in the second part of that verse, namely the guilt of
the Jewish leaders. He again reminded them that God had
raised from the dead the person whom they had killed by
crucifixion. It is not clear whether *God . . . raised Jesus* refers
to his bringing Jesus on to the stage of history (Bruce, *Book*,
p. 121) or to his raising him from the dead; *cf.* 3:26; 13:33f.
The latter seems more probable. What Peter is emphasizing
is that it was the ancestral God of the Jews who had done this.
For the Jewish leaders to kill Jesus was to act against the God
whom they claimed to worship. Nor could they shift the responsibility, if they were so inclined, by attributing Jesus'
death to the Romans, since they had themselves been responsible for giving Jesus what could be regarded as a Jewish form

of execution, described in the Old Testament as hanging on a gibbet (Dt. 21:22f.; *cf.* Acts 10:39; 13:29; Gal. 3:13); one may wonder whether there is a hint of the idea, developed by Paul, that a person who so died was regarded as being under the curse of God (Dt. 21:23).

31. This crucified man, however, was the one whom God had *exalted* to sit *at his right hand* (2:34; Ps. 110:1) and to be a leader and saviour (3:15) through whom the people of Israel might have the opportunity of repentance and of receiving forgiveness of their sins. Here is the offer of salvation to the very people who had crucified Jesus; the apostles use the opportunity provided in court to preach the gospel to their accusers and judges. The description of Jesus resembles that of Moses in 7:35, and the implication is that the former now replaces the latter as the mediator of salvation to Israel. This is the first occurrence outside the Gospels of the description of Jesus as a *Saviour*, although the motif of salvation has already been used (2:21; 4:9, 12). It is a title which tends to be restricted to the later books of the New Testament (Paul uses it for the first time in Phil. 3:20), and hence it has been suggested that here Luke is using a rather late vocabulary; in view, however, of the widespread use of the terms 'save' and 'salvation' in the early church, this is a precarious assumption, and it may simply be the case that the New Testament writers had no occasion to use the title earlier.[1] The statement that God *gives* repentance is significant; the thought is that through his appointment of Jesus as Saviour, God gives to sinners an opportunity to repent which they would not otherwise have had.

32. The brief gospel message is confirmed by the witness of the apostles who could claim to have seen the risen Jesus. Along with them the Spirit is also named as a witness (1 Jn. 5:7); the thought appears to be that the gift of the Spirit to the church is a further testimony to the reality of the exaltation of Jesus, since the Spirit is regarded as the gift of the exalted Messiah. Peter adds pointedly that it is those who *obey* God (verse 29!) who receive the Spirit.

33. Peter's words did nothing to commend his point of view to his hearers – at least, to the Sadducean element in the

---

[1] See further E. M. B. Green, *The Meaning of Salvation* (London, 1965), pp. 136–151.

Sanhedrin. They were roused to fury (7:54) and were of a mind to have the apostles put to death. Whether they could have had any legal grounds for doing so is not clear.

34. But at this point there was a somewhat surprising intervention. In the Gospels the Pharisees appear fairly consistently as the opponents of Jesus (*e.g.* Lk. 5:21, 30; 7:30; 11:53; 15:2; 16:14), and Jesus himself certainly criticized strongly their religious behaviour which he regarded as hypocritical (*e.g.* Lk. 11:39–52; 12:1; 16:15; 18:9–14). The Pharisees, as represented by the scribes, also formed part of the Sanhedrin which condemned Jesus to death (Lk. 22:2; *cf.* Mt. 27:62). Nevertheless, there are signs of a more favourable attitude to Jesus on the part of some of the Pharisees in Luke (Lk. 7:36; 11:37; 14:1). In none of the Gospels are they directly named in connection with the condemnation of Jesus, and in Acts we find some Pharisees who became Christians (15:5; 23:6); Paul claims that in belief the Pharisees stand closer to the Christians than do the Sadducees (23:6–9), and some of the scribes side with him against the Sadducees who are represented as the real opponents of the Christians (23:9). It is, therefore, perhaps not so strange that a leading Pharisee rose to warn against adopting extreme measures with the Christians. *Gamaliel* I (who is confused in Jewish tradition with his grandson Gamaliel II) was a leading Pharisaic teacher who belonged to the more moderate 'school' founded by Hillel and who was renowned for his piety. He moved that the court should go into closed session.

35. As in 4:15–17 the problem arises as to whether Luke had access to reports of what was said in the Sanhedrin behind closed doors; we cannot expect a word-for-word account of the proceedings although it is remarkable how easily secret information can become public property. Essentially, however, Gamaliel was making a plea for restraint and caution in deciding what to do about the apostles. He claimed, by citing two examples, that movements of human origin would come to nothing without any interference by the Jewish authorities; whereas, if the movement were inspired by God, it would be dangerous to take action against it. More precisely, he contended that once the leaders of mass movements had been killed, their followers soon lost enthusiasm for their cause; now that Jesus was dead, there was no need to take action against his disciples.

36. Gamaliel's choice of historical examples causes some difficulties. He first of all refers to a man called *Theudas* who claimed to be *somebody* (*i.e.* a prophet or a messianic pretender) and raised 400 followers. When he was put to death (by the Romans), his followers were dispersed and nothing came of the affair. Now Josephus (*Ant.* 20:97f.) relates: 'During the period when Fadus was procurator of Judea [AD 44–46], a certain imposter named Theudas persuaded the majority of the masses to take up their possessions and to follow him to the Jordan River. He stated that he was a prophet and that at his command the river would be parted and would provide them an easy passage. With this talk he deceived many. Fadus, however, did not permit them to reap the fruit of their folly, but sent against them a squadron of cavalry. These fell upon them unexpectedly, slew many of them and took many prisoners. Theudas himself was captured, whereupon they cut off his head and brought it to Jerusalem.' It is obvious that this could be a fuller account of the same incident. There are two problems: (1) Since Gamaliel was speaking well before AD 44 (the year in which Herod Agrippa I died, 12: 20–23), a reference to the Theudas mentioned in Josephus would be anachronistic on his lips. (2). Gamaliel goes on to describe the rising of Judas *after this*; but the rising of Judas took place in AD 6 *before* the Theudas incident in Josephus. So, it is argued, Luke makes Gamaliel commit an anachronism and put the two stories in reverse chronological order. It has been argued that Luke was led to his error by misreading Josephus who goes on after the Theudas story to mention the sons of Judas and then to explain parenthetically who this Judas was and how he had led a revolt against Rome. But this supposition is highly unlikely, since Josephus' works were not published till c. AD 93, and since Luke cannot possibly have got the details of his story (the 400 men) from him. No plausible explanation of Luke's alleged error has been offered. There is, therefore, much to be said for the suggestions either that Josephus got his dating wrong or (more probably) that Gamaliel is referring to another, otherwise unknown Theudas. Since there were innumerable uprisings when Herod the Great died, and since 'Josephus describes four men bearing the name of Simon within forty years and three that of Judas within ten years, all of whom were instigators of rebellion' (cited by

Knowling, p. 158), this suggestion should not be rejected out of hand.

37. *Judas the Galilean* was a rebel against the new taxation arrangements which came into force when Archelaus was deposed in AD 6 and the Romans took over direct rule of Judea (Jos., *Ant.* 18:4, 23; 20:102). Only in Acts is it recorded that he was put to death, which is entirely probable. On the relation of the census taken for taxation purposes mentioned here with that mentioned in Luke 2:1f., see commentaries on Luke.

38. Gamaliel draws the moral from his two examples. The Sanhedrin should take no action against the Christians. Haenchen (p. 257) doubts the probative value of the examples: the followers of Theudas and Judas needed to be put down by the Romans! But Gamaliel's point may be that the Sanhedrin should leave such measures to the Romans. For if the Christian movement is merely of human origin, it will come to nothing. *This plan* will mean the apostles' plan to disobey the Sanhedrin, while *this undertaking* will be the whole Christian action in preaching and healing.

39. On the other hand, if the Christian movement has its origin in God, it will overcome human opposition. Worse still, the Sanhedrin may find itself in the position of *opposing God* and thus standing under his judgment. It has been noted that the Greek constructions in the two parallel clauses in verses 38b and 39a are slightly different, and this raises the question whether there is a subtle difference in force between the two conditional sentences. According to Bruce, the first 'if' clause has the force 'if it turn out to be', but the second 'if' clause expresses what Luke considers more likely and therefore puts more directly: however, 'we cannot argue that *Gamaliel* regarded the second alternative as the more probable; the interplay of conditional constructions belongs to Luke's Gk., not to Gamaliel's Aram.' (*Acts*, p. 149).

40. Gamaliel's arguments had the effect of restraining the Sadducean members of the Sanhedrin. When the apostles were recalled before the court, they were again admonished not to speak in the name of Jesus and the admonition was emphasized by a beating. This was the Jewish punishment of 'forty lashes less one' which could be inflicted by the Sanhedrin or the officials of a synagogue for offences against the Jewish law (22:19; 2 Cor. 11:24; Mk. 13:9). It was no soft option; people were known to die from it, even if this was exceptional. It was meant to be a serious lesson to offenders.

41–42. Not only did the punishment not deter the Christians (verse 42). It also filled them with joy. They had suffered ignominy and physical pain, and therefore in a very real sense they cannot have been feeling happy. Yet at the same time their reaction was one of joy because they had been regarded by God as worthy to take their share of suffering for the sake of the gospel, or, as it is put here, for the sake of the Name (21:13; 3 Jn. 7), *i.e.* of Jesus. Here we have a concrete example of that 'rejoicing in suffering' which should be the hallmark of the Christian under persecution (1 Pet. 4:13; *cf.* Mt. 5:11f.; Rom. 5:3f.; 2 Cor. 6:10; 1 Pet. 1:6f.). Finally, as might be expected, the experience did nothing to diminish the ardour of the apostles' witness to Jesus as the Messiah. The Sanhedrin could probably do little to stop them evangelizing in their homes. But they also continued their activities in the temple, apparently without molestation for the time being.

III. THE CHURCH BEGINS TO EXPAND (6:1 – 9:31)

a. The appointment of the Seven (6:1–7)

The first five chapters of Acts have seen the establishment of the church in Jerusalem and the beginnings of opposition to it because of its preaching of Jesus. In the next main section of Acts we see the missionary work of the church beginning to expand in various ways. First, we have the story of the increase in the church in Jerusalem and its spread among Greek-speaking Jews; this led to the martyrdom of Stephen (6:1 – 8:3).[1] Secondly, we have the spread of the church to Samaria (8:4–25). Thirdly, there is the conversion of an Ethiopian (8:26–40). Fourthly, there is the conversion of Saul, who was to be the most significant Christian missionary to the Gentiles (9:1–30). The Jewish persecution of the Christians comes to a peak in the death of Stephen, but at the same time this incident leads to the geographical spread of the church and hence to the beginnings of witness outside the strict limits of Judaism; the ground is being prepared for the critical question of the place of non-Jews within the church.

The narrative begins with a criticism of the arrangements

[1] M. Hengel, 'Zwischen Jesus und Paulus', *ZTK* 72, 1975, pp. 151–206.

for the care of the poor in the church by the Greek-speaking Christians, as a result of which the Twelve, who had hitherto looked after this matter (4:35), realized that their burden of work was too great and that they were being distracted from their primary duty. Seven men were therefore appointed to take charge of the work, and were installed by the laying on of hands. It is noteworthy that spiritual qualifications were sought in men appointed to such tasks within the church.

It seems probable that the men appointed were drawn from the Greek-speaking part of the church which had raised the original complaint. Two of them, Stephen and Philip, proceeded to distinguish themselves by the same kind of evangelistic activity as the Twelve. We shall also discover that what Stephen said was open to the interpretation that he was critical of the temple and the law. These facts have suggested to many scholars that the complaint about the poor relief was but a symptom of a deeper problem, namely that the Aramaic-speaking Christians and the Greek-speaking Christians were dividing into two separate groups, the latter being more radical in its attitude to Judaism, and that what we really have in this incident is the appointment of a set of leaders for the Greek-speaking Christians.

Some suggestion of this kind is inherently probable, although there is no need to go as far as some scholars who reckon with two virtually separate groups in the early church, each with its own distinctive theological outlook. It would seem rather that the two groups were in close contact, even if they worshipped separately in their own languages, and that the Twelve had a general authority over the whole church, while the Seven were leaders of the Greek-speaking section. Although Luke depicts them formally as being in charge of the poor relief, he does not disguise the fact that they were spiritual leaders and evangelists.

1. Luke indicates how the problem within the church came to a head partly as the result of its increasing number of members. The terms *Hebrews* and *Hellenists* (9:29; 11:20 mg.) are obviously to be defined as contrasts. After much discussion there is a growing consensus that the Hebrews were Jews who spoke a Semitic language but also knew some Greek. It can be safely assumed that nearly every Jew knew at least a little Greek, since it was the *lingua franca* of the eastern Mediterranean world. The Semitic language which they spoke

125

was most probably Aramaic rather than Hebrew itself. By contrast, the Hellenists were Jews who spoke Greek and knew little or no Aramaic. These groups would tend to worship as Jews in their own languages, and this practice would carry over when they became Christians. The former group would be principally of Palestinian origin, while the latter would be principally Jews of the Dispersion who had come to settle in Jerusalem. The latter group were more open to syncretistic influences than the former, but it should be emphasized that they had a strong sense of their Jewishness; Hellenistic Jews were strongly attached to the temple.[1] The complaint which the Hellenists made concerned the lack of attention to their *widows* in the provision made by the church for the poor; it has been noted that many widows came from the Dispersion to end their days in Jerusalem. They would not be able to work to keep themselves, and, if they had exhausted or given away their capital, they could be in real want.

2–4. It is only here that Luke refers to the apostles as *the twelve* (but see 1:26; 2:14), probably because of the impending contrast with 'the Seven'. They responded to the criticism which was ultimately directed against themselves by recognizing that the combined task of teaching and poor relief was too great for them. In fact they were able to fulfil neither part of it properly. Their care of the poor had come under criticism, and they themselves felt that they were not devoting proper attention to their prayer and their service of the Word. It is not necessarily suggested that *serving tables* is on a lower level than prayer and teaching; the point is rather that the task to which the Twelve had been specifically called was one of witness and evangelism. The solution to the problem was the appointment of a new group of leaders to *serve tables*. Although the verb 'serve' comes from the same root as the noun which is rendered into English as 'deacon', it is noteworthy that Luke does not refer to the Seven as deacons; their task had no formal name. The choice of seven men corresponded with Jewish practice in setting up boards of seven men for particular duties. The men chosen were to be distinguished by their possession of *wisdom* (6:10; 7:10, 22) and the *Spirit, i.e.* a

[1] See I. H. Marshall, 'Palestinian and Hellenistic Christianity', *NTS* 19, 1972–73, pp. 271–287.

wisdom inspired by the Spirit; we may recognize a parallel
with the appointment of Joshua (Nu. 27:16–20).

5–6. The proposal made by the Twelve was put before a
church meeting and gained their approval. The choice of the
seven candidates was made by the members of the church,
and not by the apostles themselves. The seven names are all
Greek, which suggests that their bearers were not Palestinian
Jews; it is true that Greek names were used by Palestinian
Jews (Andrew, Philip), but, apart from Philip, these are unlikely names for Palestinians. *Stephen* and *Philip* come first in
the list by reason of their subsequent importance in the story,
and we are prepared for the significance of Stephen by the
fuller description of him as a man of faith. The last-mentioned
name is that of a proselyte, who would rank as a proper Jew.
The Philip listed here is a different person from Philip the
apostle (see 8:5; 21:8f.). After the men had been chosen, they
were placed in front of the Twelve who appointed them to
their task by praying for them and placing their hands upon
them.[1] The whole story is reminiscent of that of the choice of
Matthias (1:15–26), but the closest parallel is the story of the
appointment of Joshua as Moses' successor in Numbers 27:15–
23 by the laying on of hands. The rite indicated a conferring
of authority, and the accompanying prayer was for the power
of the Spirit to fill the recipients (*cf.* Dt. 34:9). A similar rite
was used in the appointment of rabbis, but there is some
uncertainty whether this goes back to the first century. See
further 8:17; 9:17; 13:3; 19:6.

7. Luke describes the effect of the new appointment in
terms of an increase in Christian witness. Using a favourite
phrase (12:24; 19:20), he says that *the word of God increased*;[2] its
proclamation increased and was effective in winning converts.
As a result the number of disciples continued to grow, and in
particular there were converts among the priests. This suggests that the work of the apostles among the 'Hebrews' was
expanding; we then hear of the work among the 'Hellenists'
in verses 8ff. The *priests* were presumably those attached to
the temple in Jerusalem, of whom there was a great number

---

[1] L. Morris, *Ministers of God* (London, 1964), pp. 59f., 88, thinks that it was
the congregation which laid hands on the Seven. There is in any case no
thought of 'apostolic succession'.
[2] J. Kodell. ' "The Word of God grew" ', *Bib.* 55, 1974, pp. 505–519.

(estimated at 18,000 priests and Levites; they were on duty for a fortnight each year according to a rota; Lk. 1:8). The theory that these were priests belonging to the Qumran community who were disaffected from the temple is improbable. *Obedient to the faith* means obedient to the call for faith contained in the gospel (*cf.* 2 Thes. 1:8).

b. The controversy over Stephen (6:8–15)

The Greek-speaking Christians now began to reach out to their Jewish compatriots with the gospel. Stephen carried on an apostolic ministry of preaching and healing. He met with opposition from members of the Greek-speaking synagogues who eventually resorted to putting up charges against him that he was attacking 'Moses and God', more specifically that he was saying that Jesus would change the laws and customs given by Moses and also destroy the temple. These charges not only angered the Greek-speaking Jews generally but also the Hebrew-speaking Jewish leaders who sat on the council and heard the charges made against him.

It is important that Luke describes these charges as false (verse 13). The subsequent speech by Stephen in chapter 7 will show why Luke thought they were false. Nevertheless, it is probable that Stephen must have said something which could have been twisted by his opponents in this manner. Certainly there was a basis in some of the things that Jesus had said for Christian teaching along these lines (Jesus' criticism of the scribal interpretation of the law, and his prophecies of the destruction of the temple). It would seem likely that Stephen went much further than the Twelve in emphasizing this teaching. If he attacked the scribal elaboration of the law, this would count as an attack on Moses, and if he attacked the Jews for tying the presence of God to the temple, this would have been sufficient to lead to the opposition which he encountered. It is noteworthy that it was the same jealous concern for the temple by Jews of the Dispersion which formed the occasion for the later arrest of Paul (21:28). Critics have noted that Luke omitted the incident about the false witnesses at the trial of Jesus (Mk. 14:57f.) and argued that he has inserted the motif here instead. The repetitiousness of Luke's account (*cf.* verses 11, 13 and 14), however, strongly suggests that he is following a source here, although he may have underlined the correspondence between the attacks on Jesus and on Stephen.

8. The description of Stephen as *full of grace and power* is probably meant to draw a parallel between him and the apostles (4:33). His gifts are due to his being filled with the Spirit – a factor which, it should be noted, was present *before* his appointment as one of the Seven. It is not clear in what sense *grace* is meant, but as in 4:33 it probably indicates the gracious power of God.

9. Stephen's activity aroused opposition from members of the synagogues, whether in the synagogue buildings where Stephen will have stood up and spoken in the name of Jesus, or outside of them. The *Freedmen* were Roman prisoners (or the descendants of such prisoners) who had later been granted their freedom. We know that a considerable number of Jews were taken prisoner by the Roman general Pompey and later released in Rome, and it is possible that these are meant here. The relation of the other names of local groups to that of the Freedmen and to one another is not certain. Different scholars have postulated any number of synagogues from one (for all the various groups) to five (one synagogue for each group). While Bruce (*Book*, p. 133) thinks of one synagogue for freedmen from the four groups mentioned, the Greek construction favours two synagogues, one for the first three groups (Freedmen, Cyrenians, Alexandrians), and one for the remaining two (Cilicians, Asians). It was natural for national groups to form their own synagogues for worship in Jerusalem,[1] and they would be attended both by immigrants settled in Jerusalem and by casual visitors.

10–11 Jesus had promised the help of *the Spirit* (Lk. 12:12) and *wisdom* (Lk. 21:15) to his disciples when they were called upon to defend themselves. The early church proved the truth of this promise. Its members were able to put up a case for their faith which could not be knocked down by argument. When Stephen's opponents could not get the better of him, they induced some people to make public charges against him, testifying that they had heard him blaspheming *against Moses and God*. Although in later usage blasphemy involved using the ineffable name of God, the New Testament usage demonstrates that at this time the term was used in a wider sense of

---

[1] Only ten men were needed to form the nucleus of a synagogue.

129

any violation of the power and majesty of God. For a closer definition of the accusations we must turn to verses 13f.

12–14. The outcry raised by the Greek-speaking Jews roused the *people* generally together with the members of the Sanhedrin, and moved them to arrest Stephen and enquire into the matter. It is strange that the priests are not named here along with the other members of the Sanhedrin. The Greek-speaking Jews set up *witnesses* to testify against Stephen in the council. They alleged (falsely, in Luke's opinion) that Stephen was continually attacking the temple and *the law*. More precisely, he was declaring that Jesus would destroy the temple and alter the customs handed down by Moses. The *customs* are no doubt the oral traditions giving the scribal interpretation of the law; these were regarded as stemming from Moses, just as much as the written law was. An attack on the oral law was thus tantamount to an attack on the law as a whole. We have no other information to show whether Stephen had begun to follow up the teaching of Jesus in this area. It is certainly not impossible. As for the attack on the temple, we know that Jesus prophesied its destruction (Lk. 21:5f.), and that this charge figured in his trial in the form that he stated that he would destroy the temple and replace it with another (Mk. 14:58; 15:29; *cf.* Jn. 2:19). The Johannine version of the saying shows that it was interpreted as referring to the replacement of material worship in the temple by the spiritual worship of the community of disciples. 'We have behind the texts at our disposal a historical nucleus in which Jesus, criticizing the temple and teaching its replacement, referred to his own person. He represented the new dimension of fellowship with God which was to outdistance the old cultus. In its negative aspect this meant a sharp criticism of the actual temple and its worship; in its positive aspect, it meant a new fellowship with God, centred on himself and replacing the temple.'[1] If this line of thought was grasped by Stephen,[2] it is easy to see how it could be understood in a negative, superficial sense by his opponents and could provide an obvious basis for a charge of attacking the temple. If this is the case,

---

[1] B. Gärtner, *The Temple and the Community in Qumran and the New Testament* (Cambridge, 1965), pp. 120f.

[2] A. Cole, *The New Temple* (London, 1950); but see R. J. MacKelvey, *The New Temple* (London, 1969).

then Haenchen's view (p. 274) that Luke has transferred the false charge against Jesus at his trial to this context falls to the ground as an unnecessary explanation of the facts. The thought that the church was the divinely intended replacement for the temple is probably to be seen in 15:16–18.

15. When the members of the court looked at the accused man, ready to hear what he would have to say for himself, he appeared to them to have *the face of an angel*. This is an unusual expression, paralleled in the apocryphal version of Esther (15:13) where Esther speaks of the glorious appearance of the king's face, like that of an angel, and in the famous second-century description of Paul as sometimes having the face of an angel. The description is of a person who is close to God and reflects some of his glory as a result of being in his presence (Ex. 34:29ff.). It is a divine vindication of Stephen, and an indication of his inspiration to make his defence.

c. Stephen's speech in court (7:1–53)

If length is anything to go by, Stephen's speech is one of the most important sections of Acts.[1] Yet the purpose of this speech is still much disputed. In form it is a lengthy recital of Old Testament history, discussing in detail what appear to be insignificant points and culminating in a bitter attack on the speaker's hearers. What is the speaker trying to do? Is the speech really a defence to the charges brought against him (6:11, 13f.)? Is its thought unique in Acts, or is it a carefully wrought contribution to the total message of Acts? And what is its structure?

We would suggest (following Bruce, *Acts*, p. 161) that two themes run through the speech: (1) Throughout their history God raised up men to act as deliverers of his people, but the Jews repeatedly rejected them and disobeyed the law given by God. After dealing with the establishment of the nation through God's call of Abraham and his promises to him (7:2–8), the speech deals with Joseph, who was rejected by his brothers but rescued by God (7:9–16), and then, at greater

[1] The literature is immense. See M. Simon, *St Stephen and the Hellenists in the Primitive Church* (London, 1958); J. Bihler, *Die Stephanusgeschichte im Zusammenhang der Apostelgeschichte* (München, 1963); Scharlemann; Wilckens, pp. 208–224; J. Kilgallen, *The Stephen Speech* (Rome, 1976); H. J. B. Combrink, *Structural Analysis of Acts 6:8 – 8:3* (Cape Town, 1979); G. Schneider, 'Stephanus, die Hellenisten und Samaria', in Kremer, pp. 215–240.

length, with Moses, who came to deliver the people but was rejected by them (7:25, 39–43). (2) The Jews had the tabernacle in the wilderness and later the temple built by Solomon, but they fell into idolatry (7:39–43) and made the mistake of thinking that God actually dwelt in the temple (7:44–50). These two themes are intermingled in the speech.

It can be seen that these two themes correspond to the charges made against Stephen. (1) So far from speaking against the law or saying that Jesus would change it, Stephen argued that in the past it was the Jews themselves who had rejected Moses and the God whom he worshipped. They offered idolatrous worship, they resisted and killed the prophets, and they failed to keep the law. (2) Stephen argued that the Jews had had in succession the tabernacle (which was moved from place to place) and the temple as places to worship God, but God himself had declared that he was not tied to these places. If, therefore, Stephen spoke of a new 'place' of worship for God, this was simply in line with Old Testament teaching.

It follows that the speech accomplishes at least three purposes: (1) It is a defence to the charges brought against Stephen. He implicitly denies that he has spoken against the law of Moses, and makes himself out to be a defender of the law. He justifies his attitude of criticism of the temple and its worship. (2) It is an attack on the Jews for their failure to obey the revelation given to them in the Old Testament and for their rejection of the Messiah and the new way of worship which he brought. (3) Consequently, the speech has its part in the total story of Acts in showing that the Jews, to whom the gospel was first preached, had rejected it, and thus clearing the way for the church to turn away from Jerusalem and the temple and to evangelize further afield, and ultimately among the Gentiles.

That the speech has been drafted by Luke who has fitted it into the total plan of Acts is not to be denied. Although the speech differs markedly in content from the other speeches to Jewish audiences which we have already read, yet in style it has affinities with the historical section of the speech by Paul in Pisidian Antioch (13:16–23), which treats in more detail the period of the early monarchy; in content it has links with Paul's speech in Athens with its condemnation of the belief that gods dwell in temples (17:24f.). In other respects also the speech fits in with Luke's general conception of salvation history.

But this does not mean that the speech is Luke's own composition without any historical basis. There are features which suggest the use of source-material. It fits admirably into what we know about Stephen from the surrounding narrative. Conzelmann (pp. 50f.) here provides a classic example of having one's cake and eating it. On the one hand, he argues that the speech is not that of a martyr in style and theme; therefore, it is a subsequent addition. On the other hand, he claims that it fits nicely into the situation as Luke sees it! Had the speech been in what Conzelmann regards as martyr style, we can be fairly confident that the same critic would have rejected it as being composed for the occasion. If it is possible that Luke had a proper historical appreciation of the situation, then clearly the speech could belong to it. It is in fact notorious that martyrs do not attempt simply to defend themselves but use the occasion to denounce or to attempt to convert their judges, a feature which will reappear in Paul's speeches later (*cf.* Stolle). Neil (p. 115) comments that 'it is unlikely that so allusive and suggestive an oration could be an extempore utterance'; if this is correct (it may underestimate Stephen's rhetorical powers), it may be that, while the speech gives the gist of what Stephen said on this occasion, Luke has put together in his own words the kind of things that Stephen said in the course of his preaching.

Many critics have recognized that in this speech source-material can be detected behind Luke's editing.[1] Certain features (see especially 7:4, 14–16, 37) have been thought to betray the use of the Samaritan version of the Pentateuch and an affinity with the outlook of the Samaritans;[2] the limitation of these to this speech would be evidence that Luke was using traditional material. The case for use of the Samaritan Pentateuch has been convincingly criticized, however,[3] and the Samaritan links are at best rather weak. Links with Hellenistic

---

[1] Wilckens, p. 208 (but he bases his case partly on the alleged incompatibility of the speech with its situation in Acts). J. Bihler, *op. cit.*, and others regard the speech as a purely Lucan composition.

[2] Scharlemann, especially pp. 36–51, uses the evidence as part of his case for the substantial authenticity of the speech.

[3] R. Pummer, 'The Samaritan Pentateuch and the New Testament', *NTS* 22, 1975–76, pp. 441–443; K. Haacker, *NIDNTT*, III, pp. 464–466.

Judaism have also been found, which would not be surprising in the thought of Stephen. Some similarities between Stephen's exegesis of the Old Testament and that practised by Hellenistic Jews like Philo may be significant, but Hellenistic Judaism in general strongly upheld the temple and the law.

Attempts to relate the outlook of the speech to that of other early Christians or early Christian groups (such as the writer to the Hebrews[1]) have not led to any certain results. It seems doubtful in particular whether we can attribute to Stephen a vision of the world mission of the church on the basis of this speech. What is unique is the critical attitude to the temple, which had evidently not been voiced earlier, and which never seems to have been shared by the Aramaic-speaking section of the church.[2]

Stephen's manner of argument with its long historical recital may strike us as strange. But it has precedents in the similar recitals of history in the Old Testament (*e.g.* Pss. 78, 105, 106). By choosing this style of presentation Stephen was able to show that the present conduct of the Jews was all of a piece with that of their ancestors and at the same time that God was still working in the same way as he had done in the past. This means that we may expect to find a deliberate use of typological language, and it is the case that some of the language used about Moses suggests a parallel between him and Jesus. Although, therefore, Jesus is mentioned only once in the speech (7:52), and some critics have argued that neither Stephen nor his speech were Christian (but rather Hellenistic Jewish),[3] a Christian outlook pervades the speech as a whole.

1–3. Stephen responds to the invitation from the high priest as chairman of the proceedings in the Sanhedrin with a courteous address to his fellow Jews. He wastes no time in preliminaries, which do not seem to have been required in the Sanhedrin but were normal in Hellenistic courts, and plunges straight into his subject with a description of how God called Abraham to be the father of the nation. He describes God as *the God of glory* (Ps. 29:3), perhaps to emphasize at the outset the transcendence of the God who does not live in a temple

---

[1] W. Manson, *The Epistle to the Hebrews*, London, 1954. See Scharlemann's criticisms, pp. 165–175.

[2] Contrast the positive attitude of James and Paul, 21:23–26; 25:8.

[3] O'Neill, pp. 89–94.

made with hands. It may be significant that he details how God appeared to Abraham *in Mesopotamia*: God's self-revelation is not confined to the land of the Jews, still less to the temple. Mesopotamia was a name applied to the 'land between the rivers', the north area between the Tigris and the Euphrates in modern Iraq, but in Hellenistic usage it was applied to the larger area including Babylonia in the south. Hence it could refer to the territory in which Ur was situated. *Haran* was situated to the north-west of Mesopotamia and lay on the 'fertile crescent' route to Palestine. The divine command to Abraham reproduced here comes from Genesis 12:1, where it is in fact spoken in Haran. Since, however, it is clear from Genesis 15:7 and Nehemiah 9:7 that God called Abraham out of Ur, it can reasonably be assumed that a divine call came to him there before he lived in Haran; and in fact this same deduction is made by Philo. It would be natural to assume that the substance of the divine message given in Ur was the same as that given in Haran, and hence there is no need to speak of Luke being in error here. The deviation from the account in Genesis 11:31 – 12:5 is quite deliberate.

4–5. So Abraham *departed* from his homeland in obedience to the divine call. At first he and his family settled in *Haran*. Indeed at this point he was presumably under the control of his *father* Terah who never left Haran. According to Genesis 11:26, 32, Terah was seventy years old when Abraham was born, and he died at the age of 205 in Haran; in Genesis 12:4 Abraham was seventy-five years old when he left Haran. This would mean that Abraham departed when Terah was 145 years old, sixty years *before* he died, and not *after* he died, as Stephen asserts. Since Philo agrees with Stephen that Abraham left Haran *after* Terah's death, and since the Samaritan version of Genesis gives the age of Terah as 145 years when he died, it is clear that Stephen here follows a variant tradition of the text of Genesis. Since Luke himself usually follows the LXX and we do not know of any Greek version of Genesis with this variant text, we may have evidence here that Luke was following a source and not freely composing the speech.

Abraham's destination was *the land in which you are now dwelling*. Implicit is the thought that God's promise to him has now been fulfilled in that his descendants are living in the promised land. For Abraham, however, it was still the *promised* land. He himself received no possession in it – *not even a foot's length,* says Stephen, using a biblical phrase from Deuteronomy 2:5. Even the promise which Abraham received must have seemed an empty one, since he had *no child* (*cf.* Rom. 4:16–22 which describes the strength of Abraham's faith in God's promise despite the seeming impossibility of its fulfilment). It is true that Abraham did purchase a burial place (Gn. 23), but Stephen rightly ignores this; a cemetery is hardly a place to live in or a symbol of a future dwelling. It is also true that he had other children before and after Isaac, but none of these was regarded as the promised heir. Only some divine intervention could bring about the fulfilment of the promise.

6–7. A further promise follows. It is introduced in a negative fashion as a prophecy that when Abraham did have descendants they would be *aliens* and slaves in a foreign land for 400 years; only after that would God judge their overlords and bring the people to serve him in Canaan. Thus the fulfilment of God's promise to Abraham is demonstrated by the fact that Stephen and his contemporaries were in Jerusalem and could worship God there. At the same time, there may again be the thought that God was with his people during their exile from Palestine. The prophecy is cited from Genesis 15:13f., and the reference is to the sojourn in Egypt. *Four hundred years* is a round figure (contrast Ex. 12:40); problems arise when we compare the chronological statement in Galatians 3:17, but these are the concern of a commentator on Galatians, since Stephen is simply following what is said in Genesis 15:13. The first part of verse 7 cites Genesis, but the second part contains wording from Exodus 3:12. That verse promised to Moses that, when the people left Egypt, they would worship God on 'this mountain', namely Horeb (Sinai), whereas Stephen speaks of *this place,* meaning Canaan. What Stephen gives his hearers is thus a paraphrase of what God said to Abraham, using scriptural language based on Exodus 3:12. He goes beyond what Genesis actually says to make this point which is not explicit there but which can reasonably be regarded as implicit.

8. As a token of the promise which he was making with him, God *gave* Abraham the rite of *circumcision.* He made a *covenant* with him, and the sign of the validity of the covenant was the act of circumcision (Gn. 17:10). The covenant was God's promise that he would be the God of Abraham and his descendants, making them the objects of his special care; on the human side, submission to the rite of circumcision was the sign of commitment to God. There is no sign of any opposition by Stephen to circumcision as such; the rite became a matter of contention only when uncircumcised Gentiles became members of the church. Lake and Cadbury paraphrased the *so* at the beginning of the second part of the verse as: 'Thus, while there was still no holy place, all the essential conditions for the religion of Israel were fulfilled' (*BC*, IV, p. 72); this is perhaps an exaggeration, but it is implicit in the narrative that Abraham received God's promise while he possessed no territory in Canaan. It was as a result of that promise, and in obedience to the command associated with it, that he fathered *Isaac* and *circumcised* him (Gn. 21:4), and so the line began which led to the birth of the *patriarchs*, the twelve sons of Jacob.

9–10. Thus Stephen reaches the story of *Joseph*, which forms the second main section of his speech (verse 9–16). It is recorded factually, and it is not clear what the theological point of the details is. Probably Stephen is showing how the prophecy in verse 6 was fulfilled, and at the same time indicating how the people, represented by Joseph's brothers, began the process of opposition to God's appointed leaders, but God vindicated his chosen ruler. So the story begins with the jealousy, or rather the envy, of Joseph's brothers when he had dreams that revealed his future superior position (Gn. 37:11), and goes on to tell how they *sold him* as a slave (Gn. 37:28; 45:4). But God was with him in his troubles and delivered him from his afflictions (Gn. 39:2, 21).[1] He gave Joseph *favour* with *Pharaoh* as a result of the wisdom which he showed in the interpretation of the king's dreams and in his plans for dealing with the approaching famine (Gn. 41:38f., 41; Ps. 105:16–22). We may note how *wisdom* was particularly associated with Egypt (7:22); Luke himself associates it with Stephen (6:3, 10), and also with Jesus (Lk. 2:40, 52).

11–13. The next part of the story is concerned to show how the family of Jacob came down to Egypt. Stephen narrates briefly what was no doubt a well-known story to his hearers, telling how the *famine* which came upon Egypt also caused

---

[1] Whether this is a typological allusion to the way in which God delivered Jesus from his afflictions and to the way in which he is with Christians in their afflictions (Acts 14:22; 20:23) is not clear.

affliction on a worldwide scale (Gn. 41:57) and affected *Canaan* in particular (Gn. 42:5). Perhaps it is seen as a form of divine retribution on Joseph's brothers; in any case it was instrumental in sending them down to Egypt to buy corn from the stores which Jacob heard were there (Gn. 42:1–5). On their *second visit Joseph made himself known* to them (Gn. 45:3).[1]

14–16. As a result of Pharaoh's coming to know Joseph's family, they were invited to settle in Egypt, and so the whole group, including Jacob, came down to Egypt. The figure of seventy-five persons is based on the LXX of Genesis 46:27 and Exodus 1:5, while the Hebrew text has 70. The larger total is arrived at by omitting Jacob and Joseph and including the remaining seven of Joseph's nine sons. In both cases the number is the total of Jacob's descendants who went *down into Egypt* or were born there. And there they all *died*. Yet, although the promise of return to the land of Canaan was not yet fulfilled, their burial in Canaan could be seen as an expression of faith that in due course God would fulfil his promise.

The relation of the story of the burial to the Old Testament traditions is complicated. According to Acts they were all buried at *Shechem in the tomb that Abraham had bought from the sons of Hamor.*(1) According to Genesis 49: 29–32; 50:13 Jacob was buried in the cave of Machpelah near Hebron which Abraham had bought from Ephron the Hittite (Gn. 23). (2) Joseph was buried at Shechem (Jos. 24:32) in land which Jacob had bought from the sons of Hamor (Gn. 33:18–20). (3) Josephus states that Jacob's other sons (and, by implication, Jacob himself) were buried at Hebron (Jos., *Ant.* 2:199), and this tradition is also found in *Jubilees* and the *Testaments of the Twelve Patriarchs*. (4) There was a local tradition at Shechem that the twelve sons of Jacob were buried there. It thus appears that Stephen differs from the Old Testament account in that he locates the tomb which Abraham bought at Shechem, not Hebron, and in that he adds the detail about the brothers of Joseph being buried there also. Bruce (*Book*, p. 149 n.39) suggests that, just as Stephen has telescoped the two calls of Abraham at Ur and Haran in verse 2 and the two divine messages in verse 7, so here he has telescoped the two

[1] The suggestion that there may be a typological reference to the *second* coming of Jesus as the time when the Jews who failed to recognize him as Messiah at his first coming will do so seems most unlikely.

accounts of purchases of land in Canaan. It seems probable that Stephen has followed a tradition, according to which not only Joseph (he, rather than Jacob, is perhaps meant by *he died, himself* in verse 15b) but also his brothers were buried at Shechem, and that he has attributed the purchase of the grave there to Abraham by including an allusion to the story in Genesis 23. The interest in Shechem and the emphasis upon it is remarkable in a speech addressed to Jews in Jerusalem, but they certainly could not contest the fact of Joseph's burial in the hated Samaritan territory. There is nothing sacrosanct about Judea as a place of burial; is there perhaps also a subtle preparation of Luke's readers for the story of the evangelism of Samaria (8:5–25)?

17–19. Stephen now comes to the third and longest part of his speech, which is concerned principally with Moses.[1] While the time of the fulfilment of the *promise* made by God (verse 7) was approaching, the offspring of Abraham were increasing in numbers (Ex. 1:7). The climax came with the rise of a new Egyptian *king* who *had not known Joseph* (Ex. 1:8). The meaning is either that he was ignorant of Joseph and his good deeds for Egypt or (perhaps more likely) that he preferred to forget about him in face of the menace which he saw in the growing might of the Israelites. He therefore got the better of them by cruelly forcing them to *expose their infants* (Ex. 1:10f., 22).

20–22. *Moses* now comes on the scene, and his life is treated in three parts, corresponding to each of the three periods of forty years that made up his life (see verse 23). The first period is that of his early life in Egypt. The description is given in terms of a formal threefold pattern and deals with his birth, his early upbringing and his education (see 22:3 and note). When he was born, he was a comely child (Ex. 2:2; Heb. 11:23). The addition *before God* may mean that he found favour with God (*cf.* 23:1) or it may reflect a Hebrew idiom and simply mean that he was a very fine child (*cf.* Jon. 3:3). After resisting the decree that they must expose their infants for three months, his parents eventually did so, but the child was discovered by *Pharaoh's daughter* who *brought him up* (Ex. 2:1–10). Although the Old Testament does not expressly relate it, Stephen follows the tradition, attested in Philo, that Moses would naturally be given a thorough Egyptian education. The

---

[1] It is not certain where the section ends. See 7:41–43 note.

statement that he was *mighty in his words and deeds* (*cf.* Lk. 24:19 of Jesus) may seem to conflict with Exodus 4:10, but we should not attach too much factual accuracy to Moses' own self-depreciatory remarks which were little more than a pretext for avoiding a task that he did not wish to undertake.

23–25. A crisis in the life of Moses came when he was *forty years old*. The age of Moses at this point is not given in the Old Testament, but Stephen's statement agrees with the opinion of some of the Jewish rabbis; the figure, therefore, is probably meant to be taken simply as a round number. 'Forty' was the age at which a person had 'grown up' (Ex. 2:11). Similarly, the Old Testament says nothing about Moses deciding to go and *visit* his fellow countrymen, although this is a natural inference from the story (Ex. 2:11). The choice of words may be meant to imply that the thought was implanted in Moses' mind by God, and that the thought was one of positive concern for the Israelites.[1] This concern expressed itself in attacking and killing an Egyptian who was oppressing one of the Israelites. According to the Old Testament story Moses hid the body in the sand and did not want anybody to know what he had done. This must have been interpreted by Stephen in terms of his not wanting anybody hostile to know what had happened and report the incident to the authorities (*cf.* Ex. 2:14). For Moses' hope, as interpreted by Stephen, was that the Israelites might recognize that they had a friend and ally in an influential position through whom God would bring them salvation, *i.e. deliverance* from their unfortunate plight as slaves. Luke would undoubtedly expect his Christian readers to see here a parallel between Moses and Jesus as the saviours of God's people, whether or not Stephen's hearers would catch the point: the behaviour of the Jews in refusing to recognize Jesus as Saviour was of a piece with their earlier rejection of Moses (7:52).

26–29. The incident was immediately followed by another one, which confirmed Stephen's interpretation of it. When Moses discovered *them* (*i.e.* the Israelites) quarrelling with one another, he tried to reconcile them by appealing to them to behave as brothers. Here Stephen generalizes the Old Testament account which is narrated in terms of Moses taking the side of an oppressed man and chiding his oppressor (Ex. 2:13).

[1] For *visit* in this sense see Lk. 1:68; 7:16.

Stephen's way of putting it emphasizes the activity of Moses as a reconciler. But his efforts were in vain; the wrongdoer vehemently attacked him for setting himself up as *a ruler and a judge* (Ex. 2:14), thus failing to realize that it was God who had so appointed him. His hostile awareness that Moses had slain the Egyptian constituted an implicit threat to him, and so Moses judged it expedient to flee the country (and the wrath of Pharaoh, Ex. 2:15) and become *an exile in Midian.* Here he settled down long enough to raise a family (Ex. 2:21f.; 18:3f.).

30–34. From Exodus 7:7 it could be deduced that *forty years* had passed since Moses slew the Egyptian.[1] Now came the decisive point in the career of Moses as he was confronted by the vision of an *angel* at *Mount Sinai* in a burning *bush.* The sight attracted his attention; it would seem that what struck him was the fact that the bush went on burning without the flame dying down, and that the mention of the angel is a metaphorical way of speaking of the presence of God in the bush (Ex. 3:2f.). When he came near the bush he heard the voice of God addressing him. Stephen reverses the order of the statements in Exodus 3:5f., so that the initial stress falls on the fact that it is the God of Moses' ancestors who is revealing himself to him; the thought of God's promises to the patriarchs is thus brought to mind. The story continues in the manner typical of a theophany; it describes the human reaction of fear and dread, and the divine reassurance which follows. To be sure, the element of fear is not wholly removed, since Stephen retains the command to Moses to treat the place as *holy ground;* here is perhaps another incidental reminder for Stephen's hearers that God's self-revelation is not confined to Jewish soil – the most important place of Old Testament revelation, Mount Sinai, was not in the promised land. Nevertheless, the main element in the revelation is the promise of God to deliver his people from their *ill-treatment* and bondage in Egypt by the hand of Moses (Ex. 3:7–10).

35–36. The narrative style is dropped at this point, and instead we have a series of statements about Moses, which are expressed somewhat rhetorically in the Greek text. Each statement begins with the demonstrative *This* (man) used four

---

[1] The verb *passed*, also used in the Greek text of verse 23, is literally 'fulfilled', and may contain the thought of God's action at appropriate intervals of time.

times over; verses 38b and 39 begin with relative pronouns. We are reminded of the similar way in which Peter speaks of 'this Jesus' in his speeches earlier in Acts (*e.g.* 2:23, 32, 36). The point of the device in the first of the statements is obvious: It was *this* very *Moses* whom the Israelites rejected in Egypt whom God appointed as a leader and redeemer. Then the following statements in verses 36, 37 and 38 lay further stress on the significant things which Moses said and did, before Stephen finally brings out again the fact that it was *this Moses* whom the Israelites refused to obey (verses 39–41). So the passage brings out not simply the Israelite rejection of Moses, but also the way in which this was a rejection of the God-given leader. Again the typological parallel with the Jewish rejection of Jesus, the One whom God raised from the dead, is implicit. This is particularly obvious in the opening statement. When Stephen gives a counter to the Israelite dismissal of Moses as *a ruler and a judge*, he insists that God sent him as *a ruler and deliverer. Ruler* is a term that could be applied to Jesus (Rev. 1:5), and a very similar term is used of him in 5:31. As for *deliverer*, this is the rendering of a Greek word (*lytrōtēs*) which is derived from a verb which means 'to redeem'. Surprising as it may seem, it is only Moses who is given the actual title of 'redeemer' in the New Testament and not Jesus. Since, however, the task of delivering Israel is assigned elsewhere to Jesus (Lk. 2:38; 24:21; *cf.* 1:68), Christian readers would detect the typological allusion here. What was God's task (Pss. 19:14; 78:35) is here delegated to his agent by the angelic voice at the burning bush. It was, therefore, Moses who actually brought the people out of Egypt to the accompaniment of miraculous signs wrought by God. The phraseology is drawn from the Old Testament, but again the Christian reader would recollect that the same language was used of Jesus and the apostles (2:22, 43; *cf.* 6:8 of Stephen himself).

37. Now the typological point becomes even clearer. Stephen reminds his hearers that it was this man, Moses, who was responsible for the prophecy about the coming of *a prophet* like himself (Dt. 18:15) which the early Christians had already begun to see fulfilled in the coming of Jesus (3:22). This early Christian usage is probably sufficient to explain why the text is quoted here, but it may be noted that the verse was an important one in Samaritan theology, and its presence here could give some weight to the cumulative argument for Samaritan influence upon Stephen.

38. For Jewish hearers, however, the climax in the description of Moses comes with the account of the gathering of the people of Israel in the desert at *Mount Sinai*. Again typology is not absent. The word translated congregation is *ekklēsia*, which Christians took over as a designation for their own community; it could be that Christians would see a certain parallelism between the presence of Moses with the Israelites on their pilgrimage through the desert and the presence of Jesus with the new people of God on their earthly pilgrimage.[1] But it is unlikely that this is part of the primary message of the passage for Stephen's Jewish hearers. The point is rather that at this assembly of the people Moses received the law, the living words of God (Rom. 3:2). This was the mark of the high privilege of Israel. The giving of the law was the sign of the covenant which God had made with them, and it was by obedience to the law that they would continue to be God's covenant people. Stephen implicitly shared this belief.

39–40. But now comes a turning point. Still continuing the Greek sentence begun in verse 38, Stephen comments how the original recipients of the law had failed to keep it. They had rejected Moses in his capacity as the law-giver, and in their hearts *they turned* back to *Egypt* (*cf.* Nu. 14:3f.). Worse still, they commanded *Aaron* to *make gods* to go before them and cast scorn upon Moses during his absence to receive the law from God (Ex. 32:1). Right from the moment when the law was solemnly given to the assembly of God's people, they rebelled against the giver and turned to idolatry. For all their protestations of loyalty to the law and the temple and their accusations against Stephen (6:11, 13f.), his hearers belonged to a nation which right from the outset had rejected the law and the true worship of God.

41–43. With this thought the speech takes a new turn, and down to verse 50 it is concerned with the twin themes of idolatry and temple-worship in Israel. The theme is developed by means of a brief historical survey which covers the period

---

[1] The motif, and especially the contrast between the situations, is worked out by the writer to the Hebrews, Heb. 12:18–24.

from the wilderness wanderings to the time of Solomon.[1] First of all, Stephen traces in greater detail the idolatry, of which he has already spoken briefly in verse 40. A Greek word found for the first time here expresses contemptuously what the Israelites did: *they-made-a-calf* (Ex. 32:4). The use of an image of a calf, or rather a bull,[2] in worship was a persistent temptation to Israel (1 Ki. 12:28) and Stephen's condemnation of it was in line with the denunciations already made by Old Testament writers (2 Ki. 10:29; Hos. 8:4–6). It was an act which involved sacrifice to an idol instead of the true God, and it also brought condemnation because it implied that gods could be made by human powers; again Stephen was echoing a powerful Old Testament motif (Pss. 115:4; 135:15; Is. 44:9–20). God reacted to such human self-sufficiency by letting the Israelites taste the full, bitter fruits of idolatry. He *turned* away (*sc.* from them),[3] just as they had turned away from him (verse 39), and he gave them up to the worship of the heavenly host. The closest parallel to this statement is found in Romans 1:24, 26, 28, although there the thought is of God giving up the heathen to the consequences of their idolatry. The *host of heaven* refers to the sun, moon and stars (Dt. 4:19) which were regarded as deities or as the dwelling places of spiritual beings. Despite the warnings given to them against such worship, the Israelites did in fact turn to it (2 Ch. 33:3, 5; Je. 8:2).

All this took place, says Stephen, in accordance with the prophecy in *the book of the prophets, i.e.* the Jewish scroll containing the twelve writings of the so-called minor prophets. He cites Amos 5:25–27 according to the LXX.[4] In the book of Amos the question 'Did you offer me sacrifices?' has been taken to expect a negative answer and to imply that Amos

[1] This division of the speech at verses. 40/41 is preferable to the usual one which makes a break at verses 44/45 (despite the continuity of the Greek sentence at this point), so that Stephen's theme is 'the time of Moses' up to verse 44 and 'from Joshua to Solomon' in verses 45–50. Verses 41–44 form a bridge between the two sections.

[2] R. A. Cole, *Exodus* (*Tyndale Old Testament Commentary*, London, 1973), pp. 214f.

[3] So most authorities; but AG suggests the alternative 'he turned them toward the heavenly bodies'.

[4] The one major change is the substitution of *Babylon* for 'Damascus'; this broadens the scope of Amos' prophecy of the exile of the northern kingdom of Israel to Assyria (east of Damascus) to include the later exile of the southern kingdom of Judah to Babylon.

thought no sacrifices were offered in the wilderness period; this is very unlikely, and it is more probable that Amos was suggesting that the people did not offer merely sacrifices but also heart-obedience to God. Stephen, however, appears to be suggesting that the Israelites did not offer sacrifices to Yahweh in the wilderness, but to other gods. Thus the quotation offers confirmation of verse 41 rather than of verse 42a. The second part of the quotation (verse 43) describes how the Israelites proceeded to take up the *tent* in which *Moloch* was worshipped and the *star* or emblem of *Rephan*; these (gods) were (represented by) images which the Israelites made in order to worship them. *Moloch* is the god who required child-sacrifice, and *Rephan* appears to be the name of an Egyptian god associated with Saturn. The LXX here differs markedly from the Hebrew text of Amos which refers to taking up 'Sakkuth your king and Kaiwan your star-god', these probably being the names of Assyrian deities. The relation of the LXX to the Hebrew text of Amos need not concern us here (the LXX is paraphrasing a difficult Hebrew text). All that needs to be said is that the Hebrew text would have made Stephen's point as effectively as the LXX; whatever version Stephen may have used, Luke has here followed his normal practice and cited the LXX. Idolatory found its due reward in exile to a land of false gods.

44–45. The quotation from Amos has taken Stephen forward in time from Moses to the later period of idolatry. Now he retraces his steps back to the time of Moses. Although the Israelites were later to take up the tent of Moloch, it was *the tent of witness* which they had *in the wilderness*, made *according to the* instructions and *pattern* which had been given to Moses (Ex. 25:40). This was a portable place of worship which the Israelites carried through the wilderness. It was taken over by the next generation of Israelites, the *fathers* who entered Canaan under Joshua and took possession of the land which had been held by the nations whom God enabled them to drive out.

46. So things continued until the time of *David*. He enjoyed the *favour* of God in that he became the ruler of a united nation enjoying secure possession of the land. David, therefore, asked if he might *find* a dwelling for the God of Jacob. The unusual wording is based on Psalm 132:4f. where David says that he will not rest until 'I find a place for the Lord, a dwelling place for the Mighty One of Jacob' (for the prose version of the

145

story see 2 Sa. 7). There is a textual problem in that *for the God of Jacob* is not as well attested as 'for the house of Jacob' and we should perhaps adopt the latter reading; in this case the word translated 'dwelling' probably means 'a place of worship'. Whether it means a tent, such as David did provide for the ark of the covenant (2 Sa. 6:17) or a more permanent building is not absolutely clear. The reply of Nathan to David's inquiry about building a temple was to affirm strongly that God had never asked for a house to dwell in, but to say that David's son would build a house for him (2 Sa. 7:5–16).

48–50. There is thus an element of ambiguity about how we are to evaluate the statement that *Solomon built a house* for God. Stephen knows that David enjoyed God's favour and (although he does not mention it) that the temple was built with God's approval (1 Ki. 8). There seems in fact to be a contrast between the tent, of which God approved, and the permanent house built by Solomon. The latter was man-made[1] (as admittedly was the tent), possibly according to human designs and not according to a divine plan, and it was easy to suppose that the transcendent God actually lived within the confines of a temple, like any idol. To be sure, the Israelites should have known better than this, since the point was made clearly enough by Solomon himself (1 Ki. 8:27) and also by the prophet whom Stephen quotes (Is. 66:1f.): the Creator of all things cannot be limited to a temple *made with hands*. Is the unspoken implication that God does dwell in a temple not made with hands, as Is. 66:2b in effect declares? Yet, if this was Stephen's thought, it is surprising that he did not go on to complete the quotation. It is tantalizing not to have the fuller information which would show clearly whether Stephen was thinking of the 'new temple' which is the Christian church. He rests on the negative point, that temple-worship imposes a false limit on the nature of God.

51–53. Stephen is nothing if not an orator, and now the style of the speech changes yet again as he proceeds to a direct attack on his audience for sharing the attitudes shown by Israel down the centuries. He uses Old Testament language

[1] This is a derogatory word used of idol worship (*e.g.* Is. 31:7; Wisdom 14:8). To apply it to the temple (*cf.* Mk. 14:58; Heb. 9:24) could well enrage the Jews.

in characterizing them as obstinate people (Ex. 33:3) who fail to show that they really belong to God's covenant. Circumcision was understood metaphorically as the cutting away of pride and sinfulness from the heart (Lv. 26:41; Dt. 10:16; Je. 4:4), and Jeremiah could describe people who were deaf to the call of God as having *uncircumcised ears* (Je. 6:10). Such obstinacy was particularly seen in *resisting the Holy Spirit* (Is. 63:10), who was regarded as speaking through the prophets and now through the Spirit-filled apostles and witnesses in the early church. There was a well-established tradition in Judaism that the Jewish people had been responsible for the deaths of *the prophets* (1 Ki. 19:10; 14; Ne. 9:26; Je. 26:20–24; Lk. 6:23; 11:49; 13:34; 1 Thes. 2:15; Heb. 11:36–38); Stephen takes up this accusation and repeats it. But he makes it more specific. The prophets in question were those who had prophesied *beforehand the coming of the Righteous One*; here *righteous* will have the sense of 'innocent' (see 3:14), but the phrase is undoubtedly meant to refer to Jesus as the Messiah; there is some evidence that the noun *coming* was used to refer specifically to the advent of the Messiah. If the Jews of olden time had shown their opposition to God by slaying the prophets, those of Stephen's own time had gone to the limit in handing over Jesus the Messiah to the Romans and so constituting themselves his murderers.

And yet even this deed is not the climax of Stephen's accusation. He reverts finally to the fact that his hearers had received *the law* of God given in the most impressive manner possible *by angels* as his intermediaries; although the presence of angels at Mount Sinai is not mentioned in the Old Testament (except in the LXX of Dt. 33:2), it was nevertheless a fixed part of Jewish tradition[1] and was accepted by early Christians (Gal. 3:19; Heb. 2:2). It was this divine law which they themselves had failed to keep; is the reference specifically to their transgression of the commandment against murder? So far from speaking against Moses, Stephen accuses his hearers of failing to obey the laws which God gave through him to Israel.

---

[1] Jos., *Ant.*, 15:136 (but the interpretation is disputed); *Jubilees* 1:29; *Testament of Daniel* 6:2.

d. The death of Stephen (7:54 – 8:1a)

Stephen's speech not unnaturally aroused hostile passion on the part of his hearers. His claim to have a vision of Jesus standing at the right hand of God exacerbated their feelings. There was an outbreak of violence, and he was taken out of the city and killed by stoning, the traditional Jewish form of capital punishment. His last words were of forgiveness for his executors, and the close collocation of a reference to Saul suggests that we are meant to infer that the words had some effect on him. The reader is being prepared for what is to follow in chapter 9.

The main problem in this section is the nature of Stephen's death. He had been tried by the Sanhedrin, but that body had no power to put anybody to death (Jn. 18:31). Yet he was executed by stoning, and not by a Roman form of execution. The possibilities are that what took place was a spontaneous act of mob violence or that Stephen was legally executed by the Sanhedrin, either because there was some kind of special permission from the Romans or because there was no Roman governor at the time and advantage was taken of the interregnum. The first of these possibilities is the more likely. But the possibility of a legal execution cannot be ruled out, especially since we have also to account for the way in which Saul could undertake persecuting missions immediately afterwards; the interregnum theory is improbable, since it is difficult to place Stephen's death (and hence Saul's conversion) as late as AD 36–37.[1]

54. The reaction of the hearers to Stephen's accusations is described in the same way as in 5:33. To gnash one's *teeth* was a sign of rage (Ps. 35:16; Lk. 13:28). Their consciences were pricked, but they were far from repenting and acknowledging the truth of what was said.

55–56. Although Stephen was a man full of the Spirit (6:5) he experienced a special filling with the Spirit which enabled him to enjoy a heavenly vision. Gazing upwards into heaven (here conceived spatially as lying up above the sky) he was able to see *the glory* that hides God from view and the figure of *Jesus standing at the right hand of God*. He cried out that he

---

[1] S. Dockx, 'Date de la mort d'Étienne le Protomartyr', *Bib.* 55, 1974, pp. 65–73, adopts this date, but at the cost of placing Saul's conversion earlier and denying that he was present at the stoning.

could see *the heavens opened, and the Son of man.* The picture is reminiscent of the baptism of Jesus, when the opened heavens were also a sign of revelation from God. The description of Jesus as the Son of man is unusual outside the Gospels; this title is found almost exclusively on the lips of Jesus himself and was scarcely used in the church as a confessional title. The point must be that Stephen sees Jesus in his role as the Son of man; he sees him as the One who suffered and was vindicated by God (Lk. 9:22), *i.e.* as a pattern to be followed by Christian martyrs, but also as the One who will vindicate in God's presence those who are not ashamed of Jesus and acknowledge their allegiance to him before men (Lk. 12:8). This probably explains why the Son of man was seen to be standing, rather than sitting at God's right hand (2:34). He is standing as advocate to plead Stephen's cause before God and to welcome him into God's presence.[1] It has been suggested that what Stephen receives is a kind of proleptic vision of the parousia or second advent of Jesus; the individual Christian finds that Christ comes to him in the moment of his death.[2] In any case, what is significant is that the dying Stephen is welcomed into the presence of Jesus; the implication is that, as Jesus was raised from the dead, so too his followers will be.

57–58. To speak in this way was blasphemy to Jewish ears. The members of the court shouted to drown out the blasphemy and stuffed their fingers in their ears so that they might not hear any more of it. Then, it would seem, all semblance of order disappeared. We hear nothing of a formal condemnation and sentence, which suggests that legal procedure was not being followed. Stephen was seized and dragged out of the town, and there he was *stoned* to death. There were formal procedures for stoning laid down later in the Mishnah, but it seems unlikely that they were followed in the first century, especially on such an occasion as this.[3]

---

[1] R. Pesch, 'Die Vision des Stephanus. Apg. 7,55f. im Rahmen der Apostelgeschichte', *Bibel und Leben* 6, 1965, pp 92–107, 170–183 (as reported in *NTA* 10, 1965–66, No. 578), has argued that the Son of man stands to *condemn* Stephen's opponents, and thus to mark the point at which the proclamation of the good news passes from the Jews to the Gentiles.

[2] C. K. Barrett, 'Stephen and the Son of man', in W. Eltester and F. H. Kettler, ed., *Apophoreta* (Berlin, 1964), pp. 32–38.

[3] So J. Blinzler, in E. Bammel (ed.), *The Trial of Jesus*, London, 1970, ch. 13.

Nevertheless, one formality could be said to have been observed. The Old Testament laid down the place of the witnesses to the act of blasphemy in the execution (Lv. 24:14; *cf.* Dt. 17:7). Here *the witnesses* are mentioned, not for their own sake, but because they laid down their garments at the feet of a man called *Saul*, who now appears in the story for the first time. The Mishnah required the victim to be stripped of his clothing; here, however, it is the executioners who divest themselves in order to perform their gruesome function more easily. There is no need to be sceptical regarding the mention of Saul here; he probably attended the Cilician synagogue (*cf.* 6:9) and so belonged to the circle of Stephen's opponents. He did not actually take part in the stoning, although he approved what was done.

59 – 8:1a. Stephen's last words were a prayer for himself and for his executioners. Like Jesus, he surrendered his spirit up; but, whereas the dying Jesus committed himself to God in the words of Psalm 31:5, Stephen committed himself to the Jesus whom he had seen in his vision. It is a striking example of a form of words originally applicable to the Father being addressed to the Son, and shows how the early Christians placed Jesus on the same level as the Father. Then Stephen prayed for pardon for his executioners, again echoing the words of Jesus (Lk. 23:34); his words stand in striking contrast to his attitude of denunciation in his speech, and illustrate how the Christian, while denouncing sin and disobedience to God in order to lead his hearers to repentance, must also have pastoral concern for them, and pray that they may be forgiven. So saying, he fell asleep (*cf.* 1 Thes. 4:14f.), the first Christian to die for the sake of Jesus.

Yet there was at least one man who remained unmoved and was not sorry to see him die. Whether Saul was a member of the Sanhedrin is not clear at this point, but 26:10 is best interpreted in this sense. It would be no easy task to convert such a man; Luke is hinting at the remarkable character of Saul's subsequent transformation.

e. The sequel to Stephen's death (8:1b–3)

This brief paragraph concludes the story of Stephen with the mention of his burial, but above all it prepares the way for the development of the narrative by indicating how Stephen's death led to the scattering of the Christians and to the con-

150

sequent spread of evangelism (8:4–40; 11:19–30); and also, by underlining the name of Saul, the persecutor of the church, it prepares readers for the wonder of his volte-face (9:1–31). The various points are linked together rather loosely: the events in verse 2 probably preceded those in verse 1, and verse 3 is really an expansion of verse 1, perhaps deliberately held back for the sake of the strong contrast with verse 2.

1b. The successful attack on Stephen was the signal for a wider attack on the church in Jerusalem, no doubt instigated by the same group that had attacked him. This is the first occurrence of the word *persecution* in Acts (except for the use of the verb in 7:52). As used here, it means harassing somebody in order to persuade or force him to give up his religion, or simply to attack somebody for religious reasons. The Christians maintained their faith and preserved their lives by flight to points where their persecutors could not be bothered to reach them. It was sufficient for them to flee to the countryside of *Judea and Samaria* in order to escape from trouble. It is significant that some of the Christians were prepared to stay in Samaria and that they did not experience opposition there from the Samaritans. It can be presumed that the opposition in Jerusalem came principally from Stephen's opponents and that it was directed mostly against his associates in the church. The *apostles* were presumably left alone; the fact that they could stay on in Jerusalem (no doubt along with other Christians) confirms the suspicion that it was mainly Stephen's group which was being attacked.

2. Despite the fact that it was dangerous to do so (this is the point in placing verse 2 after verse 1), there were pious men in the church who were prepared to give *Stephen* a proper burial. It was normal to bury executed criminals,[1] but later Jewish codification of the law forbade open mourning for them; if this prohibition was in force in the first century, the mourners were in effect mounting a public protest against the execution of Stephen, and would have been exposing themselves to considerable risk. The word *devout* is elsewhere used of pious Jews (2:5; Lk. 2:25), but it is later used to describe Ananias, admittedly as 'a devout man according to the law'

---

[1] Archaeological discoveries at Giv'at ha-Mivtar have demonstrated this; see *NIDNTT*, I, p. 393.

(22:12), although he was a Christian. It can be assumed that Christians are meant here.

3. A different kind of religious zeal was demonstrated by *Saul* who took a leading role in the persecution of the church. He went round the houses of Christians and haled them off *to prison*, not even sparing the women. Saul's activity is fully confirmed in broad terms by his own unimpeachable testimony (1 Cor. 15:9; Gal. 1:13, 22f.; Phil. 3:6; 1 Tim. 1:13).[1] No doubt the Roman authorities connived at what was going on; in any case the attack need only have been of short duration (long periods of rigorous persecution tend to be rare), and many Christians may have slipped back to Jerusalem once things cooled down.

f. The gospel spreads to Samaria (8:4–25)
The scattering of the Christians led to the most significant step forward in the mission of the church. One might say that it required persecution to make them fulfil the implicit command in 1:8. As the Christians moved to new areas they found a ready response to the gospel, and this is exemplified by the way in which the Samaritan people responded to it. The preaching of Philip was accompanied by the kinds of signs which had been seen in the ministry of Jesus and the apostles, and there was a powerful response to the call for baptism. This was all the more remarkable since the people to whom Philip preached had previously been under the spell of a religious charlatan called Simon. The successful mission led to a visit by Peter and John who discovered that the converts had not received the Spirit and who laid hands on them that they might do so. Even Simon sought to gain something, not just the gift of the Spirit, but the gift of bestowing the Spirit on others; but he had to be sharply warned against the sinful, unrepentant attitude which this request showed.

The story is significant in two ways. First, it records the reception of the gospel by the Samaritans, a people whom the Jews cordially hated and regarded as heretical; the feeling of hostility was, however, mutual. Although we might be tempt-

[1] In the light of these clear references in his own writings to activity which can only have taken place in Jerusalem and its neighbourhood, Paul's statement in Gal. 1:22 that he was 'still not known by sight to the churches of Christ in Judea' some three years after his conversion cannot mean that the latter had never seen him.

ed to see in the mission to Samaria the church's first attempt to evangelize Gentiles, this would be a wrong interpretation. To the Jews the Samaritains were not Gentiles but schismatics, part of the 'lost sheep of the house of Israel' (Jervell, pp. 113–132). For Luke they were people who kept the law and showed a greater piety than many Jews (Lk. 10:33–37; 17:11–19), although they could also show hostility to the disciples of Jesus (Lk. 9:52–56). Behind the narrative, therefore, we may well see the overcoming of the hostility between the Jews and the Samaritans through their common faith in Jesus, and it is in this sense that the story may be seen as a step towards the greater problem of bringing Jews and Gentiles together. If this is correct, it may provide the clue to the undoubted problem presented by the fact that the Samaritan believers did not receive the Spirit until the apostles laid hands on them. They were thus brought into fellowship with the *whole* church, and not merely with the Hellenist section of it. This explanation is preferable to the view that the Samaritans had not responded fully to the preaching of the gospel. Other views, such as that the Spirit could be received only by the laying on of apostolic hands, go against the general trend of Luke's picture in Acts (*cf.* 9:17).

Secondly, the story features Simon the magician who later became infamous as a Gnostic heretic. There is great uncertainty whether Simon really was a Gnostic who held at least some of the heretical views attributed to him by later writers, or was merely a magician and charlatan to whose name later Gnostic beliefs were attached.[1] It is certainly curious that some of the more radical of New Testament scholars (such as Haenchen, pp. 303, 307), who would be very cautious of attributing any of the church's christology to the mind of Jesus himself, are so ready to believe that second-century Gnostic beliefs were already held by Simon in the first half of the first century. It seems more likely that certain claims of the historical Simon enabled his later followers to regard him as a Gnostic, although he himself had not reached this stage.

4. The story begins by showing how the persecution of the church in Jerusalem was turned to good effect. Those who were driven from their homes or felt it wise to leave them

[1] See W. A. Meeks, 'Simon Magus in Recent Research', *Religious Studies Review* 3, 1977, pp. 137–142, for a survey of the voluminous research.

preached the Word as good news as they went about from place to place. It is interesting that this particular movement is not attributed to any specific guidance from the Spirit, such as occurred at other crucial stages in the expansion of the church. It seems rather to have been regarded as the natural thing for wandering Christians to spread the gospel; perhaps opportunities for doing so arose naturally, as the people into whose midst they came asked them why they had left their homes.

5. One of the people who went to Samaria (8:1)[1] was *Philip*, who is clearly the member of the Seven named in 6:5. His preaching about the Messiah would certainly have aroused at least the interest of his hearers, since the expectation of the coming of a future deliverer (known as the *ta'eb* or 'restorer') was a firm part of Samaritan theology (Jn. 4:25); this expectation was based on Deuteronomy 18:15ff., and the expected person had more the character of a teacher and giver of the law than a ruler.

6–8. There was something of a mass movement among the people as they listened intently to Philip's message. Their attention was aroused by what they heard and saw. Philip had the same ability as the apostles to perform miraculous *signs* which acted as a confirmation of his message. Like Peter (5:16) he could exorcise evil *spirits*, and the people could hear the cries that came from the possessed victims when the demonic powers left them (*cf.* Lk. 4:33; 9:39; Mk. 1:26).[2] The people could also see for themselves how people who had been *paralysed or lame* were now able to walk; again Philip's activity matches that of Peter (3:1–10) and Jesus. Such curative miracles brought rejoicing to the people. As yet, however, nothing is said of the people actually believing the gospel, and, although it is said that Jesus could not heal where there was no faith (Mk. 6:5f.), we know that there could be healing without

[1] The RSV has *a city of Samaria*. The oldest MSS have '*the* city of Samaria', which GNB paraphrases as 'the principal city of Samaria'. If the latter text is correct, the phrasing is somewhat odd, and the GNB rendering is a not altogether satisfactory attempt to deal with it. The possible towns are Sebaste (Herod the Great's new name for Old Testament Samaria), Shechem, or possibly Gitta, the birthplace of Simon. Whatever be the identification, it has no significance for the story as such.

[2] The first part of verse 7 is awkwardly expressed in the Greek text, as if Luke had failed to give the text a final revision, but the meaning is clear.

an appropriate response of faith and gratitude to God (Lk. 17:17–19).

9–11. But before the conversion of the people is recorded, Luke turns his readers' attention back to what had been happening before Philip arrived. There had been a man called *Simon* in the town who had claimed to be somebody great and gained credence by his magic powers. The people were sufficiently deceived by him to say that he was *the great power of God*. The facts about Simon are hard to disentangle from later legend. We have reliable information from Justin Martyr, himself a native of Samaria, that Simon lived there and later moved to Rome where he continued his mischief. Later, Irenaeus records how he travelled around with a certain Helen, a former slave, and said that she was an incarnation of 'Thought' (a Gnostic power). Hippolytus, another writer about heresies, tells a nice story about how Simon was worsted in a disputation with Peter. At last Simon said 'that if he were buried alive he would rise again on the third day. Commanding a grave to be dug, he ordered his disciples to heap earth upon him. They did as he commanded, but he remained in it until this day. For he was not the Christ.' What degree of truth there is in these and other stories is hard to assess. Certainly Luke is the earliest writer to give us information about him, and we must take seriously the claim which he puts on Simon's lips, and which was corroborated by the people. It is hard to be sure exactly what Simon claimed to be, but at the very least he said that he was some kind of heavenly power. It is improbable that he claimed to be the Messiah. Haenchen (p. 303) thinks that he claimed to be 'the Great Power, namely God'. K. Haacker (*NIDNTT*, III, pp. 456–458) argues convincingly that 'the great power' is a designation of divinity, and 'of God' is Luke's explanatory addition. It is also possible to think of the great power of God as a Gnostic being, an emanation from the supreme God. But it seems more likely that Simon claimed to be divine, and that later Gnostics interpreted this in their own way. In any case, Luke presents him solely as a magician who deceived the people by his tricks, and it is his role as a magician which is discredited in the story.

12. The effect of Philip's preaching was that the people paid attention to him (verse 6) instead of to Simon (verse 11). They *believed Philip* as he preached the *good news* of *the kingdom* *of God and the name of Jesus.* This is an interesting combination of themes, showing how the early church saw the message of Jesus being continued in its own message, but at the same time increasingly spoke about the means by which God's kingly power was being manifested in their own time, namely through the mighty name of Jesus. It has been thought significant that Luke says that the people believed Philip rather than that they believed in the gospel or in Jesus. The construction used is *pisteuō* with the dative, which is said by Dunn (*Baptism*, p. 65) to indicate intellectual assent rather than commitment of heart. The construction is used in 16:34 and 18:8, however, of genuine faith in God. The point is rather whether belief in Philip as he preached the gospel is to be understood as inadequate faith. The people proceeded to be baptized, and one would expect that Philip was satisfied of their sincerity in so doing; nothing in the story suggests that he was inadequate as an evangelist. On the whole, there is no clear evidence that the people were merely superficial in their belief.

13. But what about Simon? He too *believed* and was *baptized.* Thereafter he clung to Philip (*cf.* the lame man in 3:11), but his attachment to him was not free from superstition and amazement: the miraculous signs which Philip was able to perform filled him with wonder and (as we may surmise from verse 18f.) a longing to have the same ability. Was, then, Simon a genuine believer? His belief certainly left much to be desired; but we need to read the rest of the story before we can evaluate his profession fairly.

14. We are not directly told what motive led *the apostles at Jerusalem* to send two of their number to visit Samaria when they received news of the favourable reception of the Word there. But the spread of the gospel to the Samaritans must have been such a remarkable step that the apostles were bound to go and see what was happening, and to come to terms with this new event in the life of the church. Later, the successful evangelism of the Gentiles in Antioch was to lead to Barnabas being sent from Jerusalem to see what was happening (11:22), and when Peter assisted at the conversion of Cornelius, the matter was discussed at a church meeting. It does look as though new advances were examined with care in the church at Jerusalem, and we certainly get the impression of a conservative body which was never responsible for any new ventures itself.

15–17. When the apostolic delegates, Peter and John,[1] arrived, they prayed that the converts *might receive the Spirit* and *laid their hands* on them to this end; for, as Luke explains, the Spirit had fallen on none of them (for the expression see 10:44; 11:15). All that had had happened was that they had *been baptized in the name of Jesus.*[2] This is perhaps the most extraordinary statement in Acts. Elsewhere it is made clear that baptism in the name of Jesus leads to the reception of the Spirit (2:38); the case is different in 19:1–7 where the twelve men at Ephesus had not been baptized in the name of Jesus. Laying on of hands is not mentioned in connection with receiving the Spirit except in 19:6, again in somewhat unusual circumstances. On the other hand, the Spirit can fall upon people *before* baptism with water (10:44–48). It is clear that reception of the Spirit is not tied to the moment of water-baptism. Why, then, was the Spirit withheld on this particular occasion? It is wholly unlikely that a *second* reception of the Spirit was conveyed by laying on of hands, perhaps accompanied by unusual charismatic gifts; verse 16 completely rules out this possibility. Nor is it likely that the Spirit could be conveyed only by the laying on of apostolic hands, since elsewhere the Spirit is given without mention of laying on of hands (2:38) or without any of the twelve apostles being present (9:17). Moreover, it can be assumed that the Ethiopian official received the Spirit without any further ado when Philip baptized him. Only two types of explanation remain. The first is that God withheld the Spirit until the coming of Peter and John in order that the Samaritans might be seen to be fully incorporated into the community of Jerusalem Christians who had received the Spirit at Pentecost.[3] This view is confirmed by the way in which, when Cornelius received the Spirit, Peter explicitly testifies that the Holy Spirit fell on him and his family just as he had fallen on the first Christians; it was the same experience (11:15–17). The second view is that the response and commitment of the Samaritans was defective, as is shown by the fact that they had not yet received the Spirit (Dunn, *Baptism*, pp. 55–68). Dunn suggests that, among other

[1] Neil, p. 122, contrasts the attitude of John in Lk. 9:54.
[2] Bovon, pp. 251f., claims that baptism and laying on of hands normally formed one act; but if so, why did Philip omit half the ceremony?
[3] G. W. H. Lampe, *The Seal of the Spirit* (London, 1967), pp. 70–72.

things, the Samaritans needed assurance that they really were accepted into the Christian community before they could come to full faith. But it must be emphasized that Luke nowhere says this. Furthermore, we are not told of any defect in the Samaritans' faith which needed to be supplied before they could receive the Spirit; Peter and John didn't preach to them, but rather prayed for the Spirit to be given to them. On the whole, therefore, the former view is preferable.[1] It is to be noted that the story presupposes that it can be known whether or not a person has received the Spirit. This would be the case if charismatic gifts were involved; *cf.* how 10:46 gives the proof for 10:45. But there is no proof that charismatic gifts were manifest every time, and other less spectacular indications, such as a sense of joy, may have been regarded as adequate evidence of the presence of the Spirit (13:52; 16:34; 1 Thes. 1:6).

18–19. Simon saw that the apostles had the ability to bestow the Spirit on other people. What he wanted was not simply that he might have the gift of the Spirit himself but rather that he might have the power to bestow it on other people. Whether the apostles had laid hands on Simon and given him the Spirit is not clearly stated, although it could well be implied by the general statement in verse 17. The passage is not concerned to speculate about whether Simon was, in later theological language, 'regenerate'. What is emphasized is his sinful desire to have spiritual power for the wrong reasons and to gain that power by the wrong method. The possession of any kind of spiritual authority is a solemn responsibility rather than a privilege, and its possessor must constantly be aware of the temptation to domineer over those for whose spiritual welfare he is responsible; he must also beware of the danger of using his position for his own ends, whether as a means of making money or bolstering his own ego (1 Pet. 5:2f.). Simon regarded the power to bestow the Spirit in a magical kind of way, and he was prepared to pay for the privilege, thereby further revealing his misunderstanding of the nature of the Spirit. When the evil practice of obtaining positions in the church by paying a price or offering

---

[1] See further M. Green, *I Believe in the Holy Spirit* (London, 1975), pp. 136–139 for the view that the ancient schism between Jews and Samaritans lies at the base of the incident.

a bribe developed, the sin gained the name of 'simony' as a result of this incident.

20–23. Peter's reply could not be more strongly phrased. J. B. Phillips boldly translated the opening phrase as 'To hell with you and your money!', which may sound like profanity, but is precisely what the Greek says. It is the utterance of a curse against Simon, consigning him and his money with him to destruction. It is thus tantamount to excommunication from the church, or, perhaps more accurately, it is in the nature of a solemn warning to Simon regarding what will surely happen to him if he does not change his attitude. The very thought of obtaining a divine gift by some kind of payment betrays a total misunderstanding of the nature of God and his gifts. We may be able to sympathize with Simon to some extent; coming straight out of paganism as he did, he could easily misunderstand the new religion which had attracted him. But the misunderstanding was serious and had to be nipped in the bud. To think in this way showed that Simon's fundamental attitudes were out of harmony with those of God (*cf.* Ps. 78:37), and therefore, so long as this was the case, he had no share *in this matter*, *i.e.* in the blessings of the gospel. (*cf.* Dt. 12:12; 14:27 for the language used). Let him therefore *repent* of his wicked attitude and pray that his evil design might be forgiven (*cf.* Ps. 78:38). Commentators have argued whether the *if possible* implies that God was likely or unlikely to forgive Simon; probably the point is simply that Simon cannot presume upon the mercy of God and take it for granted. As a final comment Peter adds that Simon's position is serious. He is *in the gall of bitterness*. This is a Hebrew way of saying 'in bitter gall', and reflects Deuteronomy 29:18 which speaks of the danger of 'a root bearing poisonous and bitter fruit' springing up; here the phrase appears to be metaphorical of a person whose idolatry and godlessness lead to bitter results for himself and the people whom he deceives (*cf.* Lam. 3:15, 19). Peter would then be saying that Simon is causing bitter judgment for himself, as befits a person who is held fast by sin (for the phrase *cf.* Is. 58:6).

24. Simon's response was to ask the apostles to *pray* for him that none of the threatened judgments might come upon him. A variant reading in some MSS adds the interesting comment that Simon wept continually as he made his request. There is no hint in the text that his request was anything but sincere, however much or little he may have understood all that was said. Later legend portrayed Simon as the persistent opponent of Christianity and an arch-heretic; there is nothing of that here, and this may well suggest that Luke's story antedates the later picture of Simon. Unlike Ananias, Simon was given an opportunity of repentance by Peter; it is difficult to be sure what difference Luke may have seen between the two men, unless he thought that Ananias had had more opportunity than Simon to realize the sinfulness of his action and thus sinned knowingly (*cf.* Lk. 12:47f.). Whatever be the case, the story indicates that there is a possibility of forgiveness even for serious sin committed by a baptized person.

25. The story concludes with a note of how the apostles themselves preached to the people and evangelized many Samaritan villages on their way back to Jerusalem. The subject of the verse is vaguely expressed, but no doubt includes Philip, and thus prepares the way for the next story about him. The comment too is very general, but is meant to show that the Samaritan mission, begun by Philip, was carried on further by the leaders of the church at Jerusalem. The reception of the Samaritans into the church was thus firmly endorsed, and in 9:31 the presence of Samaritans in the one church is taken for granted by the narrator.

g. The conversion of an Ethiopian (8:26–40)

Philip also figures in a second story which is again concerned with the missionary expansion of the church. Where the preceding story was concerned with Samaria and a mass movement, here there is a single convert, who comes from the far south. In the former story, there was no special divine guidance leading to the evangelistic venture, but here at every stage the Spirit can be seen overruling what happens. The story is concerned with the conversion of a Gentile; whether he was a proselyte is not certain. Since, however, the man returned to his own, distant country, the episode evidently aroused no immediate problems for a church that had not yet clarified its attitude to Gentile converts. The issues raised came to a head only at a later stage as a series of events forced the church to recognize and come to terms with what was going on. The story is included here both because it is about Philip and because it forms part of the gradual progress of the church towards the Gentiles. Historically it shows that the

Hellenists, rather than Peter, took the lead in bringing the gospel to the Gentiles. The actual conversion is interesting, since the Ethiopian is led to faith by the realization that the prophetic Scriptures are fulfilled in Jesus. Philip is able to act without any need for his efforts to be supplemented by the apostles.

On the assumption that the story is historical, it must rest on the reminiscences of Philip himself. It has, however, obviously been recast by Luke who stresses the elements which he found particularly significant – the way in which God responds to those who fear him in every nation (10:34f.), the fulfilment of the prophecy of God's Servant in Jesus (3:13), and the place of the Spirit in the work of evangelism. The way in which the story is told bears some structural resemblances to another story in which a Stranger joined two travellers and opened up the Scriptures to them, took part in a sacramental act, and then disappeared from view (Lk. 24:13–35).

26. The story is set in motion by an angelic command *to Philip* which took him away from the scene of successful evangelism and led him to a place which must have seemed wholly inappropriate for further Christian work. The use of the *angel of the Lord* as a messenger is reminiscent of his role in the Old Testament (2 Ki. 1:3, 15). It is not clear why the angel is replaced by the Spirit as a divine messenger in verse 29 (*cf.* 5:19; 10:3; 12:7–23; 27:23); in Jewish thought the two appear to have been closely associated (23:9). What is important is that in this way Philip's journey and the subsequent action are seen to have been instigated by God and thus to have been part of his intention. The church did not simply 'stumble upon' the idea of evangelizing the Gentiles; it did so in accordance with God's deliberate purpose. Philip was directed to go *toward the south* (RSV text). The Greek phrase, however, can also be translated 'at noon'.[1] Although none of the recent translations adopt this rendering in their text, it could be the right one, since it helps to make the divine command to Philip all the more unusual and perplexing: at noon the road would be deserted of travellers because of the heat.[2] The road in

---

[1] This is the literal meaning; since the sun is due south at midday, the phrase came to have a geographical meaning.

[2] For this and other points in the story see van Unnik, pp. 328–339.

question went south from Jerusalem to Hebron and then west towards the coast at Gaza. *This is a desert road* is Luke's comment that underlines the strangeness of the command.

27–28. So Philip did what he was told; he obeyed instantly – and, strange to relate,[1] he met another traveller. The man came from the country now known as Sudan (rather than modern Ethiopia) where he was a eunuch employed in the court service of the queen mother, who was known by the hereditary title of Candace and was the effective ruler of the country. The term *eunuch* normally indicates a person who has been castrated; such people were forbidden entry to the temple by the Jewish law (Dt. 23:1), although Isaiah 56:3–8 offered them a better deal in the future. If the man was a eunuch in this sense, he could not have been a proselyte. The term could also be used, however, to refer simply to a court official. This may be the sense here, but the piling up of terms in the sentence suggests that the word is meant to have some independent meaning alongside *minister*, and Luke's use of Old Testament language suggests that he may well have intended his readers to see a fulfilment of Isaiah 56:3–8. In the same way he may also have seen a fulfilment of Psalm 68:31. The high position of the official as the royal treasurer is emphasized: this was no insignificant convert! He had come to Jerusalem in order *to worship* there; he was, therefore, at least a 'God-fearer' (see 10:2 note). Even if he could not be a full proselyte, he served God to the best of his ability. He had probably been in Jerusalem on the occasion of one of the pilgrim festivals and was now on his way home, riding, as befitted his status, in a chariot and beguiling the journey by reading from a scroll containing part of the Jewish Scriptures.

29–31. For the second time in the story Philip receives a divine command. We may presume that in normal circumstances an ordinary person would not accost a traveller of higher social rank, and therefore Philip needed the inward assurance that this was what he must do. The chariot would have been in fact an ox-drawn wagon and would not have moved at much more than walking pace, so that it would cause no difficulty for Philip to run alongside it and call out to the occupant. As he approached the chariot Philip heard the voice of somebody reading – whether of a slave reading

---

[1] The narrative is structured to underline this point.

aloud to his master or of the eunuch himself.[1] He recognized what was being read, and proceeded to ask the eunuch whether he understood what he was reading. For an answer the eunuch confessed his need of an interpreter and invited Philip to undertake the task. He will have presumed, perhaps from his clothing or accent, that he was a Jew and therefore probably able to help him. But the general principle which he annunciates is significant. The Old Testament cannot be fully understood without interpretation. It needs a key to unlock the doors of its mysterious sayings. Jesus had provided such a key for the disciples (Lk. 24:25–27, 44–47). Now Philip was being called upon to help the eunuch in the same way.

32–33. The passage which the eunuch was reading provided a golden opportunity for the evangelist. We can indeed see the hand of God throughout this narrative in the way in which Philip was guided to the right place and met a man who was also being prepared by God for the encounter. It was, therefore, no accident that at the precise moment when Philip heard him he was reading from a passage which was ideally suited as a starting-point for the Christian message. Isaiah 53:7f. comes from a passage of prophecy which refers to a Servant of God who suffers humiliation of all kinds and bears the consequences of the sin of others; he thus makes some kind of atonement for their sins and is finally exalted by God. It is much debated as to how first-century readers would have understood the text, and the eunuch's uncertainty may well have been typical. The particular verses cited are obscure in their meaning. They describe how the Servant remains silent just as an animal may make no noise when confronted by the knife of the slaughterer or shearer. He makes no protest although he is humiliated and deprived of justice, and finally put to death.

34. Strangely the eunuch does not ask what the verses mean; he begins by asking whether the prophet is describing his own experience or that of somebody else. Since Jeremiah could describe his own sufferings in a manner remarkably like this (Je. 11:18–20), it is not surprising that some scholars have surmised that in the present case also the prophet was referring to his own experience. And since elsewhere in the same

[1] In ancient times people generally read aloud, rather than silently as we do today.

general context God addresses the people of Israel as his servant (Is. 44:1f.), it is again not surprising that the Servant has been identified as Israel, or a part of the nation, or Israel as God intended her to be. Both of these types of view were current in Judaism. What is not clear is whether the Servant was equated with the expected 'Son of David' who would establish God's final rule in Israel. In our view there is some likelihood that this step was taken by some Jews,[1] and above all that Jesus saw himself as fulfilling the role of the Servant.[2]

35. The phrase 'to open one's mouth' is used when a significant or weighty utterance follows. Here, then, is the climax of the conversation as Philip takes his point of departure from the passage and declares the good news of Jesus. Clearly his first step was to show that *Jesus* was the person who fulfilled the prophecy. A description of the general character of Jesus, and the way in which he suffered unjustly and was condemned to death, would prove the point. No doubt Philip said more. He must have shown how the story of Jesus was good news. We do not know whether he expounded the rest of Isaiah 53 to him. It has been observed that, so far as Luke himself is concerned, he records little reference to the sin-bearing and atoning work of Jesus, and it has been concluded that he attached little significance to this in his own theology. Here too, it has been observed, it is curious how the verses from Isaiah 53 which are actually quoted speak of the unjust suffering of Jesus but not of his bearing the sins of others and his suffering on their behalf: is this silence significant? To put the question in this way of course is to assume that Luke's choice of citation was his own and was not dictated by the actual facts of the story as he had revealed them from Philip or some intermediate source, and this is a dubious assumption. Since elsewhere Luke refers to Jesus' suffering for others (20:28; Lk. 22:19f.), it seems doubtful whether we are entitled to draw any conclusions from the silence of the present passage on this point.[3]

36. The fact that Philip said much more to the eunuch than is briefly hinted at in verse 35 is apparent from the fact that

[1] See J. Jeremias, *TDNT*, V, pp. 654–717.
[2] R. T. France, 'The Servant of the Lord in the Teaching of Jesus', *Tyn.*B 19, 1968, pp. 26–52.
[3] See Marshall, *Luke*, pp. 169–175.

when the travellers reached a stream, the eunuch's reaction was to ask for baptism. Obviously, then, Philip must have spoken to him along the lines of Peter's sermon in Acts 2, especially verse 38, regarding the appropriate response to the Christian message. In the same way, it can be assumed that the eunuch must have given Philip some evidence of his faith in Jesus. There was, then, no reason why he should not be baptized. But the lack of any clear mention of these things led some early scribe to 'improve' the story by including the additional matter which appears as verse 37 in the AV and as a footnote in modern versions of the text: 'And Philip said, "If you believe with all your heart, you may." And he replied, "I believe that Jesus Christ is the Son of God." ' The content of the addition is perfectly sound theology, but the style is not that of Luke and the MS evidence is weak.

38. Satisfied that the eunuch was ready for baptism, Philip was agreeable to his request. The eunuch halted his chariot, and the two men went down into the stream, where Philip administered baptism to him. There is not sufficient evidence to indicate whether the baptism took place by the immersion of the eunuch in the water or by the pouring (affusion) of water over him as he stood in the shallow water; if the New Testament leaves the precise mode of baptism obscure, perhaps we ought not to insist on one particular type of practice.

39. As the text stands, it describes how *the Spirit* snatched Philip away as the two men came up out of the water. This is an abrupt ending to the story, and it is considerably eased by a longer form of the text which reads: 'And when they came up out of the water, the *Holy* Spirit *fell upon the eunuch, but the angel* of the Lord caught up Philip. . . ' Since in the Greek sentence the word for 'Holy' comes after 'Spirit', it can easily be seen that the whole of the italicized phrase might have dropped out of the text by accident. If so, the longer form of the text could have been the original wording, in which case the story would have related explicitly how the gift of the Spirit followed upon the eunuch's baptism. Although the MS evidence for the longer text is weak, it could be original. The phrase 'Spirit of the Lord', however, is found in 5:9 and Lk. 4:18, and the picture of the Spirit (rather than an angel) transporting a person is found in 1 Kings 18:12; 2 Kings 2:16; Ezekiel 3:14; *et al.* In any case, the fact that the eunuch went on his homeward journey rejoicing allows us to infer that he had received the Spirit.

40. Meanwhile Philip arrived in *Azotus*, the next major town north of Gaza on the coast road. From this point onwards there were settlements and Philip preached in them as he made his way northwards to *Caesarea*. Caesarea appears to have been Philip's home; at any rate, when he next appears in the Acts at a much later date, it is here that he is settled (21:8).

h. The conversion and call of Paul (9:1–19a)

Philip disappears abruptly from the story, and equally abruptly the young man called Saul reappears, hot on the trail of Christians. On his way to Damascus he experienced a blinding light and heard the voice of Jesus commanding him in effect to cease persecuting him and to be prepared to do something new. Meanwhile a disciple in Damascus was prepared to go and meet him and convey to him both healing for his blindness and baptism as a Christian. To Ananias it was revealed that Saul was to be a witness for Jesus before both Gentiles and Jews and to suffer for the sake of Jesus.

The substance of the story is told twice more, in Paul's[1] speech before the crowd in Jerusalem in 22:3–16, and in his testimony before Agrippa and Festus in 26:4–18.[2] These two accounts are given in the first person, and they show a certain amount of variation in what they omit and add by comparison with the present version of the story. While past critics have debated whether Luke had as many as three separate versions of the story, the current tendency (associated with the assumption that Luke did not have precise reports of the several speeches of Paul) is to claim that Luke had one account of the story and that he has presented it in three different ways. If this is correct, it would follow that we do not have the problem of harmonizing two or more versions of the story that might be significantly different from one another, but rather that the differences are merely literary; Luke himself saw no problem in them.

[1] In what follows we shall in general use Saul's better-known name of Paul, although Luke himself does not begin to use it until 13:9.

[2] On the conversion of Paul and Luke's picture of him generally see Burchard; Löning; Stolle; G. Lohfink, *The Conversion of Paul* (Chicago, 1976).

The fact of Paul's conversion and calling to be a missionary is not in any doubt. He himself refers to it in 1 Corinthians 15:8f.; Galatians 1:12–17; Philippians 3:4–7; and 1 Timothy 1:12–16. These passages describe the way in which Paul had been a persecutor of the church but had a vision of Jesus as a result of which he was called to be an apostle (*cf.* 1 Cor. 9:1) and summoned to preach to the Gentiles. From Galatians 1:16f. it can also be deduced that immediately after his calling he went to Damascus, and then, after a visit to Arabia, returned to Damascus. The account in Acts gives fuller details of this event, and it should be clear that the Lucan and Pauline versions of it are in essential agreement on the basic features. The problems that arise concern the way in which the story is told in Acts. Any account of what actually happened must have come ultimately from Paul and Ananias. Is the story in Acts comprehensible as a narrative based on the words of Paul, although he never goes into such detail in his letters? We cannot see any real difficulty in answering this question affirmatively. The story, however, shows a number of features in common with the Jewish legends (1) of Heliodorus, whose attempt to take money from the temple treasury was thwarted by the vision of a heavenly rider which made him fall to the ground (2 Maccabees 3), and also (2) of the conversion of Aseneth, the Egyptian wife of Joseph (in the Jewish romance, *Joseph and Aseneth*). Probably the most that can be drawn from these resemblances is that the way in which the story has been told has been influenced by the forms of Jewish legends, but the basic historicity of the story remains unaffected. It must, however, be observed that the differences between the three accounts in Acts, especially in the way in which the divine commission is given to Paul by Jesus on the road in chapter 26, but only at a later stage by Ananias in Damascus in chapters 9 and 22, demonstrate that on each occasion Luke is not trying to give us an account of what happened in precise detail but rather the general nature and significance of the event.

1–2. The story begins by reminding us of the persecuting activity of Paul which was described in 8:3. The implication is that he was not satisfied with the results of the campaign in Jerusalem itself but was *still* anxious to do more. He was going about saying what he would do to the Christians if they did not cease their activities, namely that he would murder

167

them. Whether he had the authority to execute them legally is problematic (see 22:4; 26:10), and perhaps the reference is, therefore, to what he would have liked to do to the Christians. Since many of them had fled from Jerusalem, he determined to pursue them and bring them back as prisoners to Jerusalem. He therefore sought authority from the *high priest* (this would be Caiaphas, AD 18–37) to go to the Jewish communities at *Damascus*. Damascus was an important town, about 150 miles (242 km) from Jerusalem, with a considerable Jewish population. It lay within the jurisdiction of the Roman province of Syria, and it formed part of the Decapolis, a league of self-governing cities. In 2 Corinthians 11:32 Paul speaks of an ethnarch of Aretas, the king of the Nabataean Arabs, who guarded the city to prevent him escaping from it. It is not clear whether this official was a representative of the king resident in Damascus to look after the interests of the Arabs there, or whether Damascus at this time was under the control of Nabataea.[1]

In any case, the Jewish communities would have had certain rights of maintaining law and order among themselves. The problem that arises is whether the high priest had authority to intervene in their affairs. Haenchen (p. 320 n.2) argues rightly that previous scholars have drawn unwarranted deductions from such passages as 1 Maccabees 15:15–21, which deals with a different and much earlier situation; when, however, he argues that Luke was among the number of those who misinterpreted 1 Maccabees, we need not go along with him. Probably Hanson, p. 112, is nearer the truth when he suggests that Paul had 'authorisation from the Sanhedrin to injure and even kidnap leading Christians, *if he could with impunity*'. The description of the Christians as 'those of the Way' is peculiar to Acts. It presupposes the use of the term 'the Way' to mean in effect 'Christianity' (19:9, 23; 22:4; 24:14, 22). Behind this term again lies the concept of 'the way of the Lord/God' (18:25f.) as the 'way of salvation' (16:17). God has appointed the way or manner of life which men should follow if they wish to be saved (*cf.* Mk. 12:14); the

[1] Some scholars have thought that the Emperor Gaius (AD 37–41) may have conferred the city on Aretas, but, if so, this would probably have been after Paul had left the city (see 11:29 note); another possibility is that Aretas has seized the city in the confusion following his defeat of Herod Antipas in AD 32.

Christian claim that theirs was *the* way of God led to the absolute use of the term, as here. It is interesting that the word was used in a very similar way by the Qumran sect (1QS 9:17f.; 10:21; 11:13), as well as by other religious groups.[1]

3–4. Paul was well on the way toward his destination when he was halted in his tracks. About noon (22:6) without any previous warning he found himself surrounded by an intensely bright *light* and heard a *voice* speaking to him. These are two features that one might expect in a divine revelation. The bright light is to be understood as an expression of divine glory, and, since it is generally held that no man can see God, it is not surprising that the effect of the light was to cause blindness. Similarly, when Peter was in prison, his angelic visitor was accompanied by shining light (12:7; *cf.* Mt. 17:5). The voice is also characteristic of a divine revelation (*e.g..* Ex. 3:1–6; Is. 6:8; Lk. 3:22; 9:35), but here it is specifically the voice of Jesus. Paul, then, can be said to have had an encounter with the risen Jesus in which he heard his voice. Elsewhere Paul speaks of God revealing his Son to him (Gal. 1:16), but he also goes further and speaks of seeing Jesus (1 Cor. 9:1; *cf.* 15:8). In view of 9:27; 22:14f. and 26:16 there can be no doubt that the present passage is meant to be interpreted in the same way. Luke, however, does not tell us in what form Jesus was seen by Paul, and it may be significant that Paul had to ask concerning the identity of the speaker. The account is of a revelation of Jesus from heaven rather than of an appearance of Jesus before his ascension, and therefore we are not to think of Jesus appearing in such a form that he might (for example) be confused with an ordinary traveller (Lk. 24:15). All the emphasis in the present narrative falls on what was said to Paul. '*Why do you persecute me?*' is a question aimed directly at the immediate purpose of Paul and indicates that while he thought that he was merely attacking a group of men for their heretical way of worshipping God, he was in reality attacking a group who had a heavenly spokesman and representative; to attack the Christians was to attack this heavenly figure.

5–6. Paul's reply was one of puzzlement. '*Who are you, Lord?*' does not necessarily indicate a recognition of the identity of the speaker; 'Sir' (RSV *Lord*) is the reverential address that one would expect to be used in replying to any heavenly figure

[1] G. Ebel, *NIDNTT*, III, pp. 935–943.

(10:4). The reply which he received showed that it was *Jesus* who was speaking, and whom he was *persecuting*. Thus the effect of the vision was to indicate to Saul that in persecuting the Christians he was persecuting Jesus (Lk. 10:16), but above all that in persecuting Jesus he was persecuting One who had now attained to a heavenly status and was thus shown to be vindicated and upheld by God. Paul's zeal for the cause of God had turned into an attack on the God who raised Jesus from the dead. Such a way of life could not continue; he must get up and go to the city where he would be given fresh instructions about his future task. It is a sovereign command, and it is assumed that Paul will obey it if he really is concerned to serve God. The conversation is reported in somewhat different terms in the parallel accounts, but there is no basic discrepancy in the general content of what is said in each scene as a whole; what is said later to Paul by Ananias in this account is equivalent to what is said to him on the road to Damascus in 26:16f.

7. The revelation was one given to Paul alone and not shared by his companions; they nevertheless were witnesses that something unusual happened (Conzelmann, p. 58). They halted *speechless* as they heard the sound of a *voice* but saw no speaker. According to 26:14 they saw the light and fell to the ground, and according to 22:9 they saw the light, but did not hear the voice. Bruce, (*Book*, p. 197) suggests that in the present passage *the voice* means Paul's voice, and that his companions were puzzled at his speaking with an invisible companion; this does not seem very likely since the comment directly follows the statement of Jesus and is close in wording to 22:9. See further on 22:9.

8–9. It would be an instinctive reflex action for Paul to close *his eyes* when he was struck by the bright light. On opening them he was still unable to see; this in itself would not be unnatural, but the way in which the condition was cured suggests that it was probably supernatural. In his weakness he needed to be *led* by his companions and so came to *Damascus*. Here he fasted *for three days*, no doubt still overcome by shock and probably by penitence as the enormity of his action increasingly dawned upon him.

10–12. Meanwhile the Lord was preparing for the next stage in his calling. A Christian called *Ananias* (*cf.* 22:12 for his good character) had a dream in which he heard the Lord addressing him; the scene is reminiscent of that in 1 Samuel 3, where Samuel heard God calling him, but in the present context *the Lord* must mean Jesus. Ananias was to go to a house in 'Straight Street' where he would find a man called Saul from Tarsus. The visit would be expected, for Saul himself was at prayer and had also been granted a vision in a dream of a man called Ananias coming to lay his hands on him and heal him. The arrangement was thus confirmed by a double dream (*cf.* the story of Cornelius and Peter, 10:1–23).

13–14. The name of Saul, however, was not unknown to Ananias, and he protested that all that he knew of this man indicated that he was an enemy of the church. News had come from many sources of the harm he had already done in Jerusalem, and it had quickly become known why he had journeyed to Damascus. The effect of the comment is to throw into relief the wonder of his conversion and to point to the contrast between his previous way of life and the new calling on which he was about to enter. We may note incidentally the two new descriptions of the Christians used here. The *saints* (9:32, 41; 26:10; *cf.* 20:32; 26:18) is a common term in Paul's writings and describes Christians as people who have been set apart for God's service and must show an appropriate character. Those *who call upon your name* echoes 2:21 (Joel 2:32) and recurs in 22:16 in a command to Paul himself to be baptized (see further 1 Cor. 1:2).

15–16. Ananias's comment might have been taken as an expression of disobedience to God; he should have realized that the Lord would know better than he did! But his remarks were entirely natural, and in the present context they serve to introduce a further statement by the Lord regarding his choice of Paul to be his servant. In 22:14–16 what is in effect a parallel to the present statement appears in the form of a divine instruction given to Paul by Ananias regarding his future role. The Lord has already decided to call Paul to his service; he has chosen him as his instrument[1] for the task of bearing his name before *Gentiles, kings* and the people of *Israel*. The thought of divine choice here corresponds with that expressed in 22:14 and 26:16 and also with Paul's own conviction in Galatians 1:15. *To carry my name* is an unusual expression

---

[1] The form of expression is Hebraic; *cf.* 'vessels of wrath', Rom. 9:22.

which signifies the bearing of witness to Jesus (*cf.* 9:27). The Gentiles, kings and people of Israel represent the three main groups before whom Paul will in fact bear witness later in the story, and the unusual order of the words is meant to stress the calling of Paul to go to the Gentiles. Such 'bearing of the name' would be no easy matter; it would involve *suffering* on behalf of Jesus – a sharp contrast to *causing* suffering for Christians (9:13). The book of Acts does not gloss over the fact that faithful witness to Jesus is a costly task in terms of the suffering that it may cause for the bearer of the good news.

17–19a. So Ananias went and did as he was bidden. He put his doubts aside, addressing Paul warmly as *brother*, and he laid his hands upon him. This act is certainly to be understood as a symbol of healing (Lk. 4:40) through the conveying of divine blessing. It is not clear whether in the present context it is also regarded as conveying the gift of the Spirit to Paul, and indeed this seems unlikely since here it precedes baptism, with which reception of the Spirit would normally be associated. At the same time Ananias indicated his commission from the same Lord who had already appeared to Paul to bring him healing and the gift of the Spirit. The return of Paul's sight was indicated by the falling away of some kind of film from his eyes (as in the story of Tobit, Tobit 3:17; 11:13). He was *baptized* by Ananias – there was no need of an apostle to perform the task – and he ended his fast.

i. Paul begins to preach (9:19b–31)

Luke emphasizes how Paul was no sooner converted and called to be a witness to Jesus Christ than he began to fulfil his commission, associating himself with the existing Christians in Damascus and preaching to the unbelieving Jews. Before long, however, his work aroused opposition, and he had to make an undignified escape from the town. On arrival at Jerusalem he found himself unwelcome among the Christians until Barnabas gave him his backing and introduced him to the apostles. Paul then joined in the witness of the church among the Hellenists until it became too dangerous for him to do so, and he nearly became a victim of the kind of persecution which he himself had once practised. Once again he had to flee, this time to Tarsus.

One item in this account receives casual historical confirmation from Paul's own evidence, the flight from Damascus

(2 Cor. 11:32f.) and this should warn us against questioning the value of the rest of it. Nevertheless, we obtain a different impression of things from Galatians 1:16–24, according to which (1) Paul did not confer with men after his conversion nor go to the apostles in Jerusalem, but (2) departed to Arabia and then returned to Damascus; then (3) three years later he went to Jerusalem for a visit lasting a fortnight during which he saw only Peter and James, and at this time he was unknown by sight to the churches of Judea; thereafter (4) he went to Syria and Cilicia. This account is accompanied by an asseveration of its truth which suggests that some people were contradicting it. There is no great difficulty about including a visit to Arabia in the pattern of events in Acts. It is more difficult to reconcile the claims that the Jerusalem Christians were suspicious of Paul three years after his conversion, that he saw 'the apostles', and that he preached openly in Jerusalem, with the statements in Galatians. Haenchen (p. 334) thinks that Luke did not know about the visit to Arabia and assumed that Paul's visit to Jerusalem took place very soon after his conversion. The matter is, however, discussed by J. B. Lightfoot[1] who explains some of the differences in terms of the different objects of the two narratives (for the details see below). It is difficult, nonetheless, to avoid the impression of some tension between the narratives.

19b–22. The brief period that Paul spent with the Christians in *Damascus* is no doubt to be placed before the visit to Arabia described in Galatians 1:16f. It is true that in the latter passage Paul says that he did not consult any man but departed immediately for Arabia, but we must not take what he says there with a crass literalness; the point is that he did not receive detailed instruction from any Christian leader either in Damascus or Jerusalem. As Acts states, he immediately began to act as a missionary instead of a persecutor. When he visited the synagogues in Damascus, it was not to hunt out Christians but *to proclaim Jesus*.

It is significant that his preaching is summed up as teaching that Jesus was *the Son of God*. Elsewhere in Acts Jesus is not described as the Son of God, except in 13:33 in a sermon by Paul. The title is, however, one that Paul uses as a key term in his theology, and it is noteworthy that it figures in the

---

[1] *Saint Paul's Epistle to the Galatians* (London, 1896), pp. 91f.

account of his calling in Galatians 1:16 and is associated with his call to be an apostle in Romans 1:1–4. It can be concluded that the effect of Paul's vision of Jesus was to convince him that Jesus was the Son of God, and that Luke is correct in stating that it was this title which figured in Paul's earlier preaching. Paul was not necessarily the first person to apply the title to Jesus. It expressed the position of Jesus as the Messiah (2 Sa. 7:14) who had been exalted by God to sit at his right hand (Ps. 2:7).

The effect of this preaching on the hearers must have been electrifying as they remembered the reason why Paul had originally come to Damascus. The words placed on the lips of the Jews to express their attitude are doubtless Luke's choice, and it is interesting that he uses the same word *to make havoc* to describe Paul's activity as Paul himself uses in Galatians 1:13, 23 (it is not used elsewhere in the New Testament). The phrase *called on this name* is Christian language (9:14) which the Jews are represented as taking up. Their opposition, however, merely served to encourage the zeal of the new convert, and they found themselves unable to refute his arguments that Jesus was the Messiah.

23–25. The *many days* of Luke's account will correspond to the time mentioned in Galatians 1:18 as elapsing before Paul went to Jerusalem; the expression 'after three years' found there is probably an example of inclusive reckoning and need refer to no more than two years. It is here that we should place Paul's visit to Arabia, after which he returned to Damascus. According to Acts the Jews were responsible for a *plot to kill* him and kept a *watch* on the city *gates* to prevent him escaping, but their murderous plans were thwarted by Paul escaping *in a basket* through the window of a house built on the city wall. In Paul's own account, however, the watch is kept by the ethnarch of King Aretas of the Nabataean Arab kingdom. The account in 2 Corinthians 11:32f. makes good sense, since, if Paul had just returned from Arabia, it is probable that his preaching had stirred up trouble among the Jewish communities there. It is equally likely that the Jews in Damascus sided with the ethnarch or even enlisted his support in their hostility to Paul.[1]

---

[1] Paul's friends are described in RSV as *his disciples*; the strangeness of this phrase had led some commentators to suggest that an original 'him' as the

26. Paul escaped safely, although he himself regarded it as something of a disgrace that he was compelled to flee in this way (2 Cor. 11:30), and he made his way *to Jerusalem* where he attempted to join the Christians. But, according to Luke, they were fearful of him because they suspected him of being a fifth-columnist. Commentators have been puzzled by this situation, since surely sufficient time had elapsed for news of Paul's dramatic conversion and his subsequent preaching activity to have reached Jerusalem. Could they have thought that Paul's apparent conversion was part of an elaborate and extended plot?

27. Whatever the case, it is wholly in character with what we learn of *Barnabas* from Acts that it should have been he who was prepared to welcome a person whom the rest of the church might have been slow to forgive for his previous attacks on them and whom they still regarded with uncertainty and fear. It was Barnabas who *brought* Paul *to the apostles* and related a story which he himself was prepared to believe and which, if true, would fully rehabilitate Paul in the minds of the Christian leaders. In particular, he told how Paul had spoken out *boldly* on behalf of Jesus and thereby placed his own safety at risk.[1] From Luke's point of view it was perhaps significant that in this way Paul was associated with the leaders of the church in Jerusalem, but Paul himself was anxious to assert his independence of them when he wrote to the Galatian Christians about his early life; he was insistent that he did not pick up his Christianity from men, and he emphasized that his visit to Jerusalem was a brief one of only a fortnight during which he saw only Peter and James of the apostles (Gal. 1:18–20).

28–29. During his brief stay Paul was in close touch with the apostles (for the phrase *cf.* 1:21) and continued to speak out openly in the name of Jesus; for Luke Paul ranked as a witness along with the apostles since he too had been called by the risen Lord to serve him. But, whatever the apostles may have done, Paul felt called to follow in the footsteps of Stephen and to witness among *the Hellenists*. Like Stephen, he

---

object of the verb 'took' (otherwise not expressed) was corrupted to 'his' in the earliest MSS(Metzger, p. 366).

[1] It may be that we should translate the sentence differently, so that it was Paul himself who gave his testimony before the apostles (Burchard, pp. 147f.).

fell foul of them, and had to escape for his own safety. This account of Paul's preaching activity has seemed difficult to square with Paul's own testimony in Galatians 1:22: 'And I was still not known by sight to the churches of Christ in Judea'.[1] It is not absolutely clear whether 'the churches in Judea' is meant to include the Christians in Jerusalem or refers merely to the surrounding countryside. An answer depends on whether Galatians 1:18f. implies that Paul merely saw Peter and James and did not visit any church meetings; had he visited the church, he must surely have met some of the other apostles, unless they were absent from Jerusalem. It seems likely, however, that in Galatians Paul is dealing with some kind of accusation that he had been involved in a mission in Judea during which he had been happy to insist on circumcision (Gal. 5:11). J. B. Lightfoot claims: 'To a majority therefore of the Christians at Jerusalem he *might*, and to the churches of Judea at large he *must*, have been personally unknown. But though the two accounts are not contradictory, the impression left by St Luke's narrative needs correcting by the more precise and authentic statement of St Paul.'[2] Since, according to Acts, Paul's activity was among the Hellenists, *i.e.* Jews from the Diaspora resident in Jerusalem, it is clear that he did not do missionary work in the country areas of Judea (see 26:19f. note).

30. As a result of the threat to his life, Paul was taken by his friends first of all to the seaport of *Caesarea* and then sent to his native town of *Tarsus*. This note fits in with his own comment that he went into the regions of Syria and Cilicia.[3] Tarsus was the capital city of Cilicia and ranked highly as a centre of learning. On Paul's links with it see 22:3 and 21:39.

31. Paul now goes off stage until he reappears in 11:25f. But an important point has now been achieved in Luke's story. All the preparations have been made for the decisive

[1] See 8:3 note. Paul must mean that he was unknown to them *as a Christian*.
[2] J. B. Lightfoot, *op.cit.*, p. 92.
[3] The fact that the two regions are named in that order in Gal. 1:21 (*cf.* Acts 15:23) need not mean that Paul worked in Syria before going to Cilicia; in fact his work in Antioch, the capital of Syria, followed his time in Tarsus. At this time Syria and Cilicia formed one province, and it was natural to name the more important partner first, without implying that Paul necessarily visited the two areas in the same order; see E. M. B. Green, 'Syria and Cilicia: A Note', *ET* 71, 1959–60, pp. 52f.

step forward in the mission of the church which took it to the Gentiles. So Luke pauses to give a general summary of the situation. Despite the opposition raised against Paul, active persecution of the church ceased with his departure from the scene, and for the time being the church enjoyed a period of *peace*. By this time it had spread throughout the whole of what we call Palestine. No specific mention has been made of evangelism in *Galilee*; Luke no doubt reckoned that the disciples of Jesus during his earthly life became members of the church and evangelized in their own neighbourhood. It is interesting that Luke speaks of *the church* throughout this whole region. The church could think of itself as one organism, or as a set of local groups in union with one another (*cf.* Gal. 1:22; 1 Thes. 2.14). It was being strengthened as it lived *in the fear* of God and with the strength given by *the Holy Spirit*, and so it continued to grow in numbers.

IV. THE BEGINNING OF THE GENTILE MISSION (9:32 – 12:25)

a. Peter's mighty works (9:32–43)

A new phase in the work and expansion of the church began when it found itself forced to decide about its attitude to those who were not Jews. The issue had already arisen in principle with the conversion of the Ethiopian eunuch, but this particular incident had no permanent effects on the policy of the church; once, however, converts were made who formed a permanent part of the life of the church, the question of their acceptability could not be delayed. Luke relates two major incidents in this connection. First, he recounts how the problem arose for the Jerusalem Christians as a result of the conversion of Cornelius and his family, and, second, he describes how the church in Antioch moved naturally and easily to the formation of a Jewish and Gentile Christian group. The fundamental decision to evangelize the Gentiles was thus taken, although the problem of whether they must be required to live like Jews continued to perplex the church for some time. Interspersed with this account we have two narratives about Peter. The first of them (9:32–43) is recounted because it probably belonged together with the story of the conversion of Cornelius and explained how Peter came to be in Joppa; at

177

the same time it illustrates the charismatic powers of the apostles, showing how Peter acted as the agent of Jesus in doing mighty works similar to those performed in the Gospels. The second narrative (chapter 12) describes Peter's imprisonment and miraculous release, after which he virtually disappears from the story in Acts (except for his appearance in chapter 15).

The two brief stories that make up the first narrative about Peter can be classified as miracle stories, told in the style of similar narratives in the Gospels. The first is told with all brevity, while the second is recounted with considerable detail. The parallels with the stories of Jesus healing a paralytic (Lk. 5:17–26) and raising the daughter of Jairus (Lk. 8:41–56) are obvious, but it is also significant that later Paul performs similar mighty works (14:8–12; 20:7–12). In both cases the effect of Peter's acts is to lead the local people to faith. Luke would have disagreed with the common modern suggestion that a faith based on miracles is not a true faith; where the healing (and judging) power of God is displayed in act as well as in word, there it is right for people to make their response to it, and the mighty work can act as a persuasive alongside the word.

32–35. Peter is represented as travelling among the churches outside Jerusalem in order to give them apostolic teaching (2:42); his activity, however, is not confined to teaching the Christians, but also includes evangelism. His travels probably covered the areas mentioned in 9:31, and on this occasion they took him to the west coast of Palestine. It is possible that he was following up the evangelism done by Philip in this area (8:40). *Lydda* (Old Testament Lod) lay on the route from Jerusalem to the coast, about 25 miles (40 km) distant. *Aeneas* was presumably a Christian; the fact that he had a Greek name (well-known from Virgil's epic poem about the survivors of the Trojan war) is not inconsistent with his being a Jew, and nothing in the narrative suggests the contrary. He had been confined to bed with paralysis for eight years (or possibly since he was eight years old). Peter was able to cure him by announcing *Jesus Christ heals you* and summoning Aeneas to get up from his bed. The command translated as *make your bed* is usually understood to mean that Aeneas must roll up his bed; but whereas in English 'Make your bed' suggests tidying it up after sleep, the Greek phrase

178

more naturally means preparing the bed in order to lie on it. The reference, however, could be to preparing a couch to sit at table in order to take a meal. This would give a parallel with Luke 8:55. In either case, the action would indicate the reality of the cure. Such a cure can be explained by those who wish to do so as psychological, since hysterical paralysis is not unknown. But the important fact is that the cure was accomplished by the name of Jesus, and this led to many conversions among the local people when they saw the healed man. Luke's *all the residents* is his way of indicating a large number; the local people may have included non-Jews in this semi-Gentile region, but no attention is directed to this point. *Sharon* was the name of the coastal plain that stretched northwards from Lydda towards Carmel.

36–38. *Joppa* (modern Jaffa) lay some 12 miles (19 km) from Lydda on the coast. Here too there was a group of Christians, including a woman called *Tabitha* in Aramaic; Luke tells us that this name had the same meaning as Greek *Dorcas*, and RSV indicates that both names mean *gazelle*. She is described as being occupied with *good works* and charitable actions; these were highly esteemed Jewish virtues which continued to be practised by Christians. While Peter was in the neighbourhood, she fell ill and died. Her friends (the Greek has a vague 'they', similar to common English usage) followed the usual practice in washing her body, but instead of anointing it and burying it, they laid it *in an upper room*, where it would enjoy privacy. These actions suggest that they had some hopes that Tabitha might be raised from the dead, and Luke's readers might be reminded of somewhat similar episodes in the Old Testament where bodies were placed in upper rooms (1 Ki. 17:19; 2 Ki. 4:10, 21). The incident may testify to a belief in some parts of the early church that Christians would not die before the return of the Lord but would be resurrected. In any case the Christians in Joppa felt sufficient faith in the possibility of resurrection to send for Peter and bid him come at once.

39–42. As soon as Peter arrived, he was taken to where Tabitha had been laid. The house was now occupied by mourners, including especially a group of *widows* who showed Peter the clothes made by Tabitha; the Greek phrase may indicate that these were the clothes that they were actually wearing. The care of widows and other needy people was a religious duty in the community, and a Christian community would naturally follow Jewish practice in caring for the poor in its midst. The demonstration may have been meant to encourage Peter to work a miracle. He now proceeded to follow the example of Jesus in similar circumstances. He sent all the people out of the room (Mk. 5:40; a detail omitted in Luke's version of the story, Lk. 8:54), and then *prayed* (2 Ki. 4:33). Then he called to the dead woman, *Tabitha, arise*. In Aramaic this phrase would be *Tabitha cumi*, which is only one letter different from Jesus' command to Jairus's daughter, *Talitha cumi* (Mk. 5:41). The coincidence has led to speculation that one story has been spun out of the other, but there is no positive evidence in favour of this view. The dead woman responded to Peter's call by opening her eyes and sitting up. Only then did Peter give her his hand and help her to stand up. The miracle was wrought purely by prayer and the word of command. Finally, Peter summoned the Christians and the widows; the phrase can mean 'the Christians, including the widows', but it is not necessary to assume that Tabitha helped only Christian widows. As with the healing of Aeneas, the news of the miracle became widely known and led to many conversions.

43. It was natural for Peter to stay on in the neighbourhood to follow up this mass movement (he will have done the same in Lydda). What is interesting is that he stays with *a tanner*. The detail is included because it gives Peter's 'address' in anticipation of the directions in the following story (10:6). Commentators have noted that the tanner's occupation was an unclean one, and that a person with Pharisaic scruples would avoid contact with such a man. We may doubt whether Peter was ever worried by such scruples, and hence whether Luke intends to record a step forward in his liberation from them.

b. The conversion of Cornelius (10:1 – 11:18)

While Peter was at Joppa, events were moving towards a new stage in his missionary career as God prepared for the entry of Gentiles into the church. Two dreams led up to the decisive encounter. First, a Roman centurion who was a worshipper of God received a divine intimation that he must summon Peter to visit him, and, second, Peter was prepared to receive this invitation by a dream in which he was shown that he was no longer to distinguish between ritually clean and unclean foods and therefore (it is implied) could feel free to eat with Gentiles. Thus Peter journeyed to Caesarea where he met with Cornelius and his family and friends, and responded to their invitation to speak to them by preaching the gospel. Even while he spoke the Spirit fell upon the assembled company in a manner that reminded Peter of Pentecost, and he realized that, if God accepted the Gentiles in this way, he should be prepared to accept them into the church by baptism. When he returned to Jerusalem, he found himself called to account for his action in eating with Gentiles (not, curiously, for baptizing them), and had to defend his action by telling the story of the unmistakable leading of God which culminated in his baptizing of the Gentiles on whom the Spirit had fallen. This not only silenced his critics but led to a recognition by the church that salvation was available for the Gentiles.

The sheer length of this story and the way in which it is in effect told twice over (see also the summary in 15:7–9) indicate the very great importance which Luke attaches to it in the context of Acts as a whole. It deals with the decisive issue in the history of the early church, namely the recognition that the gospel is for the Gentiles as well as the Jews, and it makes clear that this was no merely human decision, but that it was the result of God's clear guidance. The obstacle to the mission to the Gentiles was that it would bring law-abiding Jews into contact with people who were reckoned unclean, and with their food which was also unclean. It is this obstacle which is overcome by the vision of Peter; no theological basis for the rescinding of the law is given, however, at this stage. Later on, the question whether Gentile converts should be circumcised and required to conform with the law of Moses in other ways was to be a sharp cause of contention, but, as Luke recognizes, this issue did not arise until the practice of admitting Gentiles to the church had begun.

The basis of the story has been much disputed. We may readily admit that the recounting of the story by Peter in chapter 11 represents the general tenor of what he would have said as conceived by Luke rather than being an exact account of his actual words. The same thing may be true of Peter's sermon in the house of Cornelius, but it is noteworthy how this sermon is nicely adapted to its context, and some features of it suggest that Luke had a basis in tradition for it (Stanton, pp. 67–85). Greater problems are raised by the suggestions that two independent items, the story of the conversion of a Gentile and the account of a vision which originally dealt with the separate issue of Jewish food laws, have been joined together, and that one or both of these are fictitious. This type of analysis of the story, presented in different ways by Dibelius (pp. 109–122) and Haenchen (pp. 355–363) has, however, been received with some scepticism by more recent scholars such as Hanson (pp. 119f.) and Wilson (pp. 171–178).[1] It has been argued, for example, that Peter's vision deals with a different subject from the conversion of Gentiles; but in our opening summary we have indicated that it had a very real relevance to Peter's situation. Again, it has been argued that Peter's subsequent refusal to eat with Gentiles (Gal. 2:11–14) is odd if he had already been convinced in principle that this was all right in God's sight; such an argument, however, fails to reckon with the possibility of vacillation (an acknowledged trait in Peter's character in the Gospels), especially in face of considerable human pressure to abandon a principle. A further argument is that Luke gives the impression that the decision to admit Gentiles to the church was taken in one crisis-event, whereas in reality it must have taken longer for the Jerusalem church to adjust itself to the idea. It then becomes possible to argue that Luke has either invented or rewritten the story, bringing out the parallelism with Jesus' attitude to a Gentile centurion (Lk. 7:1–10), and giving Peter the credit for the decisive action. The miraculous elements in the story are implicitly rejected, and Haenchen (pp. 362f.) goes so far as to suggest that the picture of God intervening decisively to guide the church, which almost acts as a pawn in his hands, is theologically unsound and should be rejected. Such thorough-going scepticism is unjustified. No doubt the Jerusalem church took some time to adjust itself to the Gentile mission; we have, indeed, little if any evidence for any further evangelism by the Jerusalem church among the Gentiles. Yet this is an inadequate basis for doubting the historicity of this incident. The most that can be said is that Luke has used this story as a means of focusing the key issues involved in the Gentile mission, without excluding the possibility that the

[1] See F. Bovon, 'Tradition et Rédaction en Actes 10, 1–11, 18', *TZ* 26, 1970, pp. 22–45, who argues for two independent traditions with a historical basis.

issue continued to be debated for some time to come. To this extent the story may be a kind of vignette in which the basic issues are dramatically presented. The essence of the story, however, is doubtless historical. It is highly unlikely that Luke invented it, or the place of Peter in it, and the way in which the Spirit fell on the Gentiles before their baptism is so unprecedented that it is hardly possible for it to be invented.

1. The first of the four scenes into which the story may be divided (10:1–8, 9–23a, 23b–48; 11:1–18) is placed at *Caesarea* (8:40; 9:30), a 'new town' built by Herod the Great which had become the centre of government for the Roman administration of Judea. Here there resided a *centurion* named *Cornelius*. The name was a common one, borne by thousands of slaves who had had freedom granted to them by P. Cornelius Sulla in 82 BC. Sherwin-White (pp. 160f.) notes that the use of this part of a tripartite Roman name fits in with the army practice of the period. A centurion corresponded to an NCO in modern army ranking. The *Italian Cohort* to which he belonged was a body of troops originally recruited in Italy. Since there were no Roman legions in Judea but only what were called auxiliary forces, the cohort will have formed part of the latter and performed garrison duties. There is inscriptional evidence that an Italian cohort was in Syria by AD 69. Haenchen (p. 346 n.2) argues that Luke has read back the conditions of a later time into the story, since in AD 41–44, while Herod Agrippa I ruled as a client king, there would have been no Roman units in Judea. But this objection ignores the possibilities that the incident described here took place before AD 41 when Roman troops certainly were present, and that Cornelius may have been retired from military service by this time.

2. More important than Cornelius's military status for Luke is the fact that he and his household were worshippers of God. The allegiance of Cornelius was far from being nominal, as was shown by his giving of alms to the poor and his frequent prayer. Nevertheless, Cornelius had not submitted to circumcision, as 11:3 makes clear. He was not a proselyte, *i.e.* a Gentile who had fully accepted the Jewish religion by undergoing circumcision, but merely a 'God-fearer' (*cf.* 13:16, 26, 43, 16:14; 17:4, 17; 18:7);[1] such people were regarded as

---

[1] This term has come to be used for Gentiles who worshipped Yahweh and attended the synagogue, but had not submitted to circumcision. The Greek

still pagans by the Jews in Palestine, but there appears to have been a more liberal attitude in the Dispersion. Possibly, therefore, Cornelius had become a God-fearer before he came to Palestine. The early church in Jerusalem shared the attitude of other Jews to such God-fearers, but Christian attitudes changed, and it is clear that Luke himself recognized the value of this step on the way from paganism to Christian conversion. Note the similarities between Cornelius and the unnamed centurion in Luke 7:1–10, especially verse 5.

3–6. The episode is set in motion by an angelic vision which came to Cornelius at *the ninth hour of the day* (3.00 pm). Since this was the hour of prayer in the temple at Jerusalem, it may be assumed that Cornelius was at prayer, and there may also be the thought that a vision in broad daylight would not be a phantom of his imagination. The *angel* addressed him by name (*cf.* Lk. 1:13, 30; Acts 9:4), and Cornelius displayed the *terror* which is the natural reaction of human beings to the supernatural and is a constant feature in stories like the present one. But there was no cause for alarm. The angel came to assure him that God had taken note of his prayers and his deeds of charity. The language used is that of sacrifices whose smoke ascends to God, and Bruce (*Book*, p. 216) thinks that Cornelius's prayers had a sacrificial efficacy before God. The language had already become traditional (Ps. 141:2; Tobit 12:12; Phil. 4:18; Heb. 13:15) in this sense, and it is this tradition which is reflected here rather than a direct allusion to Leviticus 2:2 (as is suggested by Bruce). The implication is that God will respond to the prayer uttered by Cornelius. But at this stage the nature of the response is not revealed. Rather Cornelius is to send to *Joppa* for a man called *Simon* – here given his Jewish name. To follow this instruction would be an act of faith and obedience.

7–8. Cornelius responded to the command by sending a group of three messengers, two servants and a military orderly who shared his faith and who would be able to explain the situation sympathetically to Peter. Since the distance was some 30 miles (48 km), it is probable that they rode, and

phrases used by Luke ('fearing God', 'worshipping God') do not have a technical sense, however, and can be used of any pious worshippers of God, whether circumcised (so probably in 13:43) or not (as here); see K. Lake, *BC*, V, pp. 84–88.

Stählin (p. 151) suggests that they may have taken an animal for Peter.

9–16. The scene now shifts to Joppa where Peter was staying, and we hear what he was doing while the messengers were still on their way. He had gone up on the roof of the house in order to seek privacy, and here he was praying at noon; Jews who took seriously the pattern of praying three times a day (Ps. 55:17; Dn. 6:10) may have used this as a set hour. Peter's thoughts would seem to have been diverted from prayer by his feeling *hungry*. It was not in fact a usual Jewish mealtime; on weekdays Jews ate a light meal in mid-morning and a more substantial meal in the late afternoon. While something was being prepared for Peter to eat, *he fell into a trance* (11:5; 22:17), and had a vision. Three factors may have governed the vision. The fact that Peter was praying means that he was in a condition to receive a divine message; Luke often emphasizes how God speaks to people when they are at prayer (*e.g.* 13:2; Lk. 3:21f.; 9:29). Peter's hunger may also have shaped the nature of his vision, and it has been suggested that, if there was an awning over the roof of the house to shield people from the sun, this may have helped to create in Peter's mind the image of a large *sheet* that was being lowered from the sky by four ropes.

The sheet contained living creatures of the three kinds recognized in the Old Testament (Gn. 6:20; *cf.* Rom. 1:23). Then Peter heard a voice telling him to kill the animals and prepare a meal; since it was a dream, we do not need to ask in detail how the command was supposed to be carried out. What mattered was the principle expressed. The contents of the sheet were animals that would be *unclean* and therefore unfit for eating in terms of the Jewish law found in Leviticus 11; whether there were any clean animals, *i.e.* those that chewed the cud and were cloven-hoofed, is not stated, but the implication is that there were none. Peter therefore protested against the command, claiming that it had never been his habit to eat anything that was common or unclean. He addressed the unknown speaker as *Lord* (RSV) or 'Sir'; we cannot deduce from this mode of address whom Peter supposed the speaker to be. The voice replied, declaring that people must no longer count as common what God had cleansed, and this happened twice before there was silence and the sheet disappeared from view. The effect of the vision was thus to announce to Peter that the distinction made in the Old Testament between foods that were 'clean', and therefore fit for human consumption, and those that were unclean, was now cancelled, so that in future Jewish Christians could eat any food without fear of defilement.

But when had God cancelled the distinction? Evidently in the moment at which this was stated. But later Christians realized that the cancellation of this law was part of the new order brought by Jesus, and that some of the things said by Jesus implied the abolition of the Jewish distinction between things clean and unclean; this was the implication of what Jesus taught when he said that it was unnecessary to wash one's hand for ritual reasons (as distinct from hygienic reasons) before a meal, and Mark commented, 'Thus he declared all foods clean' (Mk. 7:19). Similarly, Paul said, 'I know and am persuaded in the Lord Jesus that nothing is unclean in itself' (Rom. 14:14), and we can take it that this principle was accepted in Corinth by the Jewish Christians who probably took their inspiration from Peter; what Paul was trying to teach them was not that ordinary food was 'clean' but that even food offered to idols and sold in the market place was 'clean', since idols were non-existent (1 Cor. 10:19). There need be no doubt, therefore, that at some early point, Peter and other Jewish Christians came to see that they could eat any kind of food and ignore the Old Testament ruling on the matter which was no longer valid.

Not all commentators have been able to see the relevance of the dream to Peter's immediate situation, and some have been tempted to treat the dream allegorically, as declaring all *men* clean, so that Peter need not be afraid of going to a Gentile household. This allegorical interpretation is forced and artificial, although it can find a basis in 11:12 and 15:9, and thus some have argued that the dream is a secondary addition to the story. It is more likely, therefore, that the point is that the Lord's command frees Peter from any scruples about going to a Gentile home and eating whatever might be set before him. It would be a short step from recognizing that Gentile food was clean to realizing that Gentiles themselves were 'clean' also.[1]

---

[1] A 'separation from uncleanness is always a simultaneous separation from unclean persons' (Schürer, II, p. 396).

17–20. As Peter was returning to consciousness and wondering what the significance of this unexpected dream might be, the messengers of Cornelius arrived at the door of what was probably quite a humble home, and inquired whether he was within. The arrival of the men at this point is clearly meant to be understood as providential. While they were still at the door inward guidance came to Peter from *the Spirit*; this was a different form of divine communication from the vision and probably implies the growth of an inward conviction. Peter was warned that three men were at the door;[1] he was commended to go with them since they had been sent by God (the Spirit speaks on behalf of God as 'I').[2] Here was the situation for which the dream was meant to prepare Peter.

21–23a. So *Peter went down* and received the messengers, making himself known to them. They repeated their message in a form calculated to make a favourable impression on Peter by describing their master as a God-fearing man who had sent for Peter in response to an angelic command and who wanted to listen to what he had to say; this last point is 'new information' for the reader, Luke having saved it up for this point to add to the literary and dramatic effect of the story, and it can be assumed that it was contained in the original angelic message to Cornelius. Since it was already too late to set out on the journey back to Caesarea, Peter received the messengers as his guests and entertained them for the night; this action probably did not go beyond what a law-abiding Jew might do.[3] Peter is able to act as host, although he is himself a guest in another man's house; Simon the tanner will also have been a Christian, and will have treated Peter with some respect as an apostle.

23b–29. The third scene in the story opens with the departure of Peter and a number of Christians from Joppa for Caesarea on the following day; from 11:12 we learn that Peter had six companions and later in the story they function as

---

[1] Some MSS have 'two men', *i.e.* regarding the soldier as a guard rather than a messenger, but 10:7 might seem to give him a more important role.

[2] The phrase translated *without hesitation* might perhaps mean 'making no distinction'. See 11:12 where a different form of the same verb is used; it is not clear whether the forms could be used synonymously in New Testament Greek.

[3] It was one thing to give a Gentile Jewish hospitality, and another for a Jew to accept Gentile hospitality (Harvey, p. 437).

187

witnesses to what had happened (10:45f.), although they may have gone in the first place simply out of curiosity. The party took the whole of one day and part of the next to reach Caesarea, and on arrival found that Cornelius was already waiting for them together with a group of his relatives and friends. It can be assumed that Cornelius knew at least something of who Simon Peter was and also of the new religious movement which was spreading throughout the country, and therefore he called together his family and others to hear what Peter had to say. Cornelius will have known roughly when to expect the visitors to arrive. His first act on meeting Peter was to kneel before him as a sign of reverence, but, as always in the New Testament, Peter refused to accept such respect which should have been offered only to God (14:14f.; Rev. 19:10; 22:9). The two men then entered the house, talking together as equals, and Peter found the group assembled to hear him. The first words of Peter were a public statement of his new willingness to meet with Gentiles and a request for an explanation of why he had been asked to come. From what Peter says it emerges that he interpreted his vision, which dealt with regarding certain foods as 'common or unclean', as a means of teaching him also not to regard any man as *common or unclean*. He had come to realize that Jewish scruples were now countermanded by God. This suggests that a new application of the vision was being made by Peter.

30–33. Cornelius's reply is essentially a recapitulation of facts already known to the reader.[1] The 'angel' of verse 3 is now described as *a man in bright apparel* (*cf.* 1:10) for the sake of variety. There are some insignificant differences in wording between the two accounts of what the angel said, which indicate once again that the New Testament writers were not concerned to give a word-for-word account of conversations

[1] Verse 30 is confused in the Greek. Literally it reads: 'From the fourth day until this hour I was praying at the ninth hour in my house, and a man stood before me'. 'From the fourth day' can mean *four days ago* (*i.e.* 'three days ago' by inclusive reckoning); the real difficulty is 'until this hour' which makes nonsense of what follows. It may be possible to translate the phrase as *about this hour* (RSV), *i.e.* it was now the same time of day as when Cornelius had his vision, but we have no evidence to support this conjecture, and it seems more likely that there is a primitive error in the text. Perhaps it was due to a scribe who supposed that Cornelius had spent four solid days in prayer; other scribes certainly took the passage in this way, and one of them added, for good measure, that Cornelius was also fasting.

and speeches. Finally, Cornelius thanked Peter for coming, and invited him to speak, commenting that their present meeting was taking place *in the sight of God*. This incidental remark indicates that when people gather together to hear the gospel (and *a fortiori* when a Christian congregation assembles), they do so in the presence of God. This appears to be the only use of this phrase in this sense in the New Testament, although the thought that men's actions are visible in God's sight is common. But for the same thought expressed in other ways we may refer to Matthew 18:20; 1 Corinthians 5:4.

34–35. Peter could have had no better-prepared and eager an audience than this, and was quick to seize on the situation as the starting-point for his address. The significance of what he says is perhaps underlined by the solemn phraseology with which Luke introduces the speech (*Peter opened his mouth*, 8:35; Mt. 5:2), but more probably this is simply a case of stereotyped ancient phraseology. Peter expresses his realization that God will accept anybody of any race who reverences him and lives righteously. God is no respecter of persons. The word which is used here is found for the first time in the New Testament and is a translation of the Hebrew phrase 'to lift (someone's) face', which meant 'to show favour' and hence 'to show favouritism'.[1] God does not have favourites. This means that, on the one hand, evil-doers cannot hope that he will show partiality to them at the judgment (Rom. 2:11; Eph. 6:9; Col. 3:25; 1 Pet. 1:17; Dt. 10:17), and, on the other hand, that no man need fear that God will not receive him out of partiality. Christians must display the same spirit (Jas. 2:1, 9). Peter does not raise the question how this attitude of God is to be squared with the teaching of the Old Testament which stressed the privileged place of Israel as God's people as a result of his election of them. It is clear, however, that the election of Israel was based solely on God's choice and not on any merits of the people, and hence there is no inconsistency in the claim that God accepts people of all nations on the same basis. If people *fear God and do what is right* (*cf.* Mi. 6:8), then they are acceptable to him. This is what Paul also teaches in Romans 2, and there are some traces of the same attitude in Judaism.[2] This does not mean that salvation is possible

[1] E. Tiedtke, *NIDNTT*, I, p. 587.
[2] K. G. Kuhn, *TDNT*, VI, p. 741.

apart from the atonement wrought by Jesus Christ, but rather that on the basis of his death and resurrection the gospel is offered to all people who are willing to receive it and recognize their need of it; had a person like Cornelius said, 'My good deeds are sufficient to win me favour with God, and I have no need of the gospel' (which is essentially what the Pharisee said in Lk. 18:11), then it would have become clear that he was not accepted by God; a good life is acceptable in God's sight only when it leads to recognition of its own inadequacy and to acceptance of the gospel (or when it would have done so, had opportunity of hearing the gospel been provided). Cornelius, however, wanted to hear the gospel.

36–38. Having established that his audience were meant to hear the gospel, Peter proceeded to proclaim it. The speech which follows is unique among the sermons in Acts in that it pays some attention to the earthly life of Jesus instead of taking up his story at the point of his rejection by the Jewish leaders and his crucifixion. The reason for this may be simply Luke's love of literary variation; in other words, he has 'saved up' this motif for this speech, and its absence from earlier ones certainly does not mean that nothing was said about it on those occasions. It may also have seemed appropriate to include this point in a speech addressed to a non-Jew who might be presumed to know less about who Jesus was than Peter's earlier audiences in Jerusalem. An apparent objection to this view is that Peter begins his remarks by saying 'You know the word . . . .', as if Cornelius was already familiar with the story and did not really need to hear it again. Wilckens (pp. 65–67) has, therefore, suggested that Luke envisaged Cornelius and his associates as being *already* converted before Peter spoke to them, so that Peter is simply confirming their existing knowledge and belief. The weak points in this theory have been exposed by Stanton (pp. 19–26), who rightly argues that Peter was supplementing Cornelius's scanty knowledge of Jesus, in exactly the same way as he does in 2:22 (where the same phrase 'you know' occurs).

The content of the speech is distinctive, and there is good reason to suppose that it is based on tradition (Stanton, pp. 67–85). This is apparent from the clumsy sentence construction in verses 36–38 (tidied up in the English versions).[1] The word-

---

[1] Literally it runs as follows: '(36) The word (accusative) [which – omitted

ing of verse 36 incorporates allusions to two Old Testament texts, Psalm 107:20, 'He *sent forth* his *word* and *healed* them', and Isaiah 52:7, 'the feet of him who *brings good tidings*, who publishes *peace*'. The message thus begins by asserting that in Jesus God has fulfilled his promise in the Old Testament to bring peace to his people, the children of Israel; *peace* is used here in its full sense as a synonym for 'salvation' (Lk. 1:79; 2:14; Rom. 5:1; Eph. 2:17; 6:15), and denotes not merely the absence of strife and enmity between man and God but also the positive blessings that develop in a state of reconciliation.[1] But this message is not confined to the Jews. Although it was *sent to Israel*, it was intended for all mankind, since, as Peter adds in an emphatic parenthesis, Jesus, the author of peace, is the Lord of all men. This last phrase is one found in pagan as well as Jewish authors, and is thus an apt one for making the point at issue.

Then Peter stresses how this message of peace came in the

---

in some MSS] he sent to the sons of Israel, preaching the good news of peace through Jesus Christ – he is Lord of all – (37) you know, the event (*or* word) which took place throughout all Judea, beginning (nominative masculine) from Galilee after the baptism which John proclaimed, (38) Jesus (accusative) of Nazareth, how God anointed him with the Holy Spirit and power, who went about doing good and healing all who were oppressed by the devil, because God was with him.'

(1) The RSV (*cf.* GNB) has retained 'which' in verse 36 and regards 'the word' as the object of 'you know' in verse 37; it then takes 'the word' in verse 37 (a different Greek word) as being in opposition to 'the word' in verse 36, and paraphrases 'took place' as 'was proclaimed', and it regards 'Jesus' in verse 38 as really belonging to the 'how God anointed (him)' clause.

(2) Alternatively, we may drop 'which' in verse 36 from the text, thus obtaining two separate sentences, verse 36 ('He sent the word. . . .') and verses 37f. ('You know the event which took place . . . , (namely) how God anointed Jesus. . . .'). This interpretation (NEB:NIV) is probably better; but neither approach is free from difficulty.

(3) H. Riesenfeld has revived a suggestion made by J. A. Bengel that 'the word' in verse 36 is in apposition to the preceding clause. He translates, 'Truly I realise that God does not show partiality, but in every nation anyone who fears him and does what is right is acceptable to him; (this is) the word which he sent to the children of Israel, proclaiming good news of peace through Jesus Christ – he is Lord of all. You know what took place throughout all Judea. . . .' On this view the good news is that God does not show partiality. This translation makes good sense of the passage. (H. Riesenfeld, 'The Text of Acts x. 36', in E. Best and R. McL. Wilson (eds.), *Text and Interpretation* (Cambridge, 1979), pp. 191–194; similarly, Jervell, p. 73).

[1] H. Beck and C. Brown, *NIDNTT*, II, pp. 776–783.

lifetime of Jesus. His hearers were already at least vaguely aware of what had been going on in the whole of Judea. It is characteristic of Luke's Gospel that it stresses that the ministry of Jesus extended to the whole of Judea including both Galilee and also the area in the south around Jerusalem which can also be called Judea in a narrower sense (Lk. 4:44; 7:17; 23:5). It is also characteristic that the ministry is said to begin in *Galilee* (Lk. 23:5) and to be associated with *John's* ministry of *baptism* (1:22; 13:24); we may compare how the earliest Gospel, that of Mark, begins at this point. Then we get the briefest sketch of what happened. *God anointed Jesus* with the Spirit; here the wording of Isaiah 61:1 is used to interpret what happened to Jesus at the Jordan, just as in Jesus' own sermon in Luke 4:18 (*cf.* Acts 4:27). The gift of the Spirit conveys *power*, and with this power Jesus was able to bring help and *healing* (Ps. 107:20) to people who were under the control of *the devil*. The idea here is that the healing miracles rescued people from the power of evil which was responsible for their suffering (Lk. 13:16). The verb *doing good* is interesting; the corresponding noun 'benefactor' was used by rulers of the time to describe themselves (Lk. 22:25), so that here Jesus is being implicitly compared with them and shown to be the true helper of the people. The motif of antagonism and opposition to the devil is also significant; it is drawn from the concept of the rule of God which Jesus came to establish over against the forces of evil opposed to it (Lk. 11:17–20). There is no mention of the preaching of Jesus at this point; this has already been referred to in verse 36, and it is noteworthy that both the preaching and the mighty works are seen as the work of God acting through Jesus as his representative.

39–41. Peter regularly refers in his sermons to the apostles as *witnesses* to the resurrection. Since, however, the apostles were people who had been with Jesus right from the beginning of his ministry (1:21f.), they could also be claimed as witnesses for the ministry as a whole, both in Judea at large and also in Jerusalem. Whereas in earlier sermons Peter had directly addressed the Jews and accused them of putting Jesus to death, this was not possible in a sermon addressed to non-Jews. The death of Jesus at the hands of the Jews is in fact mentioned almost in passing, although its importance is underlined by the way in which it is regarded as having been foretold in the Old Testament; the phrase *by hanging him on a tree* is undoubtedly an echo of Deuteronomy 21:22f. (also cited in 5:30), a passage which Paul saw as having a 'fulfilment' in the case of Jesus (Gal. 3:13).[1] It was this Jesus, crucified by the Jews, whom God *raised* from the dead *on the third day*.[2] Then God allowed him to be seen by a select group of witnesses whom he had chosen beforehand for the purpose. The resurrection appearances were not made to the people at large. The reason appears to have been that those who saw Jesus were constituted to act as witnesses to the many people who could not see him, and this obligation was not laid on people who were unfit for it but only on those who had been prepared by lengthy association with Jesus and by sharing his work of mission. The reality of their experience of him is stressed by the note that they *ate and drank* with him (1:4; Lk. 24:30, 43).

42–43. After the resurrection Jesus *commanded* the apostles *to preach to the people* (*i.e.* the Jews) and as part of their message to testify that Jesus had been appointed by God to act as *judge* of all men, both *living and dead*. This function of Jesus is also attested in 2 Timothy 4:1 and 1 Peter 4:5, but it is not specifically mentioned in any of the summaries of what the risen Jesus *commanded* his disciples to proclaim; it may, therefore, be a deduction from his earlier teaching that the Son of man would sit at the right hand of God and share his task of judgment (*cf.* Jn. 5:22, 27). Finally, Peter declares that in accordance with prophecy *everyone who believes* in Jesus can have *forgiveness of* their *sins* (cf. Lk. 24:46f.). We cannot be certain what prophecies Peter may have had in mind, but possible texts include Isaiah 33:24; 53:4–6, 11; Jeremiah 31:34; Daniel 9:24.

44. Peter's reference in verse 43 to every one who believes in him need refer only to 'every one in Israel who believes in him', but in view of verses 34f. a wider meaning is probably intended. In any case, before he had a chance to say anything more, *the Holy Spirit* came upon those who heard the message. Since elsewhere the gift of the Spirit comes to people who repent and believe (*cf.* 11:17f.), the implication is twofold: first, that the Gentiles present responded to the message with

---

[1] See M. Wilcox, ' "Upon the Tree" – Deut. 21:22–23 in the New Testament', *JBL* 96, 1977, pp. 85–99.
[2] This and 1 Cor. 15:3 are the only references outside the Gospels to the resurrection taking place on the third day.

faith; and, secondly, that God accepted them and sealed their faith with the gift of the Spirit. Once Gentiles had been given an opportunity to hear the message, they responded, and God received them. This verse marks the end of religious particularism.

45–46a. Now Peter's companions play their part in the story. Whether or not Peter was surprised by what happened, they certainly were. It was one thing to make an attempt to preach to Gentiles; it was quite another to see the sermon interrupted by the clear signs of their conversion and reception of God's gift. There could be no mistake about what had happened. Just as the first Jewish believers had received the Spirit and praised God in other tongues on the day of Pentecost, so now these Gentiles received the identical gift of God. We cannot tell for certain whether the gift of *tongues* was the inevitable accompaniment of the coming of the Spirit; the facts that it is mentioned so infrequently and that Paul thinks of it as a special gift not bestowed on all members of the church indicate that it was probably not an invariable sign of conversion. The reception of the gift on this occasion stressed the reality of the conversion of the Gentiles over against all possible doubt. (It is true that the gift of tongues can be counterfeited; it is not so easy to counterfeit genuine praise to God. The whole context rules out any thought of deception.) Would not Gentiles, freed from their religious inferiority, have felt their hearts strangely warmed and expressed their emotion in an unusual fashion?

46b–48. If God had welcomed the Gentiles, it only remained for the church to do so. Baptism had become the outward sign of reception into the people of God. It was the sign of cleansing from sin, and so of forgiveness (2:38), but at the same time it was seen as the outward accompaniment and sign of being inwardly baptized by the Spirit; the latter did not replace water-baptism. Since the Gentiles had been baptized with the Holy Spirit, it followed that they were eligible to be baptized with water. So Peter put his question to the Jewish Christians with him, as representatives of the church. It is possible that the use of the verb *forbid* (also used in 8:36 with reference to the Ethiopian eunuch) reflects a stereotyped phrase used at baptism. There was no objection raised, and so Peter gave instructions for the converts to be baptized. Although Bruce (*Acts*, p. 228) thinks that this refers to a com-

194

mand to the converts ('Be baptized'; *cf.* 2:38; 22:16), it is perhaps more likely that the command was addressed to the other Christians present to perform the rite. We may compare how Paul too did not usually perform baptisms himself, although he was the founder-evangelist of the church at Corinth (1 Cor. 1:14–17); it was not necessary to have baptism carried out by an apostle. It may also be noted that the narrative does not imply that Cornelius or his friends were circumcised; indeed it positively rules it out (*cf.* 11:3). Finally, the new fellowship in the church between Jews and Gentiles was cemented during a brief stay by Peter with Cornelius. At the same time, this interval allowed news of what had happened to reach Jerusalem before Peter himself arrived back.

11:1. The story of the conversion of Cornelius would be incomplete from Luke's point of view without the addition of the fourth scene in which the effects of the incident on the church are described. Luke's concern is with the *apostles* as the leaders of the church and the *brethren* as its ordinary members (1:15), and he speaks of the church *in Judea* (8:1; 9:31), which consisted of the group in Jerusalem together with the Christians scattered in the neighbouring area. It was the reaction of these Jewish Christians to the response of the Gentiles to the gospel which was all-important for the future.

2–3. It was, therefore, *the circumcision party* which questioned Peter about what had happened, as soon as he had returned to Jerusalem. The RSV rendering here is misleading; the Greek phrase simply means 'those belonging to the circumcision', *i.e.* 'those who were of Jewish birth' (NEB). There is no suggestion that there was a definite 'party' in the church at this stage, especially before the issue of circumcision had arisen in such a way as to lead to people taking sides on it. Nevertheless, centuries of Jewish practice made them critical of what Peter had been reported as doing, especially his action in eating with Gentiles. Even though the Gentiles had become converts, the problem still existed. If Jewish Christians felt bound by the Jewish food laws, there could not be fellowship with Gentile Christians (or contact with non-Christian Gentiles) unless the Gentiles were circumcised and observed the Jewish food laws themselves. That this problem was no figment of Luke's imagination is seen by the way in which the problem was still a live one at the time of the incident reported in Galatians 2:11–14 (when even Peter went back on his earlier practice). Behind the strong feeling of the Jewish Christians there may have been the fear that, if they ceased to follow the practice of Judaism, they might find themselves under attack from their fellow Jews, just like Stephen and his associates. The situation is thus perfectly plausible, and there is no need to share the scepticism of Dibelius (pp. 109–121) who contests that the problem of eating with Gentiles played any part in the original story.

4–17. Peter's reaction to the question was to tell the audience the whole story *in order* (for this last phrase *cf.* Lk. 1:3), in the belief that when they heard it properly (instead of the fragmentary and possibly garbled reports that they had already received) they would be bound to see that God had led him to this action. So the story is briefly retold with little significant difference from the earlier narrative, except that it is considerably abbreviated and told in the first person from Peter's point of view.

The account naturally begins with Peter's own experience, rather than that of Cornelius, and describes how he fell into a trance while at prayer and saw the vision of the sheet being let down from the sky, full of various living creatures (the account here includes 'beasts of prey', *i.e.* wild animals, along with the others mentioned previously). The account of the conversation between the heavenly voice and Peter is repeated without significant variation. Immediately after the dream three men arrived to invite Peter to go to Caesarea, and Peter heard a message from the Spirit telling him to go with them *making no distinction* (see 10:17–20 note), *i.e.* without treating them any differently (*sc.* from Jews). Along with his six friends he therefore went to *the man's house*; 'the man' is of course Cornelius, and he is not named, since both Peter's hearers (who already knew something of the story) and Luke's readers would recognize who was meant. One must demur, therefore, from Haenchen's statement (p. 355) that the account would not have been intelligible to Peter's audience. Likewise, there is no reason to see any 'sizeable self-contradictions' between the two accounts. Haenchen sees such a contradiction in the fact that in verse 11 the six Jewish Christians from Joppa are already in Simon the tanner's house when the messengers of Cornelius arrive; the point is in any case absurdly trivial, but nothing in chapter 10 proves that the men were not in the house at the time. In verse 13 Cornelius briefly describes how

196

he had seen *the angel*, a manner of narration which is again meant for Luke's readers and need not mean that Peter spoke unintelligibly to his audience. It is only here, however, that we learn that the angelic message promised to Cornelius that he would hear a message explaining how he could be saved, along with his household (verse 14). This detail explains Cornelius's statements in 10:22, 33. The angel speaks the language of the early Christian preachers (*cf.* 16:31) when he talks about *being saved*, but this phraseology was already familiar in the Old Testament and would cause no difficulty to Jews or proselytes. A further difficulty has been seen in the fact that Peter says that the Holy Spirit fell on the audience *as I began to speak*, while in chapter 10 he has preached for some time before anything happens. But this too is merely an apparent difficulty. The point of Peter's statement here is simply that he had not finished what he wanted to say, and the force of the verb 'begin' cannot be pressed in Hebraizing Greek.

Peter's comment brings out the fact that the experience of the Gentile converts was the same as that of the original recipients of the Spirit *at the beginning*, *i.e.* on the day of Pentecost. It is significant that he compares the experience of the Gentiles with that of the group in the upper room, rather than with that of the first converts from Judaism: there is nothing that might suggest a status as 'second-class citizens' for the Gentiles. Further, Peter sees in the experience of the Gentiles a fulfilment of the saying of Jesus in 1:5 when he reminded his disciples of the fact that, while *John* had *baptized with water*, they would be *baptized with the Holy Spirit*. Two things followed from this recollection. The first was that the reception of the Spirit by the Gentiles was to be regarded as being baptized with the Spirit (on the meaning of this term see 1:5 note), since it was the same kind of experience as that of Pentecost, which was the first fulfilment of Jesus' prophecy. Secondly, if the Gentiles had been baptized with the Spirit, then they should *a fortiori* be eligible to be baptized with water. This deduction may not seem immediately obvious, since the saying in verse 16 (*cf.* 1:5) seems to contrast baptism with water and baptism with the Spirit; but it is probable that the saying means 'John baptized (merely) with water, but you shall be baptized (not only with water but also) with the Holy Spirit.'[1]

---

[1] Marshall, *Commentary*, pp. 145f. (following J. Jeremias).

The church, which carried out baptism with water, was thus under compulsion to baptize believing Gentiles; otherwise, it would have been hindering God from carrying out his will. It emerges incidentally from this statement that Peter assumes that the Spirit is given to those who believe on the Lord Jesus Christ; baptism with water is bestowed in response to the confession of faith, and, although the bestowal of the Spirit was the evidence that faith was present, it is probable that the baptism of the Gentiles included their confession of faith.

18. Peter's argument proved convincing. Not only was incipient criticism reduced to silence, but rather the audience expressed their praise to God that he had granted *to the Gentiles* as well as the Jews the opportunity of repenting of their sins and thus of obtaining eternal life (5:20; 13:46, 48). This opportunity was provided in the preaching of the gospel.

Peter's argument implicitly claimed that Gentiles were full members of the church, and therefore that circumcision and keeping of the law were unnecessary for salvation; it also contained the wider implication that the Jewish distinction between clean and unclean foods and people was obsolete. But this was an earth-shattering idea for Jews, and was not to be accepted without much heart-searching and controversy. Luke does not take up this theme immediately, and we do not know how far the full implications of Peter's action were immediately realized in Jerusalem. As the next section of Acts will show, the initiative in the Gentile mission passed to Antioch, and it is not clear how far the church at Jerusalem was prepared to follow Peter's lead. We should not take verse 18 to imply that the church at Jerusalem forthwith entered zealously into a mission to Gentiles; indeed, it never seems to have done so, and as a result it lost its importance in course of time.

c. The church at Antioch (11:19–30)

While these developments were taking place in the mission area of the Jewish church, the Hellenistic Jewish Christians who had been forced to leave Jerusalem at the time of Stephen's death had scattered northwards as far as the great metropolis of Antioch. They spread the gospel as they went, but it was only at Antioch that they began to speak to non-Jews and to win many converts. The church began to grow rapidly. The news prompted the church in Jerusalem to send a delegate to see what was happening. The appointed visitor, Barnabas, had no doubts about the value of the work that was being done, and actively joined in, summoning Paul from Tarsus to help in the work. The church's evangelism made such an impact that the local people dubbed its members 'Christ-people'. The members of the church were conscious of their ties with Jerusalem, and when they heard a prophecy of a forthcoming famine they sent a gift of money to aid the church.

There can be no doubt that the formation of the church at Antioch was an event of great significance in the expansion of the church and its mission to the Gentiles. It can be confidently assumed that the Gentile converts were not required to be circumcised or keep the law, and they probably formed a sizable group in the church, although there is no firm evidence that they formed the majority. The question of the Jewish law arose only when visitors from Jerusalem tried to enforce it (Gal. 2:11–14).

Earlier commentators regarded the information in this section as stemming from an 'Antioch-source', possibly mediated to Luke by Silas. It may have originally included 6:1 – 8:4, the story of Stephen, to which there is a link in 11:19. More recent commentators, such as Haenchen, (pp. 368–372) have doubted this hypothesis. They point to the lack of concrete details in the section and the presence of Luke's own vocabulary and ideas. Haenchen suggests that Luke had only a few historical reminiscences, including the facts that Barnabas came from Jerusalem and was active in the church, and journeyed later with Paul to Jerusalem. In reality, says Haenchen, Barnabas and Lucius of Cyrene were the founders of the church, but Luke has told the story in such a way that Barnabas is given a different role as the 'inspector' from Jerusalem. Haenchen (pp. 375–379) also finds the visit of prophets from Jerusalem at this early date difficult, and in particular he argues that the prophecy of a famine was unfulfilled, and that the Christians of Antioch were unlikely to send help to Jerusalem in this connection; he therefore postulates that Luke has wrongly dated Agabus's prophecy, and that he has mistaken the details of Paul's activity in taking up a collection for the Jerusalem church. Luke has thus constructed a false picture of a church remaining in close touch with Jerusalem and indeed almost subservient to it.

This reconstruction is sheer speculation, and its value stands or falls with the question of whether the difficulties which Haenchen finds in the existing narrative are real ones or not. One is tempted to say that Luke cannot win either way: if the narrative is lacking in concrete details, he is said to have no sources at his disposal, and if he paints a detailed picture of an episode, it is dismissed as legendary embellishment. The narrative is in fact reasonably detailed, and there is nothing incredible about its main features. In particular, Haenchen's suspicion that the Hellenists driven out of Jerusalem would not have hastened to send aid to 'the murderous city' not only might suggest that he doesn't believe that Christian charity is a reality but also overlooks the fact that it was to the *church* that the gift was being sent. As for the problem of Paul and Barnabas's journey to Jerusalem with the gift and the timing of the whole affair, this is best solved by adopting the equation of this visit with that recorded in Galatians 2:1–10, a solution which Haenchen rejects without convincing grounds.

19. Luke's introduction to the section takes the reader back to 8:2–4, which described how the death of *Stephen* led to a wave of opposition to the church and the scattering of many Christians. In all probability these were Jews who had links with the Dispersion, and it was natural for them to move to areas outside Judea, including the three places named. *Phoenicia* (modern Lebanon) was the area that stretched along the coast in a narrow strip from Mount Carmel for a distance of about 150 miles (242 km) its main towns were Ptolemais, Tyre, Zarephath and Sidon, and we hear later of Christian groups in three of these places (21:3, 7; 27:3), no doubt formed at this time. *Cyprus*, which has already been mentioned as the home of Barnabas (4:36), had had a Jewish element in its population at least since the second century BC (1 Macc. 15:23); it was to be the first place evangelized by Barnabas and Paul when they later went out as missionaries together (13:4–12). This means that there were Christians in Cyprus before the arrival of Barnabas and Paul, a fact which is not in tension with Luke's account in 13:4–12 even if he does not mention it there (*pace* Conzelmann, p. 67). The third place mentioned is the most important for the future development of the story. *Antioch*, the capital city of the Roman province of Syria, had grown rapidly to become the third largest city in the Empire (after Rome and Alexandria) with a population estimated at around 500,000. It was founded by Seleucus I and named in honour of his father Antiochus (the same honour was attached to the names of some sixteen cities; *cf.* 13:14). There was a large Jewish population.[1]

20–21. The exiled Jews in their new home at first preached the gospel only to their fellow Jews. The decisive change was initiated by some of the Jews from *Cyprus and Cyrene* who preached the good news of Jesus to the *Greeks* also in Antioch.[2]

There can be no doubt that a successful period of evangelism among Gentiles was initiated, and that observance of the Jewish law was not required of the converts. What we do not know is how the church was led to take this step. It required divine intervention to persuade Peter to take the same action, but here it seems to have happened almost casually without any issues of principle arising at the outset or later. Probably the matter can be explained quite simply by noting that the likelihood of Gentiles being associated with the synagogues was far higher in the Dispersion, so that the church would be brought up against the problem of their place in evangelism much more frequently and directly than in Judea itself. If some of the evangelists were themselves proselytes, this would make the step all the more natural. It must be assumed that the new Christian group quickly lost contact with the synagogues, so that it was not compelled to observe the Jewish law, as was the case in the predominantly Jewish setting of Jerusalem. We do not know whether the conversion of Cornelius had taken place earlier and was known of in Antioch, so that it could have acted as a precedent.

22–24 There is nothing surprising in the fact that *news* of what was happening at Antioch reached *the church in Jerusalem*, since there was no doubt considerable traffic between the two cities. On previous occasions (8:14; *cf.* 9:32) the leaders of the church at Jerusalem had sent representatives to follow up

[1] The site has been excavated in recent years; see G. Downey, *Ancient Antioch* (Princeton, 1963).

[2] Luke must mean Gentiles, but the text is uncertain. Instead of 'Greeks', the majority of the MSS (including Codex Vaticanus) have 'Hellenists', the word used in 6:1 and 9:29 to designate Greek-speaking Jews. The textual arguments in favour of the latter reading are very strong; if adopted, it must refer to the Greek-speaking mixed population of Antioch (Metzger, pp. 386–389).

mission work outside the city, and this particular occasion clearly demanded that they show their interest. It is not necessary to assume that their action was motivated by suspicion, still less by hostility. At the most, it may have been necessary to do something to placate a group of right-wing Jewish Christians in Jerusalem who were to cause difficulty at a later stage and who may already have been opposed to the admission of Gentiles to the church without circumcision being demanded of them; nothing suggests that this group was dominant in the church, but the leaders did their best to conciliate them (see Hanson, p. 130).

The basic sympathy of the church in Jerusalem with the news of what was happening in Antioch may be deduced from the choice of *Barnabas* as their delegate. Although he came of a Dispersion family, he was regarded with complete confidence in Jerusalem and acted as a pivot or link between the Hebrew and Hellenistic elements in the church. His character was well adapted for this function, for he was outstanding for the Christian quality of his life; no other man is described by Luke as *good* in Acts, and in his spiritual gifts he stood on a level with Stephen. He could not help seeing the hand of God in the growth of the church at Antioch, and rejoiced at this evidence of divine grace. So far from urging any legalistic demands upon the new converts, he rather instructed them to remain firm in their faith; here we see how Barnabas merited being called 'Son of encouragement' (4:36). The fact that Barnabas had the spiritual insight to recognize that God's plan was being fulfilled at Antioch was of decisive significance for the growth of the church.

25–26. Barnabas recognized the rich potentialities of the situation for further advance, and saw the need of additional help in evangelism and teaching. He therefore hunted out his old friend Paul who was at work in *Tarsus* and persuaded him to join in the work at Antioch. Did Paul feel that he had accomplished all that he needed to do in Tarsus? We simply do not know, and we do not hear of any later contacts he had with the city, but Paul must have spent a considerable period of time there, and in his later missionary campaigns his practice was to stay long enough in any given place to establish the church and then move on elsewhere. The work that Barnabas and Paul did in Antioch is described as teaching the church, but this could refer to evangelism as well as to the upbuilding of existing converts.

One important result of all this activity was that for the first time the disciples became known as *Christians*.[1] Luke specially mentions this because 'Christian' had become a familiar term in certain areas at the time when he wrote. Early in the second century the name is attested for Rome, Asia Minor and Antioch, and nothing prevents the view that it first came into use at Antioch. The ending of the word (*Christianos*) indicates that it is a Latin word, like 'Herodian', and that it refers to the followers of Christ. 'Christ' will then be understood as a proper name, although its original use was as a title, 'the Messiah', for Jesus. The verb *were called* implies in all probability that 'Christian' was a nickname given by the populace of Antioch, and thus 'Christ' could well have been understood as a proper name by them, even if at this stage the Christians themselves still used it as a title; it was not long, however, before the title became increasingly more like a name for Jesus. It is likely that the name contained an element of ridicule (*cf.* Acts 26:28; 1 Pet. 4:16, its only other New Testament uses). The Christians preferred to use other names for themselves, such as 'disciples', 'saints' and 'brothers'.

27–28. One important feature of the early church was the activity of *prophets*, charismatic preachers who might be attached to a local church or engaged in an itinerant ministry (13:1 note).[2] Their functions were various and included both exhortation and foretelling of the future; they may well have given expositions of the Old Testament, using their spiritual insight to show how its prophecies were being fulfilled in the events connected with the rise of the church. Their activity was connected with the new sense of inspiration associated with the gift of the Spirit to the church. There is nothing surprising about such men coming from Jerusalem to Antioch (although Haenchen, p. 376, is most perplexed by them). We learn, however, nothing about the purpose or results of their visit except for the fact that one of them, named *Agabus* (he reappears at 21:10), forecast a *famine* that would extend *over*

---

[1] W. Grundmann, *TDNT*, IX, pp. 536f.
[2] E. E. Ellis, 'The role of the Christian prophet in Acts', *AHG* pp. 55–67 (Ellis pp. 129–144); D. Hill, *New Testament Prophecy* (London, 1979), pp. 94–109.

all the world, *i.e.* the Roman Empire. Famines were part of the Christian expectation for the last days (Lk. 21:11), and this prophecy may have been a warning that the end must be near, but nothing is made of this in the text. To be sure, there was not one Empire-wide famine during the reign of Claudius (nor at any other time); there were, however, 'frequent famines', according to the historian Suetonius, and this is an adequate fulfilment of the prophecy. There was certainly famine in Judea *c.* AD 46, and Josephus tells how Helena of Adiabene sent corn to relieve the hunger among the poor in Jerusalem. J. Jeremias noted that the Jews followed the law of the seventh, fallow year during this period, and argued that if the dearth coincided with the effects of a fallow year, the famine would be all the greater; he therefore suggested that the famine should be associated with the sabbath year which was celebrated in AD 47–48.[1] The prophecy could, of course, have been a few years earlier.

29–30. The prophecy encouraged the Christians in Antioch to send a collection of money to enable their brothers in Judea to buy up food against the coming crisis. This was an act of Christian fellowship, in which the members of the church took part voluntarily according to their means. The money was sent to the elders of the church. This is the first mention of *elders* in the church at Jerusalem, and it has caused surprise that they are mentioned, and not the apostles, who were in charge of the poor relief earlier. But in fact the apostles had delegated this duty to others (6:1–6), and it may be that the 'Seven' people appointed to look after this task had now become known as 'elders' by analogy with the name given to leaders in Jewish synagogues. They functioned alongside the apostles (15:4, 6, 22f.; 16:4; 21:18). The collection was brought by Barnabas and Paul. It has been objected that they would have been unlikely to be in Jerusalem during the persecution of the church described in the immediately following section: could they have remained unmolested? But we are not specifically told that they were in Jerusalem at this precise point; the chronology remains open.[2] More important is the relationship of the present narrative to that in Galatians 1–2 where

[1] J. Jeremias, 'Sabbetjahr und neutestamentliche Chronologie', *ZNW* 27, 1928, pp. 98–103.
[2] Knox, p. 36.

Paul summarizes his early relationships with the church in Jerusalem. Apart from his visit to Jerusalem after his unceremonious departure from Jerusalem, he mentions one visit to Jerusalem, on which he was accompanied by Barnabas and Titus, and during which he discussed the problem of preaching the gospel to Gentiles; he was asked to 'remember the poor', the very thing which, he says, he was eager to do (Gal. 2:1–10). Is this visit to be equated with the one in Acts 11? The following objections can be raised: (1) Acts 15 relates the story of a further visit to Jerusalem at which the question of the Gentiles was the explicit subject of discussion. While the accounts in Acts 15 and Galatians 2 differ in detail, it is arguable that they refer to the same incident, and that it is unlikely that the ground was gone over twice. There is, however, nothing improbable in the fact that a difficult subject had to be discussed more than once before agreement was finally reached, as anybody who has ever worked on a committee will realize. (2) Galatians 2 deals with a theological controversy, while Acts 11 is concerned with a gift of money. But we can understand Luke saving up the controversy for chapter 15. Moreover, Galatians 2:10 can mean that Paul was already eager to help the poor, and was in fact doing so.[1] If so, there is no real conflict between the passages. We therefore regard it as most probable that the visit recorded here is the same as that in Galatians 2:1–10.[2]

---

[1] Despite Haenchen's denial (377f.) this is the probable interpretation of the verse; see D. R. Hall, 'St Paul and Famine Relief: A Study in Galatians 2:10', *ET* 82, 1970–71, pp. 309–311.

[2] F. F. Bruce, 'Galatian Problems. 1. Autobiographical Data', *BJRL* 51, 1968–69, pp. 292–309. See further 15:1–35 note. Chronological difficulties have been raised by R. Jewett, *Dating Paul's Life* (London, 1979). He argues that the Gal. 2 visit to Jerusalem cannot have taken place as early as our theory requires, and places this visit (which he equates with the visit recorded by Luke out of chronological order in Acts 15) *after* Paul's ministry in Corinth. This view assumes that the three years and the fourteen years of Gal. 1:18; 2:1 lead to a total of seventeen years, and that Paul's escape from Damascus (Acts 9:23–25) cannot have taken place before AD 37. Both of these assumptions are questionable. Paul may be using inclusive reckoning in Galatians, and his escape from Damascus could have taken place before AD 37 if we follow Bruce, *Acts*, p. 205, in arguing that there was a representative of king Aretas in Damascus (2 Cor. 11:32f.) before AD 37. Jewett's claim that the Acts 11 visit to Jerusalem is fictitious and the Acts 15 visit is to be equated with that in Acts 18:22 attributes unbelievable inaccuracy to Luke. On Jewett's chronology see also 15:36–41 note.

d. The imprisonment and escape of Peter (12:1–25)

Although Luke tells us nothing about what happened when Barnabas and Paul visited Jerusalem, he fills up the space between their departure (11:30) and return (12:25) with an account of how Herod Agrippa I tried to curry favour with the Jews by executing James and attempting to execute Peter. Luke's narrative shows how Herod's plan was thwarted by the direct intervention of God. God acted, however, in response to the prayers of the church, although when Peter was released from the condemned cell, the church could scarcely believe that its prayers had been effective. If the story underlines the relationship between prayer and the action of God, it also shows how God acts to bring retribution upon those who oppose his work and exalt themselves; those who set themselves up against God ultimately perish.

Such are the bare bones of the story. It is more difficult to see its place in the general pattern of the history of the church as recorded selectively by Luke. What is the function of this chapter in the narrative as a whole and what light does it shed on Luke's picture of the church? A number of different possibilities arise. At first sight the story is unnecessary to the developing theme of the expansion of the church; had it been omitted, we should not have noticed the loss. Perhaps, therefore, the story has been told simply because it formed part of the traditions which Luke had inherited about Peter (*cf.* 9:32–43). It may, however, serve historically to tell how Peter was forced to leave Jerusalem and thus to hand over the leadership of the church to James (although we should note that Peter is still active in the church in Jerusalem in Gal. 2:9 and Acts 15). Another function of the story may be to indicate the way in which the career of Peter ran along lines similar to those of Jesus and of Paul: the theme of imprisonment and death (real or threatened) is common to all three. It is less likely that we should trace a deliberate typological parallelism with the story of Jonah, although the evidence for this interpretation has been soberly presented by Williams (pp. 152f.).

From Luke's point of view the emphasis would appear to be on the triumphant progress of the gospel (12:24) which is not hindered by the death of one apostle or the imprisonment of another. When the church prays, the cause of God will go forward, and his enemies will come to naught, even if this does not exempt the church from suffering and martyrdom;

Luke's belief in the victory of the gospel is thoroughly realistic and recognizes that though the word of God is not fettered, its servants may well have to suffer and be bound (2 Tim. 2:9).

The basic historicity of the story is not in doubt. The facts that Peter was imprisoned and that he escaped are perfectly probable, although rationalists may want to insist that an originally 'natural' escape has been elaborated into a miracle. See on 5:19.

1. The timing of the events in this chapter is determined absolutely by the death of Herod which took place early in AD 44; their dating relative to the visit of Barnabas and Paul to Jerusalem is disputed, since it is uncertain whether the famine relief was brought so soon before the actual famine; see 11:29–30 note. *Herod* in this context is Herod Agrippa I, a grandson of Herod the Great, who after a somewhat tempestuous youth was granted ever-increasing areas to rule by the Emperors Gaius and Claudius; by AD 41 he had acceded to a kingdom of similar extent to that of his grandfather.[1] He did his best to win the favour of the Jews and especially cultivated the Pharisees.

2. It is entirely in keeping with what we otherwise know of him that Herod should have attacked some of the leading members of the church. James, the son of Zebedee, was executed; it is possible that Herod was conniving with the Sanhedrin which was taking severe measures against the church, but we cannot be sure on this point. Thus was fulfilled the prophecy of Mark 10:39, at least in respect of James. The view of J. Wellhausen and others that John his brother was executed at the same time (and therefore could not have written the Fourth Gospel) is baseless supposition; as C. K. Barrett drily commented, 'we cannot martyr the apostle for our convenience in handling critical problems'.[2] Luke does not speculate over why James perished but Peter was rescued; it would be highly perverse to deduce from verse 5 that prayer was offered for Peter but not for James.

3–4. The execution of James was effective in Herod's pur-

---

[1] It had been divided up in the interim period into three basic parts: Judea, ruled by Roman officials; Galilee and Perea, ruled by Herod Antipas; and the areas north-east of Galilee, ruled by Herod Philip.

[2] C. K. Barrett, *The Gospel according to St John* (London, 1955), p. 87.

pose, and he therefore proceeded further in the same direction by arresting *Peter*. Since it was the time of the feast of *unleavened bread*, which followed directly upon the passover, so that the two festivals were regarded as virtually one, no immediate action could be taken. We may compare the similar problem that arose when the Jewish leaders were contemplating the arrest of Jesus (Mk. 14:1f.). The utmost precautions were taken against any attempt to release the prisoner; the details serve to emphasize the wonder of the actual escape. Four groups, each of four soldiers, were deputed to guard the prisoner; the comment fits in with an otherwise attested Roman practice of changing the guard during each of the four watch-periods into which the night was divided. The rest of the story makes it clear that the imprisonment was in Jerusalem, where Herod was no doubt resident for the festival period (*cf.* Lk. 23:7).

5. The essential lesson of the story is presented in this carefully balanced verse: *Peter was* being *kept in prison, but earnest prayer* was being *made* for him. The prayer was manifestly for his release. The view that the early church believed that its Lord would return at the time of passover, and that it was praying for him to come on this particular passover to deliver Peter[1] is not even hinted at in the text. It was fervent prayer which was offered, like that offered by Jesus in Gethsemane (Lk. 22:44), expressive of the church's concern for Peter rather than of a feeling that, if God is to answer prayer, he must be pressed and persuaded by spectacular feats of devotion. At the same time, if the church knew how its Lord himself had prayed, it would have had to pray: 'Nevertheless, not our will, but yours, be done' (*cf.* Lk. 22:42).

6–11. As the imperfect tenses in verse 5 make clear, Peter's imprisonment and the early church's prayer lasted for several days. The story moves to the night before the day on which Herod intended to bring Peter out of prison and take him before the people (verse 4) for trial and summary execution. Luke describes the method of imprisonment in more detail. Peter was handcuffed to a soldier on each side in the prison, and the door was guarded by sentries. During the night – the regular time for such events – *an angel of the Lord*

---

[1] A. Strobel, 'Passa-Symbolic und Passa-Wunder in Apg. 12.3ff.', *NTS* 4, 1957–58, pp. 200–205.

entered the prison and the place *shone* with a supernatural *light*. Peter was asleep, untroubled by the thought of what he expected to happen the next day, and had to be awakened by a nudge on his side. As he stood up, the fetters holding him to the soldiers fell off his hands. Half asleep, he heard the angel tell him to put on his daytime clothing preparatory to leaving the prison. He walked out of the open door of the prison, following the angel and not unnaturally thinking that he was dreaming it all. There were three gates to be traversed before Peter reached freedom. The story does not make it clear whether the first two were open or closed, but the implication is that they were open while the guards were sleeping. The third door was the massive outside door of the prison, and it swung open of its own accord, letting Peter and the angel pass out and along the street. Once they had walked away from the immediate vicinity of the prison, the angel disappeared, and Peter realized that he was really and truly free, thanks to divine intervention.

The story is plainly regarded by the narrator as miraculous at every point. It can be argued that it is a legend, especially since several of the motifs in the story can be paralleled from other ancient stories, some of which would have been current knowledge in the first century (5:19 note), and it can be claimed that in a world of such superstitions it would be only natural for Christians to believe that their God could do the same kind of things as other deities. On this view a story of a release from prison by human agencies may have acquired legendary features in the course of telling. It is impossible to prove the point either way. The person who believes in the reality of the supernatural will not find it difficult to accept this story as it stands, along with other, similar stories in the Bible and Christian history. In this particular instance there is no element in the story which forbids such a view of it.

12–17. Once Peter realized that he was free, and also no doubt that he was in danger if he remained where he was, he made moves to get out of harm's way without delay. First, it was necessary to inform his fellow Christians of what had happened. He knew that he would find friends in the home of *Mary, the mother of John Mark*, and thither he went. The lady of the house is identified by the reference to her son who figures in the narrative almost immediately (verse 25), and who may have been Luke's informant on this and other epi-

sodes in the history of the early church. It has been conjectured that this house was the one where the disciples gathered
at Pentecost (1:13 note), but there is no positive evidence in
favour of this guess. Although it was late at night, many
people were assembled together and were spending their time
praying; here we have one of the incidental references which
show that early Christians prayed by night. Their prayers
were interrupted by a knocking at the door, and a servant
went to see who was there; the house is envisaged as having
an entrance-way separating the main room from the street. It
would be normal to enquire who was at the door before opening it, lest a marauder might enter. When the servant girl
heard Peter's voice in response to her query, she was so surprised and overjoyed that she ran back into the house to tell
her exciting news without opening the door. The people in-
doors refused to believe her story. First, they said that she was
out of her mind. When they could not shake her story, they
thought that it must be Peter's *angel*. This curious reference
must be to some kind of 'heavenly' counterpart to a person,
having the same physical appearance. The Jews believed that
people had guardian angels (see Mt. 18:10 for an echo of this
belief), and there is some evidence (admittedly much later
than the New Testament and not altogether easy to interpret)
that guardian angels were thought to bear the image of the
persons whom they protected.[1] The supposition of the people
in the house was in this case false, since it really was Peter
himself; Luke says nothing to indicate that the supposition
rested on a sound doctrine of angels, and it is most likely that
it is nothing more than a Jewish superstition which he cites
but does not necessarily corroborate. When Peter eventually
did gain admission, he lost no time in hushing the excitement
of his friends. He satisfied their natural curiosity by explaining
how he had been set free, and then he asked them to pass on
the news to the other Christian leaders before he set off into
the night to a secret hiding place.

The *James* mentioned here is the brother of Jesus (Mk. 6:3)
who later figured as the leader of the church in Jerusalem
(15:13; 21:18); Paul regarded him, along with Peter and John,
as one of the three 'pillars' of the church (Gal. 2:9). He had
been a witness of a resurrection appearance of Jesus (1 Cor.

[1] SB, II, p. 707.

15:7), and hence Paul recognized him as an apostle (Gal. 1:19). It seems probable that from an early stage he was one of the leaders in the church, and at some point he took Peter's place as the recognized leader. The present passage need not express more than that he was Peter's deputy at this stage. We do not know how it was that James came to occupy this position rather than one of the twelve apostles. One possibility is that he himself was one of the Twelve, and is to be identified with James, the son of Alphaeus (in which case he was Jesus' cousin rather than his brother). It is more probable that his kinship with Jesus and his natural gifts of leadership combined to establish his position in the church. As for the apostles, it is likely that they had gone into hiding in view of what had happened to James, the son of Zebedee, and Peter; James himself was probably also in hiding. The *brethren* can simply mean the other members of the church, but it is just possible that the word has here the technical sense of the leaders in the church.[1] As for Peter, the text may imply merely that he went into hiding until it was safe for him to return to Jerusalem (*i.e.* after the death of Herod); he is again present in the church there in Galatians 2:1–10 and chapter 15, but otherwise he plays no further part in Acts. At some point he went to Antioch (Gal. 2:11–14), and this visit may have taken place at this time. Suggestions that he went to Rome at this point[2] or that the story is a pictorial representation of Peter's death and departure to heaven are quite fanciful.

18–19. The discovery of Peter's escape was not made until morning, by when Peter was safely out of harm's way. When the news was reported to Herod and he could gain no satisfactory explanation from the guards, he acted in typical ancient fashion by holding them responsible for the prisoner's escape and executing them. When his visit to Jerusalem was over, he left *Judea* (here used in the narrow sense of the area around Jerusalem) and went to *Caesarea*, the official capital town of the province. The detail is included to change the scene for the immediately ensuing episode.

20–23. The Jewish historian Josephus records how Herod celebrated games in Caesarea in honour of the Emperor, which

[1] E. E. Ellis, 'Paul and his Co-workers', *NTS* 17, 1970–71, pp. 437–452.
[2] J. Wenham, 'Did Peter go to Rome in AD 42?' *Tyn.B* 23, 1972, pp. 94–102.

were attended by the leading men of the kingdom. When Herod entered the theatre, clad in a glittering silver garment, his flatterers addressed him as a god: 'May you be propitious to us, and if we have hitherto feared you as a man, yet henceforth we agree that you are more than mortal in your being.' The king accepted their flattery. Then looking upward he saw an owl perched on a rope and took it as a symbol of ill fortune. At the same time he was seized by violent internal pains and was carried into his palace where he died after five days of illness (Jos., *Ant.* 19:343–350). It is clearly the same story which Luke tells us here. A new feature, however, is the information about Herod's quarrel with the coastal cities of *Tyre and Sidon*, free self-governing cities, that were economically dependent on Judea. We know nothing about the reason for the quarrel, and are simply told that the people sought to appease Herod through the mediation of his chamberlain. As a result they were able to obtain an audience of the king, and this must have taken place on the occasion of the festival in honour of the Emperor. The story, although unattested by Josephus, is doubtless reliable, since Luke had no conceivable motive for inventing such details which contribute nothing to his main narrative purpose.

The *appointed day* will be that for the audience of the king, and it fell on the occasion of the festival. It is not certain whether the festival took place in March (AD 44 – *i.e.* before the passover in that year, in which case Peter's escape took place nearly a year earlier at passover AD 43) on the anniversary of the founding of the city, or in August AD 44 on the occasion of the Emperor's birthday. When the public assembly was held, at which the ambassadors of the two cities would appear, Herod gave an address, and then the people cried out that he was *a god, and not* a *man*. Immediately afterwards, as both sources agree, he was struck down by illness. Luke ascribes the sudden onset to *an angel of the Lord*; here the phrase is applied to the ultimate divine origin of a natural disease, and it shows that Luke is not thinking of a visible appearance of a human or heavenly figure (contrast verses 7–11). The point is that God himself acts against those who usurp his position and claim divine honours for themselves. The cause of Herod's death is not certain. *Eaten by worms* can be taken quite literally (*cf.* 2 Macc. 9:9), although it appears to have been a stock phrase in describing the deaths of tyrants. Appendicitis leading to peritonitis would fit the symptoms described by Josephus, and with the lack of medical hygiene in the ancient world roundworms could have added to the king's sufferings. Neil (p. 152) suggests a cyst produced by a tapeworm.

24. At intervals Luke has commented briefly on the progress of the church (6:7; 9:31), and he now does so once again, to demonstrate that despite the attacks on the church from outside, *the word of God* continued to spread (for the language see 6:7). This was more important than the fact that the persecutor of the church suffered retribution for his deeds. The work of God went on despite the death of James and the departure of Peter.

25. The final verse in the chapter should perhaps be regarded as the beginning of the next section, but it can also be seen as rounding off the story of events in Jerusalem and making the necessary change of scene for the next part of the story. It mentions briefly how Barnabas and Paul performed the service for which they had come to Jerusalem (11:29) and then returned to Antioch. The only link with the intervening story is the mention of *John Mark*, who accompanied them back to Antioch; he was, as we learn incidentally from Colossians 4:10, the cousin of Barnabas, and this relationship explains why he now went to Antioch and became the companion of Barnabas and Paul in their missionary work.[1]

V. THE MISSION TO ASIA MINOR AND ITS AFTERMATH (13:1 – 15:35)

a. The call to mission (13:1–3)

Acts 13–14 contains the account of the first period of missionary activity carried on by Paul along with Barnabas. Of all

---

[1] A puzzling feature of the verse is that, while most MSS say that Barnabas and Paul returned *from* Jerusalem (so RSV), the oldest and best MSS (including codices Vaticanus and Sinaiticus) have the phrase *to* Jerusalem. This phrase is so strange in its context that it has strong claims to being the best-attested reading, but it surely produces an impossible sense if we take the verse to mean that Barnabas and Paul returned *to* Jerusalem. Either there is a primitive error in the text (rightly amended in the later MSS) or we must translate 'Barnabas and Saul returned, having fulfilled their mission at Jerusalem' (with Gk. *eis* equivalent to *en* and an unusual word-order). See Metzger, pp. 398–400.

Paul's missionary work this period has the best claim to being called a 'missionary journey', as is customary on Bible maps. The later periods were much more devoted to extended activity in significant key cities of the ancient world, and we gain a false picture of Paul's strategy if we think of him as rushing rapidly on missionary *journeys* from one place to the next, leaving small groups of half-taught converts behind him; it was his general policy to remain in one place until he had established the firm foundation of a Christian community, or until he was forced to move by circumstances beyond his control. The same basic pattern was in fact followed on this missionary *campaign* in Asia Minor (*cf.* 13:50; 14:3, 5–7, 20).

The importance of the present narrative is that it describes the first piece of planned 'overseas mission' carried out by representatives of a particular church, rather than by solitary individuals, and begun by a deliberate church decision, inspired by the Spirit, rather than somewhat more causally as a result of persecution.[1] Luke thus describes in solemn detail how the missionaries were appointed at a church meeting under the guidance of the Spirit. He is well aware that he is describing a crucial event in the history of the church.

1. The narrative begins by describing how the church in Antioch was served by a group of prophets and teachers. Five names are listed. First comes *Barnabas*, who as a Christian leader from Jerusalem may have been regarded as the most important of the group, or perhaps the Christian of longest standing (for the way in which the first converts might become the leaders of the church see 1 Cor. 16:15f.). Secondly, there is *Symeon*, a man bearing a Jewish name and therefore in all probability a Jew; his other name, *Niger*, is Latin and means 'dark-complexioned'; in view of the way in which he is mentioned just before a Cyrenian, it has been thought that he too came from Cyrene and is to be identified with the Simon who carried the cross of Jesus (Lk. 23:26), but, if so, it is surprising that Luke has spelled the two names differently from each other. Thirdly, there is *Lucius* from *Cyrene*, who was presumably one of the founder-members of the church (11:20). It has been conjectured that Lucius should be identified with Luke himself, an identification that was made by at least one early

[1] E. Best, 'Acts 13:1–3', *JTS* 11, 1960, pp. 344–348.

214

scribe, but it is improbable.[1] Fourthly, we have *Manaen*, a Jewish name meaning 'comforter' who was an associate of *Herod* Antipas; the term *member of the court* could refer to a boy of the same age brought up as a companion of a prince or, more generally, to a courtier or friend of a ruler; whatever the precise meaning, it could be that Manaen was Luke's source of information for material about Herod Antipas which is not found in the other Gospels. Finally, there is Paul, here given his Jewish name of *Saul*, as has been Luke's usual practice up to this point (see verse 9 note). Luke does not tell us which of these men were *prophets* and which were *teachers*. The probability is that the dividing line was not very clear, both groups being involved in exposition of the significant of the prophetic Scriptures and in exhortation; the prophets, however, had also the gift of charismatic utterance. We may contrast the teaching activity of Barnabas and Paul (11:26) with the inspired messages of prophets like Agabus (11:27f.).

2. It is not clear whether the subject of the sentence is the prophets and teachers or includes the members of the church in general. Since the list of names in verse 1 is primarily meant to show who was available for missionary service, and since changes of subject are not uncommon in Greek, it is preferable to assume that Luke is thinking of an activity involving the members of the church generally; this will fit in with the fact that elsewhere similar decisions are made by the church as a whole (1:15, 6:2, 5; *cf.* 14:27; 15:22). On this view the members of the church were assembled together to serve the Lord and fast. The verb *worshipping* means serving God, and is a Greek word originally used of doing public service at one's own expense and then applied in the Greek Old Testament to the cultic service of the priests and Levites in the temple (*cf.* Lk. 1:23). The thought here is that the church serves God when it gathers together, and, since elsewhere *fasting* is associated with prayer, it is likely that prayer is regarded as the 'cultic' activity of the church. Fasting, or voluntary abstinence from food, is also associated with prayer in 14:23 in the appointment of local church leaders, but otherwise is not attested as a practice of the early church (see, however, 2 Cor. 6:5; 11:27 for Paul's own personal experience). Here it marks

---

[1] Although 'Luke' is a Greek form for the Latin name 'Lucius', it was a very common name.

out the special significance of the occasion, when the church felt it necessary to lay aside even the demands of hunger in order to concentrate on serving God and receiving his guidance.

To a church waiting on the Lord his word now came. The *Spirit* is named as the author, since it is he who appoints leaders in the church (20:28) and guides the church at crucial points. But the Spirit speaks through human agencies (4:25), and it must be assumed that one of the prophets in the church received the message which called the church to put aside two of its leaders for a task to which God was calling them. It has often been noted how the church had to be willing to give up the service of two of its most outstanding teachers for the sake of God's work elsewhere. The nature of the task[1] is not revealed at this point, possibly for literary effect, but it is clear that missionary work must have been indicated; whether the missionaries were given directions for their route at this point or later (13:4) is not stated. Luke's main point is to emphasize that mission is inaugurated by God himself.

3. The departure of the missionaries was preceded by a further session of prayer and fasting, this time no doubt a period of intercession for their future work. Then the missionaries were commissioned by the church by the *laying on of hands* (6:6), an act of blessing in which the church associated itself with them and commended them to the grace of God (14:26), and not an ordination to life-time service, still less an appointment to the apostolate.

b. Evangelism in Cyprus (13:4–12)

There had already been some evangelism in Cyprus (11:19) and some members of the church in Antioch had family ties with the island, including Barnabas himself (4:36). From a human point of view, therefore, it was natural for the mission to start there, but the missionaries felt guided by the Spirit to do so. A pattern of establishing contact with the synagogues was followed, but the main interest of the story is centred on Paul's audience with the Roman governor and his confrontation with a magician who opposed the preaching of the gospel. The story shows how there was sympathetic interest in the gospel from the Roman governing class, and also how the

---

[1] For this use of *work* to indicate evangelism and mission *cf.* 14:26; 15:38.

power of the gospel was superior to that of pagan magic. At the same time Luke shows how Paul came to assume the leading position in the mission; whatever Barnabas's excellences in other ways (especially as a Christian teacher), he had to recognize that Paul possessed in an unusual measure the gifts of an evangelist.

The general historicity of the whole missionary campaign has been questioned by some radical critics; others hold that it really took place, but after the events reported in Acts 15 (Haenchen, pp. 438f.) The former of these views can be cheerfully dismissed from consideration, since not even Haenchen is prepared to go that far, and it is completely improbable that Luke invented the details – including the unimportant details – of the story (Hanson, p. 118). For the latter view see 15:1–35 introduction.

So far as the present incident is concerned, the general background is perfectly plausible. Some doubts have been expressed about the conversion of the Roman governor, but there is no compelling reason for disbelieving the story. The story of Paul's miraculous powers is also calculated to arouse scepticism, but it would be quite credible in a first-century context, in which Christians believed that their faith was superior to the powers of darkness and evil.

4–5. Luke emphasizes once again that it was under the direction of the Spirit that the missionaries set out, and were brought into a situation of conflict with the force of evil (verse 9); are we intended to see a parallel with the equipping of Jesus with the Spirit at the outset of his ministry followed by his conflict with Satan (Lk. 3:22; 4:1f., 14)? Since Antioch lay some 16 miles (26 km) from the sea, Barnabas and Paul set off from the nearest seaport, *Seleucia*. It was a journey of about 60 miles (96 km) to Cyprus, a large island about 140 miles (223 km) long and 60 miles (96 km) broad. It was important economically for its copper mines and had been annexed by the Romans; by this time it had become a senatorial province. It had been colonized earlier by settlers from Greece, and *Salamis* on the east coast was a Greek city. There was also a substantial Jewish population, as is indicated by the comment that there was more than one synagogue. Barnabas and Paul began their mission work by preaching *in the synagogues*; this was a pattern that was to be frequently followed (13:14, 46; 14:1, 16:13 (see note); 17:1, 10; 18:4, 19; 19:8; 28:17). Not only did it follow the principle of 'to the Jew first' but also it made practical sense in establishing a point of contact for the gospel.[1]

Whether the preaching was effective in this case is something we are not told. Instead, we have the comment that *John* was assisting them. The reference is to John Mark (12:12; 13:13; 15:37–39). It comes in very oddly at this point. Clearly Luke has included it to explain the later references to his departure from the group, but the problem is why he did not do so at the outset of the story. Is there a hint that John was not sent by the Spirit, and that this was why he failed to finish the course? Or does Luke avoid saying directly that he had been sent by the Spirit in order to avoid the suggestion that later he withstood the guidance of the Spirit? But John was merely a helper, and not in the same group as the prophets and teachers listed in 13:1–3, and hence it was not necessary to name him there. Further, it was Paul's practice to take young men with him as his assistants in the work, and there is no good reason to doubt that this particular appointment was made in good faith. Since Barnabas belonged to Cyprus, and later took John back there with him, it is possible that John himself had family links with the island and that this was why he was chosen to accompany the other missionaries. It may be this family link with Cyprus that led to his being named at this particular point in the story. John's role as a servant is uncertain. Commentators differ as to whether he was to help the missionaries on a practical level (*cf.* the use of the corresponding verb in 20:34; 24:23) or in the work of the gospel, but both could be meant; it is unlikely that Luke here means to designate him as a 'servant of the word' (Lk. 1:2).

6–12. From Salamis the missionaries moved westwards to the seat of government, *Paphos.* Here the interest centres on Paul's meeting with a Jew who made his living by practising magic and claiming to be a *prophet.* He was probably the same kind of person as Sceva, who claimed to be a Jewish high priest in Ephesus (19:14). Although Jews were forbidden to practise magic, it is clear that this law was not universally

---

[1] This pattern has been dismissed as totally unhistorical by Schmithals, pp. 46–62, but his view (based on a dubious interpretation of Gal. 2:7–10) falls foul of Paul's perfectly clear statement in 1 Cor. 9:20f.

observed. Luke would have regarded the present culprit as a practitioner of what we now call black magic rather than as a conjuror. His name, *Bar-Jesus*, means 'son of Joshua'. Later he is called *Elymas*, which according to Luke means 'magician'.[1] The use of two names has been regarded as an indication that two sources have been used here, but there are no other signs of this in the story, and many Jews had more than one name; Luke saw significance in *both* of the names.

The magician formed part of the retinue of the Roman governor of the island, who is correctly titled as a *proconsul*. Earlier identifications of *Sergius Paulus*, such as that he is the same person as L. Sergius Paullus who was a curator of the River Tiber, are weakly based; but it is possible that he is the Q. Sergius (Paulus) mentioned in a recently discovered inscription from Cyprus.[2] He is described as a man of understanding, the implication being that he was not taken in by the magician but was open to hearing the gospel. So he called for the missionaries to visit him; it can be assumed that he had received some news of their doings. The magician, fearful lest he should lose his position, did his best to oppose what they said. His open opposition to the gospel led Paul to take strong action against him. He addressed him not as a 'son of Jesus' but as a *son of the devil*, a man full of trickery and evil, who was thwarting the ways of God (for the phraseology see Je. 5:27; Gn. 32:11; Pr. 10:9; Hos. 14:10), and pronounced the judgment of God upon him in the form of an attack of blindness. The character of the judgment suggests an analogy with what had earlier happened to Paul himself, and the phrase *for a time* suggests that it was meant to be merely temporary; hence the judgment was probably meant to be a warning and intended to act as a stimulus to conversion, although we do not know whether it achieved this result. The unfortunate magician was afflicted with a mistiness of the eyes and his consequent blindness was evident from his need of somebody *to lead him by the hand*. The superior power associated with the *teaching* of the Christian missionaries astounded the proconsul to such an extent that he was prepared to believe their mes-

[1] Elymas has been explained as a Semitic name, akin to Arabic *'alīm*, 'wise', or perhaps derived from an Aramaic form *hālōmā*; see L. Yaure, 'Elymas – Nehelamite – Pethor', *JBL* 79, 1960, pp. 297–314.
[2] B. van Elderen, 'Some Archaeological Observations on Paul's First Missionary Journey', *AHG*, pp. 151–161.

sage. The phraseology suggests conversion; it is strange, however, that we are not told any more of the story than this, and this may suggest that the conversion was not a lasting one. Luke tells the story more to show how Paul overcame the power of magic than to indicate how a Roman governor was converted.

In the course of the story two significant incidental features occur. First, Paul occupies the leading role, a fact which is recognized by the way in which the *Barnabas and Saul* of verse 7 is replaced by 'Paul and his company' in the first verse of the next section (verse 13). Secondly, having called him Saul up to this point, for the first time Luke refers to him as *Saul, who is also called Paul* (verse 9) and thereafter consistently calls him Paul. As a Roman citizen Paul would have borne three names, the third of which (his *cognomen*) would have been the Latin 'Paullus'; what his first two names were, we do not know. A Roman citizen could have a fourth name (his *signum* or *supernomen*) given at birth and used as a familiar name; in Paul's case this could have been his Jewish name 'Saul', which he would use in a Jewish environment. The change in name here to the form which Paul uses in his letters corresponds to his entry into a mainly Gentile environment. Luke observes the coincidence that the governor of Cyprus was also called Paul, but there cannot have been any connection between this fact and Paul's own name which he had received at birth.

c. Evangelism in the synagogue at Pisidian Antioch (13:13–52)

We are not told why the missionaries departed from Cyprus after what cannot have been a very long stay; there is no specific reference to spiritual guidance at any point of this missionary tour. It may seem surprising that Paul and his companions then made their way to the somewhat out-of-the way towns in the centre of Asia Minor. In fact they lay on an important line of communication. The first centre of activity was Antioch of Pisidia, the leading town in the area, where Paul followed his practice of seeking a point of contact for the gospel in the synagogue. A friendly welcome gave him the opportunity to speak on the sabbath.

The address which Luke records is of considerable length and can be summed up as a historical survey designed to root the coming of Jesus in the kingly succession of Judah and to show that the career of Jesus was in fulfilment of prophecy: it culminates in an appeal to the hearers not to repeat the error of the people of Jerusalem who had rejected Jesus. The general pattern is similar to that of the other speeches in the first part of Acts, the same basic elements being present. To a certain extent the speech is complementary to that of Stephen; the earlier speech rehearses the history of Israel from the patriarchs to Solomon, with particular emphasis on the first part, while the present speech concentrates on the period of the monarchy and culminates in the presentation of Jesus which is missing from Stephen's speech. This careful avoidance of repetition between the two speeches in their broad sweep of Old Testament history may be due to Luke's literary skill, but it is also dictated by the entirely different purposes of the speeches given by two different speakers, the former dealing with Moses and Jesus in a warning manner, while the latter deals with David and Jesus in terms of promise. The speech is based on the Old Testament and shows similarities to Jewish methods of interpretation. It may well be a midrash on 2 Samuel 7:6–16, *i.e.* an exposition of the passage in order to bring out its continuing significance by applying it to a contemporary event, the resurrection of Jesus, and by interpreting it in the light of other scriptures.[1]

Paul's speech was effective in convincing both Jews and proselytes in the synagogue, so much so that great crowds came together the following week to hear more. But other Jews were envious of Paul's success and opposed the message. Their rejection led Paul to pronounce openly the principle that he would now go to the Gentiles, which he did with significant results. Further opposition forced him to leave an infant church before he had time to consolidate his work.

The story is related at length to give a typical and significant example of Paul's experiences. But there is no need to claim

---

[1] M. Dumais, *Le langage de l'évangélisation. L'annonce missionaire en milieu juif (Acts 13, 16–41)* (Tournai/Montreal, 1976). J. W. Bowker, 'Speeches in Acts: A Study in Proem and Yelammedenu Form', *NTS* 14, 1967-68, 96–111, makes the more elaborate suggestion that Paul is following the typical pattern of a synagogue sermon based on a reading from the law (Dt. 4:25–46 is suggested), a reading from the prophets (2 Sa. 7:6–16 is suggested), and an introductory text (1 Sa. 13:14): the text formed a bridge between the two readings, and the sermon was meant to elucidate the text. In this case the sermon began unusually with an introduction (verses 16–21) before the text. *Cf.* Wilckens, pp. 232f.

that it is an 'ideal' scene, which never concretely happened, and to accuse scholars who take the narrative seriously of being naive. Although the content of the sermon may not have been repeated word for word, yet Paul and his companions did report on their experiences to the church at Antioch in Syria (14:27).

13–15. Luke quickly covers the voyage of the missionaries from *Paphos* to the coast of Asia Minor and the subsequent journey from the coast to the interior (about 100 miles, 160 km). *Pamphylia* was a coastal district which had been a separate Roman province from 25 BC to AD 43 and had then been united with Lycia. The missionaries probably landed at Attalia (*cf.* 14:25) and made their way some 12 miles (19 km) inland to *Perga*, a Greek city with an important temple to Artemis and a large theatre and stadium. Nothing is said about any missionary activity here. Luke merely records how John Mark left the party at this juncture. Did he resent the fact that Paul was now the leader, while his cousin Barnabas was relegated to second place? Or did he not want to go further than Cyprus? Or did he lose courage? Or was there some other reason? We simply are not told, but it is clear from 15:38 that Paul regarded his defection as a serious matter, while Barnabas was prepared to make allowances for him.

The remaining missionaries went on to *Antioch*. Seleucus I founded several cities and named them all in honour of his father Antiochus (*cf.* 11:19 note). This particular town had received the status of a Roman colony and was the leading city in the area known as Phrygia Galatica. It was not in fact in the district of Pisidia, but since there was yet another Antioch in Phrygia on the River Maeander this one was known as 'Antioch towards Pisidia'. Here the missionaries went to the synagogue and took their seats in the congregation. Luke sets the scene by providing what is, along with Luke 4:16–21, the earliest known description of the essential features in a synagogue service. After the opening prayers (not mentioned here) the central act was a reading from *the law, i.e.* the first five books of the Old Testament; this was followed by a lesson from *the prophets*, and then, if there was a competent person present, a sermon related to the lessons. There was usually one 'ruler' in charge of the arrangements, but here there were at least two (a possibility that seems to be attested in a Jewish inscription).[1] They invited Paul to speak, perhaps because they had already had some contact with him before the service.

16–20. Paul responded to the invitation. He followed what was probably the practice in Hellenistic synagogues by standing to teach,[2] and he emphasized his message with gestures. His opening words indicate that the audience consisted of Jews and God-fearing Gentiles (10:2 note). He plunged straight into a survey of Jewish history, the purpose of which was to show that Israel was chosen by God and provided by him with a land and with rulers; this succession of rulers had come to a climax in the sending of Jesus as a Saviour. The account begins with the divine choice of the patriarchs and passes swiftly to the growth of their descendants to form a mighty nation during their stay in Egypt. The verb *made . . . great* refers to the increase in numbers and strength of the people (Ex. 1:7, 9). Then Paul refers quickly to the way in which God exercised his power to bring the people out of Egypt (for the phraseology see Ex. 6:1, 6; Ps. 136:11f.), and then brought them through the wilderness. The Greek verb *bore with* differs by one letter from the variant reading 'cared for' (RSV mg.), and both are possible translations of the underlying Hebrew verb (Dt. 1:31). Although the former is the better attested reading here, the latter gives the better sense; it has been suggested that the former reading represents a Hellenistic spelling of the latter.[3] Next, God cleared the way for the people into Canaan by driving out seven nations who then occupied the land (Dt. 7:1). The period of *four hundred and fifty years* is difficult to interpret.[4] It seems best to take it of the sojourn in Egypt (400 years), the wilderness wanderings (40 years, verse 18), and the occupation of the land (10 years). The needs of the people were cared for by the provision of the judges, the last of whom was *Samuel*.

21–22. When the people *asked for a king* (1 Sa. 8:6), God supplied their request and gave them *Saul*. The *forty years*

---

[1] W. Schrage, *TNDT*, VII, pp. 844–847, especially pp. 846f., citing *Corpus Inscriptionum Iudaicarum*, II, p. 803.

[2] Philo, *Spec. Leg.* 2:62.

[3] See also R. P. Gordon, 'Targumic Parallels to Acts XIII 18 and Didache XIV 3', *Nov.T* 16, 1974, pp. 285–9.

[4] One widespread form of the text shifted the expression to verse 20 so that it refers specifically to the period of the judges, but this would conflict with 1 Ki. 6:1.

assigned to his reign are probably drawn from Jewish tradition (*cf.* Jos., *Ant.* 6:378); the text of 1 Samuel 13:1, which is corrupt, gives the impossible figure of two years. But Saul was *removed* from his rule as being unfit for his task, and was replaced by David. David had divine credentials for his task, which Paul proceeds to quote. The citation is a composite one. *I have found (in) David* comes from Psalm 89:21, while *a man after my heart* comes from 1 Samuel 13:14. *Who will do all my will* is similar in wording to Isaiah 44:28 (where the phrase is used of Cyrus), but it has been observed that the wording could be a translation of the targum to Psalm 89 which paraphrases 'a man after my heart' by 'a man doing my will' (Wilcox, pp. 21–24). If this observation is correct, it would show that this part of the speech could have had an Aramaic origin. The point of the quotation is to establish the place of David as the ideal king of Israel.

23–25. It was thus from David's descendants that God could be expected to fulfil his promises to the people. The promises in question are those made to David that he would have offspring who would rule after him for ever (2 Sa. 7:12–16; *cf.* 22:51; Pss. 89:29, 36f.; 132:11f., 17). This offspring is identified as *Jesus*, and his function is described as that of a *Saviour*. Here Paul's language echoes that of Peter (5:31). The term was one applied in the Old Testament to the judges (Jdg. 3:9, 15), but more especially to God (*e.g.* Ps. 27:1 LXX), and it may be significant that the related noun 'salvation' is used in Psalm 89:26.

At this point there comes a reference to the work of *John* the Baptist which appears to be something of a digression. Paul states that the appearance of Jesus was preceded by that of John who proclaimed *a baptism of repentance* and who disclaimed that he himself was the person for whom the Jews were looking; rather he was the humble servant of the One who was to come (Lk. 3:15f., Jn. 1:20, 26f.). The reference may be explained by the fact that the ministry of John was the beginning of the new era (10:37); John is cited as a witness to Jesus, but the main purpose appears to be to confirm that John himself was not the coming one. He was finishing his task when Jesus appeared and was content to take a humble role in relation to him. It may be that there were some people who honoured John too highly, and that it was necessary to remind them that John had disclaimed any honour (*cf.* Jn. 1:8; 3:28–30).

26–29. The speech now makes a fresh beginning, marked by a repetition of the opening address to the hearers with slight variations in wording. The point is that the message about the Saviour (*cf.* verse 23) is directed to them and demands their attention. Paul regards his hearers as in a separate category from those who had already heard of Jesus and rejected him, and the rest of the speech is in effect an appeal to them not to throw away their opportunity of *salvation* by following the example of the people *in Jerusalem and their rulers* who had rejected Jesus and condemned him to death. They had done so because they failed to recognize who Jesus was and to appreciate the significance of the prophetic witness of the Old Testament which they regularly heard as it was read to them in the synagogues; in fact they themselves had unwittingly *fulfilled* those very prophecies by rejecting Jesus (*e.g.* Ps. 118:22; Is. 53:3). True, they had no real grounds for condemning Jesus to death in the way they did, but they nevertheless handed him over to the Roman governor to be executed. The part played by the Romans in condemning and executing Jesus is almost passed over in silence here, as Paul emphasizes how the Jews contributed to the fulfilment of all that had been prophesied concerning the death of Jesus, and then took his body down and buried it (Lk. 23:53).

30–37. Over against the hostile action of men (which was nevertheless part of the divine plan) is now placed the action of God himself in raising Jesus from the dead (*cf.* 2:24; 3:15; 4:10; 5:30; 10:40), and this is immediately followed by a reference to the repeated appearances of the risen Jesus to his followers. It is stressed that these followers were the people who had been with Jesus throughout his ministry; they had come up *from Galilee to Jerusalem* with him before the crucifixion, and they were thus qualified to be *witnesses to the people* (10:39, 41). Paul does not mention his own experience of the risen Jesus at this point; the reason may be that he is thinking primarily of the witness of the apostles to the Jews in Palestine (*the people*, verse 31), whereas he himself was a witness to the Gentiles. Rather his role is that of an evangelist, one who brings the good news to the Jews of the Dispersion and the God-fearers that the promises of God made to the ancestors of the Jewish nation have now been fulfilled by God through his action in raising Jesus from the dead. The promises are those referred to in verse 23, and Paul now proceeds to cite them, quoting three texts which found their fulfilment in Jesus. When Paul refers to *us their children*,[1] he is presumably thinking primarily of the Jews in his audience, but in view of the emphasis in verses 16 and 26 on the God-fearers as part of the audience, it is difficult to avoid the impression that they are regarded as the spiritual offspring of the fathers (*cf*. Rom. 4:11f.).

The first of the three texts cited is from Psalm 2:7, a psalm that describes the opposition of the nations and their rulers to the Lord's anointed one, *i.e.* the ruler of his people. The ruler tells what God decreed and said to him: 'You are my son, today I have begotten you.' In its context this refers to the way in which God legitimates the king as his son, in the same way as a father would accept his wife's child as being really his son and so promise him loving care and protection; the idea of begetting is purely metaphorical. The Psalm was recognized as applying supremely to the Messiah (*Psalms of Solomon* 17:26), and early Christians applied it to Jesus (4:25f.; Lk. 3:22; Heb. 1:5, 5:5). The divine utterance at the baptism of Jesus probably reflects these words. But it was the raising of Jesus from the dead which was regarded as his being brought to new life by the power of God, and hence it was possible to see the 'begetting' in the Psalm as being spiritually fulfilled in the resurrection. It is often argued that it was the use of verses such as this one which enabled the church to regard Jesus as being adopted by God as his Son at the resurrection (and that only at a later stage did the church come to believe that Jesus was already God's Son during his earthly life). But it is highly unlikely that the early church saw the resurrection as a begetting and then used this idea to argue that Jesus became God's Son at the resurrection. On the contrary, it was because he was known to be God's Son that Psalm 2 could be applied to him and then seen as foreshadowing the resurrection. The thought is close to that in 2 Samuel 7:14–16 and may imply the universal and eternal reign of the One whom God thus honours as his Son.[2]

[1] The text is confused, the best MSS having 'to our children', and there may be a primitive corruption.

[2] We have assumed that the verb 'raise' in verse 33 applies to the resurrec-

The second and third quotations are closely linked. Paul is concerned in verse 34 with the fact that when God raised Jesus from the dead he entered upon a new existence which would not lead back to death and the consequent corruption of his body. The word *corruption* is taken from Psalm 16:10, which has already been cited to similar effect in 2:25–28 in Peter's sermon at Pentecost, and is now cited again as the third of Paul's quotations (verse 35): verses 36f. then make the point that clearly Psalm 16 cannot be applied to David himself; he served the will of God *in his own generation*,[1] and died an ordinary death which led to corruption, but Jesus' body did not suffer corruption after death.[2]

But we have passed over verse 34b which contains the second quotation, taken from Isaiah 55:3. Here the prophet promises to God's needy people, 'I will make with you an eternal covenant, the sure holy things of David' (LXX), *i.e.* 'the sure manifestations of God's grace (promised to) David'. Paul's quotation differs from the LXX by using the verb *give* instead of 'make' and omitting the reference to the covenant. The use of 'give' may be related to the use of the same verb in verse 35 (RSV *let*, literally 'give') and a further similarity between the two texts which is not immediately obvious in the English translation is that 'holy things' and 'Holy One' are both translations of the same Greek word.[3] The combination of the two texts may be due to this verbal link. What, then, is the point of the quotation? (1) Verse 34 may be seen as conveying to God's people (*you*, plural) the fulfilment of the promises that God made to David for the future. These promises would be of salvation through the Messiah expressed in forgiveness and the like. But it is hard to see the link with verse 35 in this case. (2) Verse 34 is a promise of the permanent dominion of the Messiah (*cf.* 2 Sa.7:16), which is possible

---

tion. Some commentators think that it refers to God's bringing Jesus on to the stage of history during his earthly ministry.

[1] Or perhaps 'on the basis of his own (natural) generation', in contrast to the Messiah who was begotten by God; K. H. Rengstorf, *TDNT*, VIII, p. 540 n. 87.

[2] It is also possible to translate: 'David served his own generation and then died according to God's will. . . '

[3] The Greek adjective *hosios* is used in Is. 55:3 to translate the plural form of Hebrew *ḥeseḏ* (RSV 'steadfast love') and in Ps. 16:10 to translate the singular form of Hebrew *ḥāsîḏ* (RSV 'godly one').

only if he lives for ever and never sees corruption (verse 35). (3) Verse 35 may be seen as defining the meaning of 'holy things' in verse 34 in terms of the Holy One who did not see corruption, so that verse 34 means 'I will restore to you the Holy One of David, the faithful one', and verses 36f. prove that the Holy One must be the Messiah, Jesus, who rose from the dead, and not David himself who suffered corruption. (4) Verse 34 refers to the divine promises, especially of preservation from death, given (not to David himself but) to the promised offspring of David, Jesus. But this view would require 'you' singular in verse 34. (5) The promise made to David in Psalm 16 has been transferred to you (Is. 55:3) and therefore cannot refer to him, but must refer to the Messiah. Of these possibilities (2) and (5) seem to offer the least difficulty.[1]

38–41. The conclusion of the argument is that Jesus, whom God raised from the dead, is the one through whom *forgiveness of sins* has become possible, and hence it is offered to the hearers. Forgiveness was an important term for the blessings offered through Jesus in the sermons of Peter (2:38; 10:43). It is less common in Paul's writings than might have been expected (Rom. 4:7; Eph. 1:7; Col. 1:14). This is because Paul preferred the idea of justification, the legal sentence of acquittal which expresses essentially the same thought, and he used this idea especially to claim that nobody could be declared to be in a right relationship with God on the basis of his attempts to keep God's law, as given to Moses (Gal. 2:16; Rom. 3:20–22). Only through believing in Jesus can a person be put in the right with God. It is precisely this idea which is expressed here by the verb *freed* (so RSV; literally 'justified', as in NIV). The passage must not be weakened to mean that Christ justifies in respect merely of those things for which the law offered no remedy; the point is that justification is not possible at all through the law. Above all, one should not miss the significance of '*every one* that believes' (10:43; Rom. 1:16; 3:22; 4:11; 10:4, 11): this offer is implicitly for Gentiles as well as Jews. Since this is God's universal way of salvation, Paul warns his hearers of the danger of despising God's offer and

---

[1] On this extremely difficult passage see especially Dupont, pp. 337–359 (view 1 above); E. Lövestam, *Son and Saviour. A Study of Acts 13:32–37* (Lund/Copenhagen, 1961' (view 2); AG p. 589 (view 5).

so fulfilling the prophecy of Habakkuk 1:5 which speaks of the danger of failing to recognize what is happening as being truly an action of God. In its original context the prophecy referred to failure to recognize the Chaldean invasion as a divine judgment; Paul applies it to the danger of failing to recognize Jesus as the Saviour sent by God.

42–43. At the conclusion of the sermon, Paul and Barnabas began to leave the synagogue, but not before a request was passed on to them that they would say more about the subject on *the next sabbath*. Many of the congregation, however, were not prepared to wait a whole week before hearing more. Once the synagogue meeting had been concluded,[1] many of the Jews and proselytes who had been present joined Paul and Barnabas, and were encouraged by them to remain faithful to *the grace of God*. This phraseology (*cf.* 11:23) suggests that these people already trusted in the grace of God, as they had come to know of it through the Old Testament, and were now being urged to continue in that basic attitude by believing in Jesus as the one through whom God's promises were being brought to fulfilment. The term *devout converts to Judaism* (literally 'worshipping proselytes') has caused difficulty to commentators who think that Luke has combined two terms, one used for proselytes and the other for 'God-fearers'. The difficulty disappears if we recognize that 'worshipping' is not being used as a technical term but as a description of the proselytes. At this stage only Jews and those fully recognized as proselytes were converted; the climax of the story, the conversion of Gentiles, followed a week later.[2] Luke's wording may perhaps be motivated by his desire to stress that it is those who truly fear God (10:2, 35) who are ready to accept the gospel.

44–47. The following sabbath the synagogue was crowded out by people from the Gentile population of the town who wished to hear the Christian message, described here as *the word of God* (4:31; 13:5, 7; *et al.*). Luke writes with pardonable exaggeration, and we should not give ourselves headaches, like some sceptical literalists, who wonder how the crowds could have been accommodated in the synagogue. The effect of the crowds, however, was to make the Jews envious of the

---

[1] It is unnecessary to take this phrase to refer to a deliberate closure of the meeting by the synagogue authorities in order to avoid a disturbance.

[2] 10:2 note; *cf.* Bruce, *Book*, p. 280; Harvey, p. 469.

missionaries; presumably their own missionary efforts had been much less successful. At the same time, they probably disagreed with the message that was being preached, and so they argued against the missionaries, and defamed (RSV *reviled*) them.[1]

It was no doubt only a section of the Jews who adopted this attitude, in view of verse 43. Nevertheless, it was plain that official Judaism, as represented by the synagogue, was rejecting the gospel. Paul and Barnabas found it necessary to speak out openly and *boldly*, declaring their intention to take the gospel to the Gentiles. They had fulfilled their duty of going 'to the Jews first'; the basis of this duty is never made absolutely clear in the New Testament, but presumably rests on the nature of Israel as the covenant people of God to whom he continued to offer his promises of salvation. Now that the Jews as a body had said No to the gospel and disqualified themselves from receiving eternal life, the missionaries were free from obligation to them and could direct their full attention to the Gentiles. But this action was not to be regarded as a kind of retaliation to the Jews' rejection of the gospel. From the beginning the missionaries had seen their task as including the Gentiles since the Old Testament had clearly stated that the task of God's Servant was to act as a light to the nations and to be a means of salvation throughout the world. This citation from Isaiah 49:6 comes from one of the passages describing the work of God's Servant who in Isaiah 44:1 is clearly identified as Israel. In Isaiah 49:5f., however, the Servant has a mission *to* Israel, and must therefore be identified as a person or group of persons within Israel. The early Christians saw the fulfilment of the prophecy in Jesus (*cf.* the citation of Is. 42:1–4 in Mt. 12:17–21, and of Is. 53:7f. in Acts 8:32–35), but the present passage asserts that the mission of the Servant is also the task of the followers of Jesus. Thus the task of Israel, which she failed to carry out, has passed to Jesus and then to his people as the new Israel; it is the task of bringing the light of revelation and salvation to all the peoples of the world (*cf.* the clear allusion to Is. 49:6 in Lk. 2:29–32).

48–52. The response of the Gentiles who heard the message

---

[1] The word *reviled* could also refer to speaking against Jesus, which to a Christian like Luke counted as blasphemy.

was immediate and wholehearted. They rejoiced at the good news and praised the word of the Lord. The latter phrase is paralleled in 2 Thessalonians 3:1 and means that glory is given to the Lord when people accept his word and believe it. Those who believed are described as those who *were ordained to eternal life*. The phrase indicates that not all the Gentiles in the town believed the gospel. It could be taken in the sense that God had predestined certain of them to believe (*cf.* 16:14; 18:10). But it could also refer to those who had already put their trust in God in accordance with the Old Testament revelation of his grace and were enrolled in his people, or perhaps it means that the Gentiles believed in virtue of the fact that God's plan of salvation included them. Whatever be the precise nuance of the words, there is no suggestion that they received eternal life independently of their own act of conscious faith. As a result of their conversion the gospel message was spread throughout the region: converts are meant to be evangelists. But the result of this was to exacerbate the feelings of the Jews against the missionaries. There were a number of upper-class *women* who worshipped at the synagogue, as was not uncommon in other cities at the time, and their influence with their husbands was obviously used by the Jews to instigate some kind of action against the missionaries as a result of which they were put under pressure to leave the town. They did not do so, however, without showing that they knew that the Jews lay behind this action and performing a symbolical action as a testimony to them. It was customary for Jews to *shake off the dust* of a pagan town *from their feet* when they returned to their own land, as a symbol of cleansing themselves from the impurity of sinners who did not worship God. For Jews to do this to their fellow Jews was tantamount to regarding the latter as pagan Gentiles. The Christians were demonstrating in a particularly vigorous manner that Jews who rejected the gospel and drove out the missionaries were no longer truly part of Israel but were no better than unbelievers (*cf.* Lk. 9:5; 10:11; Acts 18:6; 22:22f.). So the missionaries moved on to the next main town, but despite this apparent setback the group of new disciples experienced the *joy* that comes from the presence of *the Holy Spirit* with believers (Gal. 5:22; 1 Thes. 1:6).

It may seem strange that after the apparently final rejection of the Jews in this chapter Paul should continue to go into the synagogues during his subsequent missionary campaigns (14:1; 16:13; 17:1, 10, 17; 18:4, 19; 28:17). Doubtless part of the reason was, as already mentioned, the suitability of the synagogues as a base of operations among the proselytes and God-fearers. At the same time, Paul was conscious of the God-given order 'to the Jew first' (Rom. 1:16f.; 2:9f.) and an intense burden lay upon his heart for his own people (Rom. 9:1–3; 10:1). It would seem that verses 46f. apply primarily to the situation in Antioch and do not rule out subsequent missions to Jews elsewhere, but at the same time Luke uses the incident to portray the general principle that was increasingly characteristic of the church's work.

d. Conflict at Iconium (14:1–7)

Luke records quite briefly the account of Paul and Barnabas's visit to the next major town, Iconium. It followed the pattern of the visit to Antioch with evangelism begun in the synagogue and leading to opposition from some of the Jews. The opposition at first merely stimulated the missionaries to continue their work, presumably outside the synagogue, but later when the unbelieving Jews and some of the Gentiles were able to gain the support of the local rulers and planned to lynch the missionaries, they found it prudent to flee to the next towns where, nothing daunted, they continued evangelism.

The brevity of the story and the lack of concrete detail, together with the apparent break between verses 2 and 3, have led to theories of expansion of an original report or, more radically, to the view that the whole account is a Lucan invention based on little more than knowledge of the fact that the missionaries visited Iconium. Luke is said to have written up the story to provide a pause between the fuller, more colourful accounts of what happened in Antioch and Lystra, and also in order to stress various points that he considered theologically important (Haenchen, pp. 421–423). Such a sceptical verdict seems to be quite arbitrary and lacking in positive proof. It is true that there seems to be a tension between verses 2 and 3, which was smoothed out by early scribes, but this is more likely to be a sign of hasty editing of a source than of literary invention. In fact the difficulty of the text seems to arise from Luke's desire to emphasize that it was precisely because of the rise of opposition that the missionaries felt they must stay as long as possible to consolidate the infant

Christian community, and departed only when they were absolutely forced to do so.

1-3. *Iconium*, modern Konya, lay on the Roman road about 90 miles (145 km) east of Antioch in the same area of the province of Galatia (the old district of Phrygia). On arrival the missionaries again commenced their work in *the Jewish synagogue* where their preaching led to the conversion of a large number of *Jews and of Greeks*. But trouble soon arose, caused by the Jews who rejected the gospel and proceeded to look for allies among the Gentiles by slandering the missionaries to them. Their efforts at persuasion were not immediately successful, and it is not until later in the story that we hear of active measures against the missionaries being planned.

Meanwhile, Paul and Barnabas decided that in view of the hostility they must spend some time in the town, and they continued to witness boldly in dependence on the power of God. Their verbal testimony was confirmed by God who enabled them to do miraculous *signs and wonders*, just as the apostles had done in Jerusalem (5:12). The phrase *word of his grace* as a description of the gospel message recurs in 20:32 in Paul's address at Miletus (see also Lk. 4:22), and Luke's use of it here may deliberately reflect the prominence of grace in Paul's message (*cf.* 13:43; 20:24). The whole of verse 3 is reminiscent of Hebrews 2:3f. where the activity of God in confirming the message by miraculous signs is also described. Even so, however, not all were persuaded by the message.

4-7. The general populace of the town became aware of the presence of the missionaries and of the differences of opinion regarding them among the Jews. There was a division among them, but some of them sided with the missionaries who are here named as *apostles* (so also in verse 14). This is the only passage where Luke refers to Paul as an apostle, a fact which is somewhat surprising in view of the emphasis that Paul himself lays on his status as an apostle. It has been argued that Luke restricts apostleship to the Twelve as persons who had been with Jesus during his earthly ministry and then been witnesses of his resurrection (1:21-25; 10:39-42). The references here and in verse 14 are then regarded as exceptions to Luke's consistent view of the matter, perhaps due to his unthinking use of an earlier source. For Luke neither Paul nor

Barnabas was an apostle.[1] If so, the Lucan authorship of Acts becomes very doubtful. It is possible that Luke uses the word here in a very general sense to mean 'the missionaries sent out by the church at Antioch' (*cf.* 2 Cor. 8:23 RSV mg.; Phil. 2:25). More probably, however, the explanation lies in the fact that by apostles Luke thinks *primarily* of the Twelve appointed by Jesus during his earthly life (Lk. 6:13; 9:1f.; 22:28–30) with a particular mission to the Jews. But Luke was well aware of Paul's apostleship, as is seen in the present passage and in the use of the cognate verb 'to send' (Greek *apostellō*) in 22:21 and 26:16f. Thus he recognizes that there was a group of apostles, commissioned by Jesus, wider than the Twelve, and he does not deny that Paul and Barnabas belong to this group.[2]

Only when an attempt was made to assault them did Paul and Barnabas decide to depart. It came from a common grouping of *Gentiles and Jews with their rulers*; it is not clear whether this refers to Jewish rulers, or Gentile rulers, or both, but both the first and third possibilities are plausible. The situation in 13:50 thus repeated itself, and it was when the city authorities began to connive at persecution that the missionaries felt they could no longer stay. They departed from the area of Phrygia into *Lycaonia*, and made their way to *Lystra*, some 18 miles (29 km) distant, and then to *Derbe*, some 55 miles (89 km) further. And still they *preached the gospel*, despite the setback they had received.

e. Evangelism of the heathen at Lystra (14:8–20)

On all previous occasions (and most subsequent ones) the activity of the missionaries began in the synagogue among Jews or Gentiles who already had some knowledge of God. The significance of the story of what happened at Lystra is that here for the first time in Acts the Christian missionaries came to a town where there was apparently no synagogue, or at least no mention is made of it. It is true that 16:3 refers to the Jews in those parts, and we may wonder whether the Jews from Antioch and Iconium would have had any success in trying to stir up feeling against the missionaries in Lystra if there had not been a local Jewish population, but, if so, they

---

[1] 1 Cor. 9:6 strongly suggests that Paul regarded Barnabas as an apostle.

[2] See especially Wilson, pp. 113–120; also D. Müller and C. Brown, *NIDNTT* I, pp. 126–137; Bovon, pp. 379–386.

play no real part in the story. The incident thus prepares for the events in chapter 15 (*cf.* 15:3), and the emphasis lies on the response of pure heathens to the gospel. On the one hand, we have the story of a healing miracle performed on a man who heard the gospel and had faith. On the other hand, we have the superstitious response of the native people to the miracle in that they regarded the missionaries as gods in human form and wished to give them due honour. This misunderstanding provided an occasion for the very briefly reported speech of the missionaries (presumably given by Paul) in which they instructed the people in belief in the one, true God. It is only at the end of the story that the Jews appear, carrying out their earlier plan to stone the missionaries (14:5) and leaving Paul for dead. His rapid recovery is not said to be miraculous.

We have seen how Haenchen criticized the Iconium story for its lack of detail. This story with its rich colour comes equally under his historical axe (pp. 429–434). The story has been regarded as an insertion in a briefer travel narrative; in 14:6 the missionaries already reach Derbe. The various episodes in the story differ in form – a healing miracle (which has parallels with Lk. 5:18–26; Acts 3:1–10; 9:32–35, showing that Paul has the same powers as Jesus and Peter) which, it is suggested, can easily be dismissed as pious legend, and a speech, which is ascribed to the hand of Luke. Haenchen also attacks the episode at a theological level, alleging that Luke has produced a story which is meant to show how the apostles behaved and were treated like 'divine men', their sufferings being overshadowed by their divine powers. The story, he claims, is full of historical improbabilities: would the people have regarded missionaries proclaiming the true God and Jesus as being themselves identical with pagan deities? Would the healing of a lame man by wandering Jews have been sufficient to persuade the local priest to offer sacrifice to them? Luke has seen some of these difficulties and tried to hide them, *e.g.* by omitting to mention that the missionaries preached about Jesus and by putting their message about belief in the one true God after the attempt to worship the missionaries, although in fact they must have said the same things in their earlier preaching.

We have already attempted to show that the theological point of the narrative lies elsewhere. As for the historical difficulties, these can be shown to be largely imaginary. It is not necessary to assume that all the people had heard or fully comprehended the first preaching of the missionaries. Tendencies to syncretism and to worship of religious propagandists are well attested features in the ancient world, not to speak of our own time also.

8–10. *Lystra* lay 18 miles (29 km) south-south-west of Iconium; it was an insignificant village which had been made into a Roman colony in 6 BC, as part of a scheme for defence against local warlike tribes. Luke has already related that the missionaries had preached the gospel in this area (verse 7). The effect of the preaching was now seen in the way in which a lame man, presumably a beggar, whose malady had been lifelong, responded to the message by believing that he could be healed; this suggests that the message included some reference to the healing ministry of Jesus. It can be assumed that the man, like most of the other inhabitants, could understand the Greek language in which Paul spoke. When Paul saw him and recognized his faith, he responded by a command that was at the same time a divine enabling to him to jump up and begin to walk (*cf.* 3:8).

11–14. The normal result of a miracle is that it produces a response from the bystanders (*cf.* 3:9f.). This is often reported quite briefly, but here it is treated at greater length and becomes the second major episode in the story. The crowds, consisting of local people, believed that Barnabas and Paul must be gods who had come to visit them, and decided that they must be honoured. The fact that the missionaries did not recognize what was in store for them is explained by the comment that the people spoke in their own native language which the missionaries did not understand. It is as natural an event as when a crowd of Welsh-speakers might comment to themselves in their own language on something said by a visiting dignitary in English. The missionaries were identified with two of the traditional Greek gods. Paul was equated with *Hermes*, since *he was the chief speaker* and Hermes was the messenger of the gods, while the role of *Zeus*, the principal Greek god, was reserved for Barnabas. It has been argued by Haenchen (p. 432) that Hermes was the messenger of the gods, not their spokesman, but the phrase that Luke uses here, *the chief speaker*, is closely paralleled in a pagan source, and it does not seem improbable that when the two gods appeared together, Hermes would be expected to act as spokesman. A legend that Zeus and Hermes had visited this region was preserved in a Latin poem by Ovid, who gives the gods their Roman names of Jupiter and Mercury (*cf.* AV, RV): they were entertained by an aged couple, Philemon and Baucis, who were unaware of the identity of their guests. It is not surprising, therefore, that archaeological evidence of the cult of the two gods side by side dating from *c.* AD 250 has been found near Lystra; Haenchen's denial that the cult existed earlier lacks any positive evidence and flies in the face of probability. Although the temple of Zeus at Lystra has not been discovered, a similar temple *in front of the city* (*i.e.* outside the city) existed in Claudiopolis, not far away from Lystra (Bruce, *Acts*, pp. 281f.). In view of all this evidence, it seems most unlikely that the gods with whom the missionaries were identified were actually local Lycaonian gods whom Luke had described in terms of the Greek gods with whom his readers would be familiar; it is, however, possible that at some previous point the Lycaonians had syncretized their own gods with the Greek gods.

If the local people had failed to honour the gods as gods on their previous visit, they were anxious not to repeat the error. The *priest* at the local temple made arrangements to offer a sacrifice to the visitors as a mark of honour. We get an interesting glimpse of the ritual of Anatolian religion, with *oxen* being led out of the city to the temple, decorated with garlands of wool and ready to be slain and offered in sacrifice. When the apostles realized what was about to happen, they acted quickly to stop it by tearing *their garments* and taking their place among the people. There is a literary parallel to this in Judith 14:16f., where the same phraseology describes the grief of Bagoas at the murder of Holophernes by Judith. But the point here is different: the tearing of the clothes is an expression of revulsion at a blasphemous attempt to regard men as divine, and the swift rush by the apostles into the crowd was their attempt to avoid being reverenced as gods and so committing sin against the true God. It has been objected that the local priest was hardly likely to mistake a couple of wandering Jewish miracle-workers for gods, but Hanson (p. 148) has produced parallel cases which show that the motif is entirely credible. The use of the term *apostles* (14:4 note) is perhaps meant to stress the role of Barnabas and Paul as mere messengers of God.

15–18. The situation demanded some explanation, and Paul was quick to seize the opportunity to give the people instruction on the true nature of God. The very brief speech-summary which follows differs considerably from the earlier sermons in Acts delivered to Jews (or God-fearers) who already believed in Yahweh and needed to be told about the coming of Jesus as the Messiah. With a pagan audience it was necessary to begin a stage further back with the proclamation of the one true God. The speech is thus most closely related to Paul's address to the Athenian philosophers (17:22–31) which treats the same theme on a more sophisticated level, as befitted an educated and cultured audience. Luke's account of the preaching at Lystra is confined to this aspect of the message; his readers could draw on their knowledge of the earlier sermons to provide what Paul was likely to have said in addition.

The speech begins very naturally where the people are and asks them to consider what they are *doing*. They should have realized that the visitors whom they were honouring were ordinary *men*, sharing the same *nature* as themselves (*cf.* Jas. 5:17). But more than that: the message which the visitors had brought was a piece of *good news*, revealing to them the existence of the *living God*, the Creator of the universe (*cf.* 4:24; 17: 24, citing Ex. 20:11), and urging them to turn from their futile idols to this God. *These vain things* is a way of describing idols found in the Old Testament (Je. 2:5), and the verb *turn* is used of conversion in 3:19 and elsewhere. In particular, the language here is remarkably close to 1 Thessalonians 1:9, which describes how the Thessalonian Christians had 'turned to God from idols, to serve a living and true God', and shows that here we have the typical phraseology used to describe the conversion of Gentiles. What is missing from the speech here is anything corresponding to the continuation of Paul's description in 1 Thessalonians 1:10, 'and to wait for his Son from heaven, whom he raised from the dead, Jesus who delivers us from the wrath to come', or to Paul's claim that his message was simply 'Christ crucified' (1 Cor. 1:23; 2:2). This omission does not mean that Paul said nothing on this matter, but rather that Luke's purpose here is to supplement his earlier accounts of the apostolic preaching by showing what more was said when pagan Gentiles were being addressed. In fact, the rest of the speech indicates that a continuation in terms of the distinctively Christian gospel must have followed. The description of what God had done in past generations cries out for a contrasting description of what he is doing now to reveal himself in a new way. In time past he had let the Gentiles live in their own ways, the implication being that he did not regard their ignorance of himself as culpable. Nevertheless, it should have been possible for men to realize that he existed, since he had given testimony to himself in the world of nature by providing *good* things for men. The sending of *rain* and the cycle of the *seasons* which cause crops to ripen meant that men were able to feed themselves and so have hearts filled with joy. The world of nature should thus have led men to recognize the existence, power and goodness of the Creator. But this 'natural' revelation of God belonged to the past; as Paul pointed out in 17:30f., it was now supplemented by a new witness by God, the good news of which Paul speaks here in verse 15, but which is not further expounded at the moment. What Paul said was sufficient to restrain the crowds from their original intention of sacrificing to the missionaries, but only just; their superstition was deeply entrenched, and the miracle had made a strong impression on them.

19–20. The incident takes a surprising turn. The Jews who had forced Paul to leave Antioch and Iconium now turned up in Lystra, and may have joined up with local Jews (not otherwise mentioned in the story) to poison the minds of the people against the missionaries. An assault followed, carried out apparently by the Jews themselves, and they *stoned Paul* and threw his apparently dead body out of the city. The change in attitude to Paul is remarkable (*cf.* Lk. 4:22/28), but by no means incredible. If the crowds did not accept the gospel, as verse 18 implies, they could easily have been persuaded that the missionaries were in fact impostors and been content to let their fellow countrymen treat them as they thought fit. In any case the historicity of the incident is beyond question; we need not doubt that this is the event to which Paul himself referred in 2 Corinthians 11:24f., and further references to it are probably to be found in Galatians 6:17 and 2 Timothy 3:11. The story does not suggest that Paul actually died and came to life again, although some have been attracted to this inference; but Luke's manner of expression, *supposing* *that he was dead*, and his failure to provide any positive indications to the contrary, indicate that there is no question of a miraculous resurrection here. There is nothing surprising in Paul going back into the city; the punishment had been administered, and he would not be molested again, provided that he departed without delay, which he did, moving on to *Derbe*. The site of Derbe, formerly identified as Gudelisin about 60 miles (97 km) south of Konya (Iconium), has now been identified as Kerti Huyuk, about 60 miles (97 km) south-east of Konya; inscriptional evidence found on the site establishes the identity.[1]

f. The return journey to Antioch (14:21–28)

Derbe marked the easternmost extremity of the missionary tour, lying as it did on the east border of Galatia. After evangelism there the missionaries retraced their steps, despite the hostile atmosphere which they had left, in order to strengthen and encourage the groups of believers which they had established. In particular, they made sure that some kind of leadership was established in order to consolidate the groups for the future. They then returned direct by sea to Antioch, where they reported on their work to the church, the emphasis lying on the way in which God had led them into successful work among the Gentiles.

There are no real historical difficulties in this section. Its importance lies in its teaching about the way in which the church must live in a hostile environment and equip itself accordingly. The other vital point is the way in which the whole missionary tour is seen as having been directed by God who had opened up the way to the Gentiles. Although it may not have been apparent during the tour, the missionaries were now able to look back over what had happened and recognize the hand of God at work. The stage was thus set for the decisive debate regarding the place of the converted Gentiles in the church (chapter 15).

21–23. The missionary tour reached its climax with successful evangelism in Derbe; there is no mention of any further

[1] B. van Elderen, 'Some Archaeological Observations on Paul's First Missionary Journey', in *AHG*, pp. 151–161; the original discovery was reported by M. Ballance, 'The Site of Derbe: A New Inscription', *Anatolian Studies* 7, 1957, pp. 147–151.

opposition from the Jews (*cf.* the silence of 2 Tim. 3:11). So the mission moved into its second phase. Paul's regular practice was to revisit the churches which he had founded, or at least to keep in touch with them by means of his colleagues or correspondence. In the present case he and Barnabas revisited each of the churches, despite the knowledge that they were returning to cities which were hostile to them; it would presumably have been possible for them to travel on overland eastwards and so reach Antioch instead of going back the way they had come. But there were no further reported incidents. Rather the missionaries were able to encourage the young believers to continue in their belief and not fall away back into Judaism or paganism, and to give them realistic warnings, based on experience, that the way to the kingdom of God is not an easy one. The *kingdom of God* (1:3, 6; 8:12) is thought of here as the future realm to be established by God into which men may enter by death or by living until the parousia of Jesus (2 Tim. 4:18). Those who set out on this road can expect to be persecuted (1 Thes. 3:2–4; 2 Thes. 1:5; 2 Tim. 3:11–13), but they stand under the protection of the Lord into whose care they were committed by the missionaries (*cf.* 20:32; 1 Pet. 4:19).

The missionaries appointed leaders in each church, here described as *elders*. This is the first reference to elders outside the church at Jerusalem; elsewhere we hear of them in the church at Ephesus (20:17), in the church order described in the Pastoral Epistles (1 Tim. 5:17; Tit. 1:5), and in James (Jas. 5:14) and 1 Peter (1 Pet. 5:1, 5). Since there is no mention of elders in the letters of Paul prior to the Pastoral Epistles, it is often argued that the reference here is an anachronism and that Paul was not in fact concerned about local church leadership to any extent. The most, however, that we may deduce from these facts is that Luke has used a term current in his own time to refer to leaders who may possibly have been known by other designations in the earlier period. Such references as 1 Corinthians 16:15f., Philippians 1:1 and 1 Thessalonians 5:12f. show that Paul was certainly concerned with local church leadership, and it is quite unnecessary to cast doubts on Luke's narrative here. The manner of appointment, involving *prayer and fasting*, was based on that practised at Antioch (13:1–3).

24–28. The return journey took the missionaries back

241

through *Pisidia*, a wild area where there was probably little opportunity for evangelism, to *Perga* (13:13f.), where we hear of evangelism for the first time. *Attalia* was the adjacent port, and from there the missionaries sailed direct to Syria and so returned to Syrian *Antioch*. Here they reported on their work to a meeting of the whole church: it was natural and right that the church which had sent them out as missionaries should welcome them back and receive a report on their activity; the keynote of the meeting was evidently praise to God, as the reports made it clear that he had opened up the opportunity for Gentiles to respond to the gospel. To be sure, the church had evangelized Gentiles for some time past in Antioch itself, but this experience confirmed that God was calling to a wider missionary work. When we read finally that the missionaries stayed for some time with the disciples, the inference would seem to be that this stay would be merely temporary; before too long God would be calling them to fresh work. But first of all an important matter of principle had to be settled.

g. The assembly at Jerusalem (15:1–35)

Luke's account of the discussion regarding the relation of the Gentiles to the law of Moses forms the centre of Acts both structurally and theologically. Once the Christian mission had begun to evangelize Gentiles who had not previously been circumcised, the problem of the conditions of their membership of the church began to arise. It had evidently been the policy of the church at Antioch and its missionaries that such Gentiles should not be required to keep the Jewish law; although this point is passed over in silence in chapters 11–14, it is clear from 15:1f. (*cf.* Gal. 2:11–14). But this policy was unacceptable to some Jewish Christians for two reasons.

First, they found it hard to believe that Gentiles could be saved and become members of the people of God without accepting the obligations of the Jewish law. One can sympathize with their position; after all, what evidence was there that the law, which represented the will of God for his covenant people, had been repealed? This was the point which was pressed by some Jewish visitors to Antioch, and it led to lively debate on the spot and a decision by the church to send representatives to Jerusalem to discuss the matter there. Here the point was reiterated by a group of Jewish Christians who still retained the attitudes of their pre-conversion days as Pharisees.

Secondly, there was also the question of how Jewish Christians, who continued to live by the Jewish law, could have fellowship at table with Gentiles who did not observe the law and were therefore ritually unclean; not only so, but any food which they served to their Jewish friends would also be unclean. This problem would be particularly acute when the church met to 'break bread'. This issue is not mentioned explicitly at the beginning of the chapter, but from Galatians 2:11–14 it is clear that it was also a live issue, and the decision reached at Jerusalem (15:20) was intended to deal with it.

Luke's account shows that the problems were raised only by a group in the church and were not felt by everybody. The representatives from Antioch found that the news of the conversion of the Gentiles was welcomed both by the churches they visited on the way to Jerusalem and in Jerusalem itself. When it came to discussion, the two foremost leaders of the church ranged themselves alongside the men from Antioch. Peter referred to his own experience through which God had shown his readiness to accept uncircumcised Gentiles into the church on the basis of faith alone and declare them to be 'clean' in heart. His speech was confirmed by Barnabas and Paul who also reported how God had manifestly shown his approval of the Gentile mission by miraculous signs. Then James, who might have been expected to take a more conservative attitude, rose to indicate that the entry of the Gentiles into the church was in accord with God's plan revealed in prophecy, and that there was no reason to have them obey the law. Nevertheless, some kind of compromise was necessary in order not to offend the consciences of the strict Jewish Christians, and he proposed that the Gentiles be asked to refrain from food dedicated to idols, from unchastity, and from meat containing blood. The meeting agreed with this proposal and formulated a letter to send to Antioch, making it clear that no more than these minimum requirements should be imposed upon the Gentiles. This was duly done, and the church at Antioch accepted the ruling. The episode, as Luke sees it, was a triumph for the Antioch church's policy that Gentiles did not need to be circumcised.

Probably no section of Acts has aroused such controversy

as this one or led to such varied historical reconstructions of the actual situation.

(1) The traditional view of the passage is that it is Luke's account of the meeting described in Galatians 2:1–10. The same people were present, the same topic was discussed, and essentially the same principle (that Gentiles need not be circumcised) was accepted. There are, however, important differences between the accounts and some unresolved problems if we regard them as referring to the same incident. *a.* Galatians 2:2 indicates that the meeting in Jerusalem was a private one, while Acts 15:22 suggests a public one. Galatians 2 stresses the part played by Paul himself in the discussion, while in Acts he makes no significant intervention in it; this difference however, could easily be due to the varied perspectives of the two accounts. *b.* More important, Galatians 2 says nothing about the actual conditions imposed upon the Gentiles and might indeed be thought to exclude the possibility of such a happening. Indeed, it has been argued that Paul would have regarded the decision in Acts 15 as a totally unacceptable compromise, and that in fact he does not appear to have known of it.[1] *c.* Again, it is arguable that the controversy in Galatians 2:11–14, when certain men from James along with Peter and Barnabas refused to eat with the Gentiles, is incomprehensible after the events in Acts 15. *d.* Paul underlines the fact that his visit to Jerusalem in Galatians 2:1–10 was only his *second* visit after his conversion, whereas Acts 15 is a description of his *third* visit (the first is in Acts 9:26–29, which corresponds to Gal. 1:18–20; the second is in Acts 11:30; 12:25). *e.* It is odd that the letter from Jerusalem is addressed only to Antioch, Syria and Cilicia (15:23) and is not mentioned by Paul in Galatians. *f.* Finally, the account in Acts 15 is said to contain historical improbabilities, *e.g.* in the speech of James whose force depends on an argument from the LXX rather than the Hebrew Old Testament. The effect of these points has been to lead modern scholars to suggest various alternative solutions.[2]

---

[1] We can dismiss the evidence of Acts 21:25, which contains information for the reader rather than for Paul. It is more significant that Paul makes no reference to the decision in 1 Cor. 8–10 and Rom. 14 when discussing this very issue.

[2] There is an enormous literature. See K. Lake, *BC*, V, pp. 195–212;

(2) The simplest view is to equate the visit in Galatians 2:1–10 with that in Acts 11:30 (see note there for our adoption of this view). This solves the decisive problem of the number of visits paid by Paul to Jerusalem (*d.* above); the visit to Jerusalem in Acts 15 is not mentioned in Galatians, most probably because the letter was written before this event. It also accounts for the differences between Galatians 2 and Acts 15 (*a.* and *b.*); they are describing different events. Further, it explains how the incident in Galatians 2:11–14 could happen (*c.*); it is evident that the decision taken in Galatians 2:1–10 was not a final or generally accepted one, and some vacillation was possible. There remain the problems of Paul's attitude to the 'compromise' in Acts 15 (*b.*), the destination of the letter from Jerusalem (*e.*), and the historical problems in Acts 15 itself (*f.*). (See below.)

(3) Those who feel the force of these difficulties adopt some kind of solution which regards Acts 15 as to some extent unhistorical or chronologically out of place. Generally speaking, it is held that Acts 15 is meant to describe the same event as that in Galatians 2:1–10. Luke, however, has rewritten the story of what happened according to his own ideas partly because of lack of reliable information and partly in order to present his own point of view. The speeches of Peter and James, like the other speeches in Acts, are his own invention, and the decision of the meeting is an intrusion into the story, since Paul would never have accepted it. The chronological problem is solved by arguing that the account in Acts 15 is a doublet of that in Acts 11:30; 12: 25, Luke having failed to realize that the two accounts which he received were variant traditions of the same event, or that the earlier account is a fictitious one. The conditions imposed on the Gentiles are held to belong to a later occasion from that which is more reliably described in Galatians 2:1–10.

(4) An important variant of this view, presented in an impressive article by D. R. Catchpole, holds that Acts 15:1–19 and Galatians 2:1–10 both describe the visit of Acts 11:30, at which agreement on the principle of the Gentile mission was

---

Knox, pp. 40–53; Dibelius, pp. 93–101; Haenchen, pp. 455–472; Hanson, pp. 153–159; F. F. Bruce, 'Galatian Problems. 1. Autobiographical Data', *BJRL* 51, 1968–69, pp. 292–309; Wilson, pp. 178–195; D. R. Catchpole, 'Paul, James and the Apostolic Decree', *NTS* 23, 1976–77, pp. 428–444.

reached before the missionary campaign in Acts 13–14. But then the Jerusalem church took the decision recorded in Acts 15:20–29 without Paul being present, and the story in Galatians 2:11–14 represents the attempt to enforce the decision in Antioch, as a result of which Paul broke off his missionary relationship with Barnabas (15:37–39).

It will be clear that the major argument for adopting either of these last two theories rather than view (2) concerns the attitude of Paul (*b*.). Would he have accepted the conditions in Acts 15:20? And if he did, why did he not appeal to them to settle the debate reflected in 1 Corinthians 8–10? A fixed point, of which advocates of views (3) and (4) have not taken sufficient account, is that Paul himself was prepared to live as one 'under the law' when associating with strict Jews (1 Cor. 9:19f.). Would he, however, have taken the further step of accepting the same conditions for his Gentile converts? He was certainly opposed to unchastity (1 Cor. 6:9), and he recommended the Corinthians not to eat meat that was actually known to have been offered to idols in the presence of Jewish Christians (1 Cor. 10:25–28); it may well be that Romans 14:13–21 deals with the question of meat which was unacceptable to Jewish Christians because it contained blood. In short, it looks as though Paul could not have accepted Acts 15:20, although he himself preferred to argue the case from first principles and not to take the ruling simply as an ecclesiastical directive.

An important point is that rules similar to those in Acts 15:20, especially in the order given in verse 29, are also found in Leviticus 17–18, where they apply both to Jews and to resident aliens. There was thus Old Testament authority for applying such rules to Gentiles, and they appear to have been accepted by Gentile proselytes and God-fearers. The question thus becomes whether Paul would have allowed Jewish Christians to impose those Jewish regulations on Christian Gentiles. Did not Paul believe that Christ had brought the law to an end, and would he not have rejected any demands that infringed on the freedom of his converts and that perpetuated the Jew-Gentile distinction? We should not, however, overlook the facts that Paul believed that his teaching established and upheld the law (Rom. 3:31), although the law was not a means of salvation, and further that he believed that 'strong' Christians must be prepared to limit their freedom for the sake of their fellow believers. Moreover, the Jew-Gentile distinction continued to exist, just like the male-female difference, even if it was of no significance 'in Christ'. Once the basic issue had been settled, namely that Gentile converts were *not* required to be circumcised and hence to keep the whole law as a means of salvation (Gal. 5:3), it seems wholly likely that Paul could assent to some measures for the sake of peace with Jewish Christians which involved no real sacrifice of principle.

If the question of Paul's attitude to the conditions in Acts 15:20 can be successfully clarified in this manner, the way is clear to consider the remaining objections to view (2). It is strange that the letter from the assembly was addressed only to Antioch, Syria and Cilicia, although Paul is said to have taken it also to Galatia (16:4 and note). This has been used as an argument for dating the events in Acts 15 before Acts 13–14. If, however, the letter was written before Galatians, it is remarkable that Paul did not use it as conclusive evidence that circumcision was not required of his converts by the Jerusalem church. It is more likely, therefore, that the letter was sent after Acts 13–14 and the composition of Galatians, and that it was directed to the areas which had been particularly upset by the visitors from Jerusalem (15:1).

Secondly, there is the problem of alleged difficulties in Luke's account of the meeting, especially in the speech attributed to James. These will be discussed below in the exposition.

It emerges that the case for view (2), namely that Acts 15 describes a different meeting from that in Galatians 2:1–10, is not only defensible but also makes the best sense of the evidence, even if it is not completely free from difficulty. Luke rightly recognized the fundamental importance of the decision reached at the meeting. In principle the need for Gentile Christians to accept the Jewish law was firmly rejected, and it was recognized that faith in Jesus was the sole condition for the reception of salvation and entry into the people of God. Luke says this as clearly as Paul. The principle was of basic significance for the future of the early church, and it remains basic for all time; no national, racial or social requirements can ever be made conditions for salvation and membership of the church alongside the single and sole requirement of faith in Jesus Christ, through whom the grace of God is brought to sinners (15:11).

1. The peaceful coexistence of Jewish and Gentile Christians which had evidently characterized the church in Antioch was interrupted by the arrival of some Christians *from Judea* who argued that circumcision was necessary for salvation. They were not denying the possibility of Gentiles being saved, but insisting that they must be circumcised. It is tempting to link this visit with that of 'certain men from James' to Antioch described by Paul in Galatians 2:12. It is true that in Galatians 2 the issue is ostensibly that of the possibility of table-fellowship with uncircumcised Gentiles, but Paul's subsequent argument in that chapter shows that he regarded the matter at issue as one of salvation by obedience to the law. Again, there is no mention in the account in Acts of the visit of Peter to Antioch in Galatians 2:11. A further problem is that the visitors to Antioch are described in Galatians 2 as coming from James, and it would seem that Paul regarded them as representing the viewpoint of James. On the other hand, in Acts 15 it is implied that the visitors went beyond their brief (15:24), and James takes the side of Paul. This suggests that James may have undergone a change of attitude at the meeting in Jerusalem, and also that the visitors to Antioch, who were of the same outlook as the Pharisaic Christians in 15:5, claimed the support of James for an attitude that was distinctly more rigorist than he himself would have adopted.

2-3. The new requirement was opposed by *Paul and Barnabas*, whose missionary work was most particularly affected by it. If Barnabas had shillyshallied on the matter in Galatians 2:13, he now once again took the side of Paul. The matter was too important to be decided locally, especially since it was being argued that the Jerusalem church demanded circumcision. It was therefore decided to send a delegation to meet with *the apostles and the elders* who were now regarded as the leading figures in the church. The travellers took the opportunity to inform the various Christian groups which they met on their way to Jerusalem of the progress of the gospel among the Gentiles. Luke's comment that this news brought *great joy* implies that the churches in question probably took the same attitude to circumcision as Paul. These congregations would have been composed of Jewish Christians (11:19), and the indication is that they were more liberally minded than some of the Jerusalem Christians.

4-5. The arrival of the visitors at Jerusalem was marked by a church meeting at which the story of the conversion of the Gentiles was again told. The emphasis is on *all that God had done*: the conversion of the Gentiles is traced to his hand, and the implication is that what had been done with his blessing must have been done according to his will. The point was not accepted, however, by certain Christians who had been *Pharisees* in their pre-conversion days, and they stated that Gentile converts should be *circumcised* and keep the rest of the Jewish law. There is nothing surprising about former Pharisees being converted – Paul was one himself – nor about their old attitudes carrying over. We probably underestimate what a colossal step it was for dyed-in-the-wool Jewish legalists to adopt a new way of thinking. Moreover, it is possible that nationalist pressure was increasing in Judea, and that Christians were having to tread carefully to avoid being thought of as disloyal to their Jewish heritage.

6. The gathering of the apostles and elders appears to be a different meeting from that described in verses 4f., although in both cases the whole church was present (verse 12).[1] It is, however, possible that verses 4f. constitute an initial summary, intended to make clear the issues involved in the debate.

7–11. The proceedings began with a general free-for-all which Luke has not recorded, although it would have been interesting to have had a statement of the legalists' point of view and their supporting arguments. In the end, however, it was the opinion of Peter and James that mattered most. Peter's comments make one basically simple point. He appealed to experience. Referring back to the incident of Cornelius's conversion some years previously (Acts 10 – 11), he claimed that God had chosen him to make known the gospel to the *Gentiles* in order that they might *believe*. Moreover, God had shown his acceptance of the Gentiles by *giving* the same gift of the *Spirit* to them as he had given to the Jewish believers. Peter referred to God as the One who *knows the heart* of all men, and he drew the conclusion that in thus pouring out the Spirit on the Gentiles God was cleansing their hearts from sin in just the same way as he cleansed the hearts of Jews. It followed, therefore, that what mattered in God's sight was the cleansing of the heart, and that outward legal observances, such as

[1] The phrase simply means that it was an open meeting, and does not imply that every member of the church was present, as Haenchen (p. 444 n. 2) wrongly assumes.

circumcision, were a matter of indifference. Moreover, to seek to impose the law on the Gentiles was to test God, in the sense of questioning his judgment to see whether he really meant it and whether men might get away with doing something different. What the legalists were trying to do was to place the yoke of the law on the Gentiles, a yoke which the Jews themselves had never been able to bear successfully.

The point here is not the burdensomeness or oppressiveness of the law, but rather the inability of the Jews to gain salvation through it, and hence its irrelevance as far as salvation is concerned.[1] On the contrary, said Peter, Jews have to *believe* in order to be saved through the grace of God, (*cf.* GNB, 'we believe and are saved by the grace of the Lord Jesus'), in exactly the same way as Gentiles; the RSV translation *we believe that we shall be saved* (verse 11) is misleading, since Peter is talking about the kind of *faith in God* that leads to salvation (*cf.* verse 7). If both Jews and Gentiles are saved in this way, clearly obedience to the law is not required of Gentiles. Nor, may we add, is obedience to the law demanded of Jews as a means of salvation (Gal. 5:6). This deduction has seemed to some scholars to be too radical to be credible on the lips of a Jewish Christian like Peter: why, then, it is asked did the Jewish Christians not give up circumcision themselves? According to Luke many Jewish Christians continued to keep the law. Jewish Christians saw no need to remove the physical evidence of circumcision (contrast 1 Macc. 1:15), and they continued to keep the law of Moses, although the evidence of the Gospels suggests that they increasingly abandoned the Pharisaic niceties of legal observance and came to realize too that in certain aspects the Mosaic law had been superseded by the new revelation of God's will in Jesus. But not all Jewish Christians came to this realization and for many the force of habit and custom in a strictly Jewish Palestinian environment remained very strong. What Peter disputed was thus the need to obey the law in order to *be saved*; whether Jews kept it for other reasons was a secondary matter.

12. Peter's remarks silenced the opposition; doubtless they were fuller than the brief report given here. The audience was ready to listen to a report from Barnabas and Paul in which they described how their work among the Gentiles had been

---

[1] J. Nolland, 'A Fresh Look at Acts 15:10', *NTS* (forthcoming).

accompanied by miraculous *signs* given by God. The allusion is to incidents of the type referred to in 14:3 (*cf.* Heb. 2:4), which placed the missionary work of the church at Antioch on the same level as the conversion of Cornelius and which demonstrated that God's blessing rested upon it. The probative power of miracles was taken for granted, although the early church knew that it had a responsibility to test whether miraculous signs were not Satan-inspired counterfeits (*cf.* 2 Cor. 11:14; 1 Jn. 4:1 and especially 2 Thes. 2:9f.).

13–15. The decisive voice in the meeting, however, lay neither with Peter nor with the delegates from Antioch but with *James*. This may have been due partly to the position which he increasingly came to hold as the foremost leader in the church (12:17), and partly also to the fact that he was regarded as a champion of a conservative Jewish outlook. In later literature he was typified as a law-abiding Jewish Christian, and there must have been something about his earlier attitude which led to Paul's remark in Galatians 2:12. His present comments, therefore, may have represented something of a change of outlook on his part. James based his argument on the comment that what Peter said was in fulfilment of prophecy. He refers to Peter by his Jewish name of *Simeon* (*cf.* 2 Pet. 1:1) – an appropriate piece of local colour – and describes the Cornelius incident as a 'visitation' by God. This term is used of a divine intervention, whether in salvation or judgment (for the former see Lk. 1:68, 78; 7:16).[1] God's purpose was *to take out of the Gentiles a people for his name.* The paradox inherent in the contrast between 'Gentiles' (or 'nations') and 'people' is striking, since the latter term was often used of the Jews as the people of God in contrast to the Gentiles. Now it is being urged that God's people includes the Gentiles. Whereas in the Old Testament Israel was God's people and not the Gentiles (Ex. 19:5; 23:22; Dt. 7:6; 14:2; 26:18f.), now the Gentiles are included.[2] Moreover, what had

---

[1] For *episkeptomai* see L. Coenen, *NIDNTT*, I, pp. 188–192.

[2] Dupont, pp. 361–365, discusses the phrase 'a people from the nations'. He observes (1) that in the LXX Ex. 19:5 refers to God taking a people (Israel) *distinct from* the other peoples, while here he takes a people *from among* the nations; (2) that the distinction between 'people' and 'nations' is found in the LXX, but not in the MT. Hence he argues that the speech is dependent on the LXX and not on the Hebrew text. This conclusion does not necessarily

happened was in accordance with prophecy.[1] James cites only one text, but he could have been thinking of more than one passage (*e.g.* Zc. 2:11)[2] when he refers to *the prophets*. In any case, however, the reference is to 'the book of the twelve prophets', *i.e.* the scroll of the minor prophets (as in 7:42), from which the citation from Amos 9:11f. comes.

16–18. This prophecy speaks of the way in which God will *rebuild* the *fallen* tabernacle *of David*, so that other men (*sc.* than the Jews) *may seek the Lord*, namely the Gentiles over whom God's name has been named. Probably the rebuilding of the tabernacle is to be understood as a reference to the raising up of the church as the new place of divine worship which replaced the temple (*cf.* 6:13f. note). The church is then the means by which the Gentiles may come to know the Lord; the reference to God's *name* may have been understood of the use of it in connection with baptism (Jas. 2:7; elsewhere the verb is used, as in Acts 2:21, of converts calling on the name of God). The quotation, however, poses certain difficulties. The wording has been influenced by phrases from Jeremiah 12:15 (*I will return* – but one word is not enough to show that Je. 15 is being quoted consciously), and from Isaiah 45:21 (*things known from of old*). Moreover, it follows the LXX rather than the Masoretic Hebrew text, from which it differs considerably in places; Amos 9:12 has 'that they may possess the remnant of Edom and all the nations who are called by my name'. The Hebrew text thus refers to the restoration of the people of David and their conquest of Edom and other pagan nations. This creates two problems: (1), the text is not understood according to its original meaning, and (2) James, a Palestinian Jew speaking in Jerusalem, is credited with citing a text that proves the point he wants to make only in its Greek version. Does this not indicate that the quotation comes from Luke, not from James, and that it is a piece of rather artificial exegesis? The following observations can be made: (1) Parts of the same text are quoted in the Dead Sea Scrolls (CD 7:16; 4QFlor. or 12f.) and applied to the current situation of the

---

follow, since the MT has a distinction between 'a people for his own possession' and 'peoples', and this could have been in James's mind.

[1] Dupont, pp. 393–419, traces this theme throughout Acts.

[2] N. A. Dahl, ' "A People for his Name" (Acts xv. 14)', *NTS* 4, 1957–58, pp. 319–327.

Qumran sect. (2) The LXX version rests on a hypothetical Hebrew text which differs only slightly in lettering from the MT; hence the differences may be due to a revision of the Hebrew text to make it relevant to a new situation. (3) We should not rule out the possibilities that James knew and used Greek (Neil, p. 173), or that he was using the Hebrew text presupposed by the LXX. (4) It has been claimed that the MT itself would support James's point, if understood of the church gaining possession of all the nations (*cf* Bruce, *Book*, p. 310). These points show that use of the quotation by James is not impossible, and that the process of reinterpreting the text of Amos was much older than the early church. On the other hand, there is no real difficulty in supposing that Luke himself has added the quotation to bring out more clearly the way in which the progress of the church is in accordance with the Old Testament prophecies.

19–20. From this argument James drew the conclusion that the church should not go on burdening Gentiles who turned to God. But how does the conclusion follow from the argument? The point would seem to be that God is doing something new in raising up the church; it is an event of the last days, and therefore the old rules of the Jewish religion no longer apply: God is making a people out of the nations and nothing in the text suggests that they are to become Jews in order to become God's people. So there are no entrance 'conditions' to be imposed upon them. Nevertheless, James has a recommendation to make, that the Gentiles should abstain from certain things which were repulsive to Jews. Four things are mentioned in the text. First, there are *pollutions of idols*. This refers to meat offered in sacrifice to idols and then eaten in a temple feast or sold in a shop. Secondly, there was *unchastity*, variously understood as illicit sexual intercourse or as breaches of the Jewish marriage law (which forbade marriage between close relatives, Lv. 18:6–18). The third element was meat which had been killed by *strangling*, a method of slaughter which meant that the blood remained in the meat, and the fourth item was *blood* itself. These food regulations resemble those in Leviticus 17:8–13. For the problems raised by these rules see the introduction to this section.[1]

---

[1] As the RSV mg. indicates, later scribes re-worded the list of forbidden things; the omission of 'things strangled' leaves three words which can be

21. James's concluding statement is puzzling. It may be regarded as saying that since there are Jews everywhere who regularly hear the law of Moses being read in the synagogues, Christian Gentiles ought to respect their scruples, and so avoid bringing the church into disrepute with them. Alternatively, the point may be that if Christian Gentiles want to find out any more about the Jewish law, they have plenty of opportunity in the local synagogues, and there is no need for the Jerusalem church to do anything about the matter.

22–29. James's proposal met with the agreement of the entire assembly. The point is worth stressing; it means that the extremist Jews had lost the argument and agreed to follow a more liberal policy. They apparently accepted their defeat without bitterness or recrimination. It was resolved to appoint delegates to accompany Paul and Barnabas to Antioch and report the findings of the meeting. *Judas Barsabbas* is not otherwise known (unless he was related to Joseph Barsabbas, 1:23), but *Silas* (otherwise known by his Latin name, Silvanus) became an important figure in the church (15:40; 1 Thes. 1:1; 2 Cor. 1:19; 1 Pet. 5:12). They were presumably elders in the Jerusalem church. Their task would be to convey and expound orally the written message which they took to Antioch.

The letter which Luke reproduces falls into the standard pattern of a first-century letter, familiar from the letters of Paul. But whereas Paul uses a Christianized form of introductory and closing greetings, here the usual secular form is retained. The letter was sent in the name of *the apostles and elders* of the church in Jerusalem. They write with authority to their Christian brothers; at this stage the Jerusalem church still felt possessed of authority to tell other churches what to do, no doubt because it was led by apostles. The addressees were the Christians in Antioch, Syria and Cilicia. *Antioch* was the capital city of the Roman province of Syria, and until AD 72 the eastern part of *Cilicia* was administered by *Syria* (9:30 note). There is no mention of the areas evangelized by Paul and Barnabas (but see 16:4).

The main body of the letter made it clear that any persons

---

understood in a moral sense - idolatry, unchastity and murder ('blood'). This alteration was probably made by scribes who no longer understood the first-century situation; in course of time the need for the prescriptions about food acceptable to Jewish Christian consciences disappeared.

who had come from Jerusalem to Antioch and advocated circumcision for Gentile converts were in no sense official representatives of the church. The church had, therefore, decided to take the step of sending delegates who would be its official representatives to put the record straight. Before naming them, however, the letter associates them with the Antioch delegates, Barnabas and Paul, and speaks of the latter in the highest terms as men who have 'devoted themselves' (NEB) to the service of Jesus; the RSV rendering *risked their lives* is perhaps too strong. The language is intended to stress the close brotherly feeling that existed between the churches. Nevertheless, the letter carries on with a firm tone of authority. The decision reached by the church was regarded as being inspired by the Spirit, who is throughout Acts the guide of the church in its decisions and actions. This Spirit-inspired decision is couched in terms of a bare minimum of requirements to be laid on the church. That is to say, the stress is on the fact that nothing more is being required than the regulations which follow; no general submission to the Jewish law, and in particular to the rite of circumcision, is being demanded. Moreover, it is recognized that what is being asked is a *burden*, even if it is a *necessary* one for the sake of harmony between Jews and Gentiles. The requirements are those with which the reader is already familiar from verse 20 with a slight change of order.[1] The message concludes with what is in essence a courteous request to accept the proposal: *you will do well* is possibly to be taken as 'you will prosper'. The final greeting is the normal one in a Greek letter. The whole letter is carefully constructed, so much so that some critics claim that it is a literary composition by Luke himself; judged by this standard, the undeniably genuine letter of Paul to Philemon, which is also a masterpiece of careful construction, could no longer be regarded as a genuine letter.

30–35. After the delegates had received their instructions from the church they *went down to Antioch* where a meeting of the members of the church was held and the letter was handed over and *read* aloud to the assembly. Its contents were regarded as an *exhortation*, the kind of Christian message which was intended to strengthen and encourage a congregation. It was greeted with joy, for its contents showed that the decisive

---

[1] The same textual variations also occur here.

point had been accepted: the Gentiles were not to be required to be circumcised and keep the law of Moses. The actual demands made by the letter were accepted apparently without demur. Judas and Silas no doubt expounded the situation in more detail, but their ministry appears to have been of a wider scope. They were recognized as men with prophetic gifts, and they used these in preaching and teaching in the church (*cf.* 1 Cor. 14:3); their ministry was similar to that of Barnabas when he first visited the church (11:23). After the lapse of a suitable period of time, they were able to return from Antioch to Jerusalem, bearing the blessing of the church: there would have been a formal leave-taking at which they were given the blessing 'Go in peace'.

Verse 34 is omitted by a weighty group of MSS (see RSV mg.). It represents an attempt by a scribe to overcome the apparent contradiction between the departure of Silas to Jerusalem in verse 33 and his presence in Antioch in verse 40; the verse, however, stands in such blatant contradiction to verse 33 which has already recorded Silas's departure, that it is undoubtedly not genuine. Meanwhile, the work of the church at Antioch continued. Paul and Barnabas taught the church and evangelized together for the last time of which we have any record. There was, however, a group of other Christians engaged in the same work, so that the way was open for the two former missionaries to resume their travels and to know that the church would be left in good hands.

VI. PAUL'S MISSIONARY CAMPAIGN IN MACEDONIA AND ACHAIA (15:36 – 18:17)

a. Paul, Barnabas, Mark and Silas (15:36–41)

After the satisfactory settlement of the Gentile question Paul raised with Barnabas the question of a return visit to the places which they had previously evangelized. At this point the possibility of evangelism in fresh territories was not raised, although the rest of the story (16:6) suggests that the idea was probably present right from the beginning. But a difference arose between the two men over the question of whether Mark should again accompany them. Paul was against the proposal, since in his view Mark had defected from the previous campaign and presumably he felt that he might do so again.

Barnabas was willing to take the risk again. The matter developed into one of principle, so that the two colleagues decided to separate, each taking one share of the territories previously visited, and Paul set off with Silas.

The reason for the contention between Paul and Barnabas has seemed so trivial that some deeper cause has been suspected. Commentators who regard Galatians 2:1–10 as a description of the events in Acts 15 are disposed to place Barnabas's vacillation on the question of eating with Gentiles (Gal. 2:11–14) at this point and to see in this the real reason for the cleavage between him and Paul. If we date this event earlier, it could be that the memory of it still lingered, and that Paul felt uncertain of Barnabas's attitude in the tricky situation in the Galatian churches.[1]

The result of the separation was that two missionary expeditions, rather than one, set out. We hear no more of Barnabas's activities. From now on the spotlight is exclusively on Paul. Moreover, what began as a follow-up visit to areas already evangelized became under the Spirit's direction a full-scale campaign that took Paul and Silas temporarily out of Asia Minor and across the Aegean Sea into Macedonia and Greece where they established churches in Philippi, Thessalonica and Corinth.[2]

36. It is probable that the period spent by Barnabas and Paul in Antioch was over the winter months and that the coming of spring, with the consequent opening up of travel routes by land and sea, stirred Paul to fresh activity. There is no mention at this stage of the Spirit's guidance regarding the future. It is arguable that Luke would not want to link the Spirit with the quarrel that developed over the future plans of the missionaries, but (as we saw in chapters 13–14) Luke

[1] See R. Bauckham, 'Barnabas in Galatians', *JSNT* 2, 1979, pp. 61–70.
[2] In his discussion of Pauline chronology (*Dating Paul's Life*; see 11:29–30 note) R. Jewett argues that the time available between the visit of Paul to Jerusalem recorded in Acts 15 and his appearance before Gallio in Corinth (18:12–16) is too short to allow for the crowded missionary travels recorded in Acts 16–18; he concludes that the visit recorded in Acts 15 actually took place after the visit to Corinth and allows a period of five years between Paul's departure from Antioch and his appearance before Gallio. While Jewett has rightly shown that some previous commentators have not allowed sufficient time for Paul's travels, the period which he suggests is excessively long; it allows for a ministry of Paul in North Galatia, which is both unnecessary and unlikely, and it gives him a longer period in Macedonia than he needed.

clearly thinks of the Spirit as being at work even when he is not specifically mentioned. Paul's proposal was for a return visit to the areas already evangelized, and in the light of the letter to the Galatians we can understand one of the reasons that made him propose this action.

37–39. Barnabas's desire to take *Mark* with them was surely motivated by the wish to give the young man another chance to prove himself. This can be traced to their family relationship, which Luke does not mention (Col. 4:10), but above all to the sympathetic character of Barnabas, of which Luke has already given his readers good evidence (9:27). Paul, however, was concerned for the mission and was unwilling to take a doubtful partner. It is a classic example of the perpetual problem of whether to place the interests of the individual or of the work as a whole first, and there is no rule of thumb for dealing with it. In this particular case a happy solution was reached in that Paul was able to choose his own companion for his part of the work, while Barnabas was able to take Mark under his wing and help him to develop as a missionary. That Barnabas's step was justified is shown by the way in which Paul later acknowledged the worth of Mark and regarded him as a colleague (Col. 4:10; and especially 2 Tim. 4:11; *cf.* 1 Pet. 5:12). Unfortunately, however, for the moment there was a sharp quarrel between Paul and Barnabas over the matter, which Luke does not attempt to hide, although he may not have given his readers the full reason for it.

40–41. Since *Silas* had previously left Antioch, we must presume either that he had returned in the meanwhile, or that Paul sent for him to Jerusalem. He was a Roman citizen (16:21) like Paul and had connections with the church at Jerusalem; both of these facts were useful qualifications for his new role as a missionary. Otherwise we know nothing about him beyond the fact of his close and fruitful association with Paul (15:22–29 note). The two men were sent on their way with the approval and blessing of the church (*cf.* 14:26), and made their way northwards by land through Syria and on into Cilicia.

b. Paul's return to Derbe and Lystra (16:1–5)

From Syria and Cilicia Paul made his way through the mountain pass known as the Cilician Gates to the area of his first missionary campaign in South Galatia. Luke has two facts to record about this visit, the enlisting of Timothy as a missionary and the communication of the decisions of the Jerusalem council to the churches.

1–3. *Derbe and Lystra* are named in the reverse order from 14:6, since Paul approached them from the east on this occasion. Since Lystra is the last-named place, it is to be presumed that *Timothy* lived there rather than in Derbe. Paul calls him 'my beloved and faithful child in the Lord' (1 Cor. 4:17), a description which suggests that he was one of his own converts. He had evidently become a Christian on Paul's earlier visit to the town. He was the son of a Jewess who had also become a Christian; *his father was a Greek*, and the way in which he is described suggests that he was not a Christian and indeed that he was already dead (16:3b; the tense of the Greek verb favours this view). In 2 Timothy 1:5 we learn that his mother was called Eunice, and that he also had a Christian grandmother called Lois; evidently the whole family had been converted. To dismiss the evidence of 2 Timothy as Christian legend at this point (Haenchen, p. 478 n.3) is unjustified. Paul's attention was drawn to the young man by the good report which was given of him by the Christians in the neighbourhood, both in Lystra itself and in Iconium, some 18 miles (31 km) away. A good reputation of this kind was an indispensable qualification for Christian leadership (1:21; 6:3; in 1 Tim. 3:7 a good reputation among people generally is a requirement in a church leader). Paul wished to have Timothy as a companion and assistant in his missionary work; his position would presumably have been the same as that of John Mark on the earlier campaign, although there is no suggestion that he was thought of as Mark's successor. There was, however, one difficulty. As the son of a mixed marriage Timothy had an anomalous position. Jews were not supposed to marry Gentiles, but if this did happen, the children were regarded as Jewish and therefore liable to be circumcised. This had not taken place in the case of Timothy; his mother had not taken her Jewish responsibilities seriously, or perhaps her husband had refused to sanction the circumcision of the child. There is no mention of a synagogue in Lystra, and it may well be that Timothy's mother had ceased to be a practising Jew. But Paul's mission was bound to bring him into contact with Jews, and it was well known among the Jews in the area that

259

Timothy had not been circumcised. Paul therefore took the step of circumcising him.

Paul's action has caused considerable controversy. According to one school of thought he was acting in an unprincipled manner, since he regarded circumcision as a matter of indifference (Gal. 5:6) and positively forbade Gentiles to submit to a rite which could be regarded as a means of salvation by works (Gal. 5:3) (Haenchen, pp. 480–482). Here, however, the circumstances were different. Timothy ranked as a Jew, but because of his mother's mixed marriage he may have been regarded as illegitimate;[1] in any case it was absolutely essential to give him good standing in the eyes of the Jews among whom he would be working. No matter of principle was involved. If Galatians was written after this incident, it is possible that Galatians 5:11 represents an attack on Paul based on a misunderstanding of this incident; but this dating of Galatians is doubtful. Other scholars think that the whole incident is fictitious, perhaps derived from Luke's misunderstanding of the attack on Paul in Galatians 5:11. To Haenchen (p. 481) it is impossible that the Paul who wrote 1 Corinthians 7:17–20 should have acted thus; why did he not go on to make Timothy keep the whole law of Moses (Gal. 5:3)? But Haenchen has confused circumcision as a means of salvation with circumcision as a legal act to remove a stigma from Timothy, and his objections are without force.

4. As the journey continued, Paul and his companions communicated to the churches *the decisions* which had been arrived at by the apostles and elders in Jerusalem. The authority of the apostolic council was regarded as binding on churches outside Jerusalem. It is true that the decisions were addressed only to Antioch, Syria and Cilicia (15:23), and it is therefore strange that they were also promulgated in South Galatia. They also became known in the province of Asia (Rev. 2:14, 20) and later in Gaul, but Paul himself made no reference to them when dealing with the problem of food sacrificed to idols in Corinth. Since the decisions explicitly relieved Gentile Christians from taking the step of circumcision, the mention of them here underlines the fact that Timothy was being treated *as a Jew*, and that his experience was no precedent for

---

[1] Jewish opinion was divided over whether the children of a mixed marriage were legitimate or illegitimate: SB IV:1, pp. 379, 383.

what Gentiles should do. At the same time, the promulgation of the decisions would act as a further means of quelling any possible Jew-Gentile conflict in the church. There is, therefore, nothing unseemly about Paul's use of the decisions here. Although they were addressed specifically to Antioch and its immediate neighbourhood, it was appropriate to promulgate them in the wider areas evangelized from Antioch. Paul's silence about them in Corinth and elsewhere, although he could insist on acting in accord with the general practice of the churches (1 Cor. 11:16; 14:33f.), suggests that he preferred to argue a case from basic principles rather than in the first instance by an appeal to authority.

5. The effect of the missionaries' visit was to establish the churches and make them more effective in evangelism. Paul's missionary strategy of following up an evangelistic campaign with a further visit (15:36) was amply justified. The description is similar to that in 6:7 and 9:31 where the establishment of the churches in Jerusalem and Judea was noted.

c. The call to Macedonia (16:6–10)

Luke does not explain what Paul's own plans for the continuation of his missionary campaign were, or indeed whether he had any. He may have intended to make for Ephesus on the west coast of Asia. But this section makes it overwhelmingly clear that Paul's progress was directed by God in a variety of ways, so that the missionaries were led into new areas of work. The whole account is related at breath-taking speed, to convey some impression of the irresistible sweep of events that took Paul to Macedonia.

6. The journey westward from Iconium is described in a somewhat puzzling fashion as going *through the region of Phrygia and Galatia* (*cf.* 18:23).

(1) The Greek construction suggests that the phrase refers to one area, 'the Phrygian and Galatian region'.[1] The area called Phrygia lay partly in the Roman province of Asia and partly in the province of Galatia.[2] The former area was known

---

[1] The objection that 'Phrygia(n)' cannot be used as an adjective in a phrase of this kind has been shown to be baseless by C. J. Hemer, 'The adjective "Phrygia" ', *JTS* 27, 1976, pp. 122–126; *idem*, 'Phrygia: A Further Note', *JTS* 28, 1977, pp. 99–101.

[2] Asia Minor was divided into a number of ethnic regions, Phrygia, Galatia and so on, and the Roman system of provinces was superimposed on this

as 'Phrygiana Asiana', and Ramsay claimed that the latter area could have been called 'Phrygia Galatica'.[1] It was the area westward from Iconium through which Paul would pass on his way to Mysia. On this view there is no record that Paul entered the ethnic area of Galatia which was inhabited by a Celtic people.

(2) K. Lake (*BC*, V, pp. 231–237) and Haenchen (p. 483), hold (with minor variations) that Luke is referring to two areas, Phrygia and Galatia. On this view Paul went through the area where the Celtic people lived, evangelized them, and later sent the Letter to the Galatians to them. This view comes to grief on the geography of the area, as Bruce has demonstrated.[2]

It is most likely that Paul did not evangelize the area of Galatia, and that, therefore, his Letter to the Galatians was sent not to the Celtic people in the north of the province of Galatia but to the inhabitants of Iconium and the other towns in the south of the province. Whether Paul's present journey was evangelistic at all is not clear from Luke's description. In any case the missionaries were directed away from their original goal of Asia, and found themselves compelled to make their way northwards. The language fits well a journey up the east boundary of Asia towards Mysia in the north-west corner of Asia Minor. How the Holy Spirit prevented the travellers from following their original plans we do not know. Presumably some inner compulsion is meant, or perhaps a prophetic utterance by one of the party.

7. Mysia was the north-west part of the Roman province of Asia; the latter extended down the whole of the west coast of Asia Minor. To the north and east of Mysia lay Bithynia, a separate Roman province linked with Pontus further east. Once again the Spirit intervened and prevented them from

---

older set of divisions. Thus the area of Phrygia was divided between the provinces of Asia and Galatia. The area of Galatia, which had been settled by a Celtic people, became the nucleus of the larger province of Galatia which included parts of Pisidia, Lycaonia and other regions.

[1] Ramsay's case is scattered through various works; see especially W. M. Ramsay, *The Church in the Roman Empire* (London, 1893); *A Historical Commentary on St Paul's Epistle to the Galatians* (London, 1899).

[2] F. F. Bruce, 'Galatian Problems: 2. North or South Galatians?', *BJRL* 52, 1969–70, pp. 243–266, especially pp. 257–258. See further C. J. Hemer, 'Acts and Galatians Reconsidered', *Themelios* 2:3, May, 1977, pp. 81–88.

turning in this direction. The Spirit is called here uniquely *the Spirit of Jesus*, a phrase which emphasizes how Jesus himself through the Spirit was guiding the progress of the gospel; again the manner of guidance remains unclear.

8. Passing through (not *by*, as in RSV), *Mysia* the travellers came down to the Roman colony of *Troas* on the sea coast, the port for Macedonia. Alexandria Troas, to give it its proper name, was an important centre, where a Christian church was later founded (2 Cor. 2:12).[1]

9. From Troas Paul might have sailed in several directions, but the matter was settled by a *vision* in which he saw a Macedonian urging him to come over to his country and help them. Dreams were a recognized means of divine communication in ancient times (see 9:10, 12; 10:3, 17; 18:9; 22:17), and Paul and his companions immediately interpreted this dream as a divine calling to take the gospel to Macedonia. This was the one kind of *help* that they knew that they could bring to the people. Paul would have deduced that the man in the dream was a Macedonian from what he said. We do not know why this form of divine guidance was adopted at this point. Psychological explanations, such as that the dream was occasioned by a visit by Macedonians (possibly including Luke) to Paul in Troas are speculative.

10. The dream was followed by an immediate attempt to cross to Macedonia. But now the narrative suddenly is expressed in terms of what *we* decided to do, and this manner of description in the first person plural continues to 16:17, after which it is resumed in 20:5. The most obvious explanation of this phenomenon is that here the narrator himself records his own part in the story. Alternatively, the narrator starts to make use of somebody else's reminiscences couched in the first person, but fails to alter the grammatical style; this explanation, however, is most improbable in the case of a consciously careful writer like the author of Acts. Haenchen (pp. 489–491) argues that the reader would naturally suppose that one of the people just mentioned (Silas, Timothy) here begins to tell the story. This is highly unlikely; no reader would naturally suppose this, but would assume that the author of the book was including himself in the story. The view that the use of 'we' is a literary means of bringing the story

[1] See C. J. Hemer, 'Alexandria Troas', *Tyn.B* 26, 1975, pp. 79–112.

to life is equally unlikely. We have then to ask which of Paul's companions might have been present on this occasion and have narrated the account; for the reasons for believing that this was Luke, see the Introduction.

d. Philippi: the first Macedonian church (16:11–40)

The arrival of the missionaries in Philippi led to successful evangelism among the women associated with the Jewish faith. It also led to persecution in this predominantly Roman town as the result of an exorcism performed by Paul. But arrest and imprisonment could not impede the progress of the gospel, but rather helped it: the release of the missionaries from their bonds in the prison by an earthquake demonstrated the power of God that was protecting them and led to the conversion of the jailer himself. At the same time the incident showed that the Roman authorities were unwilling to press charges against the missionaries. Although they were forced to leave the town probably sooner than they had intended, they were able to leave behind a small group of Christians, which Paul was later able to revisit without any molestation (20:1f., 6).

The story of Paul's visit to Philippi is vividly told and illustrates the trials of the Christian missionary in a Roman environment where the gospel affected the vested interests of local people. As a result of the visit there was formed a Christian church with which Paul had exceptionally warm relations, reflected in the tone of his later letter to the Philippian Christians. This and other writings confirm the essential historicity of the story. Thus Philippians itself testifies to the continuing hostility which the church faced in its pagan environment, and Paul could tell his readers that they were 'engaged in the same conflict which you saw and now hear to be mine' (Phil. 1:30; *cf.* 1:27–29; 2:17). It is perhaps surprising that we read nothing about Lydia or the jailer in the letter; but in fact no names of Philippian Christians are mentioned except those of two ladies engaged in a tiff (Phil. 4:2) and Clement. But the general picture of a church in which women were Paul's fellow workers agrees well with the presentation in Acts. In 1 Thessalonians also we have important first-hand evidence for Paul's suffering and shameful treatment in Philippi (2:2) before he went on, as Acts relates, to Thessalonica. As 2 Corinthians 11:25 shows, illegal beatings by magistrates were not uncommon for Paul.

The story in itself has the ring of historicity. The opening part (verses 11–15) is from the we-source, and nothing stands in the way of its reliability. Similarly, there is no reason to question the general account of the missionaries' arrest, imprisonment and release (verses 19–24, 35–40); as our comments will show, the details regarding the legal procedure are perfectly credible. But historical doubts have been raised over the two parts of the narrative where supernatural elements occur, the account of the exorcism (verses 16–18) and the earthquake in the prison (verses 25–34). Haenchen (pp. 499–504), who offers the fullest recent analysis from a sceptical point of view, has to concede that stories about Paul's activity as an exorcist and the conversion of his jailer were probably current in Philippi, but argues that these have been 'embroidered' by Luke in order to glorify Paul and also to turn the account of the magistrates' injustice into an indirect apology for Paul. Some of the difficulties mentioned by Haenchen are discussed below. The exorcism story need not cause any great difficulty, since Paul lived in a world where exorcism was not uncommon (*cf.* 19:13) and there is no reason why he should not have practised Christian exorcism in cases of bondage to evil; to be sure, some modern readers may want to offer a different diagnosis of the girl's condition, but there is nothing to prevent acceptance of the story as it stands. As for the story of the prison, here it can be objected that similar motifs can be found in other, legendary material (especially Euripides, *Bacchae*, and the *Testament of Joseph*), and that the earthquake seems to have had no effect on the magistrates or the rest of the town. Haenchen concludes that the story could be dropped from the narrative without any loss of continuity. The cumulative force of these objections should not be underestimated, but it may be questioned whether they amount to an overwhelming case against the historicity of the story. The existence of fictional parallels to details in the story cannot disprove it, and it is hard to see why the story of the earthquake should have been invented if there were not a basis of truth to it.[1]

11. Paul and his companions were able to make a quick sea journey from Troas, via the island of *Samothrace* (where they probably made an overnight stop), to *Neapolis* in a couple

[1] Earthquakes were common enough in the area (*BC, TV*, p. 197).

of days; the distance of 125 miles (200 km) could easily be accomplished in this time with a favourable wind, although the return journey in 20:6 took five days. Neapolis, modern Kavalla, was the port for Philippi, some 10 miles (16 km) away.

12. *Philippi* was an ancient town which had been renamed by Philip of Macedon *c.* 360 BC. It was the site of the defeat of Julius Caesar's murderers, Brutus and Cassius, by Antony and Octavian (the later Emperor Augustus) in 42 BC. The town then became a *Roman colony, i.e.* a settlement for veteran Roman soldiers who possessed the rights of self-government under Roman laws and freedom from taxes. Further veterans were settled there after the defeat of Antony and Cleopatra at Actium in 31 BC. According to RSV it was *the leading city of the district of Macedonia*, which as it stands is a meaningless phrase. Macedonia was unusual as a Roman province in being divided into four subprovinces, of which Philippi belonged to the first, although its capital city was Amphipolis. The Greek text is confused, the manuscripts offering several different versions of a phrase that had evidently been garbled at an early stage, but the rendering in GNB and TNT, 'a city of the first district of Macedonia', probably represents the intended sense. Luke's description betrays local knowledge (Sherwin-White, p. 93) and is intended to prepare the way for the account of Paul's first encounter with a Roman situation and the Roman local administration.[1]

13. Paul's missionary practice usually took him to the synagogue in the first instance to proclaim the coming of the Messiah to the Jews and proselytes who gathered there (13:4–5 note). He did not start his missionary work, therefore, until the *sabbath* when he went to the Jewish meeting place. The RSV text, *where we supposed there was a place of prayer*, implies that Paul and his companions did not know for certain where the Jews met, and that they had not been lodging with Jews. This would not be surprising if Jewish worship was being practised by a mere handful of women, at least one of whom was a proselyte; the missionaries would be dependent on what

[1] See further R. P. Martin, *Philippians (New Century Bible)*, London, 1976), pp. 2–9. W. Elliger, *Paulus in Griechenland* (Stuttgart, 1978), summarizes the archaeological information available about Philippi, Thessalonica, Athens and Corinth.

vague information they could pick up from the local people. The text is again uncertain, however, and it is possible that originally it read 'where prayer was accustomed to be made', in which case nothing is said about any difficulty in finding the place. A synagogue could be established only where there were at least ten men. Since there is no mention here of men, it is probable that *place of prayer* here simply means a place where the women gathered by custom to pray (perhaps in a house); the phrase, however, can be used to mean a synagogue building. It was probably outside the town because the authorities would not allow the Jews to meet inside it. The proximity of the place to a river (the Gangites, or the Crenides, a stream within a sabbath day's journey of the town) may have been in order to have water for Jewish ritual purification.

14. Among the women gathered for prayer was one who came from *Thyatira* (Rev. 2:18–29), a town in the part of Asia Minor called Lydia; the woman had been called after the area from which she came, and she was involved in selling goods made with the purple dye for which Lydia was famed. There was a Jewish community in Thyatira, and there or elsewhere *Lydia* had become an adherent of the Jewish religion. She now responded to the message of Paul which was no doubt concerned with the coming of the Messiah in the person of Jesus (*cf.* 17:3). Her conversion is attributed to the fact that *the Lord opened her heart* (for the phrase *cf.* Lk. 24:45; 2 Macc. 1:4) and thus set his seal on the obedience of the missionaries in crossing over to Macedonia at his bidding.

Luke underlines that conversion is due to the action of God who opens the hearts, *i.e.* the minds, of men and women to receive his Word. This view of things is exactly the same as we find in Paul who says that people do not believe because their minds have been darkened by the god of this world (2 Cor. 4:4), but that they are converted when the gospel comes to them 'not only in word, but also in power and in the Holy Spirit and with full conviction' (1 Thes. 1:6). To be sure, this way of looking at the matter does not lessen the responsibility of the missionary to beseech and entreat people to receive the Word (2 Cor. 5:20; 6:1), nor does it in any way remove the responsibility of the hearer to repent and believe the gospel.

15. It is not clear whether the baptism of Lydia followed immediately upon her initial conversation with Paul. But there certainly cannot have been any long interval, so that her baptism was indeed the outward expression of the salvation which she received and the faith which she showed. The act of baptism also embraced her household. Advocates of infant baptism eagerly seize on this verse and similar ones (11:14; 16:33; 18:8; 1 Cor. 1:16) and argue that the possibility (and in some other cases the probability) that the households included small children is high. Their opponents point out that children, and in particular infants, are never expressly mentioned. In the present case, the fact that Lydia was engaged in business strongly suggests that she was single or widowed, and the members of her household would have included any servants or dependants whom she had living with her.[1]

The conversion of Lydia was immediately followed by her offer of hospitality to Paul and his party; she was thus quick not merely to follow the early Christian practice of being hospitable (Rom. 12:13; 1 Tim. 3:2; Heb. 13:2; 1 Pet. 4:9; 3 Jn. 5–8), but also to share material goods with those who teach the Word (Gal. 6:6; *cf.* 1 Cor. 9:14).

16. The second part of the story takes us out of the world of Judaism into contact with the popular superstition of the Hellenistic world. On one of Paul's visits *to the place of prayer*, he and his companions were met by a *slave girl* who had the gift of second sight, and made money for her owners by telling fortunes. Her gift is attributed by Luke to *a spirit of divination*, literally 'a spirit, a Python'. The latter word originally meant a snake, and in particular the snake which guarded the celebrated oracle at Delphi and which was said to have been slain by Apollo. The word was also used to mean a ventriloquist. Ventriloquists acted as fortune-tellers, the unusual character of the sounds which they produced no doubt having a numinous effect; they were probably thought to be inhabited by a demon. In the present case the girl presumably spoke like a ventriloquist and had the gift of clairvoyance, and therefore Luke has described her as having a spirit (*i.e.* an evil spirit), namely one capable of ventriloquism.

17. The girl met Paul and his companions in the street and shouted after them that they were *servants of the Most High God*,

[1] Those who are interested may compare representative statements of the two views in J. Jeremias, *Infant Baptism in the First Four Centuries* (London, 1960), pp. 19–24, and G. R. Beasley-Murray, *Baptism in the New Testament* (Exeter, 1972), pp. 312–320.

proclaiming *the way of salvation*. The description of the supreme God in this way is found elsewhere on the lips of pagans (Lk. 8:28), but it was also in use among Greek-speaking Jews; probably pagans copied the usage of Jews when referring to their God. *Salvation* was a common term for the content of the Christian message (4:12; 13:26, 47). The girl's cry could thus have depended simply on what was common knowledge about the activity of the missionaries in Philippi. Nevertheless, the story is told in a manner like that of the exorcism stories in the Gospels, in which the demon-possessed proclaim their knowledge of the identity of Jesus (Lk. 4:34, 41; 8:28) as a means of showing their would-be superiority over him. It seems likely that Luke attributed the girl's knowledge to the supernatural insight of the demon-possessed. Elsewhere in the New Testament the lines between demon possession, mental unbalance, and charlatanry are equally hard to draw.

18. The effect of the girl's proclamation, which was repeated over a few *days* whenever she met Paul, was to give the missionaries some unexpected publicity. Paul made no attempt to deal with the situation on the first occasion for reasons which are not clear. The girl's cries may not have seemed dangerous at first; indeed there is no suggestion that she was hostile to the missionaries. But it became clear to Paul that she was in the grip of an evil *spirit*, and he proceeded to exorcise the spirit by means of the name of Jesus. The story does not tell whether the girl became a convert; Luke's interest was solely in the effect of the incident on the fate of Paul and his companions. Consequently, we cannot draw conclusions about the problem of exorcism in the modern church from this incident. What is clear is that the exorcism deprived the girl of her ability or willingness to tell fortunes.

19. Whether or not the girl's *owners* were with her during the exorcism, they quickly discovered that not only the spirit had left the girl, but also their source of profit (Luke has deliberately used the same verb for humorous effect in verses 18 and 19), and they knew who was responsible for it. As in the later case in Ephesus (19:23–27), the effect of the gospel was to ruin the business of those who traded on or made use of human superstitions and vice. So the owners, no doubt with the help of friends or bystanders, promptly acted in their own cause by seizing Paul and Silas and dragging them to the town square where they could present their case against them before the magistrates. The other members of the party (Timothy and Luke) were not involved in the scene (the use of 'we' ceases in verse 17), either because they were of less importance than the principals or simply because they were elsewhere at the time. (Or were only the fully Jewish members of the party arrested, as Bruce, *Book*, p. 335, suggests?) The town square was the business centre; it has been excavated by archaeologists.

20–21. The *magistrates* are referred to by a general title as 'rulers' in verse 19, but here they are more specifically named. Their proper title was *duoviri*, as is attested by inscriptions. The Greek word used here, *strategoi*, may simply be the nearest Greek equivalent to this word (Sherwin-White, pp. 92f.), but it also could be used to translate the more grandiloquent title of *praetores*; older commentaries suggest that the magistrates may have affected this title (in the same way as they did at Capua in the first century BC; Bruce, *Book*, p. 335), but it is unlikely that this archaic usage was still current. It is significant that when the accusers make their charge, the economic considerations retreat into the background and other pretexts are found. The charge in fact falls into two parts. The first is that Paul and Silas were causing a public disturbance. This was backed up by a comment that they were Jews, so as to take account of the anti-Jewish feeling which was not uncommon at the time (see 18:2, 12–17). The second part of the charge was that Paul and Silas were advocating non-Roman customs. This put the exorcism into the broader context of missionary activity. We see here the specifically Roman self-consciousness found in a colony. The Romans were officially not supposed to practise foreign cults, although in practice they might do this so long as these did not offend against Roman customs. The principle was clearly a flexible one which could be invoked as necessary. During the first century and onwards it was used when foreign cults led to criminal practices; here the complaint is the archaic-sounding one that the cult in question was 'un-Roman'. It has sometimes been argued that the Jews were banned from proselytizing, but this does not appear to have been the case (Sherwin-White, pp. 78–83).

22. The crowd who had gathered to witness the proceedings sided with the owners of the slave girl; they were no doubt moved by the emotive language of the accusations. The next step after the laying of a charge by private individuals was for the *magistrates* to arrest the accused and hold them in custody pending the hearing of the case before the proconsul. In the present case the arrest was accompanied by beating the prisoners. They were stripped of their clothes as a preliminary (again following normal Roman practice) and then beaten *with rods* by the lictors who attended the magistrates (*the police*, 16:35 RSV; they carried bundles of rods (Latin *fasces*) as a sign of the magistrates' authority). This was doubtless one of the three instances of being beaten to which Paul referred in his catalogue of apostolic hardships in 2 Corinthians 11:25. The beating should not have been imposed on Roman citizens, but at this point the authorities were ignorant of Paul's status. The infliction of the beating shows that the magistrates simply assumed the guilt of the missionaries and took advantage of the anti-Jewish feeling of the crowd to adminster summary justice; possibly their intention all along was simply to keep the prisoners overnight and then send them packing.

23–24. The beating was severe and was followed by imprisonment. The command to *the jailer to keep them safely* has its dramatic purpose in preparing the reader for the miraculous escape of the missionaries: no matter how securely men bind them, God can set them free. On a historical level the magistrates may possibly have feared that such prisoners, who had displayed supernatural powers, needed to be guarded especially carefully. The jailer therefore placed them in the inmost and securest part of the prison, and took the further precaution of fastening their legs securely in wooden *stocks*.

25. There was no sleep for the missionaries that night, thanks to their pain and their uncomfortable position. But in the midst of their suffering they displayed their trust in God and their joy by *praying and singing* praise to him. Here we have a concrete depiction of the Christian ideal of 'joy amid suffering' (Rom. 5:3; Jas. 1:2; 1 Pet. 5:6). The prayers offered may have been simply of praise to God; there is no suggestion that the prisoners prayed for release, although the fact that the other prisoners heard them is perhaps meant to convey the point that they would then regard the miraculous release which followed as an answer to the missionaries' prayers to their God.

26. In answer to the joyful confession by the missionaries there suddenly came an *earthquake* which shook the prison building, causing the *doors* to fly open and the bonds securing the prisoners to the walls to be loosened. Escape thus became possible, although presumably the *fetters* would still be attached to the prisoners' arms or legs. The point of the story, however, is that the prisoners made no attempt to escape. The miracle served a different purpose.

27. The attention shifts from the prisoners to the *jailer* who was roused from his sleep by the earthquake; seeing the open doors he drew the conclusion that the *prisoners* had already *escaped*, and was about to commit suicide. Attempts to provide a rational account of his behaviour are perhaps in vain. Why did he not first look more closely to see what had happened? Although he stood in danger of capital punishment if the prisoners escaped through his negligence, why should he have feared punishment when their escape was due to a natural disaster? But the man knew of the supernatural powers of Paul and Silas, and his wits were deranged in face of the supernatural; he did not know what he was doing (*cf.* Mk. 9:6 and the sheer terror of the women at the tomb of Jesus, Mk. 16:8).

28. The jailer was interrupted in his action by the *voice* of Paul from within the prison telling him that all the prisoners were safe. Commentators have puzzled over how Paul knew that nobody had escaped and that the jailer was about to kill himself when, as verse 29 shows, the jailer himself needed a light to see what was happening. Is this meant to be an example of supernatural insight, or has the author simply not thought about the problems of the narrative? But is it so difficult to conceive that Paul could hear what was going on in his immediate surroundings, or that there was sufficient light in the place to give a hazy view of what was happening? We are dealing, as so often, with a condensed story in which the narrative is limited to the points significant for the author's purpose, and he does not bother to furnish the details which attract the interest of a historian anxious to reconstruct the scene in every particular.

29–30. The jailer called to his aides for torches, and rushed into the jail where he went straight to Paul and Silas whom he regarded as the causes of the whole shattering event. His question to them is surprising in its immediate context, and can be understood only in the light of the reputation which Paul and Silas had gained in Philippi for their proclamation of 'the way of salvation' (verse 17). The supernatural confirmation of the messengers and thus of their message led the jailer to give them the reverence due to divine agents (verse 29) and to seek the salvation which they claimed to offer. The question can hardly refer to being *saved* from punishment by his superiors over what had happened in the prison, since the prisoners were all safe; we do not have a case of reinterpretation on a spiritual level (compare the way in which 'water' is understood both on a literal and on a spiritual level in Jn. 4:10–15, or the way in which 'save' can be used both of physical and of spiritual healing in the Gospels, Lk. 7:50; 8:48). Rather the jailer is forced by the supernatural confirmation of the message to realize that he must come to terms with the God proclaimed by Paul and Silas.

31. The missionaries' answer is the classical statement of how one may be 'saved', namely by *believing in the Lord Jesus*. It reflects the early Christian confessional statement, 'Jesus is Lord' (Rom. 10:9; 1 Cor. 12:3; Phil. 2:11), but brings out particularly the necessity of trust and committal to Jesus as Lord (*cf.* 9:42; 11:17). Jesus is Saviour to those to whom he is Lord. At the same time, it becomes clear that the way of salvation associated with 'the Most High God' (16:17) is by believing in Jesus. Not only so, but the gift offered to the jailer is also offered to his whole *household*. The New Testament takes the unity of the family seriously, and when salvation is offered to the head of the household, it is as a matter of course made available to the rest of the family group (including dependants and servants) as well (*cf.* 16:15). It is, however, offered to them on the same terms: they too have to hear the Word (16:31), believe and be baptized; the jailer's own faith does not cover them.

32. But all this needed fuller explanation than could be given in a brief formula, and so there and then the jailer and his family were given Christian instruction. The urgency of the gospel took prior place over considerations of comfort for the prisoners. We may note in passing that it is not enough simply to face people with gospel proof-texts; there is normally need for careful instruction adapted to their particular situation and for personal, pastoral care if the task of evangelism is to be successful and lasting in its effects (1 Thes. 2:7f.).

33–34. The effect of the jailer's change of heart was seen, first, in his care for the physical needs of the missionaries; he did what he could to assuage the effects of their beating the previous day (*cf.* Mt. 25:36; Heb. 10:34). Thereafter he and his family were baptized without delay in the prison itself. Note that although Paul and Silas put the preaching of the gospel before their own personal comfort, the jailer saw to their needs before being baptized. The jailer's care for his prisoners was further emphasized by taking them into his house where he provided for their needs in a meal that was at the same time an expression of Christian fellowship and joy at his and his family's conversion. The meal may have included a celebration of the Lord's Supper, but Luke does not say so explicitly. Thereafter, it can be presumed, the missionaries had to return to their place in the prison. The other prisoners, likewise, would have been fastened up again; but Luke is silent on these unnecessary details of the story (although some early scribe added a comment to this effect in the western text of verse 30).

35. When *day* came, *the magistrates sent* their servants, the lictors, to the prison to authorize the release of the captives. They no doubt regarded the beating and night's imprisonment as sufficient exercise of their authority over the trouble-makers; to have sent them on to a higher court for so trivial an offence would have been to make themselves a laughing-stock.

36. The news of release was given to the jailer who in turn communicated it to the prisoners inside the prison. It was the jailer himself who bade the missionaries depart *in peace*, taking up the Jewish form of greeting which had become part of Christian usage (Lk. 8:48).

37. For Paul and Silas to have departed in this way, however, could have set a dangerous precedent for the future treatment of missionaries and also could have left the Christians in Philippi exposed to arbitrary treatment from the magistrates. The magistrates had erred. They had not only *beaten* and imprisoned the missionaries without checking up properly on the accusations against them, but they had also not considered whether they might be *Roman citizens*. Roman citizens were expressly exempted from the penalty of beating, although there was little to stop a local magistrate, far from supervision, from exceeding his powers. It would seem that no opportunity had been given to Paul to protest his Roman citizenship the previous day. In a famous earlier case a Roman citizen had been beaten by the orders of Verres, the notorious governor of Sicily, even while he cried out '*Civis Romanus sum*'. Such injustice could not be overlooked. Paul demanded a public apology: let the magistrates who had ordered the imprisonment personally bring it to an end.

38–40. The news brought by the lictors put the magistrates in a quandary, since they knew that if an account of what had happened reached a higher authority they would be in for trouble. So they made the best of a bad situation by personally coming and conciliating the missionaries (RSV *apologize* is perhaps an over-translation). Nevertheless, they still required them to leave the town, perhaps because they feared continued disturbances; after all, they had to fear not only the reaction of the missionaries to their illegal punishment but also the continuing attitude of local people like the slave girl's owners who might create fresh trouble for them. It is not clear whether the magistrates had the legal right to expel the missionaries, but they certainly had the effective power to do so (Sherwin-White, pp. 77f.). The story is rounded off with the release of the missionaries, their final visit to Lydia and the other members of the infant church, and their departure. Presumably Luke stayed on (see 20:5f.).

e. Thessalonica and Beroea (17:1–15)

From Philippi Paul moved on directly to the capital city of Macedonia, Thessalonica, where he had a successful mission in the Jewish synagogue, winning converts among the Jews and the Gentile adherents. When trouble arose this time, it sprang from the jealousy of the Jews at Paul's success with the Gentiles. Not being able to lay their hands on Paul, they took his friends before the city authorities and accused them of treason. The magistrates dealt with the matter by binding the accused over to keep the peace, and the Christians responded by sending Paul and Silas away to the neighbouring town of Beroea. Here, nothing daunted, they again campaigned in the synagogue with similar encouraging results until a deputation of Jews from Thessalonica incited the crowds against the Christians. Once more it was judged expedient for Paul to depart, and he made his way to Athens.

The narrative presents no insuperable historical problems, although we need to add the evidence of 1 Thessalonians to get a full picture of events. Haenchen (p. 513) claims that 1 Thessalonians does not suggest that the Jews caused the trouble for Paul in Thessalonica; it was due rather, he main-

275

tains, to a Gentile anti-Christian movement: 'you suffered the same things from your countrymen as they (*sc.* the churches in Judea) did from the Jews' (1 Thes. 2:14). Against this view it must be insisted that 1 Thessalonians 2:15f. refers to *Paul's* experiences at the hands of the Jews, undoubtedly with reference to what his readers knew of his experiences in Thessalonica; verse 14 will then refer to the Gentile and Jewish opponents of the church in the town.

1. The great Roman highway, the Via Egnatia, began at Neapolis and ran through Philippi, *Amphipolis* (16:12 note), *Apollonia* and *Thessalonica*, and then on westwards across Macedonia to the coast of the Adriatic Sea at Dyrrachium, from where travellers could cross to Italy. Paul's missionary campaigns were greatly eased where good highways, the motorways or autobahns of the ancient world, aided his progress. The missionaries made their way some 33 miles (53 km) to Amphipolis, 27 miles (43 km) to Apollonia, and then 35 miles (56 km) to Thessalonica; if these distances are meant to represent each a single day's journey, the travellers must have made use of horses (see 21:15), but Luke may be simply noting the main towns through which they passed. If missionary work took place in these towns, Luke does not mention it; possibly they did not possess synagogues (there is no evidence of any), or possibly Paul was concerned to reach the main city of the province and work there. *Thessalonica*, like Philippi, was an ancient city which had acquired a new lease of life in the Hellenistic era. It was made a free city by the Romans in 42 BC and had the appropriate rights of self-government on a Greek, rather than a Roman, pattern (Sherwin-White, pp. 95–98). It had a Jewish population, probably more than sufficient to establish a *synagogue*. Recent archaeological evidence indicates that later there was a Samaritan synagogue in the town.

2. Paul's customary visit to the synagogue in a strange town (13:4–12 note) was not simply to engage in worship but to evangelize among those who attended its services (*cf.* Lk. 4:16). He continued this activity in Thessalonica for three sabbaths (RSV mg.). His total stay in the town, however, may have been longer, since we know that he received at least one gift from Philippi (Phil. 4:16)[1] and that he had to work to keep himself (1 Thes. 2:9).

[1] For the correct translation of this verse (mistranslated in most recent

3. Luke has no vivid conversion stories to tell from Paul's visit to Thessalonica, and he has already indicated at some length the kind of discourse that Paul would give in a synagogue setting (13:16ff.). He therefore contents himself here with a general summary of Paul's evangelism. It was based on the Scriptures, the common authority accepted by Jews and Christians, and it was conducted by means of argument. He opened up the meaning of the Scriptures (Lk. 24:32) and brought forward what they said as evidence for his case. Probably to the great astonishment of the Jews he claimed that it was *necessary* for the Messiah to *suffer* (*i.e.* to die, 1:3 note) and thereafter *to rise from the dead*, and then he argued that since Jesus fulfilled these conditions he was the Messiah. The necessity lay in the will of God, as accepted by Jesus (Lk. 9:22) and revealed in the Scriptures (Lk. 24:26f.). Since Paul makes essentially the same statements about the Messiah in 1 Corinthians 15:3–5, a passage which is based on early Christian tradition, it is clear that he was not pushing a line of his own here, but was simply repeating what was commonly accepted Christian teaching. We can be reasonably sure that the Scriptures used would include Psalms 2, 16, 110; Isaiah 53; and possibly Deuteronomy 21:23 (see 26:23 note).

4. Paul's preaching was effective. His converts included some of the Jews together with a considerable number of the Gentile adherents of the synagogue, and women. The latter are described as *leading women*, which may mean that they belonged to the upper class in the town; alternatively the phrase can mean 'wives of the leading men', a sense made explicit in some early textual witnesses. Either way, this would not be surprising, since we know that Jewish women were to be found in upper-class society, and even Nero's mistress and wife, Poppaea, was reputed to have Jewish sympathies (Jos., *Ant.* 20:195). When Haenchen (p. 507) comments that it is strange that these influential women could not avert the persecution of Christians here or in Beroea, he evidently overlooks the fact that in both cases the persecution was caused by the Jews (with whom these women had presumably little if any influence) rather than by the city authorities. Luke tells us

---

versions except JB) see R. P. Martin *Philippians* (*Tyndale New Testament Commentaries*), London, 1959), pp. 180f.

that the converts *joined Paul and Silas, i.e.* probably that they formed a separate group and met apart from the synagogue, evidently in the house of Jason (17:5).

5. Paul's successful drawing away of the Gentiles roused the envy of the *Jews*. The Gentiles were potential converts to Judaism, but Paul had proved more effective than the synagogue in persuading them to take the step of full commitment. Many Gentiles who were attracted by the more spiritual aspects of Judaism were unwilling to take the step of circumcision and were content to remain as God-fearers. So the Jews resolved on action. There appear to have been two types of course open to them. Since Thessalonica was a free city, it had a popular assembly (described in this verse as *the people*, Gk. *dēmos*) before whom charges could be laid. The Jews attempted to bring Paul and Silas before this assembly. They did so by enlisting the aid of a group of idle loafers who were willing to create an uproar; by this means the Jews could incidentally gain ammunition for a charge that the missionaries were disturbers of the peace and so present a more compelling charge to the assembly. The unruly mob gathered outside *the house of Jason* where they hoped to find Paul. Jason was evidently Paul's host; Haenchen (p. 512) makes the attractive suggestion that possibly he merely gave the missionaries work and shelter in the first instance and then was converted through his contacts with them. We do not know whether he was a Jew or a Gentile; if the former, his Jewish name may have been Joshua, with Jason as a somewhat similar-sounding Greek name for use in a Greek environment (*cf.* Jos., *Ant.* 12:239).

6. But the plan of the Jews misfired, since the missionaries were not at home. In their frustration the mob seized the people whom they could find in the house, Jason himself and some of the Christians (here described from the author's point of view as 'brothers'). Instead of taking them before the assembly, however, they now adopted the other possible course of action and took them before the magistrates. These men are given the title of 'politarchs', an unusual designation used for non-Roman city officials in Macedonia; inscriptions have confirmed the accuracy of the terminology used here. The reason for the change of action is not clear, but possibly it seemed more appropriate to arraign the Thessalonian citizens themselve before the magistrates, or they may have feared that the town assembly would have been more sympathetic to the townsfolk. They raised the charge that the people who had been causing upsets throughout the world had now come to their city. The language is, of course, wildly exaggerated, but it at least suggests that news of the trouble in Philippi had already made its way to Thessalonica, and possibly too something was known or guessed of the missionaries' earlier travels from Palestine via Asia Minor. *Turned the world upside down* is not quite the sense, however much we may like to think that this *ought* to be the effect of the gospel; 'caused trouble everywhere' (GNB) is the right meaning.

7. Now comes the heart of the accusation. Jason is harbouring the missionaries and sympathizing with them; he is implicated in the general charge that they are *acting against the decrees of Caesar* by proclaiming *another king, i.e.* emperor, namely *Jesus*. This is an apt description of the positive content of the gospel with its claim that Jesus is Lord (*cf.* 16:31); it indicates how the focus had shifted very naturally from the proclamation of the 'kingdom' in the ministry of Jesus to the proclamation of the 'king' in the evangelism of the early church. The Christian claim could easily be misunderstood as an implicit attack on the emperor (despite 1 Pet. 2:17), especially when the claims of Christ were seen to be incompatible with those of the emperor. What is not so clear is the reference to *decrees of Caesar* in this context. Sherwin-White (pp. 51, 96, 103) observes that the decrees of Claudius were concerned with Jews who were 'fomenters of what is a general plague infecting the whole world'.[1] This is not quite the same thing as denouncing treason against the emperor, and hence he concludes that Luke's account is garbled. The answer to the problem, however, may have been found by E. A. Judge, who argues that Paul's preaching could have been construed as a prediction of a change of ruler. There were imperial decrees against such predictions. Oaths of loyalty to Caesar could be regarded as demanded by his decrees, and these would be enforced by the local magistrates.[2]

8–9. On this view the local *people* and magistrates may well

---

[1] Letter of Claudius to the people of Alexandria (Barrett, *Background*, No. 45).
[2] E. A. Judge, 'The Decrees of Caesar at Thessalonica', *Reformed Theological Review* 30, 1971, pp. 1–7.

have been *disturbed* by the accusation, although the latter, as
officials of a free city, may not have been disposed to take it
too seriously: let the Romans themselves deal with such matters! So the magistrates contented themselves with *taking security* from Jason, *i.e.* binding him over not to let Paul stay any
longer with him and being responsible for seeing that he did
not return to the city. The phrase used is a Latinism, and the
procedure is an attested one.

10. Presumably because of the fear of further mob violence
the Christians sent Paul and Silas away secretly *by night*; there
is no mention of Timothy who reappears in the story at 17:14.
The missionaries went to *Beroea* (modern Verria) about 45
miles (72 km) west-south-west of Thessalonica.[1] Possibly Paul
went no further in the hope that he might return fairly soon
to Thessalonica; however, as he later recorded, 'Satan hindered us' (1 Thes. 2:18). The time, however, was not spent in
rest or idle waiting. Nor was Paul discouraged by his recent
experiences. He made straight for the *synagogue* to commence
evangelism.

11–12. The account of Paul's reception at Beroea is the
classical description of a more well-disposed and open-minded
(RSV *more noble*) response by the Jews to the gospel. They were
zealous to hear what Paul had to say, and so they met with
him *daily* (and not merely on the sabbath). Nor did they accept
what he said thoughtlessly and uncritically, but they themselves examined the Scriptures to see whether the case which
Paul developed from them (as in 17:2f.) was sound. Here was
no mere emotional response to the gospel, but one based on
intellectual conviction. The result was that a considerable
number believed, both Jews and also well-to-do *Greek* men
and *women*; the order of the words suggests that the women
are particularly prominent in the new Christian group.

13. Even among the Jews who remained unpersuaded there
was apparently no hostility to the missionaries. Trouble en-
sued only after *Jews* from *Thessalonica* found out that Paul was
there and created trouble by *stirring up the crowds* in the same
way as they had done previously. Sherwin-White (pp. 97f.)
observes that legal action against the missionaries in Thessa-

[1] The commentators are curiously confused about its location, some giving
the distance as 35 miles (56 km) or even stating that it was due south of
Thessalonica and situated on the Via Egnatia.

lonica would not be valid elsewhere, and there was no kind of general policing of the province to follow up criminals from one town to another. Consequently, the only recourse open to the Jews was to repeat their former efforts.

14–15. The Christians decided that it would be best for Paul, who was obviously the centre of the attack, to depart, and they despatched him to the coast. From there he took ship, along with some Beroean companions, to *Athens*.[1] Silas and Timothy had remained behind, but Paul sent back instructions for them to join him. Although Acts does not say so, they appear to have fulfilled his instructions and rejoined him in Athens, from where he sent them back to Macedonia (probably to Philippi and Thessalonica respectively), and then they rejoined him when he had reached Corinth (18:5; 1 Thes. 3:1–6).

f. Athens: the Areopagus address (17:16–34)

Paul's speech at Athens has sometimes been regarded as the high peak in his missionary career in the eyes of Luke. It is more probable that we should see in this scene simply Luke's presentation of Paul's encounter with cultured paganism. He gives us an illustration of the kind of approach which Paul made to the educated pagan, but at the same time has to admit that the gospel was 'foolishness to the Greeks' or at least to most of them (*cf.* 1 Cor. 1:22–24).

The picture of the city painted by Luke has impressed different scholars as being remarkably true to life or as a brilliant literary product. There was in fact at Athens a blend of superstitious idolatry and enlightened philosophy. Paul's speech, which is delivered before the philosophers, has often been thought to be rather irrelevant to their concerns, since it was directed more against popular idolatry. In fact, however, it would have been very relevant to Epicureans, who thought it unnecessary to seek after God and had no fear of his judgment, and to Stoics, whose concept of God was pantheistic. Paul in fact uses the insights of the philosophers in his attack on the beliefs of the Athenian populace; the Epicureans attacked superstitious, irrational belief in the gods, expressed

---

[1] This is the meaning of the Greek text translated in RSV. Some MSS have 'as if toward the sea' in verse 14, suggesting that Paul's friends concealed their intention of enabling him to depart by land.

in idolatry, while the Stoics stressed the unity of mankind and its kinship with God, together with the consequent moral duty of man. What Paul was doing was to side with the philosophers, and then demonstrate that they did not go far enough.[1]

The speech can be divided up in various ways. After an introduction designed to attract the attention of the audience and to state the theme (verses 22f.), the main portion falls into three parts: (1) God is lord of the world; he does not need a temple or human cultic ritual (verses 24f.); (2) Man is God's creation; he needs God (verses 26f.); (3) God and man are related; therefore idolatry is foolish (verses 28f.). There follows a conclusion, calling on men to abandon their ignorant ideas of God and to repent (verses 30f.; Dibelius, p. 27).

There has been much discussion over (1) the historicity of the scene generally; (2) the theological character of the speech; and (3) the relation of the speech to Paul's thinking, as revealed in his Letters.[2] The historical difficulties are chiefly concerned with the nature of the assembly before which Paul appeared and with his reference to the altar dedicated to an unknown God; these points will be discussed below. The problem regarding the theological character of the speech is whether it is to be regarded as being 'as alien to the New Testament (apart from Acts 14.15–17), as it is familiar to hellenistic, particularly Stoic, philosophy' (Dibelius, p. 63), or as being essentially based on Old Testament and Jewish thinking (B. Gärtner). Recent discussion has illumined the kinship between the speech and Hellenistic Jewish religious propaganda, and shown that it belongs to a type of approach which clothed essentially Jewish beliefs in a Hellenistic form. It has always been good missionary policy to express the gospel in terms that would be intelligible to the hearers without thereby altering the essence of the message. It has often been claimed that Paul's view of 'natural theology', as seen in Romans 1,

---

[1] C. K. Barrett, 'Paul's Speech on the Areopagus', in M. E. Glaswell and E. W. Fasholé-Luke, *New Testament Christianity for Africa and the World* (London, 1974), pp. 69–77.

[2] See especially Dibelius, 26–83; N. B. Stonehouse, *Paul before the Areopagus* (London, 1957), pp. 1–40; B. Gärtner, *The Areopagus Speech and Natural Revelation* (Uppsala/Lund, 1955); W. Nauck, 'Die Tradition und Komposition der Areopagrede', *ZTK* 53, 1956, pp. 11–52; Wilson, pp. 196–218; F. F. Bruce, *Paul: Apostle of the Free Spirit*, (Exeter, 1977), pp. 236–247.

is different from the view presented here, and that the approach expressed in this speech is un-Pauline. Such a view is undoubtedly too extreme. The difficulty is that we do not have any full statements from Paul himself (as opposed to what Luke tells us) regarding the content of his missionary preaching; what we have in his Letters is teaching for his converts. Consequently, it is impossible to be sure that Paul could not have expressed himself in the way described here. Bruce rightly comments that Paul could well have expressed the essence of Romans 1–3 to pagans along the general lines indicated here, and similarly W. Nauck concludes his study by claiming that there is little reason to doubt that the basis of the Areopagus address is a sermon Paul actually delivered in Athens. Nauck, however, admits that Luke has given the speech a different accent from Paul. This is a fair assessment of the speech; it is a summary in Luke's language of the kind of thing that Paul said to Gentile audiences and, in particular, to his audience in Athens.

16. Although *Athens* had once been the intellectual centre of the ancient world, it was now in a period of decline. It was a free city and had a famous university, but it tended to live on its reputation. When Paul arrived, he was not so much impressed by the culture as irritated by the evidences of idolatry. 'He found himself confronted by a veritable forest of idols', with vast numbers of images of Hermes all over the city and especially at the entrance to the *agora* (RSV *market place*) through which he probably walked.[1]

17. Paul directed his attention in the first place, as was his custom, to the Jews and 'God-fearers' (10:2 note) whom he met in the synagogue. He also spoke to anybody whom he happened to meet in the market place. It is unusual for Luke to describe Paul as going directly to the pagans (*cf.* 14:8), and there is no reason to follow Conzelmann (p. 96) in assuming that the verse represents a fictitious Lucan pattern ('to the Jew first') rather than rests on historical report. The description is reminiscent of the activity of Socrates who argued with anybody who would listen to him, although for Luke 'argue' means 'preach' rather than 'debate' (20:7, 9).

18. Paul's hearers included adherents of the *Epicurean and Stoic* philosophies. The former, who took their name from their

[1] R. E. Wycherley, 'St Paul at Athens', *JTS* 19, 1968, pp. 619–621.

founder Epicurus (341–270 BC), tended to be materialistic in outlook. For them either the gods did not exist, or they were so far removed from the world as to exercise no influence on its affairs. They taught a rudimentary atomic theory, and in their ethics they stressed the importance of pleasure and tranquillity. They have often been falsely represented as sensualist in outlook, but in fact they had a lofty view of 'pleasure' and scorned sensualism.

The Stoics, founded by Zeno (340–265 BC), took their name from the *stoa* or colonnade where he taught. They stressed the importance of Reason as the principle which was inherent in the structuring of the universe and by which men ought to live. They had a pantheistic conception of God as the worldsoul, and their ethics stressed individual self-sufficiency and obedience to the dictates of duty.

Their initial impression of Paul was not favourable. They dismissed him contemptuously as a *babbler*; the word designated a bird picking up scraps in the gutter, and hence came to be used of worthless loafers (the kind of person who today would pick up cigarette ends and smoke them) and also of persons who had acquired mere scraps of learning. There would appear to be a deliberate echo of the tradition about Socrates when Paul is said to proclaim strange *divinities*; here the word 'demon' is used in its neutral, Greek sense. The divinities in question were *Jesus* and *Resurrection*, the latter possibly being understood as the name of a goddess, although a contemptuous dismissal of the idea of resurrection, as taught by Paul, is just as likely an interpretation.

19. Paul was taken to the *Areopagus* to find out more precisely what he was teaching. In ancient Athens there was a council which used to meet on the *Areopagus*,[1] a hill overlooking the *agora*, and which had once had important judicial functions. It still retained its importance as the chief court in Athens in the first century.[2] Its meeting place was either on the hill or in the Stoa Basileios, whose site was near the northwest of the *agora*.[3] Commentators are not certain whether Luke

[1] Gk. *Areios Pagos*, literally Ares' Hill. Since Ares, the Greek god of war, was equated with the Roman god Mars, the alternative name Mars' Hill is also found (Acts 17:22 AV).

[2] T. D. Barnes, 'An Apostle on Trial', *JTS* 20, 1969, pp. 407–419.

[3] C. J. Hemer, 'Paul at Athens: A Topographical Note', *NTS* 20, 1973–74, pp. 341–350.

meant to describe: (1) a meeting of the court to 'try' Paul's
teaching, whether formally or informally – and, if so, whether
the court was meeting on the hill or in the Stoa Basileios[1]; or
(2) an unoffical gathering of Athenians generally on the Areopagus hill.[2] In favour of view (2) are the facts that Paul's
speech does not look like a legal defence and that there is no
hint of any legal proceedings. The argument that the hill was
not large enough to hold a crowd is false. The reference to
Dionysius the Areopagite (verse 34), however, suggests that
Luke meant to describe a meeting of the court, no doubt in
public session and not necessarily taking the form of a legal
trial.

20–21. The occasion gave Paul an opportunity to spell out
his views. His audience recognized that he was teaching
strange things which they had not heard before, and they
wanted to know what it all meant. In a rare aside Luke
comments that the Athenians themselves and visitors to the
city were moved by sheer curiosity to hear something *new*, and
that they had nothing better to do with their time than to
enjoy intellectual titillation. Luke implies that they were not
greatly concerned about the truth of what they heard; his tone
is distinctly sarcastic.

22. Paul begins by commending the Athenians for being
very religious. This word could be used in a positive sense or in
a derogatory fashion. It is most likely that Paul meant it in a
good sense, to provide a way in to his address that would
engage the attention of the audience.[3] Nevertheless, Luke also
uses the corresponding noun in what is perhaps a slightly
derogatory sense in 25:19, and it is likely that he intended his
readers to perceive the irony of the situation (*cf.* verse 16). For
all their religiosity, the Athenians were in reality thoroughly
superstitious and lacking in knowledge of the true God.

23. As proof of his statement Paul relates how he had been
observing the various objects of worship in the city; here again
the word could be understood positively by the hearers, but
at least to Jewish readers it would have a derogatory nuance
('idols'; Wisdom 14:20; 15:17). One such had particularly

---

[1] The former view is defended by Barnes, the latter by Hemer.

[2] Dibelius, pp. 67–69; Haenchen, pp. 518f.; W. G. Morrice, 'Where did Paul
speak in Athens?', *ET* 83, 1971–72, pp. 377f.

[3] K. Grayston, *Theology as Exploration* (London, 1966), pp. 3–6.

occupied Paul's attention: a wayside altar with the inscription *to an unknown god*. He eagerly seized on this inscription as a way of introducing his own proclamation of *the* unknown God. There was, to be sure, no real connection between 'an unknown god' and the true God; Paul hardly meant that his audience were unconscious worshippers of the true God. Rather, he is drawing their attention to the true God who was ultimately responsible for the phenomena which they attributed to an unknown god. But what was this inscription? The Greek traveller Pausanias (*cf.* AD 150) tells us that near Athens there were 'altars of gods both named and unknown', and other writers speak of altars to unnamed or unknown gods. Later, however, Tertullian and Jerome bear witness to an altar 'to unknown gods' and the latter asserts that Paul deliberately altered the wording to suit his purpose. Some of these cases may have been where altars were placed on graves that had been disturbed in order to placate whatever gods or demigods might take vengeance on the desecration. On the basis of this evidence some scholars categorically deny that there could have been an altar 'to *an* unknown god'. Such a denial is over-confident. Bruce (*Book*, p. 356) rightly comments that 'if there were two or more altars each bearing an inscription "TO AN UNKNOWN GOD", these could well be referred to comprehensively as "altars to unknown gods." ' This is certainly possible, even though later writers could not find the precise altar which Paul had seen; in any case, it could have disappeared in the following century.

24. Paul's proclamation is concerned with the God who made the universe and all that it contains, and who is therefore *Lord of heaven and earth*. His language is based on the Old Testament description of God (*e.g.* Is. 42:5; Ex. 20:11), but what he said would also have been accepted by the Greek philosopher Plato. The Old Testament does not employ the word *world* (Gk. *kosmos*), since there is no corresponding term in Hebrew; rather it speaks of 'the heaven and the earth' or 'the all' (Je. 10:16). But the word was used in Greek-speaking Judaism (Wisdom 9:9; 11:17; 2 Macc. 7:23), and it is not surprising to find it here (*cf.* Rom. 1:20); Paul employs the language that we would expect a Greek-speaking Jew to use, especially when addressing pagans. A God who is Creator and Lord clearly does not live in a temple made by human hands (*cf.* 7:48; Mk. 14:58; the phrase was used of man-made idols in contrast with the living God, Lv. 26:1; Is. 46:6). There is perhaps an echo of Solomon's prayer at the dedication of the temple when he recognized its inadequacy as a house for God (1 Ki. 8:27). Again, this was a sentiment that would be accepted by Stoic philosophy.

25. Such a God has no *need* of men to supply him with anything; on the contrary it is he who is the source of life. The folly of caring for the gods was pointed out in the Old Testament (Is. 46:1; Je. 10:5) and by the Jews in their polemic against pagan idolatry (Letter of Jeremiah 25), but again the insight was shared by educated pagans, and numerous examples of the sentiment can be quoted (Dibelius, pp. 42–44). The description of God as the source of breath is drawn from Isaiah 42:5 (*cf.* Gn. 2:7) but Paul has utilized the triad of *life* and *breath and everything* from current terminology. Since the word for 'life' (*zoē*) was popularly associated with 'Zeus', the name of the supreme Greek god, it is possible that Paul was indirectly saying, 'Not Zeus but Yahweh is the source of life'. Dibelius (pp. 42–46) and Haenchen (p. 522) have urged strongly that here the thought is thoroughly Hellenistic and not based on the Old Testament. But the thought was certainly present in Greek-speaking Judaism (2 Macc. 14:35; 3 Macc. 2:9), and it has its roots in Psalm 50:7–15; if the language and thought represent a development from the Old Testament and a use of Greek terminology, it is hard to see why this makes the statement foreign to the spirit of the Old Testament.

26. From the description of God Paul turns to the way in which he has created mankind. The RSV takes the verb in the sense *he made* (*i.e.* let) them *live*, but more probably it refers to God's act of creation, as in verse 24. *From one* will then mean 'from Adam' as the ancestor of mankind. It is debated whether we should translate *every nation of men* (RSV) or 'the whole race of men'. Dibelius (pp. 27–37) argues that the former translation would give a biblical view of the history of individual nations stemming from Adam, while the latter (which he adopts) gives a Hellenistic view of 'humanity . . . seen cosmopolitically as the sum of the inhabitants of the earth'. But Stählin (p. 234) correctly observes that the latter idea is biblical, and that the New Testament is concerned more with the fate of men as a whole than with the individual nations. The debate continues into the translation of the next phrase. Do

287

the *allotted periods* ordained by God for mankind mean the divinely appointed periods for the individual nations to flourish (Dt. 32:8; Dn. 2:36–45; Lk. 21:24) or the seasons of the year (as in 14:17)? And do *the boundaries of their habitation* refer to national boundaries (*cf.* Dt. 32:8); or to the natural boundaries which God has set between the land and the threatening sea (Ps. 104:5–9; Job 38:8–11)? If the latter possibilities are accepted, the verse could be an exposition of Psalm 74:17 (*cf.* 1QM 10:12ff. where natural and national boundaries are mentioned together). But the former possibilities are perhaps to be preferred (Wilson, pp. 201–205). The point in any case is the goodness of God in providing for the needs of mankind.

27. God's purpose in all this was that men *might seek after him* in the hope of touching him and finding him. The language can be taken Hellenistically of the philosophical search for what is true or divine, without any certain hope of success. But it is better taken in the Old Testament sense of the thankful and reverent longing of the whole man for the God whose goodness he has experienced (for the vocabulary of seeking and finding God see Is. 55:6; 65:1; Ps. 14:2; Pr. 8:17; Je. 29:13; Am. 9:12 LXX). The unusual element is the word *feel after* which is perhaps suggestive of men groping in the darkness in order to find God. This groping takes place despite the nearness of God to men, of which Paul goes on to speak, and it may indicate the sinful failure of man to find God to which Romans 1:20f. point. Nevertheless, the main point is that seeking should not be difficult since God *is not far from each one of us*. This was a thought current in Stoic philosophy, but there it was taken in an impersonal, intellectual sense. Paul's concern is with the living God of the Old Testament (Ps. 145:18) who is near to his worshippers despite his transcendence and greatness (Je. 23:23f.).

28. Paul confirms this point by two statements which have a pagan origin but could be used to support a Jewish-Christian doctrine of God. The first of these is punctuated as a quotation in RSV, but the identification of its source poses problems. A Syriac writer called Isho'dad (ninth century) cited a passage in which Minos of Crete addressed his father Zeus and attacked the Cretan belief that Zeus was buried on the island: 'They fashioned a tomb for thee, O holy and high – the Cretans, always liars, evil beasts, slow bellies! But thou art not dead; thou art risen and alive for ever, for in thee we live and move and have our being.' The second line of this quotation appears in Titus 1:12, and a Christian writer (Clement of Alexandria) ascribes it to Epimenides of Crete. This would then appear to be Paul's source. Unfortunately there is a complicating factor in that Paul's wording is neither in poetic metre nor in the expected Greek dialect; it is possible, therefore, that Paul is simply giving the general sense of the quotation.[1] The words are not expressly said to be a citation, although the phrase *as even some of your poets have said* may perhaps refer backwards as well as forwards. But the plural form 'poets' may have been chosen because the following words are in fact found in more than one poet. As quoted by Paul, they come from Aratus, but they are also found in a slightly different form in Cleanthes, *Hymn to Zeus*. Paul thus takes over pagan Greek poems, expressive of Stoic philosophy, and applies them to God. A process of 'demythologization' was already under way in that for the Stoics 'Zeus' meant not the supreme god in Greek polytheism but the Logos (Reason; *cf.* verse 18 note). Paul was prepared to take over the glimmerings of truth in pagan philosophy about the nature of God. But whereas the Greeks thought of the divine *nature* of man, Paul would have thought of the way in which man is the *image* of God. It is God who is the source of man's life.

29. On the basis of the fact that man is God's offspring, Paul now draws his conclusion that idolatry is forbidden. Small images of gold and silver (19:24, 26) and massive temple idols of marble are alike wrong. For if men are like God, it follows that an inanimate image cannot portray the living God; if men possess the spirit of God, they must surely recognize that God is Spirit and not capable of material representation. Here Paul was at one with Old Testament and Jewish thought (Gn. 20:4; Dt. 5:8; Is. 44:9–20; Wisdom 13:5; 15), and in opposition to Greek thought. Although Haenchen (p. 525) claims that what Paul was saying merely attacked Greek popular religion and not sophisticated philosophy, it remains the case that there was still a considerable attachment to polytheistic and idolatrous practices alongside a more philosophical outlook.

30. Until the coming of the revelation of God's true nature

[1] We may perhaps compare how Callimachus imitated the same lines in this Hymn to Zeus.

in Christianity men lived in *ignorance* of him. But now the proclamation of the Christian message brings this time to an end so far as those who hear the gospel are concerned; they no longer have any excuse for their ignorance. God was prepared to *overlook* their ignorance, but now he will do so no longer, and calls on *all men everywhere to repent*. Some commentators have claimed that this is not the thought of Paul who alludes only in passing to God's overlooking of human sin and speaks of justification by faith rather than of repentance in view of the judgment to come. But this verdict is false. The summary of Paul's gospel, as preached to Gentiles, in 1 Thessalonians 1:9f. shows precisely the same stress on repentance as here, and it is possible that Paul used the language of justification more especially in relation to Jews and proselytes who trusted in the law as the means of salvation. We should probably also draw a distinction between what Paul says in theological discussion in Romans 1:18ff. about the way in which God gave up mankind to sin and its consequences, and the way in which he would stress the mercy of God who makes allowance for human ignorance when actually preaching the gospel to pagans (*cf.* Rom. 3:25f.).

31. The urgency of Paul's appeal for repentance is underlined by his claim that God has appointed *a day* for judgment of the world.[1] Using Old Testament language Paul emphasizes that it will be a righteous judgment (Ps. 9:9). It will be conducted by God's agent, *a man whom he has appointed*. This is an unusual form of statement, since elsewhere the majesty and exaltation of the judge are stressed, but the form of expression has been chosen in order to introduce the next statement which gives decisive confirmation of the fact of judgment: the appointment of the judge has already taken place and is to be seen in the fact of his being raised from the dead by God. With these words Paul reverts to the themes of his earlier preaching in Athens, 'Jesus' and 'resurrection'. He treats the resurrection as historical fact, and he uses it as proof of the divine appointment of Jesus as judge. Behind the statement lies the thought of the new status given to Jesus by the resurrection (*cf.* Rom. 1:4), which was interpreted by the early church as exaltation to lordship and consequently to judicial

[1] Possibly there is an echo of Jesus' teaching about the Son of Man (Neil, p. 192).

authority. These thoughts, however, are not developed; we already know of them from the earlier examples of preaching the Christian message in Acts, and Luke has here concentrated on what was distinctive in Paul's address to the philosophers of Athens.

32. Paul's return to his starting-point provoked the scorn of some of his hearers. Although Greeks believed in the immortality of the soul, the idea of a bodily *resurrection* was alien to their thinking, since the body was increasingly regarded as earthly and evil in comparison with the soul which was the seat of the divine in man.[1] Not only was the cross 'folly to Gentiles', but so also was the resurrection. Others of Paul's hearers said that they would *hear* him on another occasion; this is often interpreted as simply a more polite form of dismissal, but the contrast expressed with the first group may suggest that this was a more positive reaction, and that these people longed that what Paul said was true.

33–34. This verdict is confirmed by the fact that after Paul had left the gathering he did gain some converts. One in particular was a member of the Areopagus called *Dionysius*. This indicates that Paul's audience certainly contained members of the court of the Areopagus, whether or not we identify the occasion as a meeting of the court. Nothing certain is known about Dionysius, although later tradition turned him into the first bishop of Athens (a fair inference since the first converts often became the leaders of the church, 1 Cor. 16:15f.). Later still he was credited with the authorship of some fifth-century Neoplatonic writings. Along with the men converted there was also a woman called *Damaris*, about whom we again know nothing. Whether a church was formed at this stage is doubtful; Paul describes some of his Corinthian converts as the 'first fruits of Achaia' (1 Cor. 16:15).

g. Corinth (18:1–17)

Corinth and Ephesus were the two most important cities visited by Paul in the course of his missionary work, and he stayed in each for a considerable period in order to establish churches which would then evangelize the surrounding areas.

---

[1] It may be significant that the Greek poet Aeschylus had depicted the god Apollo as denying the resurrection on the occasion of the inauguration of the Court of the Areopagus (*Eumenides*, 647f.; Bruce, *Book*, pp. 363f.).

His activity was again threatened by the Jews who, as in Philippi and Thessalonica, sought the support of the civic authorities in thwarting the work of the missionaries. The appeal was unsuccessful and Paul was able to continue his work without hindrance. From his letters to the church, however, we find that Paul had problems of a different sort in Corinth, internal dissensions and the growth of unbalanced ideas more dangerous to the growth of spiritual life than persecution from outside. Luke makes no mention of these troubles (which probably broke out after Paul's departure); he is more concerned to describe the founding of churches (but see 20:29f.).

1. *Corinth* was at this time the capital city of the Roman province of Achaia. The famous city of classical times had been destroyed by the Romans in 146 BC, but a new city had been created by Julius Caesar. It was situated strategically on the narrow isthmus between the Greek mainland and the Peloponnesian peninsula, and was a centre of communications, both north-south along the isthmus and also east-west between the two ports of Cenchreae (18:18; Rom. 16:1) and Lechaeum. As a commercial centre, it had attracted a Jewish minority, and the remains of the inscription over the door of a synagogue dating from this period have been found.[1] The town had a bad reputation for immorality, which is amply reflected in 1 Corinthians. The importance of the town made it Paul's obvious goal after his departure from Athens.

2. Whatever motives led Paul to Corinth, and whatever feelings of discouragement he may possibly have experienced as he left Athens,[2] his arrival at Corinth was attended by encouragement. First of all he met up with a Jewish couple, *Aquila* and *Priscilla*. They were Jews of the Dispersion, the husband bearing a Roman name ('Eagle'), as did also his wife, Priscilla being a diminutive form of 'Prisca' (Rom. 16:3; 1 Cor. 16:19; 2 Tim. 4:19). Prisca is more frequently named before her husband, which suggests that she was the more important figure from a Christian point of view. Although Aquila hailed from *Pontus*, he had been resident in Rome, but had been compelled to leave by an edict of the Emperor

---

[1] Barrett, *Background*, No. 48.

[2] 1 Cor. 2:3 should not be interpreted as reflecting on Paul's experience in Athens.

Claudius. This edict was associated with the Jews rioting *impulsore Chresto*, 'at the instigation of Chrestus' (according to Suetonius), a phrase which may well refer to trouble arising in the Jewish community as a result of the preaching of *Christus*.[1] The edict is probably to be dated in AD 49–50, although there is some uncertainty about this. In any case, it can hardly have been carried through effectively against the whole Jewish population in Rome, and those who were expelled no doubt trickled back to the city later on. Assuming that Romans 16 is addressed to Rome,[2] then by the time of its composition Priscilla and Aquila were already back in Rome after their visits to Corinth and also to Ephesus (18:18f.).

3–4. The indications are that the couple were already Christians before they met up with Paul; otherwise Luke would surely have told of their conversion. Christianity must have come to Rome quite early as a result of the frequent movements of travellers to and from the capital city (*cf.* 2:10). There was an added link between the couple and Paul in that they shared the same *trade*. Since rabbis were expected to perform their religious and legal functions without demanding a fee, it was necessary for them to have some other source of income. Paul's occupation was as a tentmaker.[3] Tents were made out of the goat's hair cloth, known as *cilicium* and manufactured in Paul's native province, or else out of leather; hence the word 'tentmaker' could refer more generally to a 'leather-worker', and this seems to be the meaning here. So Paul was able to reside with Aquila and Priscilla, support himself by sharing in their work, and enjoy Christian fellowship with them. Now began a period of evangelism in which Aquila and Priscilla no doubt assisted Paul. As usual, Paul made use of the sabbath services in the synagogue to *argue* (17:2) the Christian case, and his evangelism was successful among both the Jews and the Gentiles who attended the synagogue.

5. The second piece of encouragement which Paul received was the arrival of his fellow workers *Silas* (here mentioned by name for the last time in Acts) and *Timothy* from Macedonia

---

[1] The words *Chrestus* and *Christus* were pronounced in the same way, and Tacitus referred to the Christians as *Chrestiani*.

[2] Not to Ephesus, as some scholars have argued.

[3] Haenchen's denial (pp. 534, 625) that Paul was a rabbi or followed the rabbinic practice is without foundation; see on 22:3.

(see 17:14f. note). As a result of their coming Paul now 'devoted himself entirely to the task of preaching' (NEB; *cf.* GNB, NIV; the RSV translation fails to bring out the point). According to 2 Cor. 11:9 Paul did not impose any burden on the Corinthian church by claiming financial support from it, since his needs were supplied by the Christians from Macedonia (*cf.* Phil. 4:15). It seems probable, therefore, that Silas and Timothy brought gifts of money which freed Paul from the need to work to support himself in Corinth; he could therefore carry out missionary work throughout the week and not merely on the sabbath. So the task of persuading the Jews that the Messiah foretold in the Old Testament was Jesus (*cf.* 17:3) was carried on all the more energetically.

6. The increase in missionary activity proved fruitful and led to opposition (possibly due to envy; *cf.* 17:5) on the part of the Jews who made statements which were blasphemous from a Christian point of view. Paul responded by leaving the synagogue, but not before he had done his best to convince the Jews of the seriousness of their plight in rejecting the gospel. As on an earlier occasion (13:51), he *shook* the dust off his *garments* (Neh. 5:13) as a sign of the breaking off of fellowship with them. This kind of action was performed by Jews against Gentiles, and its present significance was to indicate that in the sight of the missionaries those who rejected the gospel were no better than the Gentiles, cut off from the true people of God. If the Jews found themselves ultimately rejected by God, the blame for this would rest entirely on themselves; Paul had preached faithfully to them, and bore no responsibility for what they did with the message. From this point onwards he was justified in bothering no more with them and turning instead to the Gentiles, both proselytes and others (13:46; 28:28).

7. Since work in the synagogue was no longer possible, Paul turned elsewhere for accommodation and found it in the house of a Gentile who was an adherent of the synagogue (*cf.* 10:2) and had no doubt been converted by Paul's ministry. *Titius Justus* is a Roman name, like those of several of Paul's other converts in Corinth (Rom. 16:21–23; 1 Cor. 16:17).[1] Ramsay

---

[1] Some MSS give the name 'Titus Justus', but it is unlikely that this is the original text, or that he is to be identified with Paul's companion Titus who is otherwise not mentioned in Acts.

produced a full three-part Roman name for him by giving him the *praenomen* Gaius and identifying him with the Corinthian Christian of this name in Roman 16:23 and 1 Corinthians 1:14 who was 'host' to Paul and the church; this is a very reasonable conjecture, although it cannot be proved. Titius's house was *next door to the synagogue*, which can hardly have made for good relations but was no doubt an effective location for influencing attenders at the synagogue.

8. The move to the neighbouring property was highly successful. Many Corinthians now heard the message, *believed* and were *baptized*, and in particular Luke mentions *Crispus* who was the (or possibly, a) ruler of the synagogue (*cf.* 13:15). He is mentioned along with Gaius by Paul as being baptized by him (1 Cor. 1:14). It must have been galling for the Jews to have their leader go over to Paul's side, and it may be that worse was to follow for them (see on verse 17). Haenchen (p. 540) finds it more likely that Crispus was converted before Paul's break with the synagogue and thinks that Paul's move to the house of Titius Justus also took place earlier. On this view Paul sought premises which he could use at other times than when the synagogue was available, and it was his success in his new location which aroused the opposition of the Jews. This is a possible reconstruction, if verse 7 is not to be regarded as coming in chronological order, but Luke's account is equally plausible and possible.

9. Luke does not supply any motivation for the heavenly *vision* which Paul received at this stage to fortify him for his continuing activity in Corinth. From his knowledge of what happened on earlier occasions in Acts, however, the reader might well conclude that Paul could expect some reprisals from the Jews in view of his success in drawing away their leader and many of their adherents. Perhaps we should also remember how Paul himself comments that on his arrival in Corinth he was 'in much fear and trembling' (1 Cor. 2:3) and in need of spiritual encouragement. Haenchen (p. 540) goes so far as to suggest that normally Paul only stayed a short while in any town and would have made a speedy departure if he had not received divine encouragement to stay longer; since, however, Paul needed no such encouragement to stay on in Ephesus in similar circumstances (19:8–10), this hypothesis is false. In fact Paul usually stayed long enough to establish a Christian church unless he was forced to move on by persecution.

Paul's vision came from *the Lord*, *i.e.* from Jesus. It is significant that the message is couched in the language used by God himself in the Old Testament when addressing his servants (Stählin, p. 245, compares 7:9; Ex. 3:12; Dt. 31:6; Jos. 1:5, 9; Is. 41:10; 43:5; Je. 1:8). The New Testament assigns to Jesus a function and status equal to those of God the Father himself. The formula *Do not be afraid* is regularly used in Old Testament theophanies in order to calm the fears of the recipient of the vision at being addressed by God. Here, however, the words are directed rather at Paul's fears concerning his own position over against his opponents in Corinth. Instead of fearing what they may do to him, Paul is to proclaim the Word fearlessly. The Greek tenses used may suggest that Paul is to *go on* preaching as he has already been doing.

10. The command is backed up by the promise that the Lord will be with Paul (Is. 43:5). This type of promise was a form of assurance to those called by God to serve him that they would be able to fulfil his command (Jdg. 6:12; Ru. 2:14; Lk. 1:28). As a result of God's protection of Paul nobody would be able to lay hands on him and *harm* him. Furthermore, God has *many people in* the *city*. The connection of thought would appear to be that since God has many people to be won for the gospel in Corinth Paul will not be prevented by hostile action from continuing his missionary work until God's purpose is complete. The expression, however, is an unusual one, since it uses the term *people* for those who are not yet converted. The saying indicates divine foreknowledge of the success of the gospel in Corinth (*cf.* 13:48).[1] Fortified by this message, Paul could look forward to its double fulfilment in his safekeeping from persecution (18:12–17) and in his successful evangelism (18:11). Luke, however, does not need to explain in detail how the promise is fulfilled, at least in regard to its second half: the fact that it was the Lord's promise is evidence enough that it was fulfilled.

11. Accordingly the reader is left to deduce from the fact of Paul's extended period of activity in preaching the Word of God that many people did join the church. The precise dating

[1] It is unlikely that the verse means that the opponents of the gospel will be restrained from harming Paul by the large number of Christians in the city.

of the eighteen-month period depends on the information given in the next verse.

12. The fulfilment of the heavenly prophecy took place when *Gallio* became *proconsul* of the Roman province of *Achaia*. Luke's narrative suggests that the Jews seized the opportunity afforded by the arrival of a new governor to make an attack on Paul. Marcus Annaeus Novatus was a brother of the famous Stoic philosopher Seneca; he was the son of a Spanish orator, and on coming to Rome he was adopted into the family of Lucius Junius Gallio and took the name of his adoptive father. Since Achaia was a second-rank province, it was governed by someone who had not yet attained the rank of consul (the senior Roman magistracy).[1] Gallio accordingly came to Achaia after being praetor and before being consul. He had a pleasant character, but suffered from ill-health. He died as a result of Nero's suspicions against the family. The date of his proconsulship can be fixed fairly accurately from an inscription found at Delphi, and it probably commenced in July, AD 51.[2]

The Jews proceeded to bring Paul before the governor when the latter was seated on his *tribunal*; this was a stone platform in the *agora* of the city whose site can still be seen. It is not clear whether Paul was forcibly dragged before the governor or appeared of his own free will to answer the charge that was to be brought against him.

13. The Jewish charge was that Paul was *persuading men to worship God contrary to the law*. If we take this to refer to persuading Jews to act contrary to the Jewish law, the question was whether the governor could be expected to enforce their own domestic laws. In this case, the force of the accusation could have been that the Christians had no right to claim the protection afforded to adherents of Judaism as a *religio licita*, *i.e.* a religion officially tolerated by the state. Bruce's suggestion (*Book*, p. 374) that they wanted to have Christianity proscribed as a *religio illicita* probably goes too far, since it is

---

[1] Between AD 15 and 44 Achaia had been governed by the legate of Moesia, and after AD 67 Nero gave it and some other areas a measure of self-government.

[2] Barrett, *Background*, No. 46. More recent discussions of the inscription do not substantially alter the dating which is probably correct within a year either way. See C. J. Hemer's article in D. A. Hagner and M. J. Harris (eds.), *Pauline Studies* (Exeter, 1980).

doubtful whether this particular category existed. It is also possible, however, that the charge was that Paul was persuading men in general to worship contrary to the Roman law; this would have been a better charge for the Jews to pursue. Sherwin-White (pp. 99–107) offers the further suggestion that the Jews may have been appealing to an edict of Claudius guaranteeing them the quiet enjoyment of their own customs, and claiming that Paul was interfering with their peace to live according to their own ways.

14. Paul was ready to offer a defence of himself, but he was cut short by the governor on the grounds that there was no case to answer. In effect Gallio was being invited to give a verdict in a case which fell outside the normal system of crimes and punishments; in this area the governor had considerable freedom of action to dispense justice according to local custom and his own wisdom. Gallio's reply was that Paul's alleged conduct did not fall into the class of crimes against the state; such charges had to be treated seriously by the governor who had a duty to investigate them.

15. On the contrary, this matter appeared to be concerned with internal quarrels in the Jewish community about the requirements of their *own law*. It was indeed a matter of mere *words* and religious terminology – so far as Gallio could see. The Jews themselves must deal with the case, insofar as they possessed the powers to do so. The governor had no intention of becoming involved in matters that were not his business. Whatever the intention of the Jews, Gallio took the law about which they spoke in their charge to be their own Jewish law, and he rightly argued that he had no call as a Roman magistrate to interfere in such a matter.

16. Gallio's final act was to drive the Jews away from the tribunal as an indication that he did not wish to listen to their complaints any further. It is not clear whether the language is purely metaphorical or implies that some degree of force was exercised by the governor through his attendants; the latter would certainly be quite possible if the Jews were slow to disperse.

17. A final incident reinforced the impression given of Gallio's attitude, and thus underlined the fact that Christians need not fear that provincial Roman governors would interfere in Jewish matters. What actually happened, however, is open to debate. According to an early textual variant (which took *they* to mean the Greek population), the Corinthian crowd who were present to witness the Jews' discomfiture before the governor, saw that they could take advantage of the latter's unwillingness to interfere, and proceeded to indulge their anti-Jewish feelings by beating up *Sosthenes, the ruler of the synagogue.* But another explanation is possible. Sosthenes may have been a Christian sympathizer; it is certainly striking that a Sosthenes appears in 1 Corinthians 1:1 as co-author of Paul's letter to Corinth, and the possibility that Crispus's successor as ruler of the synagogue was also converted to Christianity cannot be ruled out. It could, then, have been the Jews who seized Sosthenes and administered the thirty-nine stripes (the regular synagogue punishment, 2 Cor. 11:24) to him, while Gallio refused to interfere in the administration of Jewish justice. On either interpretation Gallio refused to intervene in matters involving the Jews. In the former case, he connived at injustice against the Jews, while in the latter he did nothing to protect Christians from synagogue justice.

VII. PAUL'S MISSIONARY CAMPAIGN IN ASIA (18:18 – 20:38)

a. Paul's departure from Corinth (18:18–21)

In the course of the next few verses Luke compresses a considerable amount of journeying by Paul which took him from Corinth via Ephesus to Jerusalem and Antioch, and then back to Ephesus where he entered upon the next main phase of his missionary work. It is difficult to see why Luke told the story in this way if it had not happened thus, but nevertheless his account raises some difficult problems regarding Paul's motives and movements.

18. It was probably Gallio's refusal to support Jewish opposition to Paul which encouraged him to stay on in Corinth for some time; he would not in any case want to give the impression of running away from the city, even if he felt that his work was now complete or that he must turn to other tasks. His immediate aim was to return to Syria, the province of which Antioch was the capital and of which Judea formed a part. We may presume that Paul had personal reasons for seeking a 'furlough' at this time. He was accompanied by Priscilla and Aquila, whose destination was Ephesus, and this may explain why he went first to Ephesus rather than directly to Syria; in fact, however, there was nothing odd about the route.

Somewhat as an afterthought Luke adds the information that when they reached *Cenchreae*, the port for sailing east from Corinth, Paul *cut his hair* as part of a *vow*. Jews made vows to God either in thankfulness for past blessings (such as Paul's safekeeping in Corinth) or as part of a petition for future blessings (such as safekeeping on Paul's impending journey); the present context inclines towards the former interpretation. A temporary Nazirite vow involved abstinence from alcohol and also from cutting one's hair. Its conclusion was marked by shaving one's hair completely off and offering a sacrifice in the temple at Jerusalem (Nu. 6:1–21; Acts 23:21–26). If this was the kind of vow undertaken by Paul, it implies that he intended to visit Jerusalem. Some scholars find it puzzling that Paul cut his hair in Cenchreae. There is no evidence that this could be done at the beginning of a vow. The alternative view would be that Paul's action there marked the end of a vow previously taken. This view is usually rejected on the ground that vows could not be terminated outside Jerusalem. In fact, however, although the sacrifice had to be offered there, the shaving of the hair was permissible elsewhere (M. Nazir 3:6; 5:4). Some scholars regard it as unlikely that the historical Paul would have held fast to Jewish practices of this kind and have suggested that the whole account is a Lucan fiction designed to show that Paul was a loyal Jewish Christian. Perhaps too commentators feel a certain embarrassment at the suggestion that Christians should make vows of this kind to God, since they imply a *quid pro quo* relationship with God. But Paul was simply expressing gratitude to God in the manner traditional at this time; he was prepared to be 'as a Jew' to the Jews (1 Cor. 9:20; *cf.* Acts 16:3; 21:23f.); his action is historically possible and theologically acceptable.

19. *Ephesus* was the main city of the Roman province of Asia, situated at the mouth of the River Cayster on an important trade route inland. It was a free city with its own assembly (19:39), and had a famous temple of the goddess Artemis. The port is now silted up and the site abandoned, but impressive ruins have been uncovered, including the theatre. The town was a meeting place of various cultural influences, and it had a large Jewish population who enjoyed special privileges.

When Paul arrived here with his companions, he *left* Priscilla and Aquila while he continued his journey. At least, that is what Luke no doubt intended to say, but as the text stands it implies that Paul left them in Ephesus while he himself went to the synagogue. It would seem that the sentence begun in verse 19 finds its continuation in verse 21b, and that the intervening words have been inserted somewhat clumsily. Haenchen (p. 547) adopts the view that Luke made the insertion in order to give Paul the credit for being the first Christian preacher in Ephesus whereas in reality there was a Jewish-Christian group there before he commenced his work. In fact, however, there can be no doubt that Paul did visit Ephesus at this time, and it is highly unlikely that he would not have seized the opportunity for evangelism.

20. But the visit was only a brief one, and Paul refused to extend it despite the favourable reception given to his message. According to the western text, he wanted to reach Jerusalem in time for 'the festival'; although the scribe may have supplied this motive from 20:16, he may have hit on the truth. If the feast was passover, Paul would have had to hurry for the period between the opening up of navigation after the winter and the festival was short (Bruce, *Book*, p. 378).

21. So Paul took his leave with a promise to return if this was God's will. His wording reflects a pagan formula taken over by Christians (21:14; Jas. 4:15), possibly as a result of the similar wording found in Matthew's version of the Lord's Prayer (Mt. 6:10).

b. Paul's journey to Caesarea and Antioch (18:22–23)

22. Although Paul's destination was said to be Syria in verse 18, in fact his journey home took him first to Caesarea. It appears that the direction of the prevailing winds made it easier for ships to reach *Caesarea* than Seleucia, the port for Antioch (13:4), which was about 250 miles to the north. Luke's narrative does not make it clear whether Paul went deliberately to Caesarea or merely as a result of the weather. When he goes on to say that Paul *went up and greeted the church*, this is usually understood as a reference to going up to Jerusalem and seeing the church there; this would fit in with the suggestion that Paul's vow could be terminated only by the offering

301

of a sacrifice in Jerusalem. If this is a correct assumption, it means that each of Paul's missionary campaigns concluded with a visit to Jerusalem, so that Paul's work began from and ended in Jerusalem in each case. Paul presumably gave an account of his work to the church there. Nevertheless, the case is not a watertight one, and it is possible that Luke simply means that Paul greeted the church in Caesarea; the question depends on whether Luke could have used the verb 'to go down' to refer to a journey from the seaport of Caesarea to the inland town of Antioch rather than from Jerusalem to Antioch. On the whole, however, the former view is preferable.

23. Paul spent some time at *Antioch* before beginning his next campaign. His goal was Ephesus, and he went there by the inland route, taking the opportunity to visit in turn the various groups of Christians formed on earlier missionary journeys and to give them spiritual encouragement. *The region of Galatia and Phrygia* is probably the area in south Galatia evangelized in Acts 13–14. Many scholars think that the reference here and in 16:6 (where a slightly different wording occurs) is to ethnic Galatia, but this is less likely. The description must at least include the churches founded in Acts 13–14.

c. The arrival of Apollos (18:24–28)

Before Luke takes up the story of Paul's return to Ephesus and his work there he inserts an account of the arrival of Apollos on the scene. The reader is thus brought up to date on what had been happening in Ephesus during Paul's absence. Apollos was to be an important figure in the church at Corinth and indeed he became the focus of some rivalry to Paul; the present passage indicates that although he himself had not been instructed by Paul, he nevertheless received his Christian education from Paul's colleagues, so that he can be assumed to have shared Paul's theological outlook, and indeed Paul himself implies this (1 Cor. 3:5–9).

24. *Apollos* is an abbreviated form of the name Apollonius. He was a native of Alexandria, and the rest of the description of his abilities fits in well with this detail. *Alexandria* was a centre of education and philosophy, and it was here that Philo, the Jewish philosopher, worked. Apollos may well have owed his eloquence and debating ability to his upbringing in Alexandria. As an educated Jew he was *well versed in the scriptures* and able to turn his knowledge to good Christian use.

25. We do not know where Apollos became a Christian. Although there is every reason to suppose that the faith would have come at an early date to Alexandria, we know nothing about its beginnings there, and the first Christianity of which we do hear was characterized by Gnostic tendencies. It would not be surprising if Apollos had picked up some garbled understanding of Christianity there. Certainly the description of his Christian status is odd. He had received Christian instruction in *the way of the Lord*, and he was able to teach accurately about Jesus. He was enthusiastic *in spirit* (Rom. 12:11), but he understood only the baptism of John. This description raises difficult questions: Does Luke mean that Apollos possessed the Spirit although he had not received Christian baptism with water? And if Apollos had not received Christian baptism, why was he not baptized like the twelve men at Ephesus (19:5)? The problem is treated by E. Käsemann[1] who argues that in the face of the heretics of his day Luke could not countenance the existence of freelance missionaries like Apollos who worked independently of the mainstream church. He therefore showed how Apollos had to be properly instructed by Priscilla and Aquila in order to be an effective missionary. He did not dare to report the rebaptism of one who was known to be possessed by the Spirit and gifted for missionary service, but he fabricated the detail that Apollos had merely received Johannine baptism, and by linking the story with that of the twelve men at Ephesus he attempted to make Apollos at least 'guilty by association'. As Haenchen (p. 551) puts it, Luke did not dare to say more than that Apollos did not 'understand' Christian baptism.

This view of the passage faces strong objections. First, in view of the heretical character of much early Christianity in Alexandria, it would not be surprising if Apollos had picked up defective ideas of the faith. Secondly, the existence of the twelve men at Ephesus shows that it was possible for people to think of themselves as disciples while merely having received John's baptism (unless with Käsemann we deny that they thought of themselves as Christians). Thirdly, Luke knew

[1] E. Käsemann, *Essays on New Testament Themes* (London, 1964), pp. 136–148.

303

that it was possible in exceptional cases for people to receive the Spirit apart from Christian baptism with water (10:44–48); Apollos differed from the twelve men in that they had clearly *not* received the Spirit, while he probably had received the Spirit. Fourthly, it is possible that there were groups of former disciples of John who had moved on to faith in the coming One without having been baptized in the name of Jesus. Did Luke shrink from recording the historical fact that so mighty a preacher as Apollos nevertheless needed to be baptized in the name of Jesus? This would lead us to exactly the opposite view of the passage from Käsemann, but on the whole it is more probable that, since Apollos had received the Spirit, he did not need to be rebaptized with water.

26. When Apollos came and started to carry on a Christian mission in the synagogue, Priscilla and Aquila recognized the shortcomings in his understanding of the faith and *took* him aside privately so that he might have a yet more accurate understanding of the faith. We can presume that he was instructed in the distinctive Pauline doctrines.

27. The teaching he received was effective, and the Christians in Ephesus gained a full confidence in Apollos, so much so that when he decided to go to Achaia, they were happy to write a letter of introduction for him to the Christians there. *The brethren* will be the Christians in Ephesus, converted as a result of the brief ministry of Paul and the work of Priscilla and Aquila; they may have included in their number Christian converts who had come to Ephesus from elsewhere. From 1 Corinthians 16:19 we learn that they met as a house church in the home of Priscilla and Aquila. RSV says that they *encouraged* Apollos to go *to Achaia*, but the text could also mean that they encouraged the disciples at Corinth to welcome Apollos. For such letters of introduction see Roman 16:1; 2 Corinthians 3:1. On his arrival Apollos soon showed his worth in building up the church, as Paul himself was later to testify (1 Cor. 3:6). *He helped those who through grace had believed* (RSV), or perhaps by his (gift of) grace he helped the believers: the text can bear either meaning, but the latter is preferable.

28. Apollos's special gift lay in debate with *Jews*, since out of his knowledge of the Scriptures he was able to demonstrate that the Messiah was Jesus (*cf.* 18:5). He was thus an effective evangelist as well as a pastor to the church.

d. The twelve disciples at Ephesus (19:1–7)

In close connection with the story of Apollos (*cf.* 19:1) Luke recounts how Paul himself found some people in Ephesus who claimed to be Christians but lacked any experience of the Spirit. He instructed them, baptized them, and laid his hands on them, with the result that they demonstrated manifest signs of the gift of the Spirit. This story has often been used as the basis for doctrines about the reception of gifts of the Spirit subsequent to conversion; but it has no real connection with these. Rather Paul was dealing with an unusual situation which required special treatment.

1. Verse 1 gives the chronological link with the preceding story about Apollos, and incidentally indicates that Paul himself was not involved in the Christian instruction of his colleague. Paul made his way to Ephesus via an inland route that brought him from the territories mentioned in 18:23. On arrival he found a group of *disciples*. These men can hardly have been Christians since they had not received the gift of the Spirit; it is safe to say that the New Testament does not recognize the possibility of being a Christian apart from possession of the Spirit (Jn. 3:5; Acts 11:17; Rom. 8:9; 1 Cor. 12:3; Gal. 3:2; 1 Thes. 1:5f.; Tit. 3:5; Heb. 6:4; 1 Pet. 1:2; 1 Jn. 3:24; 4:13). Consequently it has been suggested that they were disciples of John the Baptist, and this agrees with the fact that they had received John's baptism. It is, however, unlikely that the word 'disciples' used without qualification can be understood to mean 'disciples of John the Baptist'. Despite this, E. Käsemann (see 18:25 note) supposes that they were disciples of John. Luke, he thinks, was unwilling to recognize that such groups existed alongside the church and therefore tried, not altogether successfully, to present them as somewhat odd Christians. Otherwise, Käsemann claims, it might appear that John had presented himself as a leader, and even as the Messiah, to his followers, instead of humbly testifying to Jesus in the way that the Gospels depict him. This understanding of the passage is wrong; John the Baptist did not need to be held responsible for any strange views held by his followers. The correct explanation of the passage[1] is that Luke has told the story from the standpoint of the principal

---

[1] K. Haacker, 'Einige Fälle von "Erlebter Rede" im Neuen Testament', *Nov.T* 12, 1970, pp. 70–77.

actor: Paul met some men who *appeared to him* to be disciples, but because he had some doubts about their Christian status he proceeded to examine their claims more carefully. Luke is not saying that the men were disciples but is describing how they appeared to Paul.

2. In view of his uncertainty Paul put a test question to them. The RSV translation *Did you receive the Holy Spirit when you believed?* assumes that the participle 'having believed' (Gk. *pisteusantes*) refers to an action at a time coincident with that of the main verb 'you received'. This is an accepted Greek construction (11:17; Eph. 1:13). Some scholars would translate, 'Did you receive the Holy Spirit *after* you believed?' with the implication that reception of the Spirit is a gift subsequent to belief in Jesus. While this is a possible understanding of the syntax, it is undoubtedly a wrong understanding of the phrase here in its context; it places an unwarranted stress on the 'after' and goes against the constant New Testament association of the Spirit with conversion. No-one can become a true believer in Jesus without receiving the Spirit (verse 1 note).[1] The group replied by denying that they had ever heard about the Spirit. This reply has been taken to imply that they knew nothing about the Spirit and therefore that John the Baptist had never mentioned the Spirit (contrary to what is reported in the Gospels, Mt. 3:11; Jn. 1:33). We should not in any case tie the teaching of John too closely to the garbled reports of it that may have been current in Asia Minor twenty years later, but the group's comment simply means that they did not know that the Spirit had yet been given (*cf.* Jn. 7:39).

3. Since the men disclaimed knowledge of the Spirit, the next stage in Paul's probing was into the nature of their baptism: *into what* had they been *baptized?* What kind of baptism had they had? Their reply was 'John's baptism'. The way in which this answer is framed suggests that various different kinds of baptism could be contrasted (as in Heb. 6:2), and it may be that Luke has compressed an answer of the form, 'We were baptized in the way commanded by John'. This confession shows that the men were followers of John the Baptist but knew something about Jesus. Somehow knowledge of Jesus separate from the Christian message about his re-

---

[1] For fuller discussion see Dunn, *Baptism*, pp. 83–89.

surrection and outpouring of the Spirit seems to have spread to Ephesus and probably elsewhere.

4. Paul therefore reminded the group of what John the Baptist himself had said. His own baptism had been associated with *repentance*: it provided a divine opportunity of repentance (*cf.* 5:31; 11:18) and at the same time had to be accompanied by the concrete fruits of repentance in the form of a changed heart and the corresponding changed way of life. But John himself had told the people of the coming of the 'stronger One', with the implication that they should believe in him (*cf.* Jn. 1:26ff.; 3:25ff.), and had promised that the coming One would baptize with the Holy Spirit. Now Paul made it clear to his hearers that the coming One was Jesus. If, however, they were already disciples, then his task was not so much to convince them that Jesus was the coming One (a fact of which John was conscious, Lk. 7:19) as to give them the news that the coming One had now poured out the Spirit.

5. Their response to the message was to be *baptized in the name of Jesus*. This is the only case recorded in the New Testament of people receiving a second baptism, and it took place only because the previous baptism was not Christian baptism in the name of Jesus. It would be wrong to conclude from this incident that people today who did not receive the Spirit at their baptism (whether as infants or adults) ought to be rebaptized in order to receive the Spirit; the characteristic and essential feature of the ceremony of *Christian* baptism is that it is performed in the name of Jesus, and the chronological relation of the gift of the Spirit to the actual rite is unimportant, as the varied order in Acts demonstrates (before baptism: 10:47; at baptism: 2:38; 8:38f.; after baptism: 8:15f.).

6. As part of the rite Paul also *laid his hands upon the men*, and thereupon *the Spirit came on them*, his presence being signified by the gifts of tongues and prophecy. Laying on of hands is also associated with the gift of the Spirit in 8:17f., but elsewhere it is not mentioned in this connection (1 Tim. 4:14 and 2 Tim. 1:6f. refer to ordination for Christian service). Some scholars have concluded that Luke regarded it as part of the rite of baptism even in those instances where it is not mentioned (Bovon, pp. 251f.), but Hanson (pp. 190f.), comments that no such association of the laying on of hands with the gift of the Spirit at baptism can be traced before AD 200, and then only sporadically. It seems more likely that the laying on of hands should be understood as a special act of fellowship, incorporating the people concerned into the fellowship of the church. This was necessary in the case of the Samaritan converts in chapter 8 to make it quite clear that they were accepted fully into the Jewish church centred on Jerusalem; and it was necessary in the present instance to make it clear to these members of a semi-Christian group that they were now becoming part of the universal church. The fact that the story demonstrates that Paul had the same authority as Peter and John to convey the gift of the Spirit is probably merely a secondary motif. The effect of the baptism was to produce 'charismatic' manifestations of the Spirit (2:4, 17f.; 10.46). It is clear from the other stories of conversion in Acts that such manifestations took place spasmodically and were not the general rule (8:17 note; 8:39; 13:52; 16:34); in the present case some unusual gift was perhaps needed to convince this group of 'semi-Christians' that they were now fully members of Christ's church.

7. The number of the group is added as a footnote; it is unlikely to have any symbolical significance.

e. Paul's work in Ephesus (19:8–22)

Luke's account of Paul's final major task as an evangelist is unusually full and vivid. The general pattern of Paul's activity in Ephesus was the same as in Corinth, but the story is told in greater detail, culminating in the account of the riot directed against Paul (19:24–41). Haenchen (pp. 558–579), however, is particularly scathing regarding the historical value of the story; he claims that it contains numerous historical improbabilities and that it represents the picture of Paul as the great and successful apostle held by the post-apostolic church rather than a historical portrait. But while the narrative raises some difficult questions, it is doubtful whether Haenchen has provided the right answers to them.

8. Paul began by returning to the *synagogue* where he had previously taught (18:19–21) and continuing his work there. Luke piles up the verbs which express the forceful and convincing character of Paul's approach, and gives the impression that his preaching was effective in converting his audience. His theme is described as *the kingdom of God* (*cf.* 8:12; 20:25). It is unlikely that this means that Paul was preaching a different message from that in 17:31; 18:5 and other places which was concerned with Jesus as the Messiah. The message was about Jesus *and* the kingdom (28:31), and Luke employs the different terms simply for literary variation.

9. Paul's association with the synagogue lasted for three months, which was longer than usual. It was brought to an end by the opposition of some of the Jews who were hardened against the message,[1] refused to believe it, and spoke against it (*cf.* 13:45; 18:6). The strength of the opposition was such that Paul felt that he could no longer use the synagogue as a base for evangelism, and he therefore moved to neutral ground, just as he had done in Corinth. *The hall of Tyrannus* was probably a lecture room or school building, and Tyrannus was the owner or the teacher; if the latter, his name must have given obvious opportunity to his pupils to speak of their teacher as 'the tyrant'! The western text adds the detail that Paul was active from the fifth hour to the tenth, *i.e.* from 11.00 am to 4.00 pm. Hanson (p. 191) argues that this trivial piece of information is unlikely to be an authentic reminiscence preserved by the western reviser; it is more probably part of an attempt to portray Paul as a Christian 'philosopher', lecturing to a class at set hours. This period of the day, however, was after the close of the morning's work, and, despite the fact that many people would take a siesta for part of it, it is historically probable that Paul was able to use the hall when Tyrannus himself was not using it and when his audience would be free to attend. Haenchen (pp. 560f.), sees problems. He questions whether Paul could have worked earlier in the day to keep himself and lectured on top of that, he doubts whether Paul's earnings would have been sufficient to pay the rent to Tyrannus, and he is puzzled by the reasons which led to the move: why did the break with the synagogue come at this precise point, and would the Christians not have been meeting separately to hold the Lord's Supper long before this? These questions arise because Haenchen presses the literal meaning of the text ('daily') to an unwarranted extent and fails to reckon that Tyrannus may have been a Christian or a sympathizer who made little or no charge for the use of his premises (especially at a time when he would not be using them himself). To be sure, it would be interesting to know in more detail what led to Paul's departure from the synagogue,

[1] On 'the Way' see 9:1f. note.

and Haenchen puts us on the right lines when he suggests that the Christians were already meeting as house groups before the break with the synagogue came; what was at issue was the use of the synagogue for evangelism.

10. Paul's ministry in Ephesus lasted for *two years* in his new base of operations (*cf.* 18:11 for a comparable period in Corinth). Luke is content to record that (speaking broadly) all the people in the surrounding province heard the gospel. Again, we would like to know more than Luke tells us, but from other information we can tell that Paul probably journeyed further afield himself (*e.g.* to Corinth) and that his colleagues helped to spread the gospel to towns which he personally never visited (*e.g.* Colossae).

11–12. Paul's preaching was accompanied by striking healings and exorcisms. They resembled the activities of Peter (5:15f.), and Paul himself refers to the signs, wonders and mighty works which accompanied his ministry (2 Cor. 12:12; Rom. 15:19; *cf.* Gal. 3:5; see also Heb. 2:4). The unusual character of Paul's powers was seen in the fact that even pieces of clothing which he had touched were taken to the sick and exercised a beneficial healing influence upon them. The rationalists have naturally found great difficulties with these reports (*cf.* 5:15). Nevertheless, it is impossible to gainsay the conviction of Paul himself that miraculous signs accompanied his ministry, although he did not personally regard these as the most important credentials of his ministry and it was possible for his opponents to play down their significance. We need not doubt then, that Paul, like Jesus, displayed miraculous powers. Granted this point, however, it is undeniably difficult to distinguish what is described here in verse 12 from primitive and crude beliefs in mana, *i.e.* in a quasi-physical power emanating from the healer and infecting his clothes so that these can be the vehicles of supernatural power. It is suprising that Luke, who is so critical of pagan magic, can allow that similar magical beliefs in a Christianized form were effective in the apostolic ministry. Perhaps we may suggest that God is capable of condescending to the level of men who still think in such crude ways, just as he did with the woman with the haemorrhage who needed, however, to be brought to a personal encounter with Jesus (Lk. 8:43–48).

13. A vigorous little anecdote acts as a foil to the report of Paul's powers and provides some indication of the kind of environment in which he worked. There were people who went around making a living by various kinds of pseudo-scientific or clairvoyant powers, including the practice of ex-orcism. They were ready to call on the names of any and every god or divinity in their invocations – and often they recited long lists of names so as to be sure of including the right god in any particular case. Even pagans used the various Jewish names of God. These Jewish exorcists (*cf.* Lk. 11:19) now proceeded to use the name of Jesus in an endeavour to rival Paul's powers. A magical formula preserved in the Paris mag-ical papyrus reads, 'I adjure thee by the God of the Hebrews, Jesus'.

14. The Jewish group who tried out this invocation were known as the seven sons of Sceva, a Jewish high priest. No person of that name ever was *the* Jewish high priest. Either Sceva was simply a member of a high-priestly family, or he assumed the title for professional purposes in order to impress and delude the public, since a high priest (or his sons) would have close contact with the supernatural; we may compare the way in which modern quacks take such titles as 'Doctor' or 'Professor'. Haenchen's claim (p. 565) that Luke really held the mistaken belief that Sceva was a high priest rests on his view that Luke would consider only a triumph over a genuine high priest (rather than over some insignificant exorcists) worth recording; but the point of the story is not the status of the exorcists but the attempt to use the name of Jesus.[1]

15–17. The attempt at invocation failed; the evil spirit in the man whom they were trying to cure confessed to knowing about Jesus and about Paul who used his name, but chal-lenged their right to use the name. Not only so, but under its influence the man turned violent and attacked them, so that they were glad to escape with the loss of their clothes. The story assumes the same kind of supernatural knowledge on the part of the possessed as we find in the Gospels (Lk. 4:34, 41; 8:28), and so takes us into an area of experience which is strange and puzzling to many modern readers. The story and presumably others like it became known among both Jews

---

[1] B. A. Mastin, 'Scaeva the Chief Priest', *JTS* 27, 1976, pp. 405–412, argues that Scaeva may have been a member of a high priest family; his sons would have been priests and thus regarded as able to perform exorcisms. Hence Haenchen's scepticism is quite unjustified.

and Greeks in the area, and the effect among a superstitious people was to cause both fear and praise for the name of Jesus. In a situation where people were gripped by superstition, perhaps the only way for Christianity to spread was by the demonstration that the power of Jesus was superior to that of the demons, even if those who came to believe in Jesus were tempted to think of his power and person in ways that were still conditioned by their primitive categories of thought; it took time for the church to purify its concept of God from pagan ways of thinking, and the tendency to let our ideas of God be influenced by contemporary, and sometimes misleading, trends of philosophical and scientific thinking is one that still confronts the church.

18–20. Nevertheless, the process of purification of Christian thinking from paganism was assisted by what had happened. Christians are not fully converted or perfected in an instant, and pagan ways of thinking can persist alongside genuine Christian experience; the history of the church in Corinth shows that Christians took some time to be persuaded that sexual immorality and idol-worship were ultimately incompatible with Christian faith (1 Cor. 6:9–11). Sooner or later there must come a point when believers realize the need to confess the sinfulness of their practices; if it is possible to go further and remove the cause of the temptation, as in this case, so much the better. The demonstration of the futility of pagan attempts to master evil spirits led many of Paul's Ephesian converts to realize that the pagan magic to which they were still attached was both useless and sinful. They therefore brought the various magical handbooks and compilations of invocations and formulae to which they were still clinging and made a final break with them by publicly burning them. The particular fascination of this kind of rubbish for the Ephesians is demonstrated by the fact that magical books were known as 'Ephesian letters'. The value of the 'rubbish' was high – corresponding to the wages of 50,000 workmen for a day's work apiece – but this is not necessarily an exaggeration in city conditions, nor when compared with what ordinary people today may spend on similar knick-knacks and frivolities. On this high note Luke ends the account of Paul's successful ministry in Ephesus, although the story of what happened in Ephesus is not yet complete.

21. Under the guidance of the Spirit Paul came to the

312

conclusion that his work of church-founding in Ephesus was at the stage where he could leave it, in order to accomplish other plans.[1] He determined to revisit Macedonia and Achaia before returning to Jerusalem. Luke leaves the reader to guess that the detour to Paul's earlier mission fields was for the purpose of encouraging the young churches as in 14:22f.; 15:36, 41; 18:23. Nor does he mention here that one of Paul's purposes was to collect the offerings that were being assembled for Jerusalem and to take them there. Hanson (pp. 194f.) correctly observes that, writing from a later perspective, Luke recognized that Paul's arrest and its sequel were more significant than the delivery of the collection to Jerusalem, although the latter seemed more important to Paul himself at the time (see Rom. 15:25–33; 1 Cor. 16:1–4; 2 Cor. 8 – 9. Luke's knowledge of the collection is seen momentarily in Acts 24:17). Looking on beyond Jerusalem, Paul also expressed his purpose of visiting Rome; more precisely he commented that he *must* see Rome, not in the sense of a tourist who says, 'I must see Venice' but in the same sense as Jesus who was conscious that the course of his life was dictated by a 'must' that had its origin in the purpose of God (Lk. 4:43; 9:22). No doubt sceptics would try to suggest that this insight into Paul's intentions represents Luke's imaginative reconstruction based on what he actually did later, were it not that Romans 15:22–24 provides first-hand evidence that this was precisely Paul's purpose at this very time.

22. Paul prepared for his journey by sending two of his colleagues on to Macedonia. Luke implies that Paul was not suddenly driven from Ephesus by the machinations of Demetrius and his friends (20:23–41): his preparations for departure had already been made. According to 1 Corinthians *Timothy* had already visited Corinth and probably returned to Ephesus (1 Cor. 4:17; 16:10, 17; this visit cannot be equated with the one envisaged here, since this would not allow sufficient time between the composition of 1 and 2 Corinthians). Some scholars have suggested that the journey here is the same as that in Philippians 2:19, which was to be followed by Paul's own visit to the area (Phil. 2:24; this view depends on the assumption that Philippians was written from Ephesus

---

[1] The phrase *in the Spirit* could also mean 'in his spirit'; *cf.* 18:25; 20:22 for a similar ambiguity; Bruce, *Acts*, p. 361, rightly prefers the former rendering.

about this time). Attempts have also been made to link 1 Timothy with this period (1 Tim. 1:3).[1] As for *Erastus*, we know of a person of this name who was 'town clerk' of Corinth (Rom. 16:23; *cf.* 2 Tim. 4:20), but it is doubtful whether a person who held an official post of this kind would have been free to move about on missionary work, and in any case the name was a common one. Haenchen (pp. 569f.), draws attention to the absence of Titus from this verse (and indeed from Acts generally), and holds that a reference to him rather than to Timothy would have been appropriate here (*cf.* 2 Cor. 2:13); he concludes, without any real evidence, that Luke's report is muddled, but at most we can say that it is incomplete.

f. The reaction of paganism in Ephesus (19:23–41)

The opposition to Paul which arose in Ephesus was like that in Philippi in springing from pagan sources. To the charge that Paul was interfering with the vested interests of those who made their living from idolatry was added the accusation that he was striking at pagan religion itself. The incident, as Luke relates, expresses the wide effects of the Christian mission, and also brings out the arbitrariness and confusion of the opposition which had no clearly concerted plan of action. It is also made clear that those who were in positions of authority were opposed to action against the missionaries, except by the proper legal processes. The story is in effect a statement that Christians do not constitute a danger to the state and a plea that they be treated with toleration in a pluralistic society; only when properly defined criminal charges can be preferred against them should they be summoned before the courts.

In his commentary Haenchen (pp. 576–579) subjects this story (like the whole of the Ephesus account) to strong criticism and alleges that it is full of historical improbabilities: (1) If Paul had threatened the existence of the cult of Artemis, we should have expected that other interested parties, including especially the priests, would have joined to oppose him. (2) It is surprising that Demetrius, who showed himself such a capable agitator among his fellow silversmiths, should have had no clear idea of what he was going to do at the assembly; in

[1] J. A. T. Robinson, *Redating the New Testament*, pp. 82–84, associates 1 Timothy with Paul's departure from Ephesus Acts 20:1.

fact he quietly disappears from the scene, and nothing happens despite the popular support which his cause enjoyed. (3) How did the Asiarchs appear on the scene so promptly to advise Paul, and why should guardians of the imperial cult have rushed to the assistance of Paul? (4) What is the point of the 'Jewish intermezzo' in the assembly? It seems unmotivated and leads nowhere. (5) The clerk's dismissal of the complaints against the Christians with a reference to the acknowledged greatness of Artemis is odd, and he ignores the fact that the Christians denied the divinity of Artemis (which would surely be the same thing as blaspheming the goddess). (6) As his principal argument, Haenchen notes that Paul himself states that he suffered an almost unbearable affliction in Asia, tantamount to a death sentence, from which only God could deliver him (2 Cor. 1:8–11). This event is not mentioned by Luke, since the present incident could hardly be described in these terms. So, Haenchen concludes, Luke did not in fact know what had happened in Ephesus, but on the basis of a few pieces of information about Ephesus and the tradition that Paul experienced some kind of tumultuous experience before his departure he decided to construct a dramatic account which would shed the maximum of glory on Paul and his successful evangelism by its ironic depiction of the futile opposition to him.

Imposing as the case may seem at first sight, it disappears under scrutiny: (1) It is improbable that the Christian mission had seriously threatened the worship at the temple of Artemis, and we must allow for some exaggeration on the part of Demetrius (and perhaps on the part of Luke; *cf.* 19:10, 17 for examples of Luke's loose use of 'all'). We do not in fact hear that Demetrius's trade had suffered any marked diminution, and he may have been guessing what might happen rather than describing what had already happened. In a pluralist, polytheistic society the priests of Artemis may well not have taken action against what may have appeared to them as a comparatively irrelevant sect. (2) Demetrius does not in fact disappear from the scene, if we take 19:38 at its face value. Luke has not recorded what he said or did in the assembly, but it seems clear that his accusations against the missionaries must have been vague and hard to prove. Demetrius emerges as a demagogue, good at rousing crowds but not very clear about what specific action he wanted taken. (3) It can be assumed that the gathering of the assembly took some little time after the protest march began, so that one or two of the Asiarchs would easily know what was going on. There is no reason why Paul should not have been acquainted with some of them, and he may have made a good impression on them, as he did on other Roman officials. We admittedly do not know how they were in the position to warn Paul not to go to the assembly, but we are equally not in a position to deny that this could have happened. (4) The fact that the 'Jewish intermezzo' is unmotivated favours its historicity. Haenchen suggests that Luke used it to show how hostile the Greeks were to the Jews (*cf.* 18:17, but see note there); but he does not explain why Luke should have wanted to show this. Even if Luke had a motive for introducing the incident, this of course does not show it was unhistorical. (5) The clerk's argument is concerned with what had actually been proved before the assembly, and his point was that the assembly was in danger of acting illegally and so arousing Roman wrath; he was therefore concerned to 'play it cool', and so he minimized the force of the accusations against the missionaries. (6) Luke's narrative of Paul's time in Ephesus is certainly incomplete. There is some reason to suppose that Paul was imprisoned there (some of the afflictions listed in 2 Cor. 11:23 may well fit into this period), and he speaks metaphorically of 'fighting with beasts at Ephesus' (1 Cor. 15:32). He suffered his 'great affliction' in Asia, which very possibly means Ephesus. This 'affliction' may well have been a severe illness which nearly killed him, rather than an experience of persecution. Both Luke's and Paul's lists of his experiences are incomplete, and therefore it is not surprising that Paul himself does not specifically refer to this episode, nor that Luke, interested mainly in the relations of Paul with his opponents outside the church, should pass in silence over his illness. It is doubtful, therefore, whether we can press the argument from silence against Luke's account here. In addition to these points we may observe that the story itself fits in remarkably well with the political situation in Ephesus, as reconstructed by Sherwin-White (pp. 83–92) who comments that 'the author of Acts is very well informed about the finer points of municipal institutions at Ephesus' (p. 87). But there are so many cases where this might be said about Luke that it becomes increasingly difficult to think that he was a writer of historical fiction remote from the events he purports to describe. Luke's account is not free from difficulty, but it must be remembered that he was recording selectively and loved a good story. There is good reason to believe that this story is well founded on fact.

23. The incident arose towards the end of Paul's stay in Ephesus, at the time when he was already making plans for his departure (20:1). One suggestion is that it occurred in the spring around the time of the annual festival of Artemis, but this cannot be proved. For *the Way* see 9:1f. note; 19:9.

24. The ringleader was a certain *Demetrius* who had a factory for making silver models of the famous shrine of *Artemis*. Artemis was the Greek name of a goddess (Latin: Diana; *cf.* AV) who had been identified in Hellenistic syncretism with an Asiatic goddess. While Artemis was a virgin goddess, the patron of hunting, the Asian goddess was a fertility goddess. She was represented as a female figure with many breasts (according to the usual interpretation of the imagery) and an image of her was placed in the great temple at Ephesus which ranked as one of the seven wonders of the world. The festival of Artemis was celebrated with wild orgies and carousing. Small terra-cotta models of the temple have survived, but so far no silver ones (which in any case were less likely to survive) have been found. It has been suggested that Luke has converted a Demetrius who is known to have been an official warden of the temple at this time into a maker of shrines, but this speculation has no basis; the name was extremely common.

25. Demetrius gathered together the members of the employers' federation (as we would call it), in order to organize a protest demonstration. He appears as a man with a nice sense of what would appeal to his fellow tradesmen, and so he put before them as the first consideration the fact that their trade, which was no doubt as profitable as the modern production of souvenirs for tourists, was in danger of going into decline.

26. Throughout Ephesus and its neighbourhood many of the worshippers of Artemis were turning to Christianity, and no longer believed in idols made by human *hands*. The early Christian missionaries had gladly taken up the existing arguments, based on the Old Testament, which were used by Jewish apologists in combatting idolatry (Is. 44:9–20; 46:1–7; Acts 17:29).

27. As a result there was a *danger* of the silversmiths' line of business getting a bad name (*i.e.* for promoting idolatry). Already with these words Demetrius is sliding over from the explicit profit motive with which he began to the kind of arguments which could be used to support this claim and indeed to replace it in appeals to a wider public. The ordinary people might not be too concerned that Demetrius was going out of business, but they might well take to heart the possibility that the *temple of Artemis* might lose its position in popular regard, and, even more, that the *goddess*, associated with Ephesus but drawing worshippers from all over the world, might be dethroned from her position.

28. Demetrius proved to be an effective advocate of his cause. His colleagues expressed their approval of his speech by responding with the cult cry shouted in the worship of the goddess: *Great is Artemis of the Ephesians!*

29. We are not told where the protest meeting was held, but evidently it culminated in a protest march through the streets.[1] A crowd quickly gathered who were sympathetic to the silversmiths, and it was decided to hold a larger-scale protest. The appropriate site for a public meeting of any size in many Greek cities was the open-air *theatre*; the one in Ephesus has been excavated and estimated to have been capable of holding 25,000 persons. The meeting that took place was an official meeting of the citizen body of the town, and its purpose would have been to persuade the city officials to take action against the missionaries. The instigators of the meeting managed to lay hold of two of them, *Gaius and Aristarchus*. The latter hailed from Thessalonica (20:4; 27:2; *cf.* Col. 4:10; Phlm. 24). There is a Gaius mentioned in 20:4, but, as the text stands, he came from Derbe in Galatia (see note on 20:4, however); it was in any case a very common name. The opponents evidently were not interested in the local Ephesian church leaders; presumably they wanted to have Paul, or at least his immediate associates who had brought this new religion into the area.

30–31. Paul, however, escaped their clutches. He was willing to appear before the citizen-body[2]; his friends, however,

---

[1] This is made explicit in the western text, which often fills out – not always correctly – details left obscure in the Alexandrian text.

[2] This is a better translation of *dēmos* than is *crowd* (RSV), although the latter word effectively describes the actual character of the company (*cf.* 17:5).

restrained him out of fear for his safety. Their persuasions were backed up by some of the *Asiarchs* who were friendly to Paul. This term could refer to 'the annual presidents, and perhaps the ex-presidents, of the provincial council of Asia, or it also covers the administrators of the various temples of the imperial cult, which were under the charge of high-priests appointed by the provincial council, or it may merely designate the city deputies to that council' (Sherwin-White, p. 90). They were thus members of a religious and political grouping of cities in Asia, and they would belong to the aristocracy. It is noteworthy that Paul had friends in this circle and that they were concerned for his safety in face of the mob.

32. The actual meeting in the theatre was somewhat disorganized and showed none of the orderly procedure of a Greek democratic city. Luke waxes sarcastic over the fact that many of the crowd did not know why they were there at all; mobs often show the same disorder and confusion.

33. There were representatives of the Jewish community present, and they probably wished to make it clear that they were in no way associated with the Christians. In an attempt to clear themselves of any possibility of coming under the same suspicions they put forward a representative called *Alexander* to speak on their behalf, and he did his best to secure attention from the noisy crowd by motioning for silence. The words *some of the crowd prompted Alexander* (RSV) are puzzling. The RSV translation implies that some (non-Jewish) members of the crowd put Alexander forward to speak when the Jews made him their spokesman. Haenchen (p. 574) takes the verb to mean 'instruct' and that the crowd 'genned up' Alexander on the actual state of affairs before he tried to speak. Bruce (*Acts*, p. 366) thinks that the crowd 'conjectured' Alexander to be the cause of the trouble.

34. The crowd as a whole, however, was by now in a hysterical mood, unwilling to listen to a *Jew*, and they shouted him down with their cultic cry for a couple of hours. If this seems incredible, we might recollect how long angry crowds today can shout abuse when somebody tries to engage in rational argument with them.

35. It was thus only with difficulty that the *town clerk* was able to silence *the crowd* (here and in verse 33, in contrast to verse 30, Luke does use the word for a mob, *ochlos*). In Ephesus and some other cities in Asia Minor, the 'clerk of the people' was the main magistrate in the city, whereas in other Greek towns he was simply an administrative assistant (Sherwin-White, p. 86). He was, therefore, the appropriate person to take control of the assembly and to receive the appeals of the silversmiths. His speech was calculated to quieten the crowd down and to urge a more cautious approach. There was, he said, no need for people to get excited over a possible decline in the reputation and fame of their goddess and of the reflected glory which the city drew from being the guardian of her cult. The term *temple keeper* was used of cities which had temples of the cult of the emperor (including Ephesus itself). When the term is applied to Ephesus as temple keeper of Artemis in the third century, the usage is an extension of the imperial use; the way in which the term is used with reference to Artemis here in Acts developed from an earlier application to the actual individuals who kept the temple, and is perfectly credible historically, although no precise inscriptional parallel has been found (Sherwin-White, pp. 88f.). Along with this dignified title Ephesus could also lay claim to a divine accreditation of the cult in the form of a *stone* that had fallen *from the sky*. This will have been a meteorite, similar to examples attested for other ancient temples, and regarded as a divinely sent image. The suggestion (mentioned in *BC*, IV, p. 450) that the clerk regarded it as 'not made with hands' and so as falling outside Paul's condemnation of idols reads too much into the text.

36. For the clerk the long-standing reputation of the city and the divine accreditation of the cult of Artemis were facts that could not be gainsaid, certainly not by the rise of the Christian groups in the area. There was, therefore, no need to deal with the matter of the missionaries in a summary fashion before the assembly. In saying this the clerk appeared not as an advocate for Christianity (far from it, in fact!) but as a defender of law and order, anxious that the city should not get a reputation for disorderliness and illegal action.

37. He pressed the point by insisting that no grounds had been offered for a charge against the missionaries. There was no properly formulated accusation for them to answer. They had not been accused of *sacrilegious* behaviour as regards the temple, nor had they spoken out against the goddess and committed what would have constituted blasphemy in the ears of her worshippers. There was, in other words, nothing of public concern at issue.

38. If, however, there was something of private concern between the silversmiths and the missionaries, then there was a recognized procedure for dealing with such a matter. Private lawsuits were to be settled in *the courts* before the magistrates. These courts were held under the presidency of the provincial governor, a Roman proconsul, who travelled round the principal cities for the purpose. The plural form *proconsuls* is slightly unusual, since there was only one official at a time holding this office, generally for one year. It may be a generalizing plural: 'there are such people as proconsuls'. G. S. Duncan proposed that the plural referred to the emperor's two representatives, Helius and Celer, who may have governed the province during the interregnum that followed the murder of the proconsul Silanus by the emperor's orders in October, 54.[1]

39. The town clerk left open the possibility that there might be something *further* at stake which concerned the town as a whole. If so, the proper procedure was to wait for a *regular* meeting of the *assembly*, which would not have been more than a week or so distant.

40–41. The clerk's final words betray his fear that the holding of an extraordinary meeting of the assembly which had turned into a near-riot might have serious repercussions. Sherwin-White (pp. 83–85) cites interesting evidence from this period which shows that the Romans were anxious to get rid of these democratic assemblies; the town clerk of Prusa addressed his assembly in remarkably similar terms, warning his hearers about the drastic consequences of reports of unruly gatherings reaching the proconsul. The clerk's appeal was successful , and the assembly *dismissed*. So far as we can tell, no further steps were taken, publicly or privately, by the silversmiths against Paul and his colleagues.

g. Paul's journey from Ephesus to Miletus (20:1–16)

Paul's plans included a return visit to Macedonia and Achaia before his journey to Jerusalem (19:21). His original plan would have been to go directly from Corinth to Palestine, bypassing the west coast of Asia, but in view of his fears of a Jewish plot against him he resolved to avoid his enemies by

---

[1] G. S. Duncan, *St Paul's Ephesian Ministry* (London, 1929), pp. 102–107.

returning the way he had come through Macedonia and down the coast of Asia via Troas. Here there occurred a notable incident in the raising of Eutychus from the dead, and thereafter Paul made his way with all haste towards Jerusalem in order to get there by Pentecost. He deliberately avoided calling at Ephesus. We have valuable commentaries on this journey from Paul's own pen in 2 Corinthians, which looks forward to the visit which he paid to Corinth, and in Romans, which was written during Paul's stay at Corinth and throws light on his immediate plans for travel. From these letters we learn of the importance which Paul attached to the collection of money which he was taking from the Gentile churches under his superintendence to help the church in Jerusalem with caring for its poorer members.

1. Paul left Ephesus after the trouble had *ceased*. The fact that he did not return again makes one wonder whether, despite the fact that no charges had finally been made against him, he considered it wiser to avoid the possibility of further trouble. Before departure, he called together the members of the church and gave them a farewell message; its content may well have been similar to the exhortation recorded in 20:18–35, which, of course, he had no expectation of giving when he left Ephesus. He then went to *Macedonia*. On the assumption that this journey is that referred to in 2 Corinthians 2:12f., Paul went north to Troas (*cf.* 16:8). Here he was able to participate in fruitful evangelism. It was during this time that the dispute in the church at Corinth had come to a head. Paul had sent Titus on there with a letter (now lost) in order to effect a reconciliation and prepare the way for his own impending visit, a visit which he was unwilling to make if he was to be confronted by a church that was still at variance with him. Paul apparently hoped to meet Titus there, but when Titus failed to keep the rendezvous Paul was so anxious about the situation that he crossed over into Macedonia, hoping to meet him the sooner.

2. On arrival in Macedonia Paul's intense worries were calmed by the arrival of Titus with good news about the church; full of thankfulness, Paul wrote a further letter to the church (2 Corinthians) and sent it by the hand of Titus and two other, unnamed colleagues who were to supervise the gathering of the collection (2 Cor. 8:16–24). Luke, however, tells us nothing of all this (19:21 note), and contents himself with reporting on Paul's ministry in Macedonia where he revisited the churches. Nor does Luke refer specifically to Paul's work in the west of Greece; according to Rom. 15:19 Paul claimed that he had preached the gospel as far as Illyricum, and this period is the most likely for this mission. From there Paul moved to *Greece* (the popular name for the Roman province of Achaia), no doubt to its chief city, Corinth.

3. Paul's stay at Corinth for *three months* was probably during the winter months when travel would have been difficult. Among other profitable activities during his enforced stay he penned the Letter to the Romans. His plan for departure in the spring by ship to Syria was frustrated by his learning of *a plot against him* instigated *by the Jews.* During this season there would probably be numbers of Jews going to Jerusalem for Passover or for Pentecost, the latter being the favourite occasion for pilgrims to visit the city; it would not have been too difficult to seize an opportunity on the boat to attack Paul. Presumably the Jews from Corinth, who had been thwarted in their earlier attack on Paul (18:12–17) were involved in the plot, but Luke has left us in the dark about the details of the plot, and how Paul came to know about it. In order to avoid his enemies Paul set off in the opposite direction northwards.

4. At this point Luke inserts a list of the people who formed Paul's travelling companions on his journey. No particular motive is apparent for the inclusion of their names. Haenchen's cynical comment (p. 583) that the reader would regard them as the appropriate entourage for such a successful missionary as Paul gives us a glimpse into his own mind rather than Luke's. It is more likely that Luke saw them as firsthand witnesses to the success of Paul's mission who would back up his report to the church at Jerusalem, where many Christians were still suspicious of what he was doing (21:20f.). In fact these were probably the persons appointed by the churches to take their shares of the collection to Jerusalem. We thus have a representative of the church at Beroea, *Sopater* (a shortened form of Sosipater; Rom. 16:21, written from Corinth, mentions a kinsman of Paul of this name). The way in which he is mentioned suggests that he would be known to Luke's readers. Next we have two Thessalonians, *Aristarchus* (already mentioned in 19:29; he accompanied Paul on the first stage of his journey from Jerusalem to Rome, 27:2) and *Secundus. Gaius* came from Derbe in Galatia; a variant reading in the western text, however, makes him a native of Doberus, a Macedonian town near Philippi, in which case he could be identified with the Gaius mentioned in 19:29 and also regarded as a representative of the Philippian church (so Bruce, *Acts*, p. 370). This view is contested (probably rightly) by Haenchen (pp. 52f.) who notes that he is linked with *Timothy*, a Galatian, in the list, and that the western text could have been due to a scribe who wanted to equate this Gaius with the one in 19:29. There were also two people from Asia (*i.e.* probably Ephesus); *Tychicus* was later associated with Paul's letters to Asia Minor (Eph. 6:21f.; Col. 4:7f.; *cf.* 2 Tim. 4:12; Tit. 3:12), and Trophimus was involved in the trouble that led to Paul's arrest in Jerusalem (21:29; *cf.* 2 Tim. 4:20). If these men were associated with the collection, one or two difficulties arise. The mention of Timothy, who was not from a local church, can be explained by his part in preparing for the collection (19:22); if Gaius was from Derbe, he may have been involved in the same way as Timothy. It is also possible that they brought gifts from the churches of Galatia, although this would have been a roundabout way to do it. It is odd that there is no mention of a representative from Philippi, unless Gaius did come from that church. It is true that in verses 5f. Paul is joined by somebody (*i.e.* Luke) from Philippi, but since Paul had not planned to return via Philippi, we should have expected that the Philippian representative would already have been present. It is also perhaps odd that when Paul does reach Philippi he is at once joined by somebody who is free to go to Jerusalem with him. Possibly there had been a plan for a rendezvous with the Philippian representative further along the route, which was then altered when Paul changed his plans. But it is simpler to suppose that the Philippian representative had already come to Corinth but does not name himself in verse 4.[1] There is no mention of a representative from Corinth itself, despite Paul's earlier suggestion in 1 Corinthians 16:3f., and we can only assume that Paul himself undertook this task. Finally, there is no mention of Titus; he was probably engaged in mission work elsewhere.

5–6. Paul's companions went on ahead of him for reasons

---

[1] This incidentally would fit in with the hypothesis that the Philippian representative, namely Luke, was the 'brother famous among all the churches for his preaching of the gospel' whom Paul had sent to Corinth, 2 Cor. 8:18.

unknown and crossed over to Troas, where they waited for the rest of the party. Now the narrative resumes the 'we' style which indicates that the author is again a member of the party. Clearly he is not to be identified with any of the persons named in verse 4. The last we-passage terminated in Philippi where this one commences, but it is possible that the author had already joined Paul before he reached Philippi. By 'we' the author apparently means 'Paul and I' – and possibly other unnamed persons; but we should note the suggestion (Haenchen, p. 582) that the 'these' in verse 5 could refer just to Tychicus and Trophimus, so that the 'we' would then include the rest of the names mentioned in verse 4. The Asians would go on ahead to prepare for the main party. Paul and the others waited till after the feast of *Unleavened Bread* before departure. It is probable that he was celebrating the Christian Passover, *i.e.* Easter, with the church at Philippi (1 Cor. 5:7f.) rather than that this is merely a Jewish time-note (*cf.* 20:16 and contrast 27:9). The journey from Neapolis, the port for Philippi (16:11), to Troas took longer than the journey in the reverse direction, no doubt owing to adverse wind conditions.

7–8. The disciples in Troas gathered together on the first day of the week (Lk. 24:1) to *break bread* and to have a last opportunity of listening to Paul. The breaking of bread is the term used especially in Acts for the celebration of the Lord's Supper (2:42; *cf.* 1 Cor. 10:16), and this passage is of particular interest in providing the first allusion to the Christian custom of meeting *on the first day of the week* for the purpose.[1] It is not altogether clear what method of time-reckoning Luke is employing. According to the Jewish method of calculating the new day from sunset, Paul would have met with the Christians on what was Saturday evening by our reckoning, and would thus have resumed his journey on Sunday morning.[2] According to the Roman method of reckoning the new day as beginning at dawn, the Christians would have met in the evening of either Sunday (the first day of the Jewish week) or Saturday (the first day of the Roman week). Since elsewhere Luke

---

[1] A Christian assembly on the first day of the week is implied in 1 Cor. 16:2, and the 'Lord's Day' mentioned in Rev. 1:10 is generally understood to be Sunday.

[2] For this view see M. D. Goulder, *Midrash and Lection in Matthew* (London, 1974), p. 177 n. 38.

reckons the hours of the day from dawn (3:1), he appears to follow the Roman method of time-reckoning and the Jewish calendar (*cf.* Lk. 24:1). Bruce (*Book*, p. 408 n. 25), argues that he regards the following morning, on which Paul intended to depart as *the morrow*, and that 'daybreak' in verse 11 signifies the beginning of the new day; hence the meeting was on Sunday evening and Paul departed on Monday morning.[1]

Paul's address to the church lasted *until midnight*. This may seem a long time by modern western standards (*cf.* also 28:23), but in some countries, especially in the Third World, services lasting for several hours with correspondingly long sermons are quite common. Added to this fact, which could have wearied some of the congregation, the upper room (1:13; 9:37) where the disciples were gathered was lit by oil lamps. The simplest explanation of the motive for mentioning these is that they emitted an odour which helped to send Eutychus off to sleep. Haenchen (p. 585 n. 2.) comments that if Eutychus, seated by a window, fell asleep, how much more must the other people in the room away from ventilation have felt sleepy; he evidently forgets that some people become sleepy more quickly than others. Surely here we have a piece of eyewitness information.

9–10. Our sympathy rests with *Eutychus*, a young lad of 8–14 years (this was the age traditionally assigned to a *lad*, verse 12) who felt unequal to the length of Paul's address and the heat; overcome by fatigue he fell asleep and plunged through the open window from the third story to the ground; *the third story* would be the 'second floor' above the ground floor by British reckoning, and the picture suggested is that of a tenement type house, common enough in lower-class dwellings in Roman towns. The boy was picked up *dead*. There can be little doubt that Luke intended to portray Paul as being able to raise the dead (like Peter, 9:36–43); Paul's comment that the boy's *life* was *in him* refers to his condition after he had ministered to him. Luke would not have devoted space to the raising up of somebody who was merely apparently dead. This, of course, still leaves it possible for those so minded

---

[1] The passage does not support the practice of Seventh Day Adventists who regard sunset on Friday to sunset on Saturday as the sabbath and the proper day for Christian worship; even if the meeting was on Saturday evening, this was not part of the Jewish sabbath.

to argue that Luke has misinterpreted what actually happened.

11. After the interruption to the meeting, Paul broke bread and ate. The description does not make it clear whether he merely ate the bread of the Lord's Supper or had a meal, but the verb *eaten* can certainly mean the latter (10:10). Haenchen (p. 586) thinks it strange that the Christians were prepared to wait until midnight for a meal and adopts the former interpretation; but he does not reckon adequately with what enthusiastic Christians might be prepared to do, and the fact that a meal accompanied the Lord's Supper at this time is well attested; 1 Corinthians 11:17ff. in fact implies that Christians might well feel hungry by the time of the church meal (verses 21, 34) and also that some probably ate a meal before coming to the church meeting. Thereafter Paul preached even longer.

12. It is only as an afterthought that Luke relates that the boy was actually restored to life and the local people were greatly *comforted*.[1] The implication may be that the boy had remained unconscious till this point; verse 10 does not necessarily imply that he became conscious at that moment. The detail, however, has roused suspicions whether what actually happened was that despite his heavy fall, which produced prolonged unconsciousness, the boy did not (as might have been expected) experience a fatal accident. The miraculous element would then be that God preserved him from what would normally have been expected to happen and so overruled during the situation in which Paul was preaching; it would have been a miracle of divine preservation rather than resurrection. To say this is not to rationalize the story; it is to attempt to do justice to the peculiar way in which the story is told. More probably, however, the apparent difficulty is due to the awkward positioning of verse 11.

13. The journey now continued, but whereas Luke and his companions went on by ship to *Assos*, some 20 miles (32 km) away, Paul chose to go by land. The sea journey was longer than the direct distance by land and could be stormy. No reason is given why Paul should have chosen to go it alone, and the detail must be historical; it is highly unlikely that Luke wanted to show the tremendous physical resilience

---

[1] Luke's *not a little* is one of his favourite Greek idioms.

of Paul as a man capable of a long tramp after a sleepless night.[1]

14–15. The travellers met up with one another in *Assos*. Paul joined the ship and it proceeded some 44 miles (71 km) further south to *Mitylene*, the chief town on the island of Lesbos. The next day they came opposite the island of *Chios*, which lies at the end of a long peninsula which juts out between Smyrna on the north and Ephesus on the south. Keeping out to sea, they bypassed Ephesus and came to *Samos*, an island off the coast to the south of Ephesus. It was close to a promontory called Trogyllia, and the western text adds the detail 'after remaining at Trogyllia', which, whether authentic or not, probably describes what the travellers actually did. Then on the next day they came to Miletus, which was 30 miles (48 km) south of Ephesus.

16. Luke explains Paul's decision to bypass *Ephesus* as due to his desire to go to Jerusalem in time for *Pentecost*. There was not a lot of time between the feast of unleavened bread, spent at Troas, and the Pentecost for the journey, although it was perfectly possible to accomplish it within the time. Paul evidently feared that if he stopped at Ephesus he would be unable to get away again in a hurry; he had therefore chosen a ship which went by a faster route. There is some force in the suggestion that Paul may have feared further disturbances if he reappeared in Ephesus (20:1 note). It may seem strange that if Paul was in a hurry he still sent for the church leaders at Ephesus to meet him at Miletus. But the explanation will be that the ship would stay in Miletus for a day or two, sufficiently long to enable a message to go to Ephesus and for the leaders to come over, and Paul had avoided also having to spend some days in a ship that was unloading and loading in Ephesus.

h. Paul's farewell address at Miletus (20:17–38)
Paul's consciousness that he would not return to Asia led him to take a last opportunity of speaking to the church leaders before he set off for Jerusalem with the probability of arrest and imprisonment there. So far as Acts is concerned, this address constitutes Paul's farewell to the churches, although

---

[1] For an interesting textual variant in this verse in the Old Syriac version see above, p. 45.

we shall hear Paul's voice frequently in the remainder of the book in defence of himself before Jews and Romans. The address thus contains the elements that would be expected in the type of farewell discourse familiar at the time.[1] There is little agreement among scholars as to how it is to be analysed, but it falls broadly into two parts. In the first section, verses 18–27, Paul looks back over his own work as a missionary. He describes how he had performed his work faithfully, then moves on to speak about the uncertainties of the future, his readiness even to die for the sake of Christ, and his conviction that his friends will not see him again. He emphasizes that he has taught them fully and that the responsibility for what they have heard now rests in their own hands. These thoughts lead over into the second section, verses 28–35, in which Paul instructs the church leaders for the future when he will no longer be with them. They are to follow his example of faithful service, and to be ready to give themselves to the service of the church as freely as he had done. They stand under God's blessing and also under the command of the Lord Jesus to give freely to help the weak.

Recent commentators, with the notable exceptions of Bruce, Williams and Neil, regard the speech as a composition by Luke and not by Paul, although they have to admit that the thought is Pauline and that Luke's way of putting things stands close to Paul's. The wording of the speech is Lucan in style, the contents are alleged to go beyond the immediate situation in their significance, and the use of himself as an example is unlike Paul. What Luke is doing is to defend Paul against accusations made in his own time (not by Paul's own contemporaries in Ephesus) and to urge the church to follow Pauline teaching and practice at a time long after his death.

It has to be admitted that the style is that of Luke who has imposed his own style on all that he wrote and did not attempt to preserve the individuality of the various speakers. But it is hard to see why Paul should not have spoken in Miletus, in the way described by Luke, and why Luke should not have had some memory of the occasion, if there actually was such

[1] H.-J. Michel, *Die Abschiedsrede des Paulus an die Kirche. Apg. 20, 17–38* (München, 1973); C. K. Barrett, 'Paul's Address to the Ephesian Elders', in J. Jervell and W. Meeks, *God's Christ and his People* (Oslo, 1977), pp. 107–121; J. Lambrecht, 'Paul's Farewell Address at Miletus', in Kremer, pp. 307–337.

a speech. Paul was capable of using himself as an example (1 Cor. 11:1), and he could use the 'type' of farewell speech as well as anybody else. He did have to endure accusations from within the churches (2 Cor. 10–13; 1 Thes. 1–2), but here in this address he is not so much responding to actual accusations as using his own life as an example to the leaders. His earnestness derives from the nature of the situation which obviously stirred his emotions deeply. In short, the denial of a Pauline basis for this address is unwarranted.

17–18. Paul's concern was with the leaders of the church, here called *elders* as in 14:23. In the address itself he describes their function as being 'guardians', *i.e.* bishops, (verse 28) and it may be that this was the term that he himself used (Phil. 1:1). The address begins with a survey of the past in which Paul called his hearers to confirm from their own memories (Greek *epistamai*) how he had lived in their midst while he was in Asia. We may compare the same technique in 1 Thessalonians 2:1f., 5, 10f.; Philippians 4:15, but the actual *word* used here is Lucan (10:28; 15:7; 22:19).

19. Paul describes his work as *serving the Lord*, just as he frequently called himself the servant of the Lord (Rom. 1:1; *cf.* 12:11; Phil. 2:22). It is also the service rendered to the church (verse 35), and this thought of service stands prior to any thought of the status that may belong to the servant. Consequently, the first characteristic of his ministry which is singled out for mention is *humility*, the refusal to claim anything for himself (2 Cor. 10:1; 11:7; 1 Thes. 2:6). The second is the *tears* which expressed his personal concern for his converts (Rom. 9:2; 2 Cor. 2:4; Phil. 3:18), and the third is the implied patience and fortitude with which he continued his work despite the temptations to give it up that arose from Jewish persecution (2 Cor. 11:24, 26; 1 Thes. 2:14–16). Here, as will be the case throughout the address, there are direct and close parallels in the writings of Paul himself which show that this was how he thought of his ministry and admonished his converts. To say with one recent scholar that 'a direct dependence on Paul can nowhere be demonstrated' is quite misleading: the total impression gained from the speech is that here we are in touch with Paul himself.

20. Paul's pastoral ministry took place in *public* meetings (such as were held in the hall of Tyrannus) and also *from house to house* (2:46; *cf.* Rom. 16:5; Col. 4:15; Phm. 2). Paul lays considerable stress on the fact that in the course of it he had not withheld any *teaching* that might be *profitable* for his hearers (*cf.* verse 27), even though it might be unwelcome (Gal. 4:16; *cf.* 2 Cor. 4:2). So strong is Paul's emphasis on this point that it has been suspected that he is replying to some accusation, or that Luke is letting Paul defend himself against later criticisms. Such self-defence was typical of farewell discourses (1 Sa. 12:2–5; the motif is frequent in the *Testaments of the Twelve Patriarchs*). Luke has not recorded any such criticisms of Paul at Ephesus, but we know that Paul was criticized in Corinth by advocates of 'another gospel' (2 Cor. 11:4), and this may be the kind of accusation in Paul's mind here.

21. Paul's summary of what he did preach is remarkably simple. Commentators have been disposed to see a chiasmus in his wording, *i.e.* he proclaimed to the Jews the need for faith and to the Greeks the need for repentance respectively. This is broadly true, since repentance and turning towards God were especially part of the message to the Gentiles (1 Thes. 1:9; *cf.* Gal. 4:8f.; Heb. 6:1), while Jews were bidden to turn from works of the law to faith. Nevertheless, faith was necessary for all converts (Rom. 10:9–13 stresses that Jew and Gentile are alike in this matter; *cf.* Rom. 1:16), and repentance was also needed in the case of Jews. The chiasmus theory is therefore uncertain. The term *repentance* is not especially used by Paul: here we have a term that is more part of Luke's vocabulary, but it acts as an equivalent for Paul's use of 'conversion' (1 Thes. 1:9).

22–23. From the past Paul turns to the impending future events which are the occasion of his address. He is on his way to Jerusalem, and this journey is characterized in two ways. It is a journey of necessity in that Paul stands under constraint by *the Spirit* (16:6f.; 19:21). He knows that he is being guided by God to go, and therefore he must obey. But it is also a journey of uncertainty: the Spirit has not revealed to him the exact purpose of the journey or what will happen to him. Something of this uncertainty is reflected in Paul's appeal for prayer in Romans 15:30–32 that he may be delivered from danger in Jerusalem and that his gifts for the church will be gratefully received. The one thing that Paul did know was that, whatever city he visited, the Spirit foretold *imprisonment* and tribulation for him. It is not clear whether this means that the Spirit prophesied persecution in Jerusalem (21:4, 11), or in every city Paul visited; probably the former is meant. The ministry of the Spirit would be through prophets, or perhaps through personal revelations to Paul.

24. If our interpretation of the previous verse is correct, then Paul did know that he would have to suffer in Jerusalem. What he did *not* know (verse 22) was whether his sufferings would lead to his death, but he emphasizes that he was prepared for that possibility. He did not regard his own *life* as a *precious* possession to be held on to at all costs. This corresponds to the attitude expressed in his letters (2 Cor. 4:7 – 5:10; 6:4–10; 12:9f.; Phil. 1:19–26; 2:17; 3:8; Col. 1:24). What did matter was that he should accomplish his course (2 Tim. 4:7) by faithfully performing the service which had been laid on him by the Lord at his conversion, namely to preach *the gospel of the grace of God* (Gal. 1:15f.; *cf.* 2 Cor. 6:1). Paul saw his task as the faithful preaching of the gospel; he felt called to do so in a wide area, and so he hoped that he would be able to go westwards to Rome (and also to Spain, Rom. 15:24, 28) to preach there; it is probable that he regarded the evangelization of the world as the essential preliminary to the coming of Christ (Rom. 11:25f.; *cf.* Mk. 13:10). Yet he was aware that the completion of this task did not necessarily depend upon him; what was important was that he should faithfully perform his particular share in the task, and it rested with God to determine how great that share would be.

25. Paul knew that his present audience would not see him again. His task of preaching the kingdom among them was complete. Several commentators have deduced from these words (taken in conjunction with verse 38) that Luke was writing in the full knowledge of Paul's death, as a result of which he never had the opportunity to return to this area. Although Luke did not record the death of Paul at the end of Acts and preferred to leave the reader with a picture of Paul proclaiming the gospel in Rome without hindrance, he had already given clear enough hints that Paul died at Rome. On the other hand, it can be urged that Paul himself believed that he no longer had any room for work in this area (Rom. 15:23) and that his future plans would take him elsewhere, so that he was extremely unlikely to return to the Aegean area. The fact that Paul's hopes of such work failed to be fulfilled and that he may have revisited this area (as the Pastoral Epistles may indicate) would simply show that Paul's fears were not realized, at least at this point. The case that Luke saw this speech as Paul's farewell address to all his mission churches is a strong one, but the evidence is not compelling.

26–27. Paul's work in Ephesus, then, is complete. He emphasizes that he has done his part faithfully, so that if anybody falls away, he will not be to blame. He boldly claims that no man's *blood* can be laid on him; for the metaphor see Ezk. 18:13; 33:1–6. The language of guilt for causing a person's death is here applied to the spiritual responsibility of the pastor for faithful presentation of the message that brings life. As the watchman who warns people faithfully of the coming of an enemy is not guilty if they choose to ignore the warning, so it was with Paul as a preacher of the gospel. Paul's assurance was derived from his confidence that he had faithfully preached the gospel in every particular; he had dealt with the whole of God's plan of salvation (*cf.* Eph. 1:11; but the thought of God's plan is distinctly Lucan).

28. Now Paul reaches the second part of his discourse. The first part has implicitly contained exhortation to his hearers in that his personal example was intended to be a pattern to them, but now he turns to direct exhortation. In the manner of a farewell discourse he deals with how they are to act when he is no longer with them. They are to pay attention to their own spiritual condition (*cf.* 1 Tim. 4:16) as well as to that of the church; it is only as the leaders themselves remain faithful to God that they can expect the church to do so likewise. The church is described as a *flock*, a familiar Old Testament metaphor for God's people (Ps. 100:3; Is. 40:11; Je. 13:17; Ezk. 34) which was taken up by Jesus (Lk. 12:32; 15:3–7; 19:10; Jn. 10:1–30). The picture is applied to the church and its leaders in John 21:15–17 and 1 Peter 5:2; Paul uses it without any particular emphasis in 1 Corinthians 9:7; but it is not one of his pictures for the church. From this usage developed the idea of church leaders as 'shepherds' or 'pastors' (Eph. 4:11), but the term which Paul uses here is *guardians* (RSV). This is the meaning of the word elsewhere translated as 'bishops' (Greek *episkopos*), a word which was used for leaders in at least some of Paul's churches (Phil. 1:1; 1 Tim. 3:1–7; Tit. 1:7). It conveys the idea of spiritual oversight and pastoral care. Such people owed their appointment to God's choice of them by the Spirit. The people described here as 'bishops' are identical with those described as 'elders' in verse 17, and in

14:23 we read how they were appointed by Paul in some of his churches with prayer and fasting, *i.e.* in dependence on the guidance of the Spirit. Their task was *to care for the church*; the RSV mg. rendering *feed* is too narrow in meaning for a word that means 'to act as a shepherd'; it refers to all the care that must be exercised in relation to the flock. The church is here called *the church of God*;[1] this is a phrase found exclusively in Paul's letters (*e.g.* 1 Cor. 1:2). The church belongs to God because he himself bought it (RSV *obtained* is weak). The thought is of the act of redemption by which the church became God's special property, and is based on the picture of God redeeming Israel in Isaiah 43:21 (*cf.* Ps. 74:2, which significantly follows a verse in which Israel is likened to a flock). The cost of redemption was (literally) his own blood (RSV mg.). It is, however, unlikely that an early Christian would have spoken of *God* shedding his own blood, and therefore we must either assume that Jesus is the subject of the clause (which is just possible, but unlikely) or that the phrase means 'the blood of his Own' (RSV mg.), which is grammatically possible and fits in with the use of the phrase *his own Son* (Rom. 8:31). Although this is one of the few places in Luke's writings which clearly refer to the doctrinal significance of the cross, we should not underestimate its importance as a statement which represented his own belief as well as Paul's.

29. Paul's concern for the church arose from his fear that, to continue the pastoral metaphor, *fierce wolves* would enter it and cause destruction. The thought is of heretical teachers coming in from outside and leading people astray, especially after Paul was no longer there to counteract them. This certainly happened in Corinth; 2 Corinthians 10–13 testifies to people who arrived in Corinth, probably after Paul's departure, and preached 'another gospel'. It also happened after Paul's death, so that, if Acts was composed after this event, Paul's words could have a broader meaning.

30. Along with such outsiders Paul also mentions the possibility of people from within the church adopting *perverse* teachings and seducing the congregation (*cf.* Rom. 16:17f.; Col. 2:8). Attempts have been made to identify the character

---

[1] The variant reading in the RSV mg. *of the Lord* represents a scribal attempt to avoid the implication that God is the subject of the following relative clause.

of these heretics more closely, but no firm conclusions can be drawn. It is sometimes thought that Luke had Gnostics or gnosticizing Christians in mind, but, since Acts contains no clearly identifiable references to Gnostic teaching here or elsewhere, we must be content with a broad reference to any kind of heresy that might arise in the church. In later years the church at Ephesus certainly had to reckon with strong heretical forces (1 Tim. 1:3; 2 Tim. 1:15; Rev. 2:1–7): Paul's warning was a timely one.

31. In face of such danger church leaders must be constantly on the *alert*, like shepherds keeping awake to watch for marauding wolves at night; the common injunction to all Christians to be watchful (1 Cor. 16:13; 1 Thes. 5:6) is here applied specifically to the leaders (*cf.* Heb. 13:17), and is reinforced by an appeal to Paul's own example. *For three years* (the rough length of his stay in Ephesus, 19:10) he had earnestly warned every member of the congregation by night and day (*cf.* 1 Thes. 2:11; 1 Cor. 4:14; Col. 1:28). *Night and day* is hyperbolical; compare 1 Thessalonians 2:9 where Paul worked with his hands 'night and day' to earn his keep.

32. Paul's final step is to *commend* the leaders to the care of *God*. This action should not be regarded as some kind of rite of ordination to their office as overseers of the flock, since they already had this status (verse 17). It is Paul's handing over to God of the responsibility which he has borne for the church, and represents a farewell act as in 14:23. The leaders are put in the hands of God and placed under *the word of his grace, i.e.* the gospel of grace (verse 24). *Grace* is a particularly Pauline word, to express the free unmerited favour of God in virtue of which he saves sinners; Luke also uses it frequently, especially to refer to the gospel message (Lk. 4:22; Acts 14:3), so that his vocabulary and that of Paul come together here, although the precise expression is Luke's. It is the Word which *builds up* Christians, *i.e.* makes them mature (*cf.* 1 Cor. 3:9–15; Eph. 4:12), and gives them an *inheritance* among all his holy people (*cf.* Rom. 8:17). This obscure phrase (perhaps based on Dt. 33:3f.) appears to refer to God's gift of a share in the blessings of his kingly rule which Paul's hearers will enjoy along with God's people as a whole. It is significant that these blessings come through commitment to the Word: Paul and Luke know nothing of the idea that church leaders stand over the Word

335

committed to them (2 Tim. 1:14) and are in control of it; on the contrary, they stand under it.

33–34. Paul is not quite finished. One last appeal follows, as he pleads with his hearers to follow his own example of selfless giving. He could say truthfully that he had been free from covetousness in not looking for any reward for his pastoral labours (1 Cor. 9:15–18). *Silver, gold* and fine clothes were accepted forms of wealth and status symbols in the ancient world. Having no wealth of his own, Paul had been content to work with his own hands to support himself, although as an apostle he might have claimed support from the churches (1 Thes. 2:6). Indeed, grateful though he was for gifts from the churches (Phil. 4:10–20), he almost seems to have been embarrassed by them. Nevertheless, such gifts from existing churches together with his own work enabled him to avoid being a burden on the particular churches in which he was working (2 Cor. 11:7–10).

35. In this way Paul sought to be an example of helping the needy (1 Thes. 5:14) and of living in accordance with the saying *It is more blessed to give than to receive*. This saying is open to misunderstanding, in the sense that the 'weak' or needy who depend on help and gifts from others may be regarded as less blessed than those who give to them; but clearly this is not what is meant, and the point is rather that it is better for a person who can do so to give to help others rather than to amass further wealth for himself. A number of similar Greek sayings indicate that this is the sense. The very existence of these parallels and the lack of Jewish ones has given weight to the suggestion that the saying is not in fact a genuine saying of Jesus but a Christianized Greek proverb. But, as Hanson (p. 206) rightly affirms, there is no reason why Jesus should not have quoted or adapted a Greek proverb in view of the strong Greek influences in Palestine. In fact the saying is expressed in a Jewish form (with the use of *blessed*), and it possibly finds an echo in *Didache* 1:5, 'Blessed is the giver . . . alas for the receiver'; the personal formulation here may be more original. Paul quotes the words of Jesus only rarely; when he does so, it is to back up some ethical instruction, as here (1 Cor. 7:10; 9:14; 1 Tim. 5:18).

36–38. The saying of Jesus brings the address to an end. It is appropriately followed by prayer on the part of Paul and all present. The usual posture for prayer was standing, but on solemn occasions kneeling was practised (see 7:60). Haenchen knows that this was the practice in Luke's time (rather than Paul's?) – but omits to tell us how he knows. A tearful farewell ensues, described in a manner familiar from the Old Testament (Gn. 33:4; 45:14; 46:29) and Jewish writings. The display of emotion with tears and kisses would be natural enough in the culture of that time. The kiss is here a sign of affection rather than the more formal 'holy kiss' of Christian worship. The last impression left by the scene is the conviction that Paul will not be able to see them again. There is a finality about his ensuing journey to Jerusalem. We may well see a certain parallel between Jesus, setting his face to go to Jerusalem to certain death, and Paul, conscious that he was going to imprisonment and not expecting to see his friends again. See further on verse 25.

VIII. PAUL'S ARREST AND IMPRISONMENT (21:1 – 28:31)

a. Paul's journey to Jerusalem (21:1–16)

The address at Miletus marks the end of Paul's missionary work according to the account in Acts. From there he journeyed to Jerusalem where he was to be arrested and imprisoned, subjected to various trials, and finally sent off to Rome to appear before the Emperor. A certain parallelism between the careers of Jesus and Paul is to be seen. Jesus too journeyed to Jerusalem, and during his journey prophesied concerning his impending sufferings; he was arrested and tried, appearing before the Jews and the Romans; and he suffered death and rose again. To be sure, in no sense does Paul literally experience death and resurrection in Acts, but some have seen in his last journey, with his salvation from possible death by shipwreck and drowning, a pattern similar to the experience of Jesus (*cf.* 2 Cor. 1:8–10).

The journey to Jerusalem is narrated in some detail, with accounts of the various stopping-places *en route*, and must rest on some kind of diary by one of Paul's companions: the 'we' style indicates that this was Luke. The significant features are the welcome given to Paul on the way and above all the prophetic warnings which reinforce his own premonition of suffering; despite them all Paul persists in fulfilling the divine plan for himself.

1. Paul and his companions had to 'tear themselves away' from their friends at Miletus. They sailed more or less due south to the island of *Cos*, and arrived a day later at *Rhodes*, the port on the island of that name. By this point they were now round the south-west tip of Asia Minor, and proceeded to sail east along the south coast to *Patara*. The western text adds the words 'and Myra', which would bring the travellers to a place some 50 miles (80 km) further east which was the more important port for sailing to Syria.[1]

2-3. At this point (Patara or Myra) Paul transferred to another *ship*. The one he had been travelling on either stopped here or continued slowly round the coast from port to port. Paul was still in a hurry with the limited time available (20:16) and therefore chose a ship which would sail direct across the open sea, a journey of some 400 miles (644 km). Luke speaks indifferently of *Phoenicia*, *Syria* or *Tyre* as its destination; Tyre was the chief town in Phoenicia which in turn was a region in Syria. The ship sighted land (Luke uses the appropriate nautical term) only as it passed south of Cyprus, and went straight on to Tyre where it was to unload its cargo.

4. After Paul's earlier haste it is surprising that he was content to spend *seven days* in Tyre. The most probable explanation is that he had made good time on the journey and now had some time in hand. It may also be that he had to wait a few days while the same ship prepared to sail further (so Bruce, *Acts*, p. 385, on the assumption that 'the ship' in verse 6 means the same ship) or while he found another boat going to Caesarea. Paul used the time of waiting to seek out the local Christians, probably the refugees and converts of the movement described in 11:19. Some of these Christians had the gift of prophecy, and by the Spirit they warned Paul *not to go on to Jerusalem*. Since, however, Paul believed that he was under divine necessity to go to Jerusalem, this prophetic warning appears to be contradictory to Paul's earlier guidance. The simplest solution is that the Christians at Tyre were led

[1] Haenchen (p. 53) thinks that the addition is a mistaken scribal addition (based on 27:5), since Patara to Myra was too long for a day's journey by sea; but the distance is no greater than from Cos to Rhodes or Rhodes to Patara, and it is difficult to see the force of his objection; the western text may well preserve correct information.

by the Spirit to foresee suffering for Paul at Jerusalem and therefore of their own accord they urged him not to go. Even this is not a wholly happy solution, since if the Spirit prophesied that Paul would suffer in Jerusalem, nothing could prevent this happening. But the possibility of disobeying God's will is a real one (raised by Paul in 26:19). The disciples at Tyre may not have been well-informed on the finer points of predestination, and could have thought it possible to say to Paul, 'If this is what is going to happen to you, don't go.'

5–6. But Paul did not act on the warning. When the ship was ready to depart, he and his companions resumed their journey, but not before a touching *farewell* scene, reminiscent of that at Miletus. The solemnity of the scene emphasized that they did not expect to see Paul again. The mention of *wives and children* in an apparently pointless fashion indicates historical verisimilitude; in such a short time Paul and his companions had attained a high place in the affections of the families with whom they had been staying.

7. The RSV rendering *when we had finished the voyage* suggests that the company left the ship at *Ptolemais*. Since this port was no more than 40 miles (64 km; a single day's journey by sea) from Tyre, it would be incomprehensible why Paul had waited a full week for a ship that merely went one day's journey when he could have travelled the same distance more quickly by land. The Greek verb, however, can mean 'when we had continued the voyage' (*cf.* NIV), which allows that they continued their journey from Ptolemais to Caesarea by ship. Ptolemais, modern Akko (Acre) had a Christian church which presumably also dated back to the period described in 11:19, and here too the travellers enjoyed fellowship and stayed overnight.

8. The next day they came to *Caesarea*, a further 40 miles (64 km) south. Here they stayed for some days with *Philip*, who was last heard of in 8:40 as having gone to this town. He is described as *the evangelist*, a term which may be meant to distinguish him from Philip the apostle. Later tradition, however, managed to confuse the two men. The title of 'evangelist' aptly described him, since although he was one of the Seven appointed to deal with the poor aid of the church, he was an effective evangelist, and probably founded the church in Caesarea.

9. Luke adds that Philip had *four daughters* who were *un-*

339

married (literally, virgins) and *prophesied*. It is not clear that Luke intends the reader to see a connection between virginity and prophetic powers, although unmarried or widowed women sometimes had a special status in the church (1 Tim. 5:3–16). What is surprising is that despite their prophetic powers the daughters did not prophesy about Paul's fate. Haenchen (p. 601) rightly regards it as a feature drawn from Luke's source.[1]

10–11. Nevertheless, there was a further prophecy about Paul. It was given by a prophet called *Agabus* who came from Judea, and who is introduced as if he was a new character, although he has already figured in the story (11:28); this suggests that Luke is recording material from the we-source in which he had not yet been mentioned. Agabus's prophecy was a combination of act and spoken interpretation and is reminiscent of the acted symbolism of some of the Old Testament prophets. Paul was wearing a *girdle* consisting of a long piece of cloth wound round his body (*cf.* Mt. 10:9). Agabus took this and wound it round *his own feet and hands* – an action which the sceptical French scholar Loisy actually believed to be impossible! He then uttered his solemn prophecy. *Thus says the Holy Spirit* corresponds to 'Thus says the Lord' on the lips of Old Testament prophets. *The Jews* would *bind* Paul and hand him over to the Romans. The action is reminiscent of the destiny prophesied by Jesus for Peter in Jn. 21:18, while the saying reminds us of Jesus' prediction that he would be delivered into the hands of the Gentiles (Mk. 9:31; 10:33). The prophecy was not fulfilled in so many words: although the Jews seized Paul, they did not hand him over to the Romans, but rather the Romans rescued him from them, while keeping him in custody. The form of Agabus's wording is no doubt meant to bring out more clearly the parallelism between the fates of Jesus and Paul. In any case, the Jews could be regarded as responsible for the fact that Paul fell into the hands of the Romans and remained in custody (*cf.* 28:17) although the latter had no particular reason of their own to charge him with any crime.

12–13. The dramatic effect of Agabus's sudden and vivid

[1] Some commentators have thought that the verse means that the daughters did prophesy about Paul, but the Greek verb used is a description of their character, not an account of a specific action.

340

prophecy was powerful. Both Paul's companions (for the first reported time) and the local people urged Paul *not to go up to Jerusalem* in view of his certain fate there. Again, as in verse 4, the feeling is a natural, if not altogether logical, one. But the incident serves to show Paul's complete willingness to do the will of God. It is hard for a man to make a sacrifice which is going to be unpleasant for himself; it is even harder when the people whom he loves are going to be hurt by his action and plead with him to act differently. The grief displayed by Paul's friends had the effect of pounding at his *heart* as they attempted to dissuade him. But for himself Paul was quite prepared not merely for what was prophesied but also for possible death at Jerusalem. It was not that there was any virtue in such sufferings for their own sake, but only if they were accomplished on behalf of the name of Jesus, *i.e.* as a necessary part of Christian service.

14. Faced by Paul's determination, his friends could only give up their persuasion and acquiesce in the *will* of God for him. Their words resemble those of Jesus in Gethsemane (Lk. 22:42), and express a readiness for whatever God may will, even if they conceal the hope that God's will may turn out to be different from what they fear; and at least in one respect this hope turned out to be justified, in that Paul did not die at Jerusalem (admittedly their fear that this would happen did not arise from any clear word of prophecy but was only their own apprehension).

15–16. So they came to the final stage of the journey. The phrase *we made ready* can, and very possibly does, mean that they saddled horses for a journey which was about 64 miles (104 km) long and would in any case be more easily accomplished on horseback than on foot. Some of the Christians *from Caesarea* joined the party, an action all the more likely if they were about to celebrate the feast of Pentecost in a Christian manner in Jerusalem. They acted as guides in *bringing* the party *to the house of Mnason*, a man who was a Christian of long standing. As the text stands, the implication is that the house of Mnason was in Jerusalem. This is probably correct, although we should note that the western text located Mnason in an unnamed village on the way to Jerusalem where Paul spent a night on the way. It is wholly probable that the journey would have taken two days, but it is doubtful whether Luke would have named Paul's host on the way and not his host in Jerusalem itself. As a Cypriot (*cf.* 4:36; 11:19f.; 35:5), Mnason probably belonged to the group of more Hellenistically minded Jewish Christians from the Dispersion with whom Paul had earlier contacts; such people were more likely to act as his hosts in Jerusalem than some of the more traditionally minded Jewish Christians.

b. Paul's arrest in Jerusalem (21:17–36)

Paul received a warm enough welcome from the Christians in Jerusalem, although Luke is silent about their reception of the collection which Paul had brought: Paul himself had worries lest his gift would not be acceptable (Rom. 15:31), and it is possible that the more right-wing elements in the church were distinctly cool towards it. In order to disarm their suspicions of Paul as an opponent of traditional Jewish Christianity it was suggested that he should take part in a Jewish vow which involved the presentation of an offering at the temple. There was no theological compromise for Paul in so doing, especially since the offering involved would not seem to him to clash with the self-offering of Jesus as a sacrifice for sin. Nevertheless, the action ended in apparent disaster, and this raises the question whether Luke possibly regarded the incident as indicating that such an action for the sake of peace was the wrong thing for Paul to do, even if it led towards the fulfilment of God's will for him. Paul was mobbed and rescued by the local Roman peace-keeping force who took him into the safety of the barracks for examination.

17. Paul's arrival in Jerusalem was followed by a welcome from the church. An unofficial meeting between members of the church and its leaders and Paul is envisaged. Haenchen (p. 607) thinks that the reference is to Hellenistic Jewish Christians, *i.e.* Mnason and his associates, since verse 22 implies that the Jerusalem Christians in general were still ignorant of Paul's arrival; this may well be the case.

18. *The following day* there was a meeting attended by *James* and *the elders*, who by this point had fully assumed the leadership of the church in Jerusalem; Paul was accompanied by the representatives of the churches who had come up to Jerusalem with him. We may assume that the presence of the latter was connected with the presentation of the collection to the Jerusalem church, although Luke lets this motive for Paul's visit appear only later in an incidental comment (24:17) addressed to Felix. From Luke's point of view the visitors were present to confirm Paul's account of his successful missionary campaign.

19. As on previous occasions (14:27; 15:3f., 12; and possibly 18:22) Paul reported back to the church on his missionary work and related in detail how God's blessing had attended his work *among the Gentiles*. The story in Acts has shown that, although Paul began his work in the synagogues and had some Jewish converts, most of his converts were drawn from the ranks of proselytes and other Gentiles who attended the synagogues, together with other Gentiles with no Jewish connections. The success of the mission is deliberately attributed to *God*: whatever doubts might still linger in Jewish minds about the Gentile mission, it was guided and planned by God.

20. Paul's audience, therefore, could do no other than glorify and praise God for what they heard (15:3). Nevertheless, they were conscious that there were still people around who were intensely suspicious of Paul, although they themselves did not share their viewpoint. There were, they said, *thousands* of *Jews* who were believers and yet zealots as far as *the law* was concerned. These will have been the same people as the converted Pharisees in 15:5. They could be described as 'zealots' in the sense that they were enthusiastic for the law as God's gift to Israel; later the term 'zealot' was to acquire a bad sense when it came to be used of those who in their zeal for the law and the traditional Jewish way of life in a country free from foreign dominion turned to violence to secure their ends. Paul himself had once been equally, if not more, 'zealous . . . for the traditions of (his) fathers' (Gal. 1:14), but had then met Jesus Christ and abandoned the law as a means of obtaining a righteous relation to God (Phil. 3:8f.). Other Jews found it less easy to abandon their previous life-style and continued to follow out the cultural expressions of Judaism.

The reference to *thousands* of believers has seemed exaggerated, if not downright unlikely, to several scholars, since Jerusalem's population was quite small; see, however, 2:41, 47; 4:4; 6:7; 9:31. A number of commentators have sought to avoid the difficulty by regarding the words *of those who have believed* as a gloss in the text: on this view James and his colleagues were motivated by fear of the non-Christian Jews in the city – a factor which must in any case have been in their minds. The emendation is unnecessary, since the existence of a traditionalist Jewish group in the church is firmly attested, although the 'thousands' of them may be a rhetorical overstatement by James.

21. These zealots for the law were ready to believe the rumours which they heard about Paul. He was accused of advising Jews who lived in Gentile communities to give up circumcision. Since they could not very well uncircumcise themselves (although some Jews literally did this, 1 Macc. 1:15), they would refrain from circumcision in the case of their children. They were also said to be abandoning *the customs* laid down in the law. No doubt it was true that Christian Jews in the Dispersion were beginning to do precisely these things: a Jew who took seriously Paul's comments to Gentile Christians in Galatians 4:9; 5:6 and Romans 2:25–30 might well conclude that he too need no longer keep the law. Paul also denied that he could be described as a preacher of circumcision – to the Gentiles (Gal. 5:11). In view of this evidence we can see how the rumours could have arisen. Nevertheless, the conclusions drawn were false. Even if Paul proclaimed that Christ was the end of the law (Rom. 10:4), there is no evidence that he actively persuaded Jewish Christians to forego circumcising their children or to give up Jewish customs. The evidence of Romans 14–15 and 1 Corinthians 8–10 shows that Paul reckoned with the existence of Jews (the 'weak' brothers) who differed from the Gentiles on what they might eat, and Paul defended the right of each group to its own views and the need for each to show toleration to the other. At Corinth Paul appears to have defended Jewish habits with regard to the veiling of women at worship (1 Cor. 11:2–16). We have seen that Paul had Timothy circumcised (Acts 16:3), and according to Acts 18:18 he himself undertook a Jewish Nazirite vow. The accusation, then, had no substance in it.

22. But the question of what to do about these false rumours remained. The other Christians, who believed these stories, would soon learn that Paul was in Jerusalem. According to the western text there would certainly be a gathering of the whole church, once the members knew that Paul had come; it was necessary to prepare for what would be said in this situation.

23–24. The leaders of the church therefore suggested something practical that Paul might do in order to make it clear that the accusations against him were false. There were *four* *men under a vow* in the church; the fact that this involved *shaving their heads* indicates that this was a Nazirite vow (see on 18:18). The termination of their vow would be accompanied by the offering of a sacrifice at the temple, and it was proposed that Paul should *pay* the *expenses* of the sacrifice on their behalf. This was an accepted act of Jewish piety; Josephus relates that Herod Agrippa I directed many Nazirites to have their heads shaved, the implication being (according to Bruce, *Acts*, p. 393 n.) that he paid their expenses. The problem is that Paul is directed to purify himself along with them. The circumstances are far from clear.[1]

Paul's action would make it clear that he lived in observance of the law, but many scholars have doubted whether the

[1] Three main solutions have been proposed: (1) Bruce (*Book*, pp. 430f.) recognizes that Paul cannot have entered upon a Nazirite vow at this point, since this would last for at least thirty days, while the men's vow was to be completed in seven days. He suggests that the four men had contracted some ritual uncleanness during their vow; in this case they would have to wait for seven days and then shave their heads before making an offering on the eighth day (Nu. 6:9f.). Bruce apparently assumes that Paul could share in the rite although he had not shared in the defilement. This view does not explain the preliminary visit to the temple for purification in verse 26. (2) Haenchen (pp. 611f.) claims that a person who came to Jerusalem from Gentile territory would be 'unclean' and unable to enter the temple. Since Paul would need to attend the temple to participate in the Nazirite ceremony, he would first need to be purified by a rite that involved sprinkling with water on the third and seventh days. Luke's source related how Paul arranged for the end of his seven-day period of purification to coincide with the termination of the Nazirite vow, and verse 26 thus relates how Paul went to the temple to give notice in advance of his intention. Luke, however, by telescoping the account, has given the impression that Paul himself shared in the Nazirite vow for seven days (*cf.* how Lk. 2:22–24 joins together the purification of Mary and the dedication of her child). (3) Stolle, (pp. 76–78) denies that as an ordinary pilgrim Paul would need to be purified to enter the temple, but agrees that he would need cleansing in order to take part in a Nazirite vow. He claims that Paul had previously made a Nazirite vow (18:18), and now proposed to offer the terminal sacrifice along with four other Nazirites from overseas. They would all require seven days for purification, and then a further thirty days (which were not in fact completed) to terminate the vow. Verse 26 then refers to the third day of the purification and verse 27 to the seventh day. The difficulties with this view are that it requires the assumption that the four men had come from overseas, and that Paul had not yet terminated a vow made several years earlier before a previous visit to Palestine. None of these three solutions is free from difficulty, but the second offers the least difficulties, provided that verse 26 can be taken to mean that Paul purified himself alone, the four men merely being present at the time (*cf.* Stählin, p. 279), and also that it was necessary for Paul to be purified in order to assist at the termination of the men's vow (*pace* Stolle).

historical Paul would have agreed to this proposal. A. Haus-rath put the objection most vividly by saying that it would be more credible that the dying Calvin would have bequeathed a golden dress to the mother of God than that Paul should have entered upon this action. Luke, it is claimed, has in-vented the incident to show that Paul was a law-abiding Jew. Even Stählin (p. 277) argues that Paul would never have accepted verse 24b, although he recognizes correctly that Paul's principle in 1 Corinthians 9:20 would have allowed him to act in this way. The truth would seem to be that Paul was prepared to live as one 'under the law' to those under the law, although he did this primarily with a view to winning uncon-verted Jews rather than to pacifying Christian Jews. The des-cription here is not Lucan invention, especially if Haenchen (pp. 611f.) is right in arguing that it comes from an earlier source.[1] It looks as though Paul was prepared to make a con-ciliatory gesture, although his own testimony remained that he no longer lived under the law of Moses but under the law of Christ (1 Cor. 9:21). Bruce (*Book*, p. 432) remarks: 'A truly emancipated spirit such as Paul's is not in bondage to its own emancipation.'

25. The fact that Paul was being asked to behave in this way in no sense implied that similar demands would be made of the Gentiles. The fundamental freedom of the Gentiles from the law had been established at the meeting described in chapter 15 whose decision is now reaffirmed. It seems strange that the Jerusalem decree should be repeated *verbatim* (*cf.* 15:20, 29) to Paul who was well aware of its contents. This part of James's speech should therefore be regarded as ad-dressed primarily to Paul's companions (assuming that they were still present), or it may be a literary device to remind the reader of the situation. Yet another possibility is that this was the first mention of the decree in the we-source, and that Luke failed to edit the source in the light of the earlier mention of the decree in chapter 15 (compare how Agabus is intro-duced in 21:10, as though he had not previously been men-tioned in 11:28).

---

[1] For Haenchen, however, the source is the we-source, which was not com-posed by the author of Acts. Those who hold that Luke was the author of the source cannot therefore use the argument in this particular form, but they can argue that as an eyewitness Luke would have got his facts right.

26. Paul accepted the request. On the next day he went to the temple to commence his own period of cleansing from ritual defilement and to give notice that the Nazirite vow of the four men would be concluded, along with his own purification, on the seventh day.

27–28. The RSV translation *When the seven days were almost completed* gives the misleading impression that Paul's troubles began towards the end of the week of purification. The Greek text, however, means that the trouble began when Paul went to the temple at the end of the seven-day period in order to complete his purification. If we take the chronological reference in 24:11 to refer to a total of twelve days from Paul's arrival in Jerusalem to his speech in Caesarea, there would not have been time for a seven-day period of purification, and so Bruce (*Acts*, pp. 394, 424; contrary to his view in *Book*, p. 433) holds that we should translate 'when the seven days were going to be fulfilled' and place the incident at the beginning of the week. The problem disappears if we follow Haenchen (p. 654 n. 2) in regarding the twelve days as the period spent in Jerusalem.

Paul's troubles were caused, not by the strict Jewish Christians from Jerusalem whom he was attempting to conciliate, but by *Jews from Asia* (*i.e.* Ephesus) who had probably come to Jerusalem as pilgrims at Pentecost. They stirred up a mob who attempted to lynch Paul. The mob quickly responded to suggestions that Paul, like Stephen before him, was attacking the fundamental symbols of Jewish national solidarity, *the people*, *the law* and the temple (*cf.* 6:13). In particular, they argued that Paul had brought Gentiles *into the temple*, thereby defiling it. It is ironical that this should have been the charge against Paul at a time when he himself was undergoing purification so that he would not defile the temple! Here is 'tragedy' in the proper, literary sense of the term.

The temple in Jerusalem was divided into several concentric rectangular courts (3:2 note). Gentiles were allowed into the outermost 'court of the Gentiles', but they were prevented from proceeding further into the 'court of the women', still less into the 'court of Israel', by a low barrier which carried notices in Greek and Latin bearing the inscription: 'No foreigner may enter within the barricade which surrounds the temple and enclosure. Anyone who is caught doing so will have himself to blame for his ensuing death.' The fact that

347

the Romans were prepared to ratify death sentences even apparently on Romans for committing this breach of Jewish temple regulations indicates how significant it was, and how much emotion attached to the Jewish ideas of the purity of the temple. It is no wonder that the charge made against Paul led to such an outburst of feeling.

29. The basis of the charge was feeble enough. The Ephesian Jews had recognized *Trophimus* (20:4) as one of their own fellow citizens, and trumped up the charge that Paul had taken him with him on his visit to the temple. Some commentators think that there may have been some substance in the charge. Bruce (*Book*, p. 436 n.) comments that Paul would not have been so stupid as to rouse Jewish susceptibilities in this way, and Haenchen (p. 616) adds that a perfectly adequate explanation of the Jews' action lies in their readiness to believe anything about Paul's lack of respect for the law. The possibility that Trophimus might have wandered of his own freewill into the forbidden area is about as likely as that somebody should wander into private rooms in the Kremlin for the purpose of sightseeing.

30. The uproar quickly spread. Haenchen (p. 616), taking Luke's *all the city* too literally, denies that so great a riot could have arisen so quickly. Lake and Cadbury (*BC* IV, p. 275), however, compare the speed with which the news of a fire or a dog-fight (!) can travel today. The crowd joined in seizing Paul and they *dragged him out of the temple*. The temple authorities promptly closed the *gates* to prevent any further trouble inside; Jeremias has suggested, probably rightly, that these were the doors separating the inner courts from the court of the Gentiles, rather than the outer doors of the whole temple complex.[1]

31-32. It would not take long for news of the disturbance to reach the Roman garrison in the city. It was located in the Fortress of Antonia at the north-west of the temple; it was high enough to enable a constant watch to be kept on disturbances below and it was connected by two flights of stairs to the court of the Gentiles. The garrison in Jerusalem was a *cohort*, nominally consisting of 760 infantry and 240 cavalry, and commanded by a *tribunus militum* (an officer of a rank similar to a major or colonel). The latter acted promptly in

[1] J. Jeremias, *Jerusalem in the Time of Jesus*, p. 210.

face of the incipient riot. Taking a strong force of soldiers under their NCOs, he *ran down* to the scene. The appearance of the Romans was quite sufficient to make the crowd fall back and leave off attacking Paul.

33–34. Paul, as being the cause of the trouble, was *arrested.* What, if anything, happened to the men attacking him is not recorded. If the tribune suspected that Paul had been breaking the temple regulations, he would not be too concerned about the Jews taking the law into their own hands; properly, however, the action against Paul should have been taken by the temple police. Paul himself was handcuffed to two soldiers – thus fulfilling the prophecy of Agabus (21:11) though not to the letter, since his feet were not bound. The tribune then attempted to find out *who* the prisoner *was and what he had done.* Haenchen (p. 617) thinks that the tribune questioned the crowd rather than Paul. Verse 37 may indicate that he did not think that Paul would understand his language. This is possible, but it is also possible that when he started to question Paul members of the crowd interrupted, anxious to get their story in first. A scene of confusion broke out (*cf.* 19:32), so the tribune decided that it would be more sensible to remove Paul to the quiet of *the barracks* where a more peaceful examination of the prisoner and his accusers could be conducted.

35–36. The crowd, however, renewed their rioting and made it impossible for Paul to walk in safety up the stairway to the barracks. He had therefore to be *carried.* Haenchen (p. 618) objects that to carry Paul would be to make him the more vulnerable to attack, and suggests that the real reason, concealed by Luke, was that he was too weak to walk after his ordeal (though not too weak to address the crowds moments after). Haenchen even questions the historicity of the handcuffs, assuming that the prisoner was barely conscious; he suggests that Luke introduced them to indicate that from this point onwards Paul was no longer a free man. All this is groundless surmise. As the crowds had cried *Away with him!* when Jesus was tried before Pilate (Lk. 23:18; Jn. 19:15), so now the crowd called out for the death of Paul (*cf.* 22:22).

c. Paul's defence before the crowd (21:37 – 22:29)

The tribune's plan of taking Paul inside the barracks for interrogation was interrupted by Paul's request to speak to the people. In his speech he emphasized that he had been

349

brought up as a strict Jew whose zeal for his ancestral religion had been displayed in his persecution of the Christians. But on his way to Damascus to carry out his task he had been confronted by a heavenly vision of bright light and heard the voice of Jesus; there came the realization that it was a heavenly being whom he was persecuting, and that he must rather serve this Lord. When he reached Damascus, he was visited by a devout Jew who confirmed that it was God who had revealed his Messiah to him and now called him to be no longer a persecutor, but a witness. Final confirmation was given when he returned to Jerusalem and went into the very temple that he was accused of later defiling and was warned by Jesus in another vision that he must escape for his own safety and go to the Gentiles. The crowd interrupted, for the speech was now more than they could stand, and showed signs of fresh rioting. So the tribune resolved to interrogate Paul by torture to get at the right story; then when Paul laid claim to Roman citizenship, which protected him against such treatment, he decided that the matter should be dealt with in the first instance by the Jewish authorities.

With this section we begin the lengthy account of Paul's imprisonment and trials both in Jerusalem and Caesarea, and his subsequent journey to Rome to face the supreme Roman court. The account is given at such length, occupying a quarter of the book, that it is manifestly of great significance in the eyes of the author. He describes several court appearances by Paul and recounts no less than three lengthy speeches by Paul, in two of which the story of his conversion is repeated from Acts 9. Luke is concerned to present Paul not only as a missionary and church planter but also as a witness on trial for the gospel. Paul faces the accusations of the Jews and stands on trial before the Romans, and in this situation he acts as a witness to Jesus Christ. His ultimate defence is that, as a pious Jew, he had been called by Jesus to serve him, and there was no other choice open to him; and he argues that Judaism, rightly understood, should culminate in faith in Jesus. His speeches unfold this case with careful variation and development.

The main core of the narrative is certainly historical, although certain aspects of the legal procedure are not crystal clear. The speeches, however, present the usual problem of authenticity. There is a detailed scheme of development in

350

them which is due to the author. We need not doubt that Luke has preserved the spirit of Paul's defence, but he has presented it in his own words. It is inherently unlikely that anybody took shorthand notes of a speech delivered in such circumstances (although witnesses may have remembered the gist of it). Paul had no time for reflection as to what he was to say, and he was hardly in a fit state to speak at all after his rough handling. No doubt in whatever Paul said on the various occasions he was guided by the Spirit (Lk. 12:11f.; 21:12–15); but it is a misuse of the doctrine of inspiration to claim that the Spirit must have revealed by abnormal means to Luke the precise words used by Paul at any given juncture.

37. As Paul was being hauled away to *the barracks*, he decided to seek the opportunity to defend himself and called out to the tribune for permission to speak to him. The latter expressed surprise that he could speak *Greek*, although it was the *lingua franca* of the ancient world. He had assumed that Paul was a rough character with no education and presumably a Jew.

38. The tribune then wondered whether he was an *Egyptian* brigand who had recently *stirred up a revolt* in the desert. According to Josephus (*Bel.* 2:261–263) there had been an Egyptian false prophet who had led 30,000 men to the Mount of Olives in order to take Jerusalem; he promised that they would see the walls of the city fall down. The governor, Felix, killed or captured his followers, while the prophet himself managed to escape. Clearly the tribune thought that this person had reappeared; the discrepancy between the number of his followers in Acts and in Josephus reflects the latter's well-known tendency to exaggeration, and the tribune's estimate will have been nearer the mark. The prophet in fact belonged to a class of people who held 'messianic' hopes (carefully played down by Josephus) and expected that God would work signs for them in the wilderness; for concrete instances of these see 5:36f. The Gospels contain warnings to Christians against being taken in by such impostors (Mt. 24:26). The tribune refers to the prophet's followers as *Assassins* (*sicarii*, so called from their use of a short dagger, Latin *sica*); this term was applied to the anti-Roman extremists who emerged during the time of Felix and were eventually responsible for the revolt against Rome in AD 66–70. Haenchen (pp. 621f.) holds that the tribune has mistakenly identified the prophet's followers

351

with this group, although Josephus carefully distinguished them. One may wonder whether the divisions were quite as sharp as all that. (At the time of writing these words, few reporters could accurately distinguish the various Irish military groups by their precise names.) Haenchen also wonders why the tribune gave up this identification of Paul once he realized that Paul could speak Greek, since Greek was the language of Egypt; but this problem arises out of a mistranslation; we should probably translate: 'Do you know Greek? Surely, then, you are the Egyptian. . . . ?'[1]

39. Paul's reply incidentally indicates that there was no connection between Christians and Jewish revolutionaries, but it is questionable whether Luke's motive in including the conversation was merely to demonstrate this. Paul was concerned to establish his respectable Jewish background and civil status: he was not the kind of person to cause a riot in the temple. He was a Jew and a *citizen* of *Tarsus*. This is not a reference to his Roman citizenship, which does not emerge until later (22:25), but to his status in a self-governing *city* to which he was proud to belong. From the time of the emperor Claudius it was possible for a man to have both Roman citizenship and local citizenship (Conzelmann, pp. 124f.).

40. Paul's request to address the crowd was granted, once he had given his credentials. From *the steps* he was able to look down on the crowd, motion for silence, and then (diplomatically) address them in their own vernacular. *Hebrew* can mean 'Aramaic' (22:6; 26:14).

The whole episode raises historical difficulties. Haenchen claims that Paul was in no fit physical condition to speak, that it is unlikely that the tribune would have given him permission to speak without some compelling reason, and that it is even more unlikely that the crowd would have been prepared to listen. To these points must be added the comments already made about the difficulties in regarding the ensuing speech as representing word for word what Paul might have said. These difficulties are probably exaggerated. They stem partly from the brevity of Luke's account. We may well have a dramatic presentation of the scene rather than a detailed photographic

[1] J. H. Moulton and N. Turner, *A Grammar of New Testament Greek*, III (Edinburgh, 1963) p. 283. The second question expects an affirmative answer.

description or taped transcript. What is significant is the teaching attributed to Paul, through which we see him as a witness to Jesus Christ.

22:1. Paul began by addressing the crowd with the same words as were used by Stephen. It can safely be assumed that some priests or other members of the Sanhedrin are envisaged as present; hence the use of the term *fathers*, although when addressing the Sanhedrin Paul simply says 'brethren' (23:1). Perhaps, however, 'fathers' is simply a term of respect to the older people present. The keynote is struck with the term *defence* (Greek *apologia*) which reappears in this section of Acts (24:10; 25:8; 26:1f., 24; *cf.* 19:33). This word does not simply mean the giving of reasoned answers to charges made in court; in the light of Jesus' words in Luke 12:11f.; 21:12–15 it also includes the concept of witness to him. This explains why we do not get a point-by-point reply to the charges made against Paul: he uses the opportunity primarily to testify to the Lord, showing how his conduct is justified by appeal to the Lord's commands. Thus Paul's speeches become a means of preaching the gospel and confronting the audience with the claim to their faith and obedience to the Lord.

2. Luke notes how the audience became the more attentive as Paul started to speak. Many Jews from the Dispersion could not speak the Hebrew or Aramaic languages: even the greatest Jewish scholar of the first century, Philo of Alexandria, could not read the books of Moses (on which he wrote extensive commentaries) in Hebrew. For Paul to address the people in their own tongue was an effective way of commanding their attention – and perhaps even some degree of sympathy. The detail underlines Paul's claim to be in every sense a Jew (Phil. 3:5).

3. Paul first of all affirms his position as a loyal *Jew*. His *curriculum vitae* follows a threefold pattern describing his birth, his early upbringing by his parents (especially his mother) and his education (by his father and other teachers).[1] This pattern is significant for the understanding of what Paul says. He was *born* in *Tarsus*, but he was brought up *in this city, i.e.* Jerusalem. Paul, therefore, was brought to Jerusalem at a very early stage in his life, and he did not, as used to be supposed,

---

[1] See the similar pattern in 7:20–22; W. C. van Unnik, *Tarsus or Jerusalem, the city of Paul's youth* (London, 1962), reprinted in van Unnik, pp. 259–320, *cf.* pp. 321–327.

spend his boyhood and adolescence in Tarsus. Nevertheless, despite leaving Tarsus at an early age, he must have maintained family contacts with it, and it was to Tarsus that he went as a missionary in the first, lengthy stage of his Christian career (9:30; 11:25; Gal. 1:21 – 2:1); he was proud to be a citizen of Tarsus. The third part of his upbringing was his education. Here the RSV rendering is wrong, and we must redivide the sentence to read: '. . . brought up in this city, and educated at the feet of Gamaliel'. Thus *Gamaliel* (5:34), a leading Pharisaic teacher from the more 'liberal' tradition of Hillel, was Paul's teacher. The phrase *according to the strict manner of the law of our fathers* is usually taken to qualify Paul's education as a rabbi, but there is some reason for taking it with the following phrase *being zealous for God*; religious zeal was expressed in meticulous observance of the law (21:20; Rom. 10:2; Gal. 1:14; Phil. 3:6). It has been denied that Paul was a pupil of Gamaliel, but on quite inadequate grounds: J. Jeremias has demonstrated that Paul not only handles the Scriptures in the rabbinic manner, but more precisely in the manner of the school of Hillel.[1]

4. Paul's statement has placed him alongside his audience as a zealous defender of the law. Now he describes how he had gone further than his audience in religious zeal. He had been a persecutor of the Christian church (here called *the Way, cf.* 9:2), even to the point of *death* (9:1). Here Paul has in mind the death of Stephen in particular; in 26:10 he refers more generally to several executions (see note there). Other Christians were jailed, and presumably released. This general picture is confirmed by 1 Corinthians 15:9; Galatians 1:13; Philippians 3:6; 2 Timothy 1:13.

5. Paul's claims could be confirmed by the Jewish hierarchy which had given him authority for his task, and in particular to extradite Christians from *Damascus* (9:1f.). Since the high priesthood was now held by a different person (Ananias, 23:2) from the time when Paul went to Damascus (Caiaphas), Paul's appeal will be to the collective memory of the present Sanhedrin regarding what its predecessors in office had done. It is possible that Caiaphas was still alive, though now deposed from office.

[1] J. Jeremias, 'Paulus als Hillelit', in E. E. Ellis and M. Wilcox, *Neotestamentica et Semitica* (Edinburgh, 1969), pp. 88–94.

6. Paul now describes in his own words what happened on the way to Damascus. His account adds to the earlier description (9:3) that his journey took place at *noon* (26:13). His experience of *light* was thus no night-time delusion; the light was strong enough to outshine the midday sun. Perhaps there is an echo of Deuteronomy 28:28f.

7–8. Paul fell to the ground, and heard a heavenly voice speaking to him. The words of the conversation are reported exactly as in 9:4f., with the single change that Jesus describes himself as being of *Nazareth*. This could be an addition to make clear to a Jewish audience the precise identity of the speaker (Lk. 24:19). It is Jesus, now alive, who is the real object of Paul's persecution. But if Jesus speaks from heaven, it follows that he has been resurrected by God, and thus in the last analysis it is God whom Paul is attacking.

9. Somewhat inconsequentially Paul interrupts his description of the conversation to point out that his companions were not able to hear what was said, although they *saw the light*. They were conscious of something unusual, but only Paul experienced the event as a divine revelation. They saw the light, but did not see it as a revelation of Jesus in glory. They heard the voice, but only as a noise, and did not make out the words.[1]

10. Peculiar to this account is the insertion of Paul's question at this point, *What shall I do, Lord?*[2] The question expresses the stupefaction of Paul as he realizes the significance of what he has been doing and recognizes that he must now change his way of life. It is not clear whether *Lord* here is beginning to have a fuller meaning for Paul than in verse 8. But this is certainly the case when Paul now goes on to explain what *the Lord* told him to do. The audience would not have recognized Jesus as 'the Lord', but Paul has fallen into his accustomed Christian way of speaking, and the choice of word indicates the new estimate of Jesus which he formed as a result of the experience. The Lord's reply is essentially the same as in 9:6,

---

[1] This distinction may be reflected in the use of the verb 'to hear' with the accusative here of the sound heard, but with the genitive in 9:7 of the source of the sound; but the fact that both constructions are used with regard to what Paul himself heard (accusative in 9:4; 26:14; genitive in 22:7) suggests that the grammatical difference may not be significant.

[2] The western text of 9:6 has a similar phrase.

355

and merely deals with the next stage in Paul's instruction about his ultimate destiny (contrast 26:16).

11. Unable to see anything as a result of the effects of the blinding *light*, Paul had to be *led* by his companions to *Damascus*. Although his companions had seen the light and fallen to the ground (26:13f.), they evidently recovered immediately (9:7); they were merely temporarily blinded by light, and had not seen a vision.

12. In the second part of his description of his calling Paul relates the role of *Ananias* (9:10–19). Paul on this occasion stresses to his audience the fact that Ananias was *a devout man* in terms of obedience to *the law* (*cf.* Lk. 1:6) and that his piety was recognized by the Jewish community in Damascus; the fact that Ananias was already a Christian disciple (9:10) is quietly omitted.

13. The account of Ananias's part in the story is considerably abbreviated, since the story is now being told from Paul's point of view. We therefore hear nothing of Ananias's own vision of the Lord, and simply learn how Paul was visited by him. The account of what happened is divided into two parts, so that first of all we hear how Ananias restored Paul's *sight* (Acts 9:17b, 18), and then, separated off for emphasis, how Ananias brought the Lord's commission to Paul and called him to signify his obedience by being baptized; in Acts 9:15f. we are told what the Lord said to Ananias, rather than what Ananias said to Paul about his commission.

14. The fact that Paul recovered his sight acted as a divine confirmation that what Ananias had to say to him was indeed a message from the Lord. The wording stresses that it was *the God of our fathers* who was calling Paul, thereby emphasizing to the audience the continuity between the Old Testament revelation and the new revelation of God through Jesus. This God had foreordained Paul to be his servant; his choice and call were prior to Paul's response (3:20; 26:16). Therefore God had revealed *the Just One* to Paul. This term (3:14; 7:52) refers to Jesus as the Messiah.

15. The purpose of the revelation was that Paul should become *a witness*, describing and proclaiming what he had *seen and heard. To all men* signifies both Jews and Gentiles (9:15; 22:21; 26:17; Gal. 1:16). Thus Paul is seen to be on trial, not merely on a charge of defiling the temple and attacking Judaism (21:28) but above all as a witness to Jesus.

16. Ananias's somewhat reproachful question *Why do you wait?* is slightly odd. The Greek phrase may simply mean, 'What are you going to do?' Paul is to get up, *i.e.* act straightaway, and submit to baptism. As in 2:38 (*cf.* 2:21) baptism is the expression of faith in Jesus by appealing to *his name*, and it symbolizes the forgiveness of sins – in this case the sin of persecution is especially in mind. Paul omits mention of the reception of the Spirit (9:17) which was not necessary in this context.

17–18. Now follows a third part of the story of the experience of Paul, peculiar to this particular version. On his return to Jerusalem (9:26–30) Paul went into *the temple* to pray. We note again this emphasis on the temple as the place where Christians continued to pray, and where Jesus Christ spoke to them. Rightly did E. Lohmeyer characterize Jesus as *The Lord of the Temple* (Edinburgh, 1961). During his prayer Paul had a visionary experience (10:10; *cf.* Rev. 1:10) in which Jesus again appeared to him and commanded him to leave Jerusalem for the sake of his own safety, since the people would not accept his *testimony* to Jesus. For the historical background to the command see 9:29f. But perhaps here there is also the thought that history is now repeating itself.

19–20. Paul, however, argued that he was the very person whom the Jews ought to hear. They would surely listen to the testimony of one who had imprisoned and beaten Christians in the synagogues. (There is no basis in the Greek text for RSV *every synagogue*; the phrase means 'in one synagogue after another'). Not only so, but Paul's part in the murder of *Stephen* was common knowledge. Here the word *witness* is beginning to be used in the way which led to its taking on the sense of 'martyr'.[1]

21. But the Lord's command stood despite the objection. Paul's departure was not intended to be simply the means of his own safety but was to effect God's previously intimated purpose of sending him 'to all men' and specifically *to the Gentiles*. Acts 9:30 relates the human side of the events leading to Paul's departure.

22. The speech of Paul is interrupted at this point by the crowd who do not want to hear any more. He has not in fact

---

[1] See A. A. Trites, *The New Testament Concept of Witness* (Cambridge, 1977), pp. 66f.

reached the point of saying anything about the immediate problem, the accusation of defiling the temple, which in the last analysis was merely a pretext for raising more fundamental issues (*cf.* 21:28a). The effect of Paul's speech is that to some extent a new motif has arisen to arouse the ire of the Jews, the mention of the Gentiles. So the crowd renewed its demand that Paul should be put to death; it was wrong that such a person should be allowed *to live*.

23. The people lent force to their demands by throwing *dust* in *the air* and waving *their garments*. The precise background of these actions is not clear. Bruce (*Book*, p. 445) thinks of excitement. Elsewhere in Acts we hear of shaking off the dust from one's feet (13:51) as a gesture used by Jews against Gentiles and by Christians against Jews who, in rejecting Christ, had cut themselves off from the true Israel. Paul's shaking of his garments in 18:6, *sc.* to remove the dust from them, may have had the same force. Against the background of these two passages the thought may be that the people waved their clothes in the air to rid them of the dust as a sign that they counted Paul a blasphemer and no longer a true Jew. Yet another possibility is that this action was a mild substitute for the stoning to which the crowd would have subjected Paul, had the soldiers not been present.

24. Whatever the situation, the tribune decided that only an interrogation of the prisoner in *the barracks* was going to get at the truth. It is probable that his command of Aramaic was not sufficient for him to get the full gist of what Paul had said; even had he understood the words he would probably have been none the wiser. So he gave orders for Paul to be *examined* under torture. The Roman practice was to examine slaves and other suspected persons by whipping them with a scourge composed of leather thongs to which rough pieces of bone and metal were attached; the fearful effects on the victim's back can be imagined. This was a far worse experience than undergoing a Jewish beating or the Roman punishment of being beaten with the lictors' rods (16:22; 2 Cor. 11:24f.).

25. When Paul realized the soldiers' intention, he at once played his trump card. It was illegal to submit a *Roman citizen* to this method of examination. (*cf.* 16:37). The Lex Valeria and the Lex Porcia were ancient laws that prohibited the beating, and even the fettering, of Roman citizens, and this right was confirmed by the Lex Julia which gave citizens in the provinces the right of appeal to Rome. There were circumstances in which a magistrate might so act against a Roman, but only after a proper trial. It is quite clear that Paul had the law on his side in this particular instance (Sherwin-White, pp. 57–59, 71–76). We do not know how a Roman proved his citizenship; at the very least a formal claim to citizenship led to a stay in the procedure.

26–28. The *centurion* in charge of the actual scourging promptly warned his superior officer, who came to question Paul for himself. Paul's statement that he was a citizen brought a sarcastic response from the *tribune*. It had cost him a lot of money to become a citizen. The point was not that the tribune doubted Paul's claim, but rather he was implying that anybody could become a citizen these days! The privilege was losing its value. The cost referred to is not that of the fee payable for the right (in fact there was none), but that of bribing the various officials (Sherwin-White, pp. 154f.). Paul, however, was able to cap his comment by claiming that he was *born a* Roman *citizen* and had no need to buy it for himself. Speculation as to how Paul's family gained citizenship is idle, and so far no light has been thrown on the problem.[1]

29. The soldiers *who were about to examine* Paul promptly ceased their attempt (doubtless on orders from the tribune), while the tribune himself was placed in a state of some fear, lest news of his contravention of the regulations might reach a superior officer. Luke takes the opportunity to underline that Christians who were Roman citizens could claim their rights as such.

The story of the incident has been criticized by Haenchen who is puzzled that the tribune who was apparently tolerant towards Paul in 21:37–40 should propose to torture him; he also finds it strange that Paul did not affirm his Roman citizenship earlier, instead of merely claiming Tarsian citizenship. This puts him in a position to declare the story fictitious. Having inserted a fictitious speech, Luke was able to reserve Paul's claim to Roman citizenship for this vivid, tense narrative, and in so doing to indicate the Roman authorities' complete uncertainty as to exactly what Paul had done that might be considered illegal (23:28f.; 25:20, 27). Even, however, if the

[1] Sherwin-White, pp. 151f., criticizes earlier suggestions without being able to offer a fresh one.

speech is a dramatic insertion by Luke, the substance of the scene is still quite credible. There is so little point, for example, in the exchange over the price of citizenship, which adds nothing to Luke's purpose (except light relief) that it is hard to regard it as sheer invention.

d. Paul appears before the Sanhedrin (22:30 – 23:10)

The tribune had grasped the fact that Paul was unpopular with the Jews, but was still no nearer discovering precisely what was the cause of the trouble; Paul's speech had not said anything about the immediate issue. In a further attempt to get at the truth he called the members of the Sanhedrin to meet with him. Instead of hearing Jewish accusations, however, the meeting heard a statement from Paul which was cut off sharply by an altercation with the high priest. Thereafter Paul again seized the chance to speak, and he successfully divided the assembly by claiming to side with the Pharisees in their belief in the resurrection of the dead, a doctrine denied by the Sadducees. A tumult broke out between the two groups, placing Paul in danger, and once again he had to be rescued from the Jews.

The whole scene has puzzled scholars, and there is scarcely a passage in Acts whose historicity has been so strongly questioned. Some have found it impossible to imagine a scene like this ever taking place, and they have sought to explain it in terms of Luke's theological purpose. Luke, it is argued, has subtly changed the issue at stake in Paul's trial from the defilement of the temple to the question whether Christianity is the true fulfilment of (Pharisaic) Judaism, and has indicated that Paul's case will not be truly decided in a Jewish court. In so doing, Luke has produced an unhistorical scene in which a Roman tribune commands the Sanhedrin to meet, no case is presented against Paul, Paul claims not to recognize the high priest, and the members of the court engage in a theological controversy of which Paul takes unfair advantage.

The element of truth in this account of things is that Luke has correctly perceived that ultimately the real issue is not whether Paul defiled the temple, but whether Judaism was prepared to tolerate Christianity, and this it was unwilling to do, being moved by irrational hatred. To a certain extent Luke as a historian may have made this issue more explicit than it appeared at the time. The individual points of difficulty in the scene are discussed below. In short, it may be claimed that the very oddity of the story as history is a pointer against invention by a writer such as Luke, and the attempt to account for it *in toto* as a fictitious narrative to suit Luke's purposes is unconvincing.

30. If the Romans were holding a man accused by the Jews of some severe misdemeanour but were unable to discover the precise nature of the charge, some further investigation would be called for. The tribune wanted to get at the truth.[1] Paul was therefore *unbound* in order that he might appear before an enquiry. His exact position is not clear. The account suggests that he was unchained only after a night in captivity, although Luke knows that a Roman citizen could not be bound without good reason. Clearly Paul was kept in custody and wore bonds (26:29), and we must assume that while in custody even a Roman citizen could be bound. Bruce (*Acts*, p. 408) probably gets the meaning in the present verse correct when he claims that nothing more is meant than being taken out of prison to face the Jewish council.

The next problem is the meeting of the *council*. Although Josephus (*Ant.* 20:202) states that the Sanhedrin could not meet without the permission of the Roman government, this is questionable (Sherwin-White, p. 54). In any case, it does not follow that the Romans could command an official meeting of it. But an official meeting may not be in mind. It is possible that this is an unofficial consultation by the tribune in order that he might know what report on the case to send to his superior officer. If the Jewish authorities had agreed that there was no case against Paul, he could have been set free. It would seem that once the Romans had intervened in the case and found that it concerned a Roman citizen, it was necessary that they themselves should deal with the matter. For this reason the tribune sought further information from responsible Jewish leaders. Haenchen (p. 640) objects that the information would more appropriately have been sought from the temple authorities, but the broader implications of the case may have suggested that a wider group should be consulted; since the Sanhedrin was the Jewish court to deal with Jewish matters

---

[1] See 21:34; 25:26 for repetition of this motif; the word translated *real reason* is from the same root as that in Lk. 1:4 where Luke sets down his own aim of enabling Theophilus to know the 'real facts' about Jesus.

of any kind, it was the proper body to consult. Objections have also been raised about the tribune's presence (with his soldiers, 23:10) at the meeting, since they were unclean Gentiles. Whatever the Jewish laws of purity actually were in the first century, however, some contact between the Jewish and the Roman authorities was essential, and there must have been appropriate procedures; the special reason given in John 18:28 for the two groups keeping apart suggests that on other occasions some kind of contact was possible. When all this is said, however, it must be admitted that Luke pictures the scene as though it were a meeting of the Sanhedrin (23:1, 6), possibly because he wants to bring out the parallelism between Jesus and Paul.

23:1. The proceedings open with a statement by Paul, although one might have expected in the first place an opportunity for the Jews to state their charges against him. In fact the Jews never do state their case in this scene. Probably this is due to abbreviation by Luke and possibly a desire to concentrate attention on Paul. The reader already knows what the charges are (21:28), and they will be repeated again in 24:5f. Luke therefore concentrates on Paul. He declares that he has nothing on his *conscience* in the sight of God (24:16). Right up to this moment he has been blameless (*cf.* 2 Cor. 1:12; 2:17; 4:2). Haenchen (p. 637) takes this to apply to the whole of Paul's earlier life, and asks: was not his connivance at the murder of Stephen on Paul's conscience? But there is no need to assume that Paul was referring to incidents so long ago as that; here he is concerned with the immediate past. It is a rejection of the charges made against him, but no evidence is produced, possibly because no evidence was produced by his accusers.

2. A somewhat bizarre interruption followed. The *high priest* at this time was *Ananias* (not to be confused with Annas, 4:6). He had been appointed *c.* AD 47, and was dismissed in AD 58–59. Later he was assassinated as a pro-Roman by Jewish guerrillas (AD 66). The Romans suspected him of being responsible for riots in Judea in AD 52, but he had been acquitted of the charge. This was the man who now ordered those nearest Paul to cuff him *on the mouth*. The incident may be meant to remind the reader of how Jesus was treated at his trial (Jn. 18:22f.), although this detail is not recorded in Luke's own account of it. Here the action is a protest against what appeared to the high priest as a lie. Perhaps Luke means us to conclude that the high priest had no rational reply to Paul and in his frustration descended to force and insult. The action is surprising on the part of a responsible official, but such things can happen in heated moments of tension even in a modern legislative assembly, and Josephus confirms that Ananias was an insolent and quick-tempered character (*Ant.* 20:199).

3. What is more surprising is Paul's reply. Some commentators note how Paul's swift reply goes against the spirit of Matthew 5:39 and his own words in 1 Corinthians 4:12. We should not dismiss out of hand the simple explanation that Paul lost his temper, with verse 5 giving something of an apology: Paul was both human and sinful, and we do not need to credit him with a sinless perfection that he himself never claimed. At the same time, Paul's prophetic consciousness may come to expression here. Ananias was undoubtedly an unworthy holder of his office, as both Josephus and rabbinic tradition attest. Paul spoke out in the name of God against his corruption, just as Jesus had spoken quite freely of Pharisaic corruption (Lk. 11:39–52). He threatened that *God* would *strike* him – a prophecy which Luke's readers no doubt saw fulfilled in the high priest's violent death. To describe him as a *whitewashed wall* was simply to accuse him of hypocrisy (*cf.* Mt. 23:27). In Ezekiel 13:10f. we hear of prophets who, as it were, daubed a rickety wall with whitewash, fondly imagining that this would make it stronger. This metaphor was still alive (*Zadokite Document* 8:12), and Paul may be making his own use of it. More openly he accuses the high priest of hypocrisy in claiming to act as a judge in accordance with the law, and yet acting unrighteously during a trial (Lv. 19:15).

4. The members of the council were astounded that Paul should call down a curse on the high priest who, in their eyes, was appointed by God to his office (*cf.* Jn. 18:22), and they called him to order.

5. Paul was well aware that one should not act in this way, as the law stated in Exodus 22:28. His words, however, are hardly a simple apology that he had transgressed the law in a fit of temper. He claims that he *did not know* that it was the *high priest* whom he had addressed. It is quite incredible that Paul did not know whom he was addressing; theories that Paul had bad eyesight, and that he did not see that it was the high priest who had given the command to strike him, or that he did not recognize the high priest in his everyday clothes lack foundation. This brings us back to the old suggestion that Paul was speaking in bitter irony: 'I did not think that a man who could give such an order could be the high priest.' This is the most probable solution, even though the ironic tone might have been conveyed more clearly. Haenchen (p. 642) rightly observes that the effect of the incident is to indicate that Paul was unlikely to get justice from a Jewish court.

6. Then the course of the action takes a sharp turn. The members of the Sanhedrin were representative of the Sadducean and Pharisaic sects. The former group comprised the priestly aristocracy, while the latter were represented by the scribes (who were mostly Pharisees). Their political and theological differences were well known. The Sadducees were sympathizers with Rome, recognizing that the maintenance of the *status quo* was to their advantage as the group in power, while the Pharisees were silent protesters against Rome. The former were conservative in theology, adhering to the letter of the Pentateuch, while the latter were progressives, ready to elucidate and 'modernize' the law by their interpretations of it. It was, therefore, the Pharisees who were open to the concept of *resurrection*, a belief which is far from being clearly or openly taught in the Pentateuch: Jesus' exposition of the law in this sense (Lk. 20:37f.) was certainly a novelty to his hearers. Paul now introduced this issue into the discussion by claiming that he was a Pharisee, and that what was really at stake was the question of belief in the resurrection. Although the issue is introduced in general terms, the real point is the possibility of the resurrection of Jesus. Earlier in Acts the leaders of the Jerusalem church had been attacked by the Sadducees for preaching the resurrection from the dead (4:1f.), and the Pharisees, or rather Gamaliel, had displayed a rather neutral attitude (5:33–39). What Paul was now in effect claiming was that one could be a Christian, while accepting the Pharisaic point of view, or more precisely, that Pharisaic Judaism found its fulfilment in Christianity. The Sadducean religion, however, needed a fundamental change in its presuppositions before it could become Christian. To be sure, the Pharisaic and Christian understandings of the law were very different, and to this extent Paul could not have claimed to be a Pharisee. The problems that arise, therefore, are whether Paul could

364

honestly have claimed 'I *am* a Pharisee', and whether his action in doing so was an unworthy attempt to win his case by dividing the assembly. Haenchen (pp. 642f.) answers both points to the detriment of Luke, and ascribes the historical inexactitude to Luke's desire to present true Judaism and Christianity as standing in continuity. To Hanson (p. 221), however, Paul, even as a Christian, was still in many respects a Pharisee, and was capable of using an opportunist argument. This latter view is historically preferable, since the former view has to pay the price of making Luke into an unintelligent writer who committed elementary historical mistakes, whereas the evidence generally suggests that Luke attempted to achieve historical accuracy.

7. The result of Paul's intervention was to throw the two parties in the Sanhedrin into dispute with one another. Haenchen objects that they were well used to each other's theological positions by this time, and that they must have realized that the real issue was Paul's attitude to the law, which would have been unacceptable to both of them. But theologians will argue on ticklish points whenever they get the chance, and argument could certainly have taken place on whether Paul's siding with the Pharisees on this issue was justified.

8. Luke prepares the way for the next part of the story by observing for the benefit of Gentile readers that the Sadducees said that *there is no resurrection, nor angel, nor spirit*. The Sadducean denial of the resurrection is well attested (Lk. 20:27), but the reference to angels and spirits is puzzling, since this aspect of their views is not attested elsewhere and angels certainly appear in the Pentateuch, which the Sadducees accepted as Scripture. A solution to the problem has been suggested by S. T. Lachs who argues that the Pharisees held that resurrection might take place as a spiritual body, *i.e.* like an angel, or as a pure spirit. Since the Sadducees denied the resurrection, they naturally also denied the possibility of a post-resurrection existence in either of these forms.[1]

9. The discussion reached the point of discord, especially when *some* (note: not all) of the Pharisaic party commented

[1] S. T. Lachs, 'The Pharisees and Sadducees on Angels: A Reexamination of Acts XXIII 8', *Graetz College Annual of Jewish Studies (Philadelphia)* 6, 1977, pp. 35–42.

that if Paul thought that he had spoken with a spirit or angel there was nothing wrong with that. This was only a minority view, and it certainly did not carry endorsement of Paul's understanding of the resurrection of Jesus. At an earlier stage the Sanhedrin had included sympathizers of Jesus (Lk. 23:50; Jn. 7:50f.); although the lines were now more sharply drawn, the possibility of some members being at least tolerant to the Christians can certainly not be ruled out, especially since the way of life of many of the Jewish Christians was not offensive to other Jews.

10. But the expression of this point of view simply exacerbated the situation, and the tribune was compelled to bring the proceedings to a halt and remove Paul from possible danger to his person. The problem of finding out the real case against Paul had not made much progress.

e. Paul is transferred to Caesarea (23:11–35)

The direction of Paul's further destiny is laid down in verse 11, and immediately afterwards the first steps towards its fulfilment are taken. The revelation that a group of Jews were plotting against Paul's life, coupled with the fact that the tribune was at a loss to know what to do next about Paul, led to his being transferred under a heavy Roman escort from Jerusalem to the Roman capital of Caesarea. Thus Paul was removed from the jurisdiction of the Jews to be placed under that of the Romans, and so he advanced a step towards his appeal to Caesar and his journey to Rome. The account is told at considerable length, and reveals Luke's delight in telling a good story, especially one concerned with travel. It depicts the lengths to which the Romans were prepared to go in ensuring justice and safety for Paul, although they are not made out to be cardboard saints and Felix in particular did not give Paul justice.

11. The decisive significance of the section is indicated by this preliminary incident in which *the Lord*, *i.e.* Jesus, appears to Paul and reassures him about the future. The vision makes it clear that what is to happen will follow a divinely initiated plan; the hand of God will guide the course of events until Paul stands before the Roman emperor. Nothing is said about the outcome of the trial before Caesar, a topic which is outside the horizon of Acts. What is significant is that the appearance of Paul before the Sanhedrin in Jerusalem is described as *witness*, and that Paul's appearance before the emperor will also be for the purpose of witnessing to Jesus. This, rather than defending himself against specific charges, is Paul's task in court. For similar visions at decisive points in the narrative see 16:9; 18:9f.; 27:23f.; in all these cases, except the first, the vision stands in the context of imminent danger and serves to encourage Paul.

12. The encouragement was quickly needed. The following day, after the tumult in the meeting with the Sanhedrin, a group of *Jews made a plot* against Paul's life. The vague description *the Jews* is made more precise in the next verse, but leaves the impression that the action of this group was typical of the attitude of the Jews generally. The identity of the group is not indicated. They were obviously fanatics, probably men with a zealot-type of outlook who were prepared to use violence against an alleged opponent of the Jewish faith, and there is nothing unlikely about the existence of such a group in the conditions of first-century Palestine. Their religious fanaticism was seen in their solemn vow to fast until they had achieved their purpose. If they broke their oath, they would regard themselves as standing under a divine curse, although they would probably not take that eventuality too seriously; even strict Jews (and these men probably did not think too clearly about the consequence of their vow) had ways and means of escaping the implications of unfulfilled vows.

13–14. The *forty* men in the plot had to find a way of getting Paul out of the barracks into a more vulnerable situation, and they therefore sought help from *the chief priests and elders*. Since the scribes (who mostly belonged to the Pharisaic party) are not mentioned, it seems that they approached the groups in the Sanhedrin most likely to favour their proposal. Haenchen (p. 649) finds some tension with the preceding scene in which a group of the Pharisees had favoured Paul, and claims that the Pharisees set the tone of the Sanhedrin; he overlooks the facts that only a small group of Pharisees were cautiously favourable to Paul, and that the chief priests held the reins of power in the Sanhedrin. The fact that according to later rabbinic teaching the Sanhedrin was not supposed to aid plotters is no proof that unscrupulous members avoided doing so in the first century.

15. The conspirators' plan was that the chief priests should arrange with the *tribune* and the Sanhedrin that Paul should be brought down again for further examination so that they might come to a more informed decision about him. In other words the Jews were to suggest to the tribune that they help him by establishing more precisely the case against Paul. The conspirators would then take advantage of Paul's journey to the place of meeting to murder him on the way. Whether the tribune would have agreed to this procedure after what had already happened is more than doubtful. It is equally doubtful whether the conspirators would have escaped with their lives if they had attempted to murder Paul. The scheme as a whole is one conceived by fanatics without too much regard to its practicability.

16. But the plot was perhaps too widely known to have much chance of success. Somehow news of it reached the ears of Paul's nephew. All attempts to learn more about this young man and how he got wind of what was happening are speculative, and we must be content to remain ignorant about Paul's family connections in Jerusalem. Certainly there is no reason to pronounce the story of the boy impossible or even improbable. Some commentators find it strange that the boy was able to go directly to Paul in the barracks and tell him the story: if the boy could get in so easily, why not a conspirator also? But other references to prison conditions at the time suggest that prisoners were easily accessible to their friends, who would bring them food and other small comforts (Lucian, *De Morte Peregrini* 12–13).[1]

17–18. On receiving the boy's message Paul naturally wished it to be communicated to the *tribune*, and asked *one of the centurions* to *take* the boy to him. Haenchen (p. 646) casts scorn on the way that Paul is able to command the centurion to do his bidding, but this is unjustified sarcasm; the apparent brusqueness of Paul's request underlines the seriousness and urgency of the situation rather than any exalted status given to Paul by Luke.

19. The fact that the tribune *took* the boy *by the hand* has also been the subject of scholarly sarcasm: 'Never was a tribune so amiable,' said Loisy. But the impression we get is rather that the lad was quite young, and the tribune's action is appropriate. The ancient world would not have seen any incompatibility between his ordering Paul to be scourged and

[1] J. Stevenson, *A New Eusebius* (London, 1957), p. 135.

368

his kindly treatment of the boy. The boy is questioned privately, evidently because he gave the impression of having secret information to convey.

20–21. The boy's message repeats what we already know, with suitable alterations in style for the occasion. He refers to the plotters as 'the Jews' which would be the appropriate term in addressing the Roman, and is not a mark of forgetfulness by a Gentile author. We also learn that the plot was to be executed the following day if possible: the plotters did not want to fast for too long! The boy gives the rest of his information in the form of a warning to the tribune not to be taken in by the Jewish request for Paul to be made available to them.

22. The tribune's reply indicates that he made up his mind as to what he should do while the boy was speaking. He may well have decided already that his proper course was to refer the case of Paul to his superior officer, since he himself did not have the necessary authority to deal with it: 'The tribune lacked the necessary *imperium* to deal judicially with prisoners of provincial status, once he had restored public order' (Sherwin-White, p. 54). The boy's news simply speeded up his action in sending Paul to Caesarea, and made it clear that he must authorize maximum security measures for Paul's safekeeping. As part of these measures it was necessary that the Jews should not hear that news of the plot had reached his ears.

23. Preparations were now made to send Paul under armed guard to Caesarea. The force was to set off at about nine or ten o'clock in the evening so as to get away from Jerusalem under cover of darkness. It was to consist of *two hundred* armed *soldiers* under their centurions, together with *seventy horsemen*, and *two hundred spearmen*. The last word translates an otherwise unknown Greek word, which is interpreted in this way in the Latin version. The total force thus comprised 470 personnel. This amounted to nearly half the Jerusalem garrison, and it has been suggested that it is a ridiculously large escort for a single prisoner. Luke, it is claimed, is romancing in his efforts to underline the importance of Paul, the scale of the danger, and the care of the Romans for their prisoner. The problem is somewhat lessened when we take into account the fact that the foot soldiers accompanied Paul only on the first, and most dangerous, part of the journey, and then returned to Jerusalem (but see verse 32 note). Even so the figures remain surprisingly high. Another attempt at a solution is to suggest that the 'spearmen' really were led horses, but this cannot be considered very probable. The difficulty may well lie in the two hundred 'spearmen', since when they are removed the rest of the force would be ample to intimidate the plotters, but it must be confessed that at present there is no clear solution of the difficulty.

24. Paul himself was to be provided with horses or mules to transport him. The plural may allow for a change of animal, but since the text does not specifically connect the animals with Paul, they may have been to carry baggage for the force as a whole.

Paul was to be brought to the governor, at this time Tiberius Claudius *Felix*.[1] He was a brother of Pallas, a freed slave who was a corrupt favourite of the Emperor Claudius, and later of Nero; after holding a subordinate post in Samaria he became governor in AD 52. He did his best to put down the rebels in Judea, but used such violence and so alienated the people that he had to be recalled (24:27). His third wife was Drusilla, the daughter of Herod Agrippa I (24:24). Felix was a freedman, and his appointment to be procurator was an unusual honour. Nevertheless, Tacitus, who could sum up a character in a terse biting phrase, commented that 'he exercised royal power with the mind of a slave': evidently he had not outgrown his lowly origins.

25. The prisoner was accompanied by *a letter* explaining the reason why he had been sent. It is the only secular letter in the New Testament. *To this effect* may be a disclaimer that the letter records precisely what the tribune wrote. It would in ordinary circumstances have been impossible for Luke to see the letter, and therefore he has used his historical skill to compose the kind of thing that the tribune would have written. The letter conforms exactly to the accepted style of composition of such documents, and the sentiments express the situation, as a Roman tribune would portray it, with accuracy.

26. The letter begins in the normal form used in the first

---

[1] F. F. Bruce, 'The Full Name of the Procurator Felix', *JSNT*, 1978–79, pp. 33–36, cautiously defends this set of names on the basis of a recently discovered inscription.

century: 'A (says) to B: *Greeting*' (*cf.* 15:23). From it we learn the tribune's name. *Claudius* will be the Roman name which he adopted when he became a citizen, and was probably chosen because it was the reigning emperor's name. *Lysias* will then be his original Greek name, which became his *cognomen* on his assumption of Roman citizenship; it may indicate that he came from the Greek-speaking coastal area or Samaria (Stählin, p. 292). The title *his Excellency* is appropriate for the procurator, since many procurators were drawn from the Roman equestrian order (an upper-middle-class social group), although Felix himself was not a member of it.

27. The tribune describes the circumstances under which Paul had come into his hands. It is a factual account of how the matter appeared from the Roman side, although the tribune twists the truth slightly in his own favour in the last phrase in the verse: it was not till after the arrest and the attempt to scourge him that the tribune learned that Paul was a Roman citizen. For a different picture of what happened see 24:6 note.

28. The seizure of Paul by the Jews was not simply a mob attempt to lynch him. On an official level the Jewish leaders wished to take proceedings against him, and therefore it was necessary that they be allowed to accuse him formally before the Romans. We may wonder why the tribune did not simply hand over Paul to the Sanhedrin to conduct its own trial of him; in effect, however, Paul was claiming Roman protection, and it was clear that any Jewish proceedings against him would quickly degenerate into a riot.

29. Despite the confusion at the enquiry, the tribune had gathered that the accusations against Paul were on a theological level, and not a criminal one. This is an important point. It shows that the original, specific charge of bringing a Gentile into the temple court (21:28b) had been quietly shelved and replaced by the more general one (21:28a); the Asian Jews, on whose evidence the charge rested, had disappeared from the scene (*cf.* 24:18f.). Now the charge seemed to refer to Paul's teachings (23:6–9), and there was nothing here that could lead to a criminal penalty from a Roman court. The insistence that Paul had done nothing worthy of death or imprisonment is significant. This is the Roman attitude all along (26:31); from Luke's stress on the point it is hard to believe that he knew that in the end Paul was executed as a result of these proceedings.[1]

30. The news of the plot against Paul led the tribune to send him to the procurator in order to settle the matter properly. If there was a real charge against Paul, it was better that it should be dealt with once and for all by proper process of law. For this purpose it was necessary that, if the Jews had any accusations against Paul, they should make them to the procurator. If they failed to do so, the case would of course lapse. The order to the accusers would naturally follow the sending of the letter; otherwise the security of the operation would have been ruined. Haenchen's suggestion (p. 648) that this is merely a Lucan device to indicate to the reader what would happen next is totally unnecessary. The formal 'Farewell' at the conclusion of the letter is omitted (although some MSS supply the deficiency).

31–32. The escort duly set off and brought Paul to *Antipatris*, a town some 37 miles (60 km) from Jerusalem (Hanson, p. 223, curiously makes it 45 miles – 72 km). Luke gives the impression that the journey was accomplished overnight. Some commentators claim that a march of this length was not possible in the time, and hold that Luke gives a misleading impression of the length or the timing of the march. Others hold that the journey was possible, admittedly as a forced march. The former view is more likely. The solution to the problem may lie in the information that the foot soldiers returned the following day to Jerusalem, leaving the mounted party to complete the journey. The full force was needed only while there was danger from the plotters, and this was most acute in and around Jerusalem itself. Although Luke certainly gives the impression that the whole force went to Antipatris, it may well be that in fact the infantry went a shorter distance and then turned back; this would then enable the mounted party to make better speed, and a journey to Antipatris would not be inconceivable.

33. Antipatris was about 25 miles (40 km) south of Caesarea, so that it was more than halfway to their destination. The soldiers handed over the message to the governor and also delivered Paul into his charge. This is the correct way to

[1] Naturally this does not rule out the possibility that Paul was executed on some other charge or as the result of a miscarriage of justice.

put the matter: it was the official communication which went to the governor, and which is therefore now mentioned first, while Paul would be kept under guard.

34–35. Whatever may be said about his general character (see 23:24 note), Felix acted in the proper legal manner on Paul's arrival. He held a preliminary interrogation of the prisoner, and first established his status by enquiring to what province he belonged. When Paul replied that he came from *Cilicia*, which was of course a different province, Felix replied that he would nevertheless deal with the case. The legal situation appears to be that it was normal for a prisoner to be tried in the province where the alleged offence was committed rather than in his home province; by the beginning of the second century, however, there certainly existed the possibility of sending a prisoner back to his home province for trial, and this procedure could enable a governor to get rid of a tiresome case. Felix did not avail himself of this possibility. Not only would it have caused bad relations with the Jews (who would have had to travel to Cilicia to make their charges), but also Cilicia at this time was not a full province, but part of Syria and came under the Legate of Syria, who would not want to be bothered with minor offences. Hence Felix really had no way out of his duty. Only a few years later the status of Cilicia changed, and it became a separate province; Sherwin-White (pp. 28–31, 55–57) indeed suggests that a later author than Luke would probably have avoided mentioning this tricky legal point altogether. So Felix agreed to take up the case, once the Jews had appealed to him. Meanwhile Paul was kept in Herod's praetorium, the palace which had been built by Herod the Great and now served as the headquarters of the Roman administration (*cf.* Phil. 1:13).

f. Paul appears before Felix (24:1–27)

Within a short time Paul's case was heard before Felix. The Jewish accusations, put by a hired advocate, dealt with Paul's activities in general terms as a fomenter of trouble and in particular with his alleged attempt to profane the temple. Paul conducted his own defence. He denied the specific charge, claiming that there was no evidence against him, and that the witnesses who had brought the original accusation were absent. On the more general charge he argued that he was simply worshipping God in the ancestral manner. Felix refused to take immediate action on such flimsy evidence, but determined to wait for a further report from Lysias. Meanwhile Paul was kept in custody. He was summoned again before Felix to talk about his religious views, and the effect was to disturb the governor's conscience. But not deeply enough. Justice was quickly forgotten, and Felix let the case drag on indefinitely in hope of a bribe. Even at the end of his governorship he still did not release the prisoner. Since Luke in general tries to present Roman justice in a favourable light, the adverse portrait of Felix will undoubtedly be historical.

1. *Five days* after Paul's arrival at Caesarea the Jewish leaders were ready to take action against the prisoner who had temporarily been snatched out of their reach. The group which arrived to prosecute him before the governor included the high priest Ananias (23:2) and some of the members of the Sanhedrin. They were represented by an advocate called *Tertullus* who would speak on their behalf just like a modern counsel. He was presumably a Jew, competent in Jewish and Roman law, but not necessarily so: it is because he is representing Jews that he speaks as if he is one of them in his speech.

2–4. When Paul's case was *called* (the phrase is the appropriate legal expression), Tertullus spoke up on behalf of the Jews. His speech is quite briefly reported, and we must presume that Luke gives us a mere resumé of it. This will explain why the opening remarks occupy nearly half the speech, and why the case against Paul appears so feeble. Luke has taken the opportunity to indicate the weakness of the case by reporting a very weak, ill-constructed speech; hidden in verse 5 there is a crude anacolouthon (lost in translation) which may be meant to suggest that Tertullus had difficulty in stringing words together. He begins in the conventional manner with some careful flattery, designed to make a favourable impression upon the governor. Felix is praised for the *peace* that extends through the province and for the *reforms* which he had *introduced*. It is true that coins issued by the Roman government made claims of a similar kind, but that was simply propaganda. In fact Felix's administration had been characterized by unrest, and the relations between Rome and the Jews had continued to deteriorate. Nevertheless, Tertullus spoke in the manner expected of him, and at the same time he prepared the way for his attack on Paul as a disturber of the Roman peace. A claim to brevity was also a conventional feature of legal speeches, as was the appeal to the judge's clemency.

5. The charge against Paul is now given briefly. Three points are made against Paul. He is first of all *a pestilent fellow*, literally a 'plague' or 'pestilence'. If the metaphor were still alive, the implication would be that Paul's influence was infectious, but it is doubtful whether the word meant anything more than a public nuisance. Secondly, Paul is accused of stirring up sedition throughout the Jewish populace in the Roman world. This was a more concrete charge, although it still lacks substance. It could certainly be argued that the *effect* of Paul's preaching was to stir up riots, whether or not he intended this; to the present day peaceable advocates of controversial viewpoints may find themselves the unwilling causes of mob action and therefore placed under restraint. Thirdly, Paul was attacked as *a ringleader of the sect of the Nazarenes*. This is the only place in the New Testament where 'Nazarene' is used to describe Christians. It was a term applied to Jesus himself (2:22), and outside the New Testament it was later applied to groups of Jewish Christians who held unorthodox views. It is quite likely that Jewish Christians may have been nicknamed after the name attached to their leader, especially if the word contained a contemptuous reference: 'Can anything good come out of Nazareth?' (Jn. 1:46); later the word could have been appropriated by some particular group of Christians.

6-7. After these general remarks Tertullus makes a specific charge: Paul even tried to desecrate the temple, the centre of Jewish piety and the symbol of the Jewish nation. As the accusation stands, the implication is that Paul's attempt was frustrated by his arrest by the Jews. This is part of the Jews' attempt to present themselves in the best light possible before the governor. Indeed, one version of the text makes Tertullus go on to say that the Jews intended to try Paul themselves, but Lysias came and snatched him out of their hands (AV, RSV mg.). This version may be correct, although the manuscript evidence is not strong and it can be argued that a reviser was trying to clarify the text.

8. The speech concludes somewhat abruptly with an appeal to the governor to examine the evidence for himself. The RSV text implies that he is to cross-examine Paul who will thus incriminate himself. This is a somewhat odd procedure to suggest, since a defendant would no doubt deny the charges. If we follow the RSV mg., then the governor is being invited to examine Lysias for general confirmation of the charge. The difficulty with this view is that the word *examining* is generally used of questioning defendants (12:19; 28:18) rather than witnesses, although the latter is possible.[1] Later, Felix was to defer the case until he had the opportunity to speak with Lysias who was absent at this point.

9. Tertullus's speech was backed up by the Jews who were present, although there does not appear to have been any formal summoning of witnesses; one wonders indeed how the Jews hoped to press their *charge* in the absence of any solid evidence.

10. Rather than examine Paul (if that is what he was invited to do), the governor proceeded to let him *speak* for himself; the nod of the head summoning Paul to do so corresponds to the status of the governor who did not need to voice his commands. Paul himself replies; he has no advocate, and sometimes he has been contrasted with the Jews who did need one, as if Luke were emphasizing his rhetorical abilities, but in fact Tertullus was present because a group of people needed a representative to speak on their behalf. Like his adversary, Paul begins with a *captatio benevolentiae*, a few words to gain the favour of the governor. He expresses himself as glad to appear before a judge with such long experience of the country and its problems. The *many years* is rhetorical and not to be taken too seriously; Felix had been at least two or three years in Judea (See 23:24 and 24:27 notes).

11–12. Paul goes straight to the specific charge with which Tertullus had concluded his speech and makes the point that he had been in Jerusalem for a mere *twelve days*.[2] That was not a long time in which to stir up much trouble, and it was also in the recent past, so that there would be no difficulty in getting evidence while it was still fresh in people's minds.

Paul claimed that during this period he had not caused any

[1] LS *s.v. anakrinō*.

[2] It is debated whether the twelve days ran from Paul's arrival in Jerusalem to his arrest (Haenchen, p. 654; see 21:27 note) or up to the time of speaking (Bruce, *Book*, p. 468). The former view makes for an easier chronology and should probably be accepted.

breach of the peace in Jerusalem in a general sort of manner. The general charges brought against his conduct 'throughout the world' (24:5) were certainly not true of his behaviour in Jerusalem. Paul had gone there in order to worship. He had not come to Jerusalem to evangelize; by the terms of the agreement in Galatians 2:7–9 he would not have engaged in evangelism in Jerusalem unless invited to do so by the Jerusalem church. *Worship* will mean offering thanks to God in the temple. The earlier narrative certainly implies this, and it need cause no historical or theological difficulties; the Jerusalem church appears to have continued to make use of the temple, just as Christians generally worshipped in the synagogues until they were made positively unwelcome.

13. As for the specific charge of profaning the temple, Paul simply denied it. He claimed that it could not be sustained by evidence. Nevertheless, Paul was not acquitted and set free by Felix, not even when the latter had a fuller report from Lysias (assuming that this was produced in due course). Paul remained a prisoner, and the question arises as to why he was kept in custody. The answer may be that Felix suspected that there was more to the matter than simply a charge about an isolated breach of the peace in the temple, and that Paul might be a public danger. The Roman authorities are bound to have been concerned over any possible causes of riot and rebellion among the Jews in the increasingly tense atmosphere of the years leading up to the outbreak of the Jewish revolt, and a Roman governor may well have decided to be on the safe side with a potentially dangerous prisoner.

14. Paul's further comments may have contributed to this impression. He was prepared to admit that his worship of God differed from that of the majority of Jews. They regarded him as belonging to *a sect* within Judaism. Paul and his fellow Christians, however, preferred to think of themselves as belonging to *the Way* (9:1f. note); it is a touch of Lucan irony that Paul had once persecuted those who belonged to 'the Way'. We may perhaps paraphrase the designation here as 'the true way of worshipping and serving God', for the Christians believed that the God of their Jewish ancestors was being rightly worshipped by them. Their understanding of true religion was based on the Old Testament, which they regarded as laying down the essentials of Christian faith and practice.

377

The church was claiming in fact that the Old Testament was a Christian book.

15. In particular, Paul states his conviction, based on his hope in God, that there will be *a resurrection* of the dead, *of both the just and the unjust*. This hope was shared with the Jews, or at least with the Pharisees, being based on such Old Testament passages as Daniel 12:2f. This passage, however, remains the only one in which Paul unequivocally asserts a belief in the resurrection of all kinds of men. Elsewhere he teaches the resurrection of the just, or rather of those who believe in Christ (1 Cor. 15:22f; 1 Thes. 4:14–16). In such passages the idea of resurrection includes the thoughts of renewal and final bliss. Elsewhere, however, the New Testament speaks of all men being raised up to face God's judgment (Mt. 25:31ff.; Jn. 5:28f.; Rev. 20:12; *cf.* Lk. 10:12; Rom. 2:5; 2 Cor. 5:10; 2 Tim. 4:1). It is this thought which is present here, and its introduction prepares the way for Paul's later remarks to Felix on future judgment (24:25).

16. When a person believes that there will be a future judgment, it is sound sense for him to endeavour to maintain *a clear conscience* as regards his duty to God both directly and also indirectly in his dealings with other people. Paul's wording reflects the common idea of human duty towards God and man (Pr. 3:4; Lk. 18:2, 4), and ties in with Jesus' summary of the law in terms of love of God and one's neighbour. It also echoes his earlier claim in 23:1 to have a good conscience, *i.e.* one that does not condemn him, not because it is insensitive but because it can detect no faults.

17. It is against this background of explanation of the Christian way as being in accord with the fundamental outlook of Judaism with its belief in God, future judgment and the importance of morality, that Paul returns to the immediate point at issue and proceeds to reply specifically to it. His own version of the story is that after an absence of several years from Judea he had returned home, and in the manner of a pious Jew from the Dispersion he brought *alms and offerings* to Jerusalem. From Paul's own account of his activities in his letters (1 Cor. 16:1–4; 2 Cor. 8 – 9; Rom. 15:25–33) we know that on this visit to Jerusalem Paul had brought with him a substantial sum of money collected from his churches 'for the poor among the saints at Jerusalem' (Rom. 15:26). It was a gift from the Gentile Christians to their Jewish brothers, a material gift as a sign of gratitude for the spiritual blessing of the gospel which ultimately stemmed from the church at Jerusalem. From the letters it is clear that Paul devoted much time and effort to this collection and regarded its reception at Jerusalem as an important part of his work. It is remarkable that this collection is passed over in silence elsewhere in Acts (19:21 note), and that this present verse is the only allusion to it. The collection is regarded as *alms*, while the *offerings* is an allusion to the payments made by Paul on behalf of the four men in 21:23-26. Luke's motive in saying so little about the collection is unknown; he evidently did not see the same importance in it as Paul did. In its present context, it may have been Paul's comment with its possible implication that he was a man of means which inspired Felix's hope of getting a bribe out of him.

18. It was when Paul was actually engaged in this pious duty and had undergone the purification ceremony that he was discovered by his opponents. It should have been obvious that a man engaged in this religious duty – a fact that could easily have been ascertained from the temple authorities – would be unlikely to be desecrating the temple at the same moment. In point of fact there had been no indication of anything wrong, no crowd had gathered, no disturbance had been caused.

19. What had happened was that *some Jews from Asia—*, but Paul breaks off in midstream. He has no need to speak about what they claimed to have done, or had actually done; for they constituted the only witnesses of his alleged misdemeanour, and they had disappeared. Let them appear and speak for themselves, if they have any charge to make. Here, as Sherwin-White (pp. 52f.) comments, Paul stood on solid ground in making a technical objection to the case against him. Roman law did not like persons who made accusations and then failed to carry them through in court. Sherwin-White further suggests that their withdrawal may indicate that the specific charge of profaning the temple was being withdrawn by the Jews in favour of the more general one of being a disturbing influence throughout the Roman world. But it is against this view that Tertullus specifically mentions the charge, although in a weak form, and that Paul found it necessary to deny it. The implication is that though the Jews

379

were conscious of the holes in their case, yet they attempted to try to carry it through.

20–21. There was, however, a further possibility. There had already been a hearing before the Sanhedrin. The Jewish elders present could at least state what had been established against Paul on that occasion. In fact, however, Paul was confident that no criminal charge had been substantiated. The one thing that had cropped up in that hearing was Paul's claim that he was on trial for his belief in the *resurrection*. This, as Bruce (*Book*, p. 471) remarks, was a theological question, on which different Jewish groups had different ideas, and it was quite outside the competence of a Roman court to condemn a man for a religious heresy. In any case, this was a point that had arisen in the course of the trial and was not the cause of the original arrest. Nevertheless, Paul's final comment serves to bring into focus the real, underlying problem, that of his belief in the resurrection (*i.e.* as 25:19 and 26:23 show, the resurrection of Jesus), and thus it paves the way for the further discussion of this issue in the subsequent interrogation of Paul.

22. The reaction of Felix was to defer a decision on the case. Two reasons are advanced. Felix himself announces his intention of waiting until he has a further report from Lysias, who would be able to give more precise details about the incident in reply to the governor's questions. Haenchen (p. 656 note 3) suggests that this is an adjournment *sine die*, an opinion which lacks substantiation. The other reason advanced for Felix's delay is that he had a fairly *accurate knowledge of the Way.* The source of his knowledge is not known, though Bruce thinks that it may have been through his wife Drusilla. As the account stands, it could suggest that Felix was acting out of sympathy for the Christians, or at least out of a desire that they should not be treated unjustly by the Jewish authorities, but his subsequent behaviour does nothing to justify this impression. He ought to have released Paul. He did, however, refuse to decide for the Jewish authorities.

23. Meanwhile, Paul was treated in the manner appropriate to a Roman citizen against whom no crime had as yet been proved. He may not have enjoyed the full measure of consideration given to Agrippa in Rome, who was handcuffed to soldiers of a humane character, enjoyed a daily bath and a comfortable bed, and could be visited by his friends with presents of food and other necessities (Jos., *Ant.* 18:204), nevertheless this description does indicate the kind of alleviation of Paul's condition that is in mind. His *friends* would of course be his fellow Christians.

24. We hear nothing more of Felix's proposal to interrogate Lysias. Instead the narrative takes a surprising turn with Felix arriving (presumably at the prison) and demanding to see Paul. He was accompanied by his wife *Drusilla*, who was a daughter of Herod Agrippa I; Felix was her second husband after he had used a Cypriot magician to persuade her to leave her first husband. The pair of them listened to Paul speaking about *faith in Jesus Christ*. The western text ascribes the desire to hear Paul to Drusilla. This may be an intelligent guess, since there does not seem to have been anything about Felix which would lead us to suspect that he had a secret interest in Christianity. It has been objected that Drusilla was no more likely than Felix to be attracted by the gospel, and that the scene is hard to reconcile with the conduct of Felix immediately afterwards. Hence it has been suggested that Luke invented the scene in order to gain the opportunity of presenting Paul as a witness before the Roman governor (see Lk. 21:12f.) and possibly also to suggest a parallel between him and John the Baptist who testified before Herod Antipas and his wife. But Paul had already had opportunity to speak before Felix earlier in the chapter. Moreover, there was no need to bring Drusilla into the story without some historical basis, especially since Luke can hardly be accused of trying to draw a parallel with Herodias whom he never mentions. The objections are groundless. Felix may have had a superficial interest in the 'strange beliefs' of the Christians.

25. But what he heard from Paul was nothing superficial. Paul did not spare him as he spoke about *justice, self-control* and the coming *judgment*, the very things that Felix and his wife needed to hear about. He had sufficient of a conscience left to feel some alarm at the Christian message, but he very quickly had as much of it as he could take, and he dismissed Paul until he had further time available. He had no intention of repenting.

26. In fact he was hoping that Paul would take the hint and offer him a bribe to set him free. The Roman governor had the freedom to leave a prisoner's case in suspense like this, but he could make the wheels of justice turn fast enough

381

when he chose to do so. But Paul provided him with no tangible motive to take action. Repeated conversations produced no effect. The taking of bribes was of course forbidden by Roman law, but it was hard to bring a governor to account for such a misdemeanour, and the custom was far from uncommon.

27. So the time rolled by, and Paul was not released. A Roman governor might well try to deal with outstanding cases before leaving his province, but this was not necessarily done. Felix certainly avoided the risk of alienating the Jews by releasing Paul (the only legal action that he could have taken). Such an action would have added to the feeling against him and could have led to charges being made against him at Rome. This may well have been the underlying principal reason for his failure to take any action earlier regarding Paul. By a slight injustice to an unpopular individual he hoped to curry favour with the Jews (he certainly needed to in view of his other conduct!); when he left the province, he did in fact avoid being impeached by the Jews (except for one group from Caesarea whose charge was quashed).

Luke presumably regards the *two years* as the period of Paul's imprisonment, but some scholars think that the reference is rather to the total length of Felix's term of office. A decision between the two possibilities depends on how long Felix was governor. Those who adopt the former view accept the theory that Felix had a comparatively long period as governor up to about AD 58–60, while those who adopt the latter view do so in view of their belief that Felix ceased to be governor as early as AD 55.[1]

g. Paul appears before Festus (25:1–12)

The Jewish leaders had not forgotten the case of Paul, although two years had slipped by, and they seized the first opportunity to take it up with the new governor. He treated the case correctly by examining it in Caesarea, the provincial capital, but at the same time he was willing to ingratiate himself with the Jews and offered to try the case in Jerusalem. But Paul was fearful about the outcome of such a trial, and, weary of the delays, now took the matter out of the governor's

[1] The case for the former date is presented convincingly by Schürer, I, p. 465 n. 42, but the latter is upheld by Haenchen, pp. 68–71.

hands by making an appeal to a higher court; it was an appeal which a governor was bound to accept.

1–2. Porcius *Festus*, who succeeded Felix as procurator, appears to have been a good ruler, although his period in office was probably too short for him to make any lasting impression on Jewish relationships with the Romans. He was probably in office from AD 58–60 to AD 62 when he died. Immediately after taking up his duties he paid a courtesy visit *to Jerusalem*. Here he would no doubt consult with the Jewish authorities and discuss with them any matters that required his attention. The members of the Sanhedrin took advantage of the opportunity thus provided to lay information before him about Paul.

3–5. They requested that Paul might be brought to Jerusalem so that the case against him might be concluded. A Roman court could sit in Caesarea or Jerusalem, but it could be that the Jews envisaged the possibility of trying Paul before the Sanhedrin without the governor taking part. Probably the former possibility is in mind in view of the fact that the case was already in Roman hands. But Luke suggests that the real reason why the Jews wanted Paul brought to Jerusalem was so that there might be fresh opportunity for a plot against his life. One is bound to wonder how the Jews hoped to succeed in such a desperate venture, but even more desperate ventures were projected and carried through in the war against Rome less than a dozen years later. Festus was unwilling to be at the beck and call of the Jews; they would have to fit in with his plans, and not he with theirs. The prisoner in question was held at Caesarea. Festus himself would be returning there from Jerusalem, and would presumably not be revisiting Jerusalem immediately. If the case was so urgent, the Jews could make the effort to come to Caesarea. So he suggested that a responsible delegation should accompany him to Caesarea where they could make their accusations against Paul in a formal manner.

6–7. Immediately after Festus had returned to Caesarea he held his court and the case of Paul was taken up. Luke does not go into details about the charges brought against Paul. They were doubtless similar to those already made by Tertullus, but it is probable that the Jews did their best to increase and strengthen them. Yet Luke comments that they could not prove them. Since the case was now two years old, it would have been difficult in any case to secure eyewitnesses to specific accusations, and so the Jews must have had to be content with generalities. It may seem surprising that they brought charges which they must have known would be difficult to sustain, but the history of litigation furnishes ample parallels of such folly.

8. Once again Paul was able to defend himself merely by denying the charges. He rejected the charges that he had attacked the Jews either by acting against their *law* or by desecrating *the temple*; we are reminded of the similar charges made earlier against Stephen (6:13). Nor, claimed Paul, had he done anything against Rome. Significantly he refers in this context to the Emperor. It was in the confidence that he had not acted against the Emperor that he would proceed to appeal to the Emperor's jurisdiction.

9. Here, as in the case of the trial before Felix, the matter ought to have come to an end with the acquittal of Paul. But, as on the previous occasion, a new factor entered the proceedings. Like Felix, Festus saw in the case of Paul an opportunity to ingratiate himself with the Jews. He therefore asked Paul whether he was willing to go and be tried at Jerusalem. As Haenchen (p. 670) drily remarks, a governor's query is tantamount to his decision. The suggestion is clearly not that Paul should be tried by the Sanhedrin and then presumably handed over to the Romans for sentence (since the Jews would regard the matter, if proved, as a capital offence). Rather Festus was willing, contrary to his earlier refusal, to hold his own court in Jerusalem, no doubt at a time to suit his own convenience. Yet the decision remains strange, since it is difficult to see what progress could be made by going over the same old ground for the third time, and therefore it is not surprising that some commentators have argued that the decision is unhistorical: Luke was trying to create the sort of decision against which Paul could genuinely appeal. On the other hand, as a newcomer to the province Festus could well have been puzzled by the whole affair and may have felt that fuller light would be shed on it if a trial took place in Jerusalem where there would be better opportunities of examining the background to the case.

10. However, Paul refused to agree. Probably what Festus proposed to do was to have some representatives of the Sanhedrin on his judicial council. It was the custom for a Roman judge to set up a group of advisers to aid him in coming to a decision, and Paul may well have feared that the chances of gaining neutral advisers in Jerusalem were nil. There was no sense in putting his head into a lion's mouth, even if he was prepared to stand up to lions when the need arose. He therefore insisted that the present court, a Roman one, was the one before which he ought to be judged; the question at issue was whether he had broken Roman law, as was in effect admitted by the Jews.

11. If Paul had committed a crime against Rome for which death was the penalty, then he was prepared to face a Roman punishment. If, however, the charges against him were baseless, then there was certainly no reason for him to be punished as a means of earning favour with the Jews for the procurator. This, however, was precisely what Paul feared might happen; Felix had already attempted to use Paul as a political pawn in this manner, and the suggestion of Festus that Paul be tried at Jerusalem pointed ominously in the same direction. If Roman justice was to be done, only one option remained open to Paul. '*I appeal*', he said, '*to Caesar.*'

From an early date Roman citizens had possessed the right of appeal against a magistrate's conduct of their case to the people. When the Roman state became an empire, the right of appeal was directed to the emperor. The precise details of the process and the limits of its applicability are unsure. By the second century it seems clear that magistrates had to send citizens charged with certain offences to Rome for trial. In other cases it appears that magistrates could try and even execute Roman citizens without any right of appeal. Sherwin-White upholds the view of A. H. M. Jones that crimes committed against statutory laws were dealt with on the spot, but that in other cases there was a right of appeal, although an accused man might not necessarily avail himself of it. When a person did appeal, the magistrate had no choice but to transfer the case to Rome. The right of appeal was presumably confined to Roman citizens.[1]

12. Festus proceeded to confer with his colleagues about

---

[1] The process described here, known as *provocatio*, should be distinguished from the right of *appellatio* (appeal *after* sentence) which was a later development, *pace* Bruce, *Book*, p. 478. See Sherwin-White, pp. 57–70, which supersedes earlier discussions, but there is still value in H. J. Cadbury's comments in *BC*, V, pp. 312–319.

Paul's demand. Although he was bound to honour an appeal, there may have been some question whether the procedure applied in this particular case. Even if the case was a clear one, it is quite probable that a magistrate would go through the formality of discussion with his colleagues. In any case, the appeal was formally granted.

h. Paul appears before Festus and Agrippa (25:13 – 26:32)

There would be an interval before arrangements could be made for sending Paul to Rome. In the meantime there was a state visit by Herod Agrippa II to Festus, and the latter took advantage of it to discuss the perplexing problem of what to do with Paul. The outcome was that a further investigation was held before an invited audience at which Paul was given the opportunity to speak yet once again in order that Festus might have a better idea of what to put in his official report on the case to the Emperor. But before the public scene Luke records a private conversation between Festus and Agrippa in which the former described the problem of Paul to the latter. Since it is highly unlikely that Luke will have had access to any observer of this private conversation, it must be assumed that here we have a clear example of Luke's policy of narrating what is likely to have been said on such an occasion; we have, therefore, evidence of Luke's dramatic skill which he will no doubt also have employed in recounting other scenes for which he had no concrete evidence.

The effect of the scene as a whole is to emphasize the uprightness of Roman legal proceedings over against the partiality and injustice of the Jews, and to show that, when measured by Roman law, Paul's behaviour appeared to be free from any guilt; mad he might appear to be, but not a criminal. There is tremendous emphasis on the climax: 'This man could have been set free if he had not appealed to Caesar.' Paul's actual defence consists of another account of his conversion experience, in which he stresses that his Christian faith is in line with his Jewish beliefs as a Pharisee and that his commission from the risen Lord is to offer salvation both to the Jews and also to the Gentiles.

The historicity of the whole scene is disputed. Haenchen (p. 678) finds it unlikely that Festus would have held a public assembly of the sort described here and professed his helplessness in performing his duty (25:26f.). He thinks that Luke has constructed the whole narrative in order to fulfil certain aims of his own, especially to deal with the question of the relationship of the church to Judaism and Rome in his own day: it was essential to reiterate that Christians were not doing anything illegal in the sight of Rome; they stood in continuity with the Jewish religion, and if the Jews were tolerated by Rome, so also ought the Christians to be tolerated. These Lucan motives may be acknowledged; what Haenchen does not appreciate is that an author can use accounts of what actually happened in order to draw lessons from them. Hanson (p. 236) rightly comments: 'There is no reason why Paul should not have been brought before King Agrippa II, not in a trial scene nor an official examination, but as an interesting case upon which Agrippa, as a prominent Jew very well versed in Jewish religion and Jewish ways, might give advice or make useful comments.'

13. Herod *Agrippa* II was the son of Herod Agrippa I whose death was described in Acts 12. He had been granted various territories in the north-east of Palestine by the Romans, and he ruled over these with the status of a king. During the troubles that lay ahead for the Jews he would do his best to intervene and preserve peace, but to no avail. *Bernice* was not his wife but his slightly younger sister. After the death of her husband, Herod of Chalcis (who was actually her uncle), she lived with her brother – a liaison which appears to have invited scandal-mongering – and later still she had an affair with Titus before he became emperor. The couple paid a courtesy visit to Festus shortly after his accession as procurator; a petty king such as Agrippa would be careful to cultivate a high-ranking Roman official.

14. At some point in a reasonably lengthy stay the conversation could easily have turned to 'talking shop' in the sort of way that Luke has imaginatively described. Agrippa was for all practical purposes a Jew – he had, for example, the right of appointing a high priest – and Festus might well seek light on a difficult case by consulting a Jew who would be free from official association with it.

15. Festus, therefore, is depicted as rehearsing the details of the case so far to Agrippa, telling the story as it would appear from the Roman point of view. His first contact with the case had been when he visited Jerusalem; the Jewish leaders had laid information against Paul and sought that Festus would settle the long-standing case by pronouncing judgment against Paul.

16. But Festus had refused to accede to this peremptory request. Roman law demanded a fair trial in which an accused person could both hear the charges and evidence against himself and then make his defence. Whatever had happened under Felix's jurisdiction – when there had in fact been precisely such a confrontation – it was necessary for Festus to re-open the matter and satisfy himself that justice was done.

17. Once the accusers had assembled, Festus had wasted no time in letting the prisoner be brought before his court. The reader will note how Luke lets Festus underline his own punctiliousness in contrast with the lackadaisical attitude of his predecessor, Felix (24:22).

18–19. Festus must have expected that a prisoner whom the Jews were so zealous to prosecute must have been charged with particularly grave crimes. When it came to the point, however, the offences seemed to him to be trivial, however emotive they may have been in the minds of the Jews. They were matters concerned with their own religion: the word used is perhaps slightly derogatory (RSV *superstition*; 17:22 note), although since Festus is represented as speaking to the man who was in effect the secular head of the Jewish faith, the word may be fairly neutral here. Probably Luke pictures Festus and Agrippa as two men of the world, the latter with a fairly formal or nominal attachment to Judaism (see, however, 26:27). More particularly, the point at issue seemed to be Paul's statements about Jesus having risen from the dead. It is interesting that by this stage the question of Paul's alleged desecration of the temple has quite disappeared from sight, and the topic of the resurrection (23:6; 24:21) has replaced it. Festus talks about it as something that he fails to comprehend, and indeed it is difficult to see how it could have become a point on which to hang a criminal charge. But this is precisely the point. The real ground of dispute is that Paul preaches the resurrection of Jesus, something which the Sadducees refused to believe on principle and which the Pharisees likewise refused to believe although they admitted the fact of a final resurrection of all men. Such an opinion might be unacceptable to the Jewish leaders, but ultimately it was a matter of 'questions about words and names and your own law' (18:15), and as such it could scarcely come within Roman cognizance as a ground for a criminal charge. The Jews had managed to convert their religious charge against Jesus into a political charge when they brought him before Pilate. They had not succeeded in proving it (Lk. 23:4, 14, 22), but they were even less successful in the case of Paul.

20. So Festus had made his suggestion of trying Paul at Jerusalem. In 25:9 his ostensible motive had been to win favour with the Jews. Here in a more private setting he claims that his motive had been puzzlement over what to do with the prisoner. Yet his puzzlement was really due to his unwillingness to declare the accused man innocent and send his accusers packing.

21. Now, however, Paul had refused to agree to this procedure and claimed his right of appeal to *the emperor*. The wording here states that Paul demanded to be kept in Roman *custody* pending his examination before the emperor. It sounds as though Paul was appealing for Roman protection against the Jews until the highest court in the empire would declare him free to maintain and propagate his beliefs.

22. Agrippa provided the way for Festus to get further light on the problem by suggesting that he himself would like an opportunity to hear Paul. His curiosity had been roused by what he had just heard, and presumably by rumours that he had previously heard. Festus was happy to grant his request forthwith. Like Herod Antipas, Herod Agrippa was intrigued to find out more (Lk. 23:8).

23. The very next day an opportunity was provided. Luke describes a state occasion in which the the visiting guests take their seats alongside the procurator to the accompaniment of considerable ceremony. Distinguished visitors from the military and civil establishment are present. The word for *pomp* came later to mean a procession, and something of the kind is no doubt meant. The scene is thus set, and then the prisoner is brought in. For Luke he is of course the main actor, and Bruce comments aptly on the fact that for Christian readers he was the real 'VIP' on that occasion. Here is fulfilment of the prophecy in Luke 21:12.

24–26. The proceedings are opened by a statement by Festus to his royal guest. It describes Paul briefly as a man who had been charged by the whole Jewish people as worthy of death. The Sanhedrin is regarded as having spoken on

389

behalf of the whole Jewish nation – a natural piece of rhetorical exaggeration. Festus, however, declares to his audience, which would have been entirely non-Jewish except for Agrippa and Bernice, that in his opinion Paul had done nothing deserving death. In view of Paul's appeal to the emperor, however, he had decided to send him to Rome. He had therefore brought him before the company generally and Agrippa in particular in order that further examination might yield some tangible basis for a charge to send with the prisoner.

27. Festus had in any case to send a report to the emperor (Nero, AD 54–68) with the prisoner. It would be absurd to send a report which in effect named no charge. Haenchen's objection (p. 678) to this verse as an impossible statement on Festus's lips arises from his failing to perceive the irony in it and is accordingly without basis. Haenchen further claims that in any case Festus had the reports of the earlier proceedings available, which would include statements of the Jewish charges against Paul, and that therefore all he needed to do was to send these to the emperor. But if Festus himself felt that there was nothing in the charges, he would be exposing himself to censure for incompetence: 'Why, then, did you not set the prisoner free?' would be the obvious question for a higher civil servant to put to him. Festus's quandary was a real one – of his own making!

26:1 Paul has already defended himself before Festus (25:8–11). It is not surprising, therefore, that Luke treats his present speech as being delivered primarily in the presence of *Agrippa*. In this way the climax of his defence is directed primarily to the Jews and not to the Romans; this chimes in with the fact that it has already been established in effect that Paul has not offended against Roman law. Agrippa has already been placed at the centre of the stage in the present scene (25:23, 24, 26), and it is he who now acts in effect as chairman of the proceedings, Festus having virtually handed over control of the meeting to him. Although Paul was chained (26:29), he was able to gesture with his right *hand* in the manner typical of ancient orators; earlier he appears to have been bound with chains on each wrist (21:33), but on this occasion he must have been sufficiently free to move his arms.

The *defence* is autobiographical in style. It begins by describing Paul's early life so as to stress that he was a fervent adherent to the Jewish faith and to pave the way for the claim

390

that the Christian faith is continuous with Judaism. Then Paul describes his initial reaction of hostility to the church. This point may be intended to indicate that he did not embrace Christianity blindly; it must have been an overwhelming conviction which led to his change of attitude. The account of Paul's conversion is given for the third time, with the emphasis falling on his call to be a witness and to bring Gentiles to salvation. It was in obedience to this call that Paul had preached to both Jews and Gentiles. And it was because of this activity that he had been arrested by the Jews. Yet nothing that Paul had said should have caused this opposition: Moses and the prophets had foretold both the suffering and the resurrection of the Messiah and also the proclamation of light to Jews and Gentiles alike. It is thus the interpretation of the hope of Israel that is the point at issue.

2–3. The speech begins with the usual attempt to secure the favour of the hearers (23:2f., 10). Paul regards himself as making a defence against *the accusations* brought by *the Jews*, and therefore he counts himself fortunate to be able to do so before Agrippa, since the latter is particularly expert in *the customs* and disputes of the Jews. He therefore seeks for a patient hearing, especially since he envisages a speech of some length.

4–5. Paul refers to his own way of life in his youth as something which was universally known. He had occupied a sufficiently prominent position in society for the Jewish leaders to know about this. *Among my own nation* could refer to life in a community of Jews in Tarsus, but, since Paul was probably brought up in Jerusalem (22:3 note), it more probably refers to the Jewish nation in Judea; *and at Jerusalem* will then give a closer definition. Paul's fellow countrymen could testify that for a long time they had known him as a member of the Pharisees. *Pharisee* (5:34 note; 23:6 note) was an umbrella term. It was used to describe those who bound themselves together in small groups pledged to live strictly according to the law, especially by maintaining the ritual purity which was demanded of priests in the Old Testament and by tithing all their produce.

6. It was, Paul claimed, for his adherence to the hope of fulfilment of God's promises to the ancestors of the Jews that he now stood on trial. The word *hope* is a key term in Paul's defence (23:6; 24:15; 26:6f.; 28:20). It refers to the believing

391

expectation that God will fulfil the promises and prophecies made in the Old Testament, and for Paul it refers specifically to the belief that these promises have been and will be fulfilled in Jesus. The question at issue is thus whether the Jews believe in the fulfilment of God's promises.

7. More precisely, the specific hope that Paul has in mind is that of the resurrection from the dead which will bring God's people into the experience of salvation. The Jews hoped to attain to this experience, which they described as 'the age to come', by their devotion to God expressed in continuous worship. The people are described as *our twelve tribes*. The idea that only returned exiles from Judah and Benjamin (the southern part of the kingdom) composed the Jewish people in New Testament times is a myth that dies hard (but see, for example, Lk. 2:36). The worship of God was carried on *by night and day* in the temple; Anna, the widow who 'did not depart from the temple, worshipping with fasting and prayer night and day' (Lk. 2:37), represents the ideal. Throughout his work Luke has emphasized how the followers of Jesus included not only sinners but also pious people who faithfully fulfilled the ordinances of Judaism (*e.g.* Lk. 1:6; 2:25; 7:4f.; 23:50; Acts 10:2). Now Paul can well ask rhetorically why he is under accusation for his loyalty to the Jewish religion and its hope.

8. The answer was of course obvious. The point at issue was Paul's belief in the resurrection. He takes the offensive by asking why it should be thought incredible that *God raises the dead*. The question is asked in general terms. For Pharisees there should have been no difficulty, since in general they did believe in the resurrection. The Sadducees did not believe in it, but they could well be asked why they regarded it as something that God could not accomplish. But of course, although Paul asks the question in general terms, the real point at issue is the resurrection of Jesus which attested that he was the Messiah: why should that be thought incredible?

9. And Paul had to confess that he himself had once shared this point of view. When he first heard that people were proclaiming that Jesus had risen from the dead and that he was the Lord and Messiah, his first reaction had been that he ought to oppose them. He puts it in terms of *opposing the name of Jesus of Nazareth, i.e.* in effect opposing what was said about Jesus by his followers. As a Pharisee he ought to have been of a different mind, if he accepted the point he has just made in verse 8. In fact he shared the blindness of heart which is the ultimate reason for unbelief (26:18; 28:26f.).

10. Paul's reaction to the preaching of the Christians was expressed with typical energy. He proceeded to attack the Christians in Jerusalem itself, right at the centre of the movement and in a place where the memory of his actions would still be present. He went out to arrest Christians and had them jailed (22:4), doing so with the *authority* of the *chief priests* to back him up. When Christians were put to death, he gave his *vote against them.* This statement raises several difficulties of interpretation. First, it is probably to be taken literally, implying that Paul was a member of the Sanhedrin. There were in fact many sanhedrins, one for each community attached to a synagogue, and membership of such a group may be implied; since, however, Paul is talking about his activity in Jerusalem, membership of the supreme Sanhedrin is no doubt indicated. Secondly, the statement implies that several Christians were put to death, although in fact only one case has been described, that of Stephen. There may have been other cases, but it is surprising that there is no mention of them. Possibly Paul is using a generalized plural for dramatic effect. Thirdly, if the statement is taken literally, it would seem to imply that the Jews had the right to put people to death, despite the clear evidence of John 18:31. The case of Stephen was probably exceptional (see 7:57f.), but it is difficult to allow for several deaths without intervention by the Roman authorities. On the whole, therefore, it seems best to take Paul's statement as being somewhat rhetorical.

11. There is, however, no difficulty in believing that in the synagogues he did punish them in an endeavour to make them *blaspheme, i.e.* to curse Christ or disown their faith (*cf.* 1 Cor. 12.3). The synagogues had powers of discipline over their members, and Paul himself suffered at their hands on several occasions: five times he received the synagogue penalty of a lashing (2 Cor. 11:24). Whether these measures were effective is not said; Paul can say only that he *tried* to make them recant. In any case, he did not confine his efforts to Jerusalem but continued them elsewhere. The expression is again a general one; we know only of his visit to Damascus, but activity elsewhere cannot be ruled out.

The best parallel to Paul's activity is provided at a later

date by Pliny, the Roman governor of Bithynia, who tells us that he brought people suspected of being Christians before his court: 'Those who denied they were, or ever had been, Christians, who repeated after me an invocation to the gods, and offered invocation, with wine and frankincense, to your image, which I had ordered to be brought for that purpose, together with those of the gods, and who finally cursed Christ – none of which acts, it is said, those who are really Christians can be forced into performing – these I thought it proper to discharge' (*Epistles* 10:96). This account is written, of course, with reference to a pagan court, but a similar kind of procedure will have taken place in a Jewish setting.

12. Thus Paul has completed the account of his zeal for the Jewish religion which led him to persecute any possible rival to it. Now comes the decisive moment in his own life. This is the third account of his experience, and it differs in some details from the earlier ones (9:1–19 note; 22:6–21). The main lines of the story are naturally the same, but the variations in telling it bring out different aspects of its significance. Something of Luke's literary ability may be seen in the way in which he varies the details of the story so that it comes over freshly to the reader each time. In each case the story begins with Paul's journey *to Damascus*, armed with authority to arrest Christians. Whereas the earlier accounts speak of 'letters', here Paul speaks of the *authority and commission* which the letters contained. In 9:2 the authority was gained from the high priest, but here it comes from the high priests, *i.e.* the leading priestly officials (9:14, 21).

13–14. It was at noon, when the sun's light would be brightest (22:6), that Paul felt himself surrounded by a light from heaven that was far brighter than the sunlight; the implication is that his companions were also aware of it (22:9). Overwhelmed by the experience they all fell *to the ground*; contrast 9:4 and 22:7 where only Paul is said to fall to the ground. Nothing is said here about Paul being blinded by the light, which in any case did not apparently affect the sight of his companions. In this particular account all the attention is concentrated on what the Lord said to Paul, and therefore questions about his blindness and the reaction of his companions are not raised; there is in fact no conclusion to the story of the conversion (contrast 9:7–9; 22:11), and Paul goes

straight on to record his response to the Lord's command
(22:19).

All the stress thus falls on the heavenly *voice*. It addressed
Paul *in the Hebrew language*, which is generally taken to mean
the Aramaic language (21:40); this fact is indicated by the
way in which Paul is addressed by the Semitic form of his
name *Saoul*, although elsewhere Luke uses the Greek form
Saulos in writing about him. The same question appears in all
three versions of the story: '*Why do you persecute me?*' But in the
present version there is an added comment: '*It hurts you to kick
against the goads.*' These words reflect a proverbial way of
speaking, attested in several Classical Greek writers, and especially in Euripides, *Bacchae*, 794f., where Pentheus, the opponent of the cult of Dionysus, is warned: 'You are a mortal,
he is a god. If I were you I would control my rage and sacrifice
to him, rather than kick against the pricks.'[1] But the proverb
was also known in Judaism (*Psalms of Solomon* 16:4), and Philo
spoke of how conscience stabs at a man (*Decal.* 87). Bruce
thinks that the point here is that Paul was struggling against
his conscience, but Hanson (p. 238) points out that in Greek
literature the proverb refers to struggling against one's destiny;
this seems the more likely interpretation. Opinions differ as to
whether the words represent exactly what the heavenly voice
said or depict graphically the consciousness of struggle in
Paul's mind as he realized increasingly that he was fighting
on the wrong side; commentators have often noted how what
he saw of Stephen's death must have made an impression on
him.

15. Paul's reply to the voice and the response of Jesus are
related more or less exactly as before. This time, however,
Paul refers to the one who spoke to him as *the Lord*; he implicitly identifies Jesus as 'the Lord', the logic being that, if
Jesus addresses him in this way from heaven, it was proof that
he had been exalted to a position of authority alongside God
(*cf.* 22:10).

16. The Lord continues to speak without interruption (contrast 22:10) and to command Paul to stand up. But whereas
in the previous accounts Paul is told to go into the city and
there receive further instructions, here the story is telescoped,

[1] P. Vellacott, *Euripides: The Bacchae and other Plays* (Harmondsworth, 1954),
p. 205.

and what God said to him through Ananias in the earlier versions of the story now becomes a further part of what was said to him on the road; such condensation of a narrative is not unknown elsewhere in the Bible (compare, for example, Mt. 9:18 with Mk. 5:22f., 35), and here it serves to concentrate attention on the heavenly command to Paul which had led to the way of life on account of which he now stood on trial. There was no need here to dwell on the part played by Ananias, either in order to relate exactly what happened, or to draw attention to the piety of the man who helped Paul (contrast 22:12). Paul is commanded not to stay in a posture of fear and reverence but to get up to do a job of work for the Lord. The reason why the Lord had appeared to him was in order *to appoint* him as a servant and witness, either to, or perhaps on the basis of, the things which Paul had already seen and would yet see. The reference here is to the vision of the risen Lord which Paul was experiencing and the future visions which he would receive (18:9f.; 22:17–21; 23:11; 2 Cor. 12:1–4, 7). The description of Paul as 'servant and witness' is reminiscent of Luke 1:2 where Luke describes how the gospel tradition was derived from those who were eyewitnesses and ministers (servants) of the word, and indicates that this group included people like Paul who had not accompanied Jesus during his earthly ministry.

17. The account of Paul's call is similar to that of the prophets of Israel (*cf.* Ezk. 2:1), and God's promise of protection to him also has Old Testament echoes (Je. 1:8; 1 Ch. 16:35). He would be safe from the people, *i.e.* the Jews, and the Gentiles; there may possibly be an allusion for Luke's readers to the safe outcome of Paul's present trial, but it should be remembered that, since God's servants are mortal, his promise applies to the safe fulfilment of their part of his work and not necessarily any further; the Lord's servant may have Paul's later experience: 'I am suffering for the gospel and wearing fetters like a criminal. But the word of God is not fettered' (2 Tim. 2:9). The work is that of an apostle: Paul is sent (Je. 1:7; Ezk. 2:3) to both Jews and *Gentiles*, but primarily to the latter.

18. His task is defined more closely in language based on the description of the Servant's commission in Isaiah 42:6f. He is to open *eyes* that are blinded by sin, to convert people and bring them out of the realm of *darkness* into that of *light*, *i.e.* from the power of Satan into the area where God reigns (*cf.* Is. 42:16 and especially Col. 1:13f. which gives a remarkably close parallel to the wording here). Those who respond to this call will obtain *forgiveness* of their *sins* and their appointed *place* among those who are *sanctified by faith* in Jesus (*cf.* 20:32). The theological language used here would probably be too deep for Agrippa to comprehend. It reflects a traditional Christian understanding of the nature of conversion, and is perhaps a summary for the reader of what Paul could have said more simply to Agrippa.

19–20. Now Paul comes to the new period in his life which resulted from his *vision* of the risen Lord. He says that he did not disobey the command, a phrase which is meant simply to underline that he obeyed it enthusiastically. Straightaway, therefore, he began to preach conversion, accompanied by the evidence of true repentance. The phraseology is reminiscent of 20:21 and especially 3:19, where the same appeal is made by Peter to Jews; the stress on producing practical evidence of repentance is paralleled in the preaching of John the Baptist (Lk. 3:8). Paul's preaching began in *Damascus* (9:19–22, 27) and continued in *Jerusalem* (9:28f.). The next phrase *and throughout all the country of Judea* is difficult. It does not fit grammatically into the sentence (the other phrases are in the dative case, while this one is in the accusative), nor does its content correspond with the earlier description of Paul's activity in Acts (Acts 9:26–30; *cf.* the strong statement of Paul in Gal. 1:22). It seems probable that the text is corrupt. The whole phrase may be a gloss by a scribe (Haenchen, pp. 686f.) or perhaps we should amend the phrase to read 'in every land to both Jews and Gentiles' (Bruce, *Book*, p. 492 note 24, following Blass). In any case, the text couples Jews and Gentiles as the objects of Paul's evangelism, and salvation was offered to both on the same terms.

21–22. It was ultimately for this reason that the Jews had seized Paul in the temple and tried to lynch him on the spot. But their efforts had been in vain. Thanks to Roman intervention Paul had been saved from their hands. But behind the protection of the Romans lay the hand of God, and thanks to his *help* Paul had been able to continue right up to the present moment to act as a witness to people in all ranks of society. In a final summary Paul reiterates the content of his message. It was, he claimed, fully in accord with what had been prophesied by Moses and the prophets in the Old Testament, and therefore should have been acceptable to the Jews (Rom. 1:2; 16:26).

23. The message is summed up in two clauses. First, the Messiah must *suffer*, *i.e.* die (1:3). But where is this attested by 'Moses and the prophets'? Paul as a Christian appears to presuppose the identification of the Messiah as the suffering Servant, but it is not certain whether this step had been taken by the Jews, and it may well be that they disputed it. Secondly, the Messiah would be the *first to rise from the dead* and would announc *light both to the* Jewish *people and to the Gentiles*. This reflects the Christian statement that Jesus was the first fruits of the resurrection (1 Cor. 15:20), and again it implies the identification of the Messiah as the Servant who would 'prolong his days' (Is. 53:10) and be a light to all peoples (Is. 42:6; 49:6; 60:3). It is clear, therefore, that the crucial point was the equation of the Messiah with the suffering Servant and the identification of Jesus as the one who fulfilled this role. The Christian argument was probably based historically on the fact that Jesus had already taken this step; its scriptural basis may have been that Isaiah 61:1f. was understood as a reference to the Servant described in the preceding chapters of the book (*cf.* the similarity of thought with Is. 42:1–7) and also as a reference to the eschatological prophet like Moses who had messianic functions.[1] By means of this 'bridge passage', therefore, the way was open to identify the suffering Servant and the Messiah.

24. Festus's comment sounds like an interruption while Paul is still in full spate, but in fact the speech has reached its conclusion. The Roman is portrayed as a man who is still unable to comprehend the subtleties of Jewish theology. All that he can do is to interrupt loudly – perhaps an element of discourtesy is implied – and suggest that Paul is raving. Paul is a clever and learned man, he suggests, but too much *learning* can be bad for a person. There is perhaps the implication that the practically minded Roman soldier has no time for the speculations of religion. Yet it would be wrong to suggest that Luke is simply painting a picture of the traditional Roman outlook, since earlier in 13:7, 12 he has shown us a Roman governor who was impressed by the gospel.

[1] Marshall, *Luke*, pp. 118–128.

25–26. Paul can only deny the charge of insanity. He claims that what he is saying is marked by *truth* and sobriety; it is not wild and speculative. For confirmation of his statement Paul appeals to Agrippa. He claims that the king has understanding of what he is talking about, and that therefore he can *speak freely*, i.e. confidently. Agrippa, he claims, cannot be ignorant of what has been going on, for it has been a matter of public knowledge. Using a well known idiom Paul insists that it has not happened *in a corner*. Certainly, if there is anything in the statistics of Christian conversions cited earlier in Acts, then the Christian movement must have been well known in Palestine, and along with it there must have been public knowledge of the Christian claim that Jesus had risen from the dead. Even King Agrippa must have heard something about it. Stählin (p. 312) thinks that Paul is exaggerating his acquaintance with the facts, since if Agrippa also believed the prophets, this would surely have led to his becoming a Christian. But this criticism assumes that Agrippa would merely need to know of the Christian claims about Jesus in order to be convinced by them, and it is obvious that this need not have been the case (*cf.* Lk. 16:31).

27. In any case, Paul attempts to call on Agrippa as a witness not merely to the facts, but also to the prophetic oracles that Christians interpreted as pointing to Jesus. If Agrippa was a worshipping Jew, he must surely have believed what *the prophets* said – and surely also accept what seemed to Christians to be the only possible identification of the fulfilment of their words. It is not quite clear what led Paul to say *'I know that you believe'*. Paul can hardly be suggesting that Agrippa did accept that Jesus was the promised Messiah. At most he must be suggesting that Agrippa believed that the prophets foretold the coming of the Messiah. But the way in which Christians saw the fulfilment of the prophecies was not necessarily the way in which Jews viewed them.

28. But Agrippa realized what he would be letting himself in for if he gave an affirmative answer to Paul's question. If he confessed belief in the prophets, the obvious follow-up would be, 'Surely then you accept that Jesus is the Messiah?' On the other hand, to deny that he believed in the prophets would be unthinkable for a loyal Jew. So he answers: *'In a short time you think to make me a Christian!'* The reply is lighthearted, but not ironic. It is Agrippa's attempt to get out of the logical trap in which he is in danger of being caught.[1]

29. Paul's reply is to express his longing that all his hearers might become Christians like himself, but without having to wear chains as a result. It is Paul's final claim that it is senseless to imprison or punish men for being Christians. The phrase *whether short or long* takes up Agrippa's reply and appears to mean 'whether it takes a short time or a long time to persuade you'.[2]

30. The session was at an end, and the platform party withdrew. Luke continues to pinpoint Agrippa as the principal figure in the gathering. *Those who were sitting with them* could mean a judge's council of assessors (25:12), but the term is probably not used in its technical sense here.

31. Luke can scarcely have had access to what was said behind closed doors by the members of the governor's entourage. But he estimates correctly that they could not have condemned Paul as guilty on the basis of the interview which had just concluded. Presumably information to this effect was sent with Paul to Rome.

32. But if Paul had done nothing to deserve death or imprisonment at the hands of the Romans, the question remains why he was not set free on the spot. Earlier, we have suggested that successive Roman governors had refused to do so in order to curry favour with the Jews. But now another factor comes into play. It is placed by Luke, on the lips of Agrippa, but this may be simply a dramatization of the situation. One

[1] The translation of the phrase is disputed: (1) The RSV rendering is supported by P. Harlé, 'Un "private-joke" de Paul dans le livre des Actes (xxvi. 28–29)', *NTS* 24, 1977–78, pp. 527–533, who argues that 'to make me a Christian' is a similar phrase to 'to make someone a proselyte' (Mt. 23:15), and translates 'In your opinion it would take a short time to make me a Christian'. (2) Bruce (*Book*, p. 494 n. 30) translates, 'In brief you are persuading me to act the Christian', and appeals to 1 Ki. 21:7 LXX for the idiom. Harlé objects that this idiom would require the present infinitive rather than the aorist. (3) The difficulties of the phrase led to confusion and simplification in the MSS, and hence to the famous AV rendering, 'Almost thou persuadest me to be a Christian'. Preachers who regret seeing the disappearance of this useful text, on which many a compelling evangelistic sermon has been developed for 'almost Christians', may be referred to Mk. 12:34 for a suitable alternative.

[2] The phrase, however, might be a play on words, referring back to verse 22, and meaning 'whether in the case of small or great people' (P. Harlé), but this seems rather forced.

might have expected that in a case such as the present one, where the prisoner's innocence was obvious, the emperor would have been glad to have been spared the nuisance of appeal proceedings. In strict law, according to Sherwin-White (p. 65) acquittal at this stage would have been possible, but 'to have acquitted him despite the appeal would have been to offend both the emperor and the province'.

Thus Paul's long-delayed desire to see Rome was brought a step nearer to fulfilment. No doubt he might have reached Rome in other ways. By going to appear before the emperor, however, he may well have hoped that he would secure a decision giving toleration to Christians which would have all the force of a test case.

i. The journey to Italy (27:1 – 28:16)

After several chapters of trials and speeches Luke brings his story to a lively conclusion by relating in considerable detail the sea voyage of Paul from Palestine to Italy. The length of the narrative in proportion to that of the book as a whole is remarkable, especially since at first sight the narrative appears to contribute little to the theological aim of Acts. Luke was perhaps guided by the literary fashion of his time: stories of sea voyages which included accounts of shipwreck were familiar in the ancient world from the writings of Homer onwards and were presumably as popular with readers then as they are nowadays. It has also been suggested that the idea of a bad man meeting his appropriate fate in death by drowning may have been in Luke's mind (28:4),[1] and that he gladly told a story which related how Paul escaped from the deep. At the same time Paul is presented as the hero of a story which is told very much as an account of his personal role, warning the sailors of disaster and then helping to encourage them in time of disaster and even contributing towards the saving of the lives of the crew and passengers. The element of divine control and protection over the life of Paul is thus emphasized. We can thus see how the story suits the literary and theological interests of the author.[2]

---

[1] G. B. Miles and G. Trompf, 'Luke and Antiphon: The Theology of Acts 27–28', *HTR* 69, 1976, pp. 259–267.

[2] The value of the passage as part of Scripture needed no proof to Christian seafarers such as John Newton.

It is not surprising, then, that its historicity has been challenged. Various scholars have suggested that the references to Paul can easily be subtracted from the account of the voyage proper (27:9–11, 21–26, 31, 33–36, 43), and that we are then left with a sea story which Luke used as the basis for his account of Paul's journey (Dibelius, pp. 204–206; *cf.* Conzelmann, pp. 146f.). The story, it is admitted, is founded on fact, and this causes Hanson (p. 243) to comment with justifiable irony: 'But what a coincidence! A story, unknown to any other writer of antiquity, describing a voyage in the same direction, and describing it with an attention to detail unparalleled in the accounts given by Conzelmann in his Appendix. What a fortunate discovery!' Not only so, but the details of the story, especially as concern the personnel involved, fit in with Luke's aim so well, that it is impossible to believe that he merely added the references to Paul. To be sure, many will find no difficulty in arguing that Luke could thoroughly adapt a story from another source to his purpose, but in the present case the fact is that the story fits in so perfectly with the exigencies of a voyage between the points described, that it is completely improbable that it has been either invented or taken over from another source. The classical treatment by James Smith of Jordanhill, *The Voyage and Shipwreck of St Paul* (London, 1856) has demonstrated the verisimilitude of the narrative, and later investigations have not overthrown this conclusion. Nevertheless, the part played by Paul in the story may seem strange: would a prisoner on his way to trial have been able to influence affairs to the extent that he did? Was Luke intent on making him out to be the hero of the hour? We may note that it is less easy than Dibelius and others suppose to cut out the Pauline references in the account; some of the details in what remains seem so closely tied to them as to be from the same source. Again, the voyage is in one of the we-sections in Acts, and thus the author is claiming first-hand information for what he is recounting. Finally, it is by no means improbable that Paul did have gifts of personality which came to the fore in conditions such as are described; Haenchen, (p. 711) scornfully compares Luke's picture of 'the strong, unshaken favourite of God who strides from triumph to triumph' with Paul's own representation of himself as despairing of his own life (2 Cor. 1:8) and then experiencing the miracle of the God who raises men from the dead (2 Cor. 1:9f.). But the contrast is not there;

the confidence of Paul in Acts 27 derives from his trust in God (27:23–25), a God who can allow men to descend into deepest need before delivering them. Paul would have had close contact with the centurion in charge of the military party, and it is far from inconceivable that the latter could have formed a favourable opinion of a man who was still not a convicted criminal, and could therefore have paid attention to what he said.

1. After the Roman governor had decided that Paul and his party (here described again in the first person plural) should be sent to Rome, arrangements were made for him and other prisoners to be taken in the custody of a centurion, along with a small body of soldiers. The description of Paul and his party being sent to Rome is loose in style; in reality it is only Paul who is under duress, unless the same is true of Aristarchus (verse 2). We are not told where Luke had been since the last occurrence of the 'we' form of narration (21:18), but it is often supposed that he stayed in Palestine, and even that he used his time in searching out information for the composition of his Gospel and the earlier parts of Acts; this is plausible, but beyond proof. The vague *they delivered* must refer to the Roman authorities. *Julius* is the 'gentilic' name of the Roman officer placed in charge of the prisoners. He is said to belong to the *Augustan Cohort*, which has been identified as the Cohors Augusta I, a regiment of auxiliary soldiers which is known to have been in Syria in the time of Augustus and which may have been in Batanea (*i.e.* 'Bashan', east of the Sea of Galilee) in the time of Herod Agrippa II. The question is whether a centurion in an auxiliary regiment would have been placed in charge of prisoners going to Rome. Ramsay (pp. 315, 348) claimed that Julius was one of a group of *frumentarii* who acted as couriers for the emperor, but it seems that during the first century these men were, as their name indicates, concerned with the corn supply from the provinces to Rome, and only later did they undertake police functions; this view should probably be dropped (Sherwin-White, p. 109).

2. The story of Paul's journey gives a fascinating glimpse into ancient sea travel. In general, ships clung to the coasts of the Mediterranean Sea and avoided sailing during the winter. The ship on which the party travelled at first came from *Adramyttium*, a port well up the west coast of Asia Minor, not far from Troas, and it was probably returning to its home port, calling at other places on *the coast of Asia* on the way; it would be the centurion's hope that at one of these places the party would be able to transfer to a ship going to Italy.

Luke adds the comment that the travellers included *Aristarchus from Thessalonica*, and the natural inference is that he was travelling home on a ship which was going into the Aegean area. He reappears in Philemon 24 and Colossians 4:10, however, as a companion and fellow prisoner of Paul; if these letters come from Paul's imprisonment in Rome, it is possible that Aristarchus was accompanying him to Rome at this point. In any case, Paul was accompanied to Rome by Luke. The mention of Aristarchus adds nothing to the story, and is a sign of authenticity.

3. The ship proceeded from Caesarea to *Sidon*, a distance of some 69 nautical miles (not land miles, as Bruce, *Book*, p. 501, implies), and thus capable of being traversed in a full day's sailing. Paul was given permission to visit *his friends and be cared for*, *i.e.* enjoy their company, perhaps be given a meal (we do not know what standard of catering was possible on ancient ships; it may not have been high) and receive some gifts to help him on his journey (*cf.* 28:14). The Greek text has literally 'the friends', which could be a designation for 'the Christians', as in 3 John 15; while this term was in use among other groups in the first century, Stählin (p. 314) suggests that the Christian use arose from that among the disciples of Jesus (Lk. 12:4; Jn. 11:11; 15:13ff.). Anybody familiar with the ways of coastal shipping knows how these boats can spend a remarkable amount of time loading and unloading cargo whenever they put in to harbour. It would be natural for ordinary passengers to go ashore and while away the time. But whereas prisoners might well have been kept on board for security, the centurion showed consideration for Paul by letting him go ashore, presumably with a soldier to keep guard on him.

4. From Sidon the direct route to Myra was by the west of the island of *Cyprus*, and it was this route which had been followed, in the reverse direction, when Paul sailed from Patara to Tyre (21:1–3). But the prevailing winds in the summer and early autumn were west or north-west, and therefore it was easier for a ship to sail round the east of Cyprus on the *lee* side, keeping close to the coast and taking advantage of the night breeze from off the shore.

5. Having rounded Cyprus, the ship had to make its way through the open sea, but probably still keeping to the coast, and moving along past *Cilicia and Pamphylia* with the help of night breezes and a westerly sea current, until it came to *Myra* (21:1 note), a seaport in *Lycia*.[1]

6. There was an important trade route from Egypt to Italy bringing corn for the vast population of Rome. Since ancient ships were not well designed for sailing against the wind, it would be natural for ships from *Alexandria* to sail more or less due north to Myra and then take advantage of the coast of Asia Minor for the next stage of the journey. The corn trade was in the hands of private owners who received special consideration from the Roman government in view of the importance of this lifeline for Rome. The centurion in charge of Paul had no doubt intended all along to make use of such a ship for the journey to Rome.

7. We must presume that the Alexandrian ship set out westwards in the reasonable hope that it would be able to reach Italy before the advent of wintry conditions made sailing impossible. But at the outset of the voyage from Myra the elements began to thwart this intention. The ship was able to proceed westwards only with great difficulty and took a long time to reach *Cnidus*, a peninsula forming the south-west tip of Asia Minor, because of the prevailing north-westerly wind. It is not clear whether the reference to the wind alludes to the difficulty of getting to Cnidus or to the difficulty of proceeding from there (RSV). The normal route would have taken the ship past Crete, possibly along the north side of the island. On this occasion the ship rounded the east tip of Crete (Cape *Salmone*) in order to continue westwards on the south (*lee*) side of the island.

8. Even so the journey was difficult, and it was hard to reach the first convenient shelter, the small bay of *Fair Havens*; it is otherwise unknown in ancient sources, but is to be identified with modern Limeonas Kalous (or Calolomonia), 12 miles (18 km) east of Cape Matala, at which point the coast curves to the north and is no longer sheltered. Fair Havens is an open bay, a poor harbour in bad weather. Luke adds that

[1] The western text notes that the voyage took fifteen days which, whether or not it is what Luke wrote, is a fair estimate of the time that might be needed.

405

it was near *Lasea*, a city which has been identified with nearby ruins and with the town of Lasos mentioned by Pliny the Elder.

9. The voyage had already taken a considerable length of time, and it seems that the ship was unable to leave the harbour because of continuing adverse conditions. The result was that by now the date at which seafaring generally came to a standstill for the winter was past. Luke states this by referring to *the fast*, *i.e.* the Jewish day of atonement. This fell on the tenth day of the month Tishri, but since the Jewish calendar was based on the moon, the position of the month varied from year to year during the general period September-October. According to Bruce (*Book*, p. 506) in AD 59 the day of atonement was as late as October 5. This would fit in with the statement of the Roman military writer Vegetius that navigation was considered dangerous after 15 September and ceased for the winter from 11 November to 10 March. The difficulty with this view is that the sailors took about a fortnight from Crete to Malta and then spent only three months in Malta before the voyage was continued. On this reckoning sailing recommenced at about the end of January or beginning of February, which is well before 10 March. This difficulty may be eased by the possibility that with favourable conditions travel might recommence in February (so Pliny the Elder), and perhaps also by Conzelmann's suggestion (p. 141) that Luke was using a Syrian-Jewish calendar which would put the tenth day of Tishri as late as 28 October. In any case, AD 59 emerges as the most suitable year for the voyage, since in the immediately preceding years the Jewish feast fell even earlier in the year.

10. At this point Paul makes his intervention in the story. It is a simple warning of danger ahead, such as might be made by anybody who took note of both the time of year and the actual presence of bad weather. To venture out to sea in these circumstances could well endanger both the *ship* and its *cargo* and also the crew and passengers. Two points are uncertain. First, it is not clear whether Paul is represented as making an inspired prophecy (*cf.* 27:21–26); if some divine revelation lay behind this commonsensical statement, we are not told of it, but the fact that Paul speaks with certainty of disaster rather than merely of the possibility may support the supposition of divine guidance behind his statement. Secondly, it is not clear to whom the statement is made. Ramsay (pp. 332–335) suggests a general council of crew and passengers presided over by the centurion. We do not know enough .bout the situation to deny this possibility, but it may seem strange that Paul, as a prisoner, would have a voice in such a discussion. One might suggest a less formal conversation, but the implication of verse 21 is that Paul was able to address the ship's company as a whole. If Paul had access to the centurion, as clearly he must have done, and was treated with some consideration as a Roman citizen under duress but not yet convicted of any crime, then it is not impossible that he could express his opinions to the centurion and even to the officers of the ship. It must be remembered that within the comparatively cramped conditions of a ship it would be difficult to keep the various groups of officers, crew and passengers entirely segregated from one another.

11. The centurion is represented as the authoritative person aboard. Ramsay suggested that the ship belonged to the imperial fleet, and therefore the military officer on board could give directions to the officers. This has been questioned by more recent scholars who hold that the ship was not under state control but merely served the interests of the state. It seems more probable, therefore, that the centurion was asked his opinion by the ship's officers, and that he deferred to their expert knowledge of sailing conditions. The captain would presumably rank below the ship's *owner* who happened to be on board; the former would be responsible for the actual navigation, while the latter had overall responsibility.

12. What weighed with the ship's officers was the fact that Fair Havens was not a suitable harbour to winter in. Evidently, then, the discussion recorded in the two previous verses was concerned merely with whether the ship should move to a better harbour along the same coast and not with the question of whether they should try to reach Italy. J. Smith (*The Voyage and Shipwreck of St Paul*, p. 84) claims that in adverse weather conditions even a journey along the coast of Crete to the next suitable harbour would have been extremely risky. The place in mind is called *Phoenix*, and it is described as looking towards the south-west and the north-west winds (RSV mg.). This phrase has been interpreted as meaning looking towards the direction towards which these winds blow, namely north-east and south-east. This would fit modern Lutro, which

407

does in fact face east. But this understanding of the Greek phrase is very unnatural, and we should think of a west-facing harbour. A suitable site on the same peninsula is modern Phineka which preserves the ancient name. It is now silted up, but was more accessible in ancient times.[1]

13. Now begins the dramatic story of the storm and shipwreck which vindicated Paul's reading of the situation. The anticipated journey was quite short – a day's cruise – and this seemed easy to achieve with a gentle south wind. The boat set off, carefully hugging the coast.

14. But the sailors had not reckoned with a sudden change in the wind. A strong gale began to blow from the land, coming down from the mountains to the north-east. The name of the wind, 'Euraquilo', is attested in a Latin inscription[2] and appears to be a hybrid formation from Greek *Euros*, the east wind, and Latin *Aquilo*, the north wind; it may, therefore, have been a sailors' term for the north-east wind.

15. The boat was caught in the resulting tempest. Ancient ships could not tack or face heavy seas, and therefore the sailors had no option but to let the boat run with the wind, away from land; Haenchen (p. 701 note 4) notes that the foresail must have been used, or else it would have been impossible to steer the boat.

16. The boat ran into the *lee* of the *island* of *Cauda*, modern Gavaho or Gozzo, some 23 miles (37 km) from Crete. Here the sailors were able, but only with great *difficulty*, to haul aboard the small *boat* which was normally towed behind the ship; in time of storm it would be in danger of being swamped or dashed against the bigger vessel. The use of the 'we' form might imply that Luke himself helped with the operation, but more probably it is the way in which a passenger or spectator identifies himself with the action taking place.

17. A further safeguard taken by the sailors is described in RSV as taking *measures to undergird the ship*. The meaning is not certain. There are two words involved. The first is a word meaning literally 'helps'. It could mean 'protective measures' in a broad way, or more specifically some kind of nautical tackle such as cables or a system of pulleys; the latter is probably the right sense to give the word here, but we have

[1] R. M. Ogilvie, 'Phoenix', *JTS* 9, 1958, pp. 308–314.
[2] C. J. Hemer, 'Euraquilo and Melita', *JTS* 26, 1975, pp. 101–111 (103).

no other sources to give us more precise information. The second word is literally to 'undergird', *i.e.* 'to tie underneath'. It has been understood (1) of ropes tied vertically round the sides of the ship to hold the planks more firmly together (Bruce, *Book*, p. 509); (2) of ropes tied longitudinally round the outside of the hull from stem to stern to strengthen it (Haenchen, p. 703 n.1); (3) of ropes tied across the boat inside the hold to strengthen it; or (4) of ropes tied longitudinally over the ship from stem to stern and tautened in order to prevent the ship breaking its back. (H. J. Cadbury, *BC*, V. pp. 345–354). In our present state of knowledge it is not possible to make a firm decision between these possibilities. All that we know for sure is that 'undergirders' were part of the equipment of Greek warships, that they were ropes or cables, usually four or six in number, and (in one case, at least) each long enough to go right round the ship longitudinally. We also know that method (1) is attested in modern times ('frapping'), and method (4) in ancient Egyptian ships (to prevent 'hogging' *i.e.* the breaking of the ship's back).

The sailors were afraid that the ship might nevertheless be blown into the Syrtis. This was an area of quicksands and shoals off the coast of Libya and was legendary on account of the danger to shipping, like the 'Bermuda triangle' today. It was still about 380 miles (611 km) distant, but the sailors were taking no chances. Their third action was to *lower the gear*. Again the meaning is uncertain. It could mean to lower or reef the mainsail, or perhaps to set it, or to lower the main yard which had been supporting the storm sail, or to jettison the spare gear on board (but 'lower' hardly means 'jettison'), or, perhaps most probably, to lower some kind of sea anchor that would slow down the ship, and cause it to make leeway to the north and so avoid the danger area.

18–19. But these measures were inadequate. The ship was making heavy weather, probably taking water on board, and so they began to lighten it by jettisoning the *cargo* (*cf.* Jon. 1:5). On *the third day* the process of lightening the ship was continued by casting the *tackle* overboard; this will refer to spare gear, perhaps the heavy mainsail and yard. The sailors are said to have done so *with their own hands*, a puzzling phrase since they had no other means than their own hands. Later MSS ease the sentence by substituting 'we cast out' for 'they cast out' and this gives better sense. Or is the point that they

409

did not have any lifting gear, such as would be available in harbour?

20. The culminating point in the description of the storm is the fact that the sailors had no idea of where they were in relation to land, or rocks or shoals. The foul weather prevented any observations of the *sun* or *stars* by which they might have made some reckoning of their whereabouts. Humanly speaking, there appeared to be no chance of survival, and despondency settled on the ship.

21–22. Now comes Paul's second intervention in the story. It is introduced by a comment on the fact that nobody was eating any *food*, although this point is not really taken up until verse 33. In the present context it further illustrates the desperate straits in which the people on the ship found themselves. There may have been little food available as a result of the storm, and the people felt too sick or too dejected to eat. All this suffering and risk might have been avoided if the ship had stayed in Fair Havens, and now Paul commented on the way in which his warning had not been heeded; his prophecy of injury and loss had come true, although in fact it had so far affected (and would in the end only affect) the ship and not the persons on board, as he had prophesied. It is this qualification of his earlier prophecy which Paul now stresses in an endeavour to encourage the people. He believes that nobody will lose his *life*, but the *ship* will be lost.

23–24. Paul gives the basis for his assurance in an account of a vision which he had had the previous night, during which an angel of God had appeared to him. The angelic message was a confirmation of the earlier revelation in 23:11 that Paul would reach Rome; it was God's plan that he should witness there (23:11) in the presence of Caesar. It therefore followed that he himself could be confident of surviving the storm at sea, but he also had been told that God had granted him the lives of all those who were sailing with him. The wording implies that Paul had prayed for his fellow travellers, and that God heard his prayer. There is a parallel to the story of Abraham, who interceded with God for the people of Sodom and pleaded that the city as a whole might be saved for the sake of the small number of righteous people living in it (Gn. 18:23–33).

25–26. So Paul could encourage his hearers to *take heart* and in effect to share his *faith* that what God promised to him would come to pass. Paul's prophecy went beyond a general hope of safety to a particular statement that they would all be cast ashore on an *island*; if there was to be a loss of the ship (verse 22), then some such turn of events would be needed to save the people on board.

This speech of Paul again stands under critical suspicion. Yet it fits in with Paul's own experience of visions from God (2 Cor. 12:1, 9); it is entirely natural that Paul should have shared his assurance with his fellow travellers, and the story is based on eyewitness testimony; we need not doubt that Paul said something like this. Haenchen (p. 709) is sceptical that Paul could deliver a set speech in storm conditions on board ship, but his conception of Paul behaving like a public orator is inappropriate to the circumstances.

27. Now comes the fulfilment of Paul's prophecy. A fortnight had passed, presumably since the ship had left Fair Havens. Calculations show that this period fits in with the time that it would take a ship to cover the actual distance involved (about 475 nautical miles or 885 km) if it was drifting in the manner described. One must also allow for some change in the wind direction, which would be natural enough. Nowadays the *sea of Adria* means the gulf between Italy and the Balkan peninsula, but in ancient usage the term was used to include the area between Sicily and Crete as well. The island of Malta lies at the western extremity of this area, due south of Sicily. The sailors recognized the approach of land, quite possibly from the noise of breakers.[1]

28. They therefore began to take soundings so as to determine what depth of water lay under the ship. Although the figures given agree with those established by modern soundings at the probable site of the wreck, Conzelmann (p. 144) nevertheless prefers to believe that they are a literary invention, on the grounds that Luke was unlikely to be standing beside the man casting the lead; this is scepticism run riot.

29. The shallowness of the water, no doubt coupled with the noise of breakers, demanded safety measures, and so the sailors let down *four anchors*. These were quite light in weight

---

[1] Codex Vaticanus has an unusual word: 'that land *was resounding*' instead of 'that land was approaching'; this conveys the probable sense accurately, and may perhaps be the original reading, although it could be a learned correction of the text.

by modern standards – hence the number – and they were let down from the stern in order to keep the ship's head from swinging round and to prepare the ship to be run ashore when it was light and a suitable opportunity and place could be found. Now all that could be done was to long and pray for light to appear.

30. The incident that now follows is variously explained. According to Luke the sailors (presumably just some of them) tried to launch the ship's boat (verse 16) in order that they might escape from the ship; they pretended that in reality they were going to lay anchors from the bow – an action that in these circumstances could be accomplished only by rowing with the anchors so that they could be dropped a little way from the bow. Many commentators argue, however, that an attempt to escape would have been sheer suicide in the stormy conditions amid darkness off an unknown shore, and that the obvious safe course would have been to stay on board until morning light. Readers of *Robinson Crusoe* will remember a very similar situation in which the ship ran aground in the early morning and the crew took to the boat and all perished except for Crusoe himself who later was able to come back to the ship and commented, 'I saw evidently, that if we had kept on board, we had been all safe, – that is to say, we had all got safe on shore.' Defoe's story indicates that men will do foolish things, although it remains posssible that the intention of the sailors was misunderstood by the passengers.

31. Whatever the sailor's intention may have been, Paul pointed out to the *centurion* the danger that if the crew left the ship the passengers would be helpless. Haenchen (pp. 706, 710) comments that, if so, Paul was responsible for the loss of the ship, since without the boat there was no other possibility than to attempt the (unsuccessful) beaching of the ship; at the same time, however, he accepts the view that the verse is a fictitious interpolation by Luke to make Paul into the saviour of the passengers. But on the other side it can be commented that it was sheer bad luck that the ship ran aground on a shoal instead of on the beach, and that it is possible that the soldiers acted precipitately in cutting away the boat (verse 32) instead of merely keeping guard over it. Luke certainly ascribes the initiative in the action to Paul and understands his action as a helpful one; it would certainly not be surprising if the soldiers and passengers acted in panic and misunderstood the sailors, especially since the motif of the crew leaving the passengers in the lurch is attested in ancient romances.

33. Now comes a further episode involving Paul. As day began to *dawn*, while the ship rested at anchor, Paul began to encourage the people on board to eat. He is represented as speaking to the ship's company generally and reminding them that they had not eaten since the disastrous storm began fourteen days previously (*cf.* verse 21). Although there is no indication that they had been fasting in order to induce whatever gods they worshipped to have mercy on them, it is possible that this motif is present, and that Paul is in effect telling them that their prayers have been answered, and there is no need to fast any longer. Alternatively, Paul is simply saying hyperbolically that they have eaten very little for a long time. Again, it may seem strange that Paul occupied such a dominant position on the ship that he could command the attention of the people generally, but a holy man, such as Paul would appear to be, would be regarded with more attention than an ordinary person in these critical circumstances.

34. Paul urges his hearers to eat, as this will be in the interests of their safety: they will not be fit for the strenuous task of getting ashore without proper nourishment. Again he assures them that they are going to be safe, by commenting in proverbial fashion that they will be preserved from danger (*cf.* 1 Sa. 14:45; Mt. 10:36 par. Lk. 12:7; Lk. 21:18).

35–36. Paul gives strength to his exhortation by personal example. He proceeds to take some *bread* and, following normal Jewish and Christian practice, to give *thanks to God* for it, and then to break off a piece and begin *to eat*. The description resembles that of the procedure of Jesus when feeding the multitudes (Lk. 9:16), celebrating the Last Supper (Lk. 22:19), and sitting at table with the disciples journeying to Emmaus (Lk. 24:30). It is, therefore, not surprising that many commentators have seen in the present incident a celebration of the Lord's Supper, or, as Luke calls it, the Breaking of Bread. Since the early church associated the Lord's Supper with a proper meal (1 Cor. 11:17–34), it is possible that Paul was in fact celebrating a Christian Breaking of Bread, in which Luke and possibly others could have shared. The action described, however, in no way goes beyond normal Jewish practice at a meal, and it takes place in the open presence of a mixed company of people. It therefore seems more probable that

Luke is simply describing an ordinary meal and not a Christian sacrament or a 'prefiguration' of such a sacrament for the benefit of those who might later become believers. Paul shared the bread with his Christian companions,[1] and thus set an example which had the desired effect on the others.

37. Somewhat inconsequentially Luke adds the information that the total complement of the ship was 276 people. Although some of the MSS offer a lower figure (76; probably due to a scribal error in copying), the number is perfectly credible, since we have an account of a similar voyage in a ship which foundered in the sea of Adria by Josephus, who speaks of 600 people being on board. The number may be mentioned to prepare for the account of how they all got ashore.

38. Having eaten their fill, the crew fell to with greater energy and proceeded to jettison the remainder of the cargo in order to lighten the ship as much as possible for running it aground; although they had jettisoned some of it earlier (verse 18), they would have had to keep some as ballast while the ship was being driven by the wind.

39. Daybreak brought sight of land, but the sailors had no idea where they were. Of greater immediate importance was the fact that they sighted *a bay with a beach* which would be a suitable spot to attempt to ground the vessel.

The traditional site of the story is St Paul's Bay on the north-east coast of Malta. At the entry to the bay there is a shoal, now sunk below its level in ancient times, which could well be where the vessel ran aground. There is thus no need for the implausible theory that the site was the island of Mljet in the Adriatic Gulf, which in any case is too far from the probable route of the ship.[2]

40. The sailors prepared to beach the ship. They slipped the anchors off the deck into the sea. They also unlashed *the ropes* which had fastened the two steering paddles for safety during the storm, and hoisted the small foresail (*cf.* verse 15; it would have been furled while the ship was at anchor), so that they could manoeuvre the ship towards the beach.

---

[1] J. Jeremias, *The Eucharistic Words of Jesus* (London, 1966), p. 133 n.6.
[2] A. Acworth, 'Where was St Paul Shipwrecked?' *JTS* 24, 1973, pp. 190–193; see, however, C. J. Hemer, 'Euraquilo and Melita', *JTS* 26, 1975, pp. 100–111.

41. But their plan went astray since the ship struck *a shoal*; the Greek has 'a place of two seas' (RSV mg.); Smith (*op. cit.*, pp. 137-139) took this to be the channel between the side of the bay and the little island of Salmonetta, which would have caused some turbulence as well as having a tenacious bottom of clay in which the ship would stick fast and be at the mercy of the waves. Haenchen (p. 708) argues for the shoal mentioned above (verse 39 note) which lies more in the middle of the entrance to the bay. He also suggests that the stern would be *broken* more by the force of the impact than by the waves (the word 'waves', RSV *surf*, is omitted in some MSS).

42. In the confusion the soldiers wanted to *kill the prisoners* to prevent them escaping; it would not be difficult for those who could swim to get ashore and take off into the countryside, from where they could be recaptured only with difficulty. There is the problem that the prisoners may have been fettered or manacled and therefore incapable of escaping, but this may not have been the case in the unusual circumstances of shipwreck.

43. Again it is Paul who provides the occasion of safety for his fellow passengers. Whatever the centurion's attitude to his other prisoners may have been, he was unwilling to put Paul's life in danger, especially in view of Paul's activity during the voyage. So he gave orders that the men should make their way to land as best they could. Those who could *swim* would easily reach the shore which was not far distant.

44. The others were to follow using planks as floats or other bits of flotsam. The Greek construction may mean, however, that they were carried by the people who could swim; this need not mean that the latter could wade through the water, carrying them on their backs, as Haenchen (p. 708) suggests, but rather that they used life-saving techniques to swim to safety with them.

28:1 Only after their safe arrival on the island did the shipwrecked party discover that it was Melita, modern *Malta* (see 27:39 note). Bruce (*Book*, p. 521) notes that the name meant 'refuge' in the Semitic language which was then spoken there, but it is dubious whether this significance was known to Luke.

2. The people of Malta were of Phoenician extraction, and their native language was a Punic dialect. Especially in a country area the people would use their vernacular rather

415

than Greek, and hence Luke refers to them as 'barbarians' (RSV *natives*), using a word which simply meant 'ignorant of Greek'; there may be a hint that they were simple, rustic people. Such people might be expected to be hostile to strangers, as Greek authors testify, but on this occasion they showed *unusual kindness* to the destitute mariners, lighting *a fire* and making the strangers welcome. Haenchen (p. 713) rightly recognizes that though the temperature would not be much lower than about 50°F (10°C), the ship's company would be wet and cold after their ordeal. He finds it difficult, however, to imagine 276 people round one fire and supposes that Luke is thinking mainly of the Christian group. Paul too appears to be quite at liberty, but this would not be surprising in the circumstances; once the group were on the island, there would be little chance for a man like Paul to escape, and in any case he clearly wanted to stand his trial before Caesar.

3. Paul was thus able to make himself useful in gathering wood for the fire, but one of the *sticks* which he was carrying turned out to be a snake when he tried to cast it on the fire. Bruce (*Book*, p. 521) cites a modern parallel from Lawrence of Arabia, where a snake wriggled out of a collection of sticks placed on a fire. The Greek word literally means a *viper*, and this has led to some sceptical comment, since there are no poisonous snakes on the island nowadays. But although the audience thought the snake was poisonous, they could have been mistaken; plenty of modern people can confuse grass snakes with vipers. In any case the modern ecology of Malta is not necessarily a guide to ancient conditions, and the people would not have thought the snake was poisonous if there were no poisonous snakes on the island.

4. Bruce (*Book*, p. 522 note 11) cites a Greek poem which tells of 'a murderer who escaped from a storm at sea and was shipwrecked on the Libyan coast, only to be killed by a viper'. In this kind of thought-world the reaction of the Maltese to Paul's experience is fully intelligible. A murderer might escape from death by drowning, but nemesis would still catch up with him. The word *justice* should have a capital letter. The thought is of the Greek goddess of Justice, but the Maltese may have referred to a corresponding deity of their own.

5–6. Paul, however, merely shook the creature off, and suffered no harm. It is not clear whether he regarded it as poisonous or not, and, if the former, whether he regarded himself as under divine protection; the promise in the longer ending of Mark, (Mk. 16:18) is probably based on this incident rather than vice versa. The Maltese people, however, continued to watch him. They fully expected that the bite would lead to some kind of inflammation or even to sudden death, but nothing of the kind happened. They then quickly *changed their minds* and decided that Paul must be *a god*.

Clearly Luke did not think of Paul as a god (14:15), yet he did think of the apostles as possessing miraculous powers. He may, therefore, have seen them as possessing some of the characteristics of the so-called 'divine men' who were known in the ancient world, although recent study has shown that this term should be used only with great caution. In the present story, however, it looks rather as if he is poking fun at the superstition which was able to swing from one extreme of opinion to another at the drop of a hat. In other words, if the 'divine man' motif is present, Luke is decidedly critical about it.[1]

7. A second story about Paul's stay in Malta follows (verses 7–10). It is a miracle story, of the same kind as is related in the Gospels, and it bears some resemblance to the story of how Jesus healed Peter's mother-in-law and then a crowd of other sick people (Lk. 4:38–41). The place where Paul landed was near to an estate which belonged to the Roman governor of the island. His title, *the chief man*, is confirmed by evidence from inscriptions. Luke gives his praenomen as *Publius* (Greek *Poplios*); the use of this name is somewhat unusual, but it is not unparalleled. The governor received the party and entertained them for three days. Whether the invitation extended to all the shipwrecked party we cannot tell, but it included Paul and the narrator.

8–10. When Publius's *father* lay ill with attacks of gastric *fever and dysentery* (which are said to be endemic to Malta as 'Malta fever'), Paul was able to heal him by prayer and the laying on of hands (9:12, 17). In the same way, Paul also cured other people on the island who had doubtless heard of what happened. The effect of Paul's healing activity was that the people of the island presented him and his friends with

[1] It will not do to follow Conzelmann (p. 147) and argue that Luke's attitude here is uncritical, by contrast with 14:11; Luke is not as inconsistent as that, especially at the climax of his book.

417

gifts, and in particular provided what they needed for the rest of their journey. The use of *us* here has been thought to suggest that Luke may have exercised his professional abilities alongside Paul. This may have been the case, but Luke is concerned simply with what Paul did.

The ending of the story is at first sight remarkable. There is not a word about the preaching of the gospel by Paul, still less about any response other than gratitude for services rendered (contrast the similar account of Paul's relationships with the governor of Cyprus in 13:6–12). But the simple reason for this may be that nobody in fact was converted during Paul's stay. Paul continues to appear in the story primarily in the role of one who helps his friends and rescues them from danger.

11. *Three months* represents the time during which navigation was at a standstill. Other ships had been caught by the onset of winter and forced to wait idly before they could complete their journeys in the spring. It was not surprising to find another ship from Alexandria waiting at Malta before continuing its journey. It too would be engaged in the transport of wheat. Some living detail is given to the story by the (useless) information that as a figurehead it *bore* the *Twin Brothers*: the sons of Zeus, Castor and Pollux, were the patrons of navigation, and their constellation (Gemini) was a sign of good fortune when seen in a storm.

12. The ship sailed first to *Syracuse*, which was the chief city in Sicily, and *stayed there for three days*; since this information is not important for the story, it is all the more likely to be authentic.

13. The statement that they *made a circuit* and so arrived at *Rhegium* on the toe of Italy is strange, since it stood in a straight line from Syracuse. The phrase may be a nautical technical term. Bruce thinks it refers to changing direction as they entered the strait of Messina. The Alexandrian MSS have a word which means 'to loose', *sc.* the anchors (*cf.* 27:40), but one would not loose anchors except in an emergency; if the text is accepted, it might perhaps mean 'to cast off' *sc.* the mooring ropes. From Rhegium the ship sailed north with a favourable wind to Puteoli at a fair speed.[1] Puteoli, modern Pozzuoli, was the principal port for the wheat trade, although

---

[1] 7½ knots, according to Haenchen, German edition.

418

later it was overshadowed by the development of Ostia, which was much closer to Rome.

14. It is not surprising that there were Christians in Puteoli with its cosmopolitan population, including a colony of Jews. Many commentators, however, find it strange that Paul had the freedom to stay with them for a whole week. Haenchen (p. 719) regards the period as a literary device to allow time for news of Paul's arrival to reach Rome and for the Christians there to send a delegation to meet him. Hanson (p. 253) suggests that the centurion had perhaps to go on to Rome to get further instructions, but surely he would already have been told what to do, unless the unexpected winter delay had led him to expect a change in plan. But the fact that no reason is given by Luke does not mean that there was none.

The last part of the verse which describes an arrival in *Rome* in anticipation of verse 16 is also puzzling. The stress may lie on the *so* – despite this long and troublesome journey; from Puteoli onwards the journey was by road and free from the risks of sea. Perhaps we should translate 'And in this way we made our journey to Rome'.[1]

15. But before Paul reached there he received a welcome. News of his arrival preceded him, doubtless sent by the Christians in Puteoli, and two groups of Christians came to meet him, one as far as Forum Appii, 43 miles (69 km) from Rome, and the other to Tres Tabernae (RSV *Three Taverns*), 33 miles (53 km) from Rome. These were well-known stopping places on the Via Appia which led from Rome via Puteoli to the south of Italy. Their arrival encouraged Paul by showing that he had friends in the capital city. The curious feature, noted by recent commentators, is that these Christians from Rome disappear once Paul reaches the city, and all his dealings are with the Jews. Some think that Luke is trying, as it were, to get the Roman Christians out of the way so that Paul appears as a pioneer missionary; unable to deny their existence, Luke solved the problem by having them meet Paul before he reached Rome (Haenchen, pp. 720, 730). But this suggestion is unnecessary. Luke describes merely what happened during the first few days after Paul's arrival in Rome, when he sought

---

[1] F. A. Mecham, 'And so we came to Rome', *Australian Catholic Review* 50, 1973, pp. 170–173 (as reported in *NTA* 18, 1973, §181) translates *houtos* as 'as follows'.

contact with the Jews, and he is not concerned about Paul's relationships with the already existing Christian church; he does, however, show that Paul was welcomed by the Christians. But his main purpose was to show how Paul behaved towards the Jews, since the question of Jews and Gentiles in relation to the gospel is one of the dominant themes of the book.

16. So Paul at last arrives at his destination; for the last time Luke writes in the first person plural. As the text stands, it tells us that Paul was given permission to live *by himself, i.e.* not in a prison but in a private dwelling (verse 30), under guard by a *soldier*. This seems to fit in with Roman practice attested at least for later times.

The western text gives a fuller explanation at this point. It reads: 'The centurion handed the prisoners over to the stratopedarch, but Paul was allowed to live by himself outside the camp . . .' This raises the question of the official procedure. The older view is that the official in question to whom the prisoners were handed over was the *princeps peregrinorum*, the commander of the camp where the *frumentarii* (27:1 note) were based in Rome. It seems, however, that this unit may not have existed before the time of Trajan in the second century. A second possibility is that the reference is to the *praefectus praetorii*, the prefect or commander of the praetorian guard, to whom prisoners from the provinces were delivered according to a letter from Trajan to Pliny. This theory is developed by Sherwin-White (pp. 108–111) who suggests that the official in question would be the *princeps castrorum*, a subordinate of the prefect. It thus is probable that the western text reflects the procedure that would be followed. For the question of the legal proceedings see verse 30 note.

j. Paul and the Jews in Rome (28:17–31)

Luke's account of Paul's activity in Rome is silent on two of the points that would most interest us: the result of his appeal to Caesar and his relationship with the Christian church that already existed in Rome. All the interest is centred on Paul's relationship with the non-Christian Jews. He summons their representatives to meet with him and explains briefly how he has come to Rome as a result of Jewish charges brought against him in Judea; this gives him the opportunity to explain the nature of the Christian message to them, but his words had a mixed reception. When they were unable to come to any agreement among themselves, Paul spoke out in condemnation of their blindness and stubbornness in refusing the gospel, and then declared himself free to take the message of salvation to the Gentiles. For the remaining two years which Luke describes Paul accordingly preached and ministered to the Gentiles. Thus the final picture which is presented to the reader is of Paul's last appeal to the Jews and his acceptance of a call to the Gentiles. The impression conveyed is that Paul felt throughout his ministry the duty to go first to the Jews and that it was when they refused the message that he went to the Gentiles. All this fits in with the emotional expression of Paul's feelings regarding his call in Romans 9–11. It also gives a climax to the book in that the missionary programme of Acts 1:8 is now brought to a decisive point: the gospel has come to the capital city, and it is proclaimed without hindrance to the Gentiles; the church is on the brink of further expansion, with Paul's hope of reaching Spain (Rom. 15:24, 28) in the background and indicating the direction for further advance. The church is thus given its marching orders: Rome is a stage on the way, and not the final goal. In principle it is free to ignore the Jews, at least for the time being (Lk. 21:24), and to go to the Gentiles.

Luke presents this picture in terms of the mission of Paul. The Jews in Rome are given the opportunity to respond to Paul's understanding of the gospel, although they must already have been familiar with the message from the Christians who had been in Rome from a very early stage (Acts 2:10). This means that Luke says nothing about the presence and activity of the church in Rome except in verses 15f., and thus a misleading impression could be given to readers of Acts. It is the same kind of concentrated account as we find in the last chapter of his Gospel where all the resurrection appearances of Jesus are presented as though they were confined to Jerusalem and its environs and took place on Easter Sunday, although there were appearances elsewhere and Luke himself later makes it clear that they continued over a period of forty days.

17. Paul's first action, once he is settled in to his new abode, is to summon *the leaders of the Jews* in Rome. We have insufficient information about the Jewish community in Rome to know precisely which officials are envisaged here. Paul

421

invites them to come to him, since he is apparently not able to visit them; his situation is one of house-arrest. He informs them of the reasons that have brought him to Rome. He claims that he had *done nothing against the* Jewish *people* or attacked their *customs* (*cf.* 25:8). Nevertheless, he had been handed over by the Jews to the Romans. The language resembles that used of Jesus in the Gospel (Lk. 18:32), and it is possible that Luke wishes his readers to see a parallel between the fates of Jesus and Paul. It has also been claimed that Luke contradicts his earlier story, in which Paul was taken out of the hands of the Jews by the Romans. But Luke is concerned with the essentials of the story, not with the details, and the account here is a fair representation of how the Jews had proceeded to prosecute Paul before Felix and Festus with a view to the Romans sentencing Paul for what were in effect Jewish offences, however much the Jews might try to claim that Paul was really a danger to Rome.

18. The Roman examination of Paul failed to substantiate the Jewish charges against him. He had done nothing that deserved death and therefore he should have been acquitted and set free. Paul says that the Romans *wished* to release him. This is slightly strange. The Roman governors in fact had made no attempt to release Paul, and it was because Festus wanted him tried in Jerusalem that Paul had been compelled to appeal to Caesar. It was Agrippa who affirmed that Paul could have been set at liberty if he had not appealed to Caesar, and Festus may be presumed to have agreed with him at that stage. Paul's statement, therefore, is something of a simplification of the earlier account.

19. The reason why Paul had *to appeal to Caesar* is said to be that *the Jews objected* to the Roman desire to set Paul free. This is evidently an allusion to the Jewish charges made in 25:2, 7, which led Festus to ask Paul whether he was willing to be tried in Jerusalem. If so, we should probably understand 25:4f. to imply that if no charge had been brought against Paul by the Jews, Festus would have set him at liberty; this would make good sense, since Festus might well have concluded that the two years' detention which Paul had already suffered was adequate punishment if he had offended the Jewish law in any way. The accounts would then be in harmony with each other. Paul makes it clear that he is not attacking the Jewish nation for the way in which its leaders had acted; this is a conciliatory speech, and Paul is allowing that the Jews had acted within their rights if they thought that he had done wrong.

20. It was, then, to inform the Roman Jews accurately about the situation that Paul had called them together. For in fact what was at issue in his trial, as he had insisted all along, was the true nature of *the hope of Israel* in the coming of the Messiah and the resurrection. It was, in other words, for being a loyal Jew, as he saw it, that Paul was wearing a Roman fetter, and this was surely something that demanded the attention of the Jews, since their religion was legally permitted by the Romans.

21. The Roman Jews professed complete ignorance about Paul and his case. They had not received any instructions from Jerusalem which might direct them to represent the Jewish cause in court against Paul, nor had any Jewish messenger from Jerusalem brought any report against Paul. There is nothing remarkable about this. Bruce (*Book*, p. 535) is undoubtedly right in arguing that the Jewish leaders were unlikely to have proceeded with the case once it had been transferred to Rome, since they would have little, if any, chance of success. No official communication about Paul would thus have reached the Jews in Rome. Very possibly the Jews in Rome preferred to remain ignorant of the case; they would not have forgotten that earlier disputes over the Messiah had led to their temporary expulsion from the city (18:2 note).

22. Nevertheless, they were interested to hear what Paul had to say for himself. They knew something of the Christian *sect* (24:14), for there was an active church in Rome, and they knew that it was often the object of attack. They presumably also had heard of Paul and his reputation as a leading missionary, and they were sufficiently curious to hear what he had to say for himself and to see why he was so out of favour with the authorities in Jerusalem.

23. A suitable *day* for a meeting was arranged, and a large group *came* to see Paul. The phrase *at his lodging* may rather mean 'to receive his hospitality'; the Jews were his guests, since he could not follow his former pattern of attending the synagogue, but the phrase does not mean that he provided them with a meal or anything of the kind. Questions as to whether Paul had a big enough room to hold them all are beside the point.

Paul's theme was not his own situation but the gospel. He *expounded* it by proclaiming *the kingdom of God* and persuading them *about Jesus*, basing his argument on the statements of *Moses and the prophets*. The subject matter thus combined the themes of the preaching of Jesus and the apostolic message about him which formed a unity: the rule of God was the rule of God's agent, the Messiah, and it was Jesus who filled this role. In a discussion with Jews the Old Testament Scriptures provided the main evidence, and the debate hung on their interpretation, and whether the facts concerning Jesus could be seen as the fulfilment of prophecy. This description of Paul's message corresponds with earlier general summaries of his arguments in the synagogues (17:2f.; 18:5) and obviously reflects his normal practice.

24–25. The result was the sort of mixed response which Paul had experienced on previous occasions. Some were persuaded by what he said, but nothing is said to suggest that they were converted to a personal acceptance of the message. Others were frankly unpersuaded. So the meeting broke up with the Jews arguing among themselves. They went off, and again there is no suggestion that any of them were sufficiently interested to return on a later occasion. But before they left Paul uttered one final word. He claimed that *the Holy Spirit* had truly spoken about them in the words which *Isaiah* had originally addressed to their ancestors; it was a case of 'like fathers, like children'. The quotation was one which was familiar to the early church. It had been used by Jesus (Lk. 8:10; *cf.* Mt. 13:13–15 Mk. 4:12;) and is quoted by John (Jn. 12:39f.), and Paul himself had used it in writing to the Romans (Rom. 11:8). Here, as in Matthew 13:14f., we get the full quotation from Isaiah 6:9f., according to the LXX. Luke perhaps deliberately abbreviated the saying of Jesus incorporating it in Luke 8:10, in order to reserve the full effect for the present context.

26–27. God's people are told that, however much they *hear* and *see*, they will never *understand* and *perceive* what God is saying to them. This is a divine judgment upon them because they themselves have made their hearts impervious to the Word of God; they have allowed themselves to become deaf and blind for fear that they might hear and see the disturbing

Word of God and so receive healing from God. God's Word brings the diagnosis of sin, which is painful to hear and accept, but at the same time it wounds in order to heal. Once a person deliberately refuses the Word, there comes a point when he is deprived of the capacity to receive it. It is a stern warning to those who trifle with the gospel.

28. In view of this the Jews must take solemn note of the fact that the message of *salvation* is now going *to the Gentiles* who will give it a more favourable response. Whether this is a final rejection of the Jews is doubtful. Paul's letters certainly indicate that he looked for a change of heart on their part in due time (Rom. 11:25–32). This may well be Luke's understanding too.[1] But for the moment the Christian mission turns to the Gentiles. Paul no longer feels under obligation to go 'to the Jews first', and Luke may well be presenting him as an example for the church generally to follow.[2]

30. For two years Paul continued to remain in his dwelling. The phrase *at his own expense* implies that he had some source of income; prisoners could in certain circumstances carry on their own trades. The variant translation 'in his own hired dwelling' (RSV mg.), while dubious as a translation, no doubt expresses the resulting situation accurately enough. The point is probably that Paul was not in a common prison but continued the manner of living described in verse 16. Though he had no freedom to move, he was still able to act as a Christian missionary, since people could come to see him; Paul could well write about 'the gospel for which I am suffering and wearing fetters like a criminal. But the Word of God is not fettered' (2 Tim. 2:9).

What happened when the *two years* were ended? The implication is that something changed at this point (Haenchen, p. 724). The various possibilities are:

(1) Luke wrote Acts at this point, and did not know what was going to happen next. It may be that he hoped to write a third volume, taking up the story at this point. The difficulty with this view is that it requires a very early (but not impossible) date for Acts. The book gives many readers the impression of being written from a later perspective.

[1] Lk. 13:35; Marshall, *Commentary*, p. 577; *cf.* Acts 1:6
[2] Verse 29 (see RSV mg.) is missing from the best MSS and looks like a scribal paraphrase.

(2) The Jews failed to appear to prosecute their case against Paul (verse 21 note). What we do not know is whether Paul would automatically have been released in this situation. Sherwin-White (pp. 112–119) has effectively rebutted the view that the prosecutors were required to appear within a specific time-limit, or else their case would lapse. But he does not appear to have refuted the possibility that if the accusers never appeared the case would eventually lapse. A more serious objection is that 23:11 and 27:24 clearly imply that Paul would appear before Caesar.

(3) Paul was tried and acquitted, or the Roman government dropped the case against him (Sherwin-White, pp. 118f., shows that the latter was quite possible).

In both of cases (2) and (3) the problem is bound up with the wider issue of whether Paul proceeded to enjoy a period of liberty before he was again arrested and eventually executed. This is the impression which we get from the Pastoral Epistles, since it is generally thought that, if they are genuine, they cannot be fitted into Paul's career at an earlier point. But this matter is much debated; some would argue that the Epistles are inauthentic and therefore of doubtful historical worth, while others claim that they can be fitted into Paul's career before the end of Acts. The one event on which there is unanimity is that Paul was executed by the Romans.

(4) The final possibility is that Paul was tried and executed at this point, but Luke was unwilling to record his martyrdom; he had given sufficient hints in advance about it (20:23–25, 38; 21:13; 23:11; 27:24), and he preferred to leave his readers with the picture of the gospel being freely proclaimed by Paul in Rome to the Gentiles. If, however, Luke knew of Paul's martyrdom or of Nero's pogrom against the Christians in Rome, it is extremely difficult to understand how he could have painted such a generally favourable picture of the Roman authorities and their attitude to Paul (23:29 note). It must be admitted, however, that Luke's picture is of the *provincial* Roman authorities, and there could be an implied contrast with the central Roman government.

The picture is ambiguous. On the one hand, it is hard to see how Paul could have been condemned to death on the evidence offered in Acts; on the other hand, Acts seems to be aware that he was going to appear before Caesar and die as a martyr.

426

31. Whatever be the truth, the fate of Paul is secondary to that of the gospel. The final picture is of Paul *preaching* to the Gentiles the same message which he had preached throughout Acts with boldness and without hindrance. All the emphasis lies on that last phrase. The implication is that the charges against Paul were false and that God backed up his proclamation.[1] Nothing that men can do can stop the progress and ultimate victory of the gospel.

---

[1] G. Delling, 'Das letzte Wort der Apostelgeschichte', *Nov.T* 15, 1973, pp. 193–204.